Lighting Technology Handbook
Erratum

P 121 Figure 6.15. The caption should read (Courtesy De Sisti Lighting)
P 126 Figure 6.20. The caption should read (Courtesy De Sisti Lighting)
P 130 Figure 6.23. The caption should read (Courtesy De Sisti Lighting)

The following credits were omitted from the second colour plate section:
Plate 4
CYM colour mixing
Courtesy High End Systems Inc

Plate 5
VL5™ Wash Luminaire Chromaticity Diagram
Courtesy Vari*Lite

Plate 6
Fixed colour wheel base
Courtesy High End Systems Inc

Plate 7
Electronics ballast
Courtesy Power Gems

Plate 8
Interior of electronic ballast
Courtesy Power Gems

Plate 9
Pearl Console
Courtesy Avolites Ltd

Plate 10
Graphics tablet
Courtesy Avolites Ltd

Lighting Technology

Dedication

This book is dedicated to four stalwarts of the lighting industry: Andy Collier, whose knowledge of the theatre is second to none; Mike Wood, who has been involved, for a number of years, with the development of systems for TV, stage and the pop industry; and John Farr, ex-Head of Lighting at the BBC, who has always passionately believed in good lighting and pictures. Finally, John Watt, who is one of the real characters of the business – who claims to know very little of the theory contained in this publication – but who could have probably written a lot of the book himself!

We also have to thank numerous friends in the industry for the provision of ideas and particularly of illustrations. Once again Brian's wife, Carole, has borne the brunt of the word processing load and the authors' lack of writing skills!

Lighting Technology

A Guide for the Entertainment Industry

Brian Fitt
and
Joe Thornley

Focal Press
An imprint of Butterworth-Heinemann Ltd
Linacre House, Jordan Hill, Oxford OX2 8DP

ℛ A member of the Reed Elsevier plc group

OXFORD   BOSTON   JOHANNESBURG
MELBOURNE   NEW DELHI   SINGAPORE

First published 1997

British Library Cataloguing in Publication Data
A catalogue record for this book is available from the
British Library.

ISBN 0 240 51449 1

Library of Congress Cataloguing in Publication Data
A catalogue record for this book is available from the
Library of Congress.

Composition by Scribe Design, Gillingham, Kent
Printed and bound in Great Britain

Contents

Acknowledgements

Avolites
BBC
British Standards
Central TV
Commission Internationale de L'Éclairage
Department of Trade and Industry
DeSisti (UK) Ltd
Elstree Light and Power
Fuji Photo Film Co. Ltd.
GE Lighting
Health and Safety Executive
High End Systems
HMSO
Meridian TV
Meteorlites
Minolta (UK) Ltd
Musco Lighting
Osram
Philips Lighting
Power Gems
Strand Lighting
Studio Design Partnership
The Institution of Electrical Engineers
The Sports Council
Varilite

1
Introduction

When we wrote *Lighting by Design* in 1991, little did we realize that in 1996 we would be completely re-vamping the original book and attempting to reflect the changes in the lighting industry. This book should really be considered as the second edition of *Lighting by Design* with additional material added to either up-date the information or cover new topics with a change of title to more accurately reflect the contents.

We are stimulated by walking through the countryside, particularly when the light streams through trees, the dawn glows and particularly when viewing a dramatic sunset. Our brain equates all of the images perceived as a very mixed bag of emotions. It's an interesting fact that dreams are manifestations of stored images. A modern digital still camera requires for a high definition picture, say 15 megabytes of information. When we think of all the facilities that the eye and brain give us it is quite mind blowing to appreciate the storage capacity of the brain – with everything automated!

Feature film is often put through a 'digitizer' to convert the optical images for manipulation on computers. Computerized television editing systems also work on a sequence of frames which are digitally manipulated from a hard disk. Hence the most dramatic development in the last five years has been the coming together of film and video picture manipulation using very sophisticated computers.

The impact of digital technology has also enabled immense advances in the lighting industry. Luminaires can now be programmed to follow the entertainer around the stage from one position to another and a phenomenal range of colour is available with dichroic filters in the digitally controlled automated luminaires in use today.

This book looks at the broad principles of practical lighting for the entertainment industry. The users of lighting systems will always justify their choice of facilities, which of course is human nature, so it is often very difficult getting to the truth about how good the individual systems are. What we have tried to do in this book is explain the fundamentals of the various component parts of any system of lighting. Lighting systems require electricity so this is a very important topic, and it can be very dangerous if not used properly. Electricity is also the cause of electromagnetic interference, so we have tried to give some guidance on this problem.

An important point to remember is that lighting can be positioned anywhere but it is only in the hands of an accomplished lighting director (designer) that it becomes an embellishment to the performance. We do not recommend specific luminaires or suspension systems as each individual lighting installation will have unique features which require consideration by a lighting consultant. However, the information given in the main body of the book, together with Appendix IV, gives many guidelines to practical solutions for the design of a complete lighting installation.

During the 1980s with the experimental work being done in high definition television, it was thought that when it was introduced, it would have a tremendous impact on the lighting levels required in studios and on location. However, with the advance of more sophisticated cameras and better CCDs the light levels used for high definition systems barely exceed those used for normal television operation. Therefore the problem that was once envisaged has almost gone away.

We must remember that lighting is not there to show off technical innovations but to enhance and embellish the performance itself. It would seem that as the shows become bland, the contraptions become more complex and this appears to be the 'Second law of entertainment'. Many major productions are absolutely full of gadgetry. One has to wonder whether this is there to embellish the performance or in fact to paper over some of the cracks. Much of the most breathtaking lighting comes from pop lighting designers, where on a broad canvas they wield large brush strokes of impact lighting and colour and movement. It is possible for a pop rig to use four million watts of lighting power and nearly as much audio – or so it appears!

It would seem that in TV, the management are willing to pay a small fortune for vision equipment, cameras, zoom lenses and sound systems but from our experience balk at the price of one Redhead, whereas the pop and theatre world appreciate the value of lighting and will invest enormous sums in special rigs and lighting systems. Over the past few years, television has moved away from main line production studios to the point where much work is commissioned in outside 'cowsheds'. With this proliferation of independent productions there has been more and more demands on lighting designers to be more innovative with smaller budgets. The problem with all this material from a multiplicity of sources appearing on British television is that, apparently, there is no overall co-ordinating technical standard as far as the pictures go; and there is a feeling in the industry that there is a lack of expertise in some areas and the training requirements are not up to scratch. Thus, programme output, as far as pictures go, varies from the very good to the simply awful. The film industry, however, seems to be going through a renaissance and the technical quality and special effects of modern films such as *Jurassic Park* and the *Star Trek* series are quite breathtaking. Much of the feature material shot for television, such as period drama, uses Super 16 film; and the results on the home viewers' screen are quite outstanding and would make one query 'is there really need for high definition television?' when pictures of this quality appear on British television as a matter of routine.

Manufacturers and suppliers of lighting equipment have to know all about their competitors to survive in a very competitive industry. The problem we've noticed is that people tend to only know about their particular area of the lighting business and hopefully this book will introduce new ideas and thoughts into other areas. Although we have been around for a long time we believe you're never too old to learn – we still learn from some of the new developments that are happening today! The one danger we see is that as gadgetry becomes more reliable, more flexible and easier to operate, there could be a danger of introducing much of this technology for technology's sake. Simple lighting, that goes unnoticed, such as a spotlight on a world class artist, can still be enough to enhance a magical performance.

It's very seldom in the lighting industry that we all get together in one place and talk about our experiences. An event which deserves much wider publicity is 'Showlight' which is a conference on lighting for entertainment which takes place every four years, usually in an interesting venue, where eminent lighting designers come along and share their experiences, usually with an enraptured audience. The fascination of the pop designer for some television lighting and the TV lighting director's appreciation of good stage lighting is interesting to observe.

One outstanding feature of being involved in the lighting industry is the overwhelming enthusiasm of all the participants and this can be from manufacturers, designers, operators and the artists themselves; for without light, our emotions are very limited.

Many people on opening this book will probably ask themselves 'Why do I need to read all this theory when I've been practising lighting for many years?' Experienced lighting directors use the tools of the trade by selecting items according to their experience over a long learning curve and several near failures over a period of some years. To all new practitioners as well as some of the old, we would say, the more you know the rules, the more you are able to break or circumvent them in order to achieve more interesting results by being able to use the tools successfully.

Light can't be bent in mid-air – it doesn't travel in curves but in straight lines. However, by shaping, colouring and moulding the beam it produces totally stunning effects in the hands of a creative lighting designer.

2
Lighting the subject

Introduction

From the time when the Savoy Theatre was first lit by electricity, the instruments used for artificial lighting have developed from very crude flood sources to the sophisticated moving light sources of today.

Lighting design

The subject may be either a performer or a static object and the lights have to be positioned and controlled to give the desired effect. Sometimes compromise is necessary due to the position of scenery, cloths, and other objects which may give rise to unwanted shadows. The choice of luminaires for the lighting designer is extremely wide and varied, but all will have their particular favourites because they know that they can produce acceptable and repeatable results from some of the devices used in the past. Lighting designers these days can use lights from another industry to give some effects that were previously unobtainable. It is now possible to see HMI Fresnels used on pop rigs and Parcans used with great effect by TV lighting designers. However, one source of illumination not used by the pop industry is the soft light, because their style of lighting requires sharp, well defined beams to give visual impact to the scene being viewed. The pop lighting designer is a great exponent of beams of light and colour which generate the most intense feelings in the audience and has to either enhance or co-exist with the music or performance. Today, it is possible to see large pop type rigs used at symphony concerts where the use of light and colour adds to the spectacle.

Pop lighting does not usually go for subtle effects but very much impact lighting. Generally, the lighting will be either synchronized or harmonized with the sound to highlight the artists performance. This is not to say that subtle lighting effects won t be used, but these will generally be for mood changes, often accomplished by the use of colour washes. Not only do the lights go on and off, or change colour in synchronization with the music, it is more than likely that the light beams are moved to give dynamic effects. Earlier pop rigs made much use of Parcans because they were a useful way of providing multi-positional changes. Today, the moving light has become very much the norm, and companies such as Vari Lite and High End Systems provide wonderfully programmed sources of illumination with positional colour and intensity changes very easily accomplished. Lighting designers in the pop industry do not have the problem of hiding lights, as generally the sets do not lend themselves to this. Indeed, it is more than likely that the rig itself becomes part of the actual scenery and to that end very elaborate systems are introduced by various pop groups; not only do we have lights moving from fixed positions, we can have lights rotating around the structure on motorized trolleys. Additionally, the shape and form of the entire rig may change, all of this controlled by sophisticated motor systems.

Historical

Evidence exists that from about 15000 BC oil lamps were being used for lighting and for many centuries this continued as the sole means of artificial light. In the eighteenth century candles became more common and also the oil lamp underwent a significant improvement by burning the wicks in a tubular glass chimney to enable a brighter light source. In 1765 at the Lonsdale coal mines near Whitehaven, surplus coal gas was piped into the mine offices to be used as a source of light and from that point in time gas lighting was gradually introduced, eventually being supplanted by the electric lamp.

The theatrical staging of drama and verse has been going on for several thousand years. In the beginning, it was staged during daylight hours to take advantage of natural light and although difficult to date, no doubt the Greeks and Romans used oil lamps to illuminate their theatrical work. The staging of drama was originally in outdoor theatres; eventually they were partly covered but still open to the elements. Theatres, such as the Globe, where Shakespeare's plays were performed, were fine in the summer but pretty bleak in the winter months. Ultimately, entertainment moved indoors and it was therefore not possible to use natural light.

Early light sources were generally floodlights with little or no finesse. As taste became more refined, so did the lighting. In modern theatres, film or TV studios as well as on pop rigs, the majority of lighting is placed at a reasonable height above the acting area. The reasons for this are quite simply that we do not wish the acting area to be full of equipment. This holds true for most lighting equipment, but in a TV or film studio the floor is also cluttered with cameras and booms, etc. As members of the human race we are conditioned that light is above us and at an average of about 45° to any standing object on earth. This fact lays down the most important ground rule for the artificial lighting of any scene. Artists throughout the ages have appreciated the light sources available to them. The sun provides a wonderful key light with warm rich colours and the blue sky provides a soft light of cool brilliance.

Human perception

In our everyday lives as human beings, we go around in illumination
that can vary from the minimum amount on a moonlit night to a
maximum of an overhead sun in the Sahara desert. Other than a
psychological difference, we are not disturbed by the differences
between gloomy, grey overcast days and the intense blue skies of
winter when the atmosphere is at its clearest. Visually, we are not
worried by a lack of shadow detail, and on other occasions we see
no problems with the intense black shadows created by sunlight. We
do become disturbed however, by green light applied to the human
skin, we also become rather unnerved by lighting when it comes
from below subjects and not from above (see Fig. 2.1(a)). Living on
the Earth, we are conditioned by the basic form of lighting which
generally consists of a mixture of sunlight and light from the blue
sky. Our experience of lighting is conditioned by the fact that in our
everyday lives we perceive fairly well balanced light, due to the sun
and the sky.

   In the absence of light from the sky, such as on the moon, we see
extremely contrasting pictures due to one light source only, namely
the sun. We feel much better when we are bathed in warm sunlight
and not standing in the cool of a grey day. Some of this is caused by
the generation of vitamins by sunlight, but mostly it is psychological.
It is interesting to note that we also feel better on a sunny day in the
middle of a cold winter. Red and yellow give us a lovely cosy feeling,
and this is probably caused by our mental stimulation with the association of the sun. It's a strange fact that as colour temperature
increases towards the blue end of the spectrum, we do not necessarily feel warmer and we actually associate blue with cool conditions.
Green has a refreshing quality, which is probably occasioned by the
response of the eye which is at its peak with the green portion of the
spectrum. We view black as a very sombre colour and associate it
with the macabre. We generally associate white with coolness and a
feeling of something that is quite unspoilt; it's interesting to note how
disturbed we are by snow when it has become muddied, as the thaw
sets in. From this short list of examples, it must become obvious that
we can associate colours with a sense of stimulation of appreciation
within the viewed scene, and many of the effects used in artificial
lighting are based upon these feelings.

   To the untrained eye, lighting, either in the theatre, television
studio, on a film set or in a huge pop rig looks somewhat similar.
However, closer inspection reveals that the luminaires used in the
theatre are somewhat different to those used for film and television
and these days will probably have more in common with the pop
industry. We find that stage lighting designers now use Parcans
together with automated luminaires using tungsten and discharge
sources. Many of the luminaires used on stage, and for that matter
in the pop world, are now being used more and more in television.

Daylight

Light in its most basic form, daylight, consists of a mixture of sunlight
and skylight. These can be analysed as the sun which provides
extremely hard light that gives well defined shadows and a sense of

Figure 2.1 (a) Underlit; (b) steep
lighting

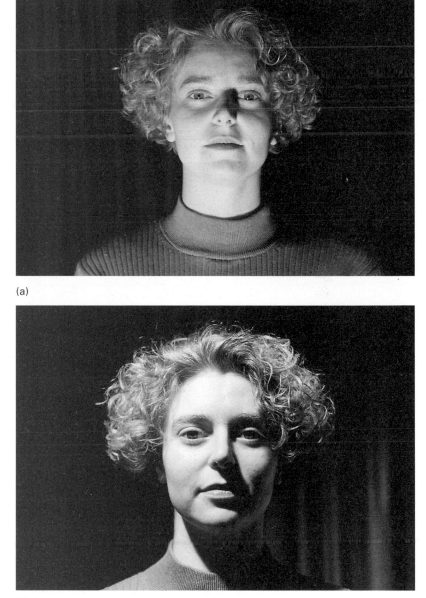

(a)

(b)

depth and the sky which gives very soft diffused lighting without any
obvious shadows. The reasons that the light behaves in different
ways is that the sun is a very small source in comparison to the
subjects it illuminates, hence it produces the hard shadows, whereas
the sky is an extremely large source in area and thus produces almost
shadowless lighting. Note the term *almost* because *no* lighting is
shadowless and if an object blocks some of the light rays it will
produce a shadow, however diffuse!

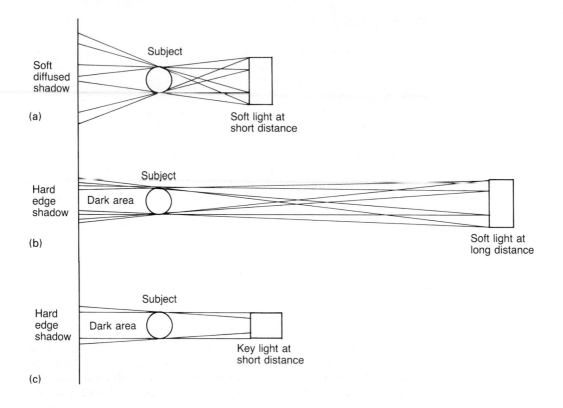

Figure 2.2 (a), (b) Soft light. (c) Hard light

Soft and hard light

'Soft' or 'hard' are relative terms. For instance, a soft light can give reasonably hard shadows, whereas a larger soft light positioned at the same distance, will produce a softer shadow. Conversely, a Fresnel lens luminaire with a brushed silk diffuser fitted can give quite a soft result when used close to the subject.

It must be remembered that both 'hard' and soft' 'light have the same physical properties. 'Hard' light consists of light rays going in straight lines from a very small source to the subject, whereas 'soft' light consists of the same light rays emerging from a larger source area going to the subject in straight lines from a variety of angles. It will have been noted in Figure 2.2 that as the light rays become more parallel to each other, so the quality of the shadow becomes more 'hard'.

Vertical and horizontal soft light

An important factor in the use of soft lights, which is often forgotten, is that they have two planes of illumination, the horizontal and vertical. If softness tests are done with a 'projected cross' system it will be found that as the width of the soft light becomes greater, so the vertical shadows become more diffuse. When the height of the soft light is increased the horizontal shadows become more diffuse. Obviously, there is a finite size to soft lights, but the most effective for many subjects are those that are reasonably wide in relation to their height.

Lighting techniques

Although on the surface, the aims of lighting for pop, theatre, film and television are extremely similar, the lighting techniques are different. In the theatre or at a concert, we view a wide scene with action accentuated by the use of the basic lighting, colour and lighting effects and unless we use some binoculars, we do not see the subjects in close up. In television and film, we are looking for most of the time at the subject detail in fairly tight close up.

What constitutes good or bad lighting is very much the opinion of the observer, but there are certain ground rules which can define the quality of lighting as perceived by the viewer of the scene. A good example of bad lighting, when shooting film and television material, is the incorrect colour of the light sources or choosing the wrong colour correction. The balance between modelling lights and fill lights has to be closely controlled or it may give problems with contrast and exposure and as well as creating 'grainy' or 'noisy' pictures. Highly saturated colours can be extremely effective in the theatre and on the concert stage but when used for television can give a very over-powering result due to the size of the screen image. Extremely steep lighting from above a person will give very distorted features on the face and for that matter if the lighting is from beneath (see Fig. 2.1(a),(b)). It has been commented that when using high definition TV systems that it is essential to have good contrast within the scene to avoid a flat result. This is also true for normal television. The use of flashing coloured moving lights in the concert hall can be extremely exciting, but if isolated close-ups are used from the scene the flashing lights, movement and their colour may become a distraction; this is quite often true at televized concerts! This is not to say that lighting has to obey a fixed set of rather boring rules but the choice of light sources, colour and special effects has to be carefully thought out and balanced against what is stimulating and what is annoying. The very best lighting for film, television and many stage productions will be largely un-noticed by the viewer and, if this is the case, the lighting designer's aims will probably have been achieved.

Lighting conventions

Most of the lighting conventions used in the film and television industry emerged from the earlier days of film when all the material was shot in black and white. It was obviously extremely important to give a sense of depth to pictures and when one sees some of the original extremely old movies that were made without the use of enhanced artificial light, and shot purely by daylight, the results are somewhat flat and uninteresting. During the late 1920s and early 1930s increasing use was made of high powered light sources in the film industry and these enabled the lighting cameramen to achieve better results than previously. Hollywood discovered that a key light placed at the correct angle could enhance the artist greatly. Thus we had 'Paramount' lighting where a hard key light was fairly low and straight onto the face, which enhanced the beauty of ladies with high cheekbones, Marlene Deitrich being one supreme example. The film makers also learnt from portrait painters and noted that a more interesting result could be given when the key light was not straight to the face, but taken to the side and thus a type of lighting known as 'Rembrandt' portraiture. Probably the pinnacle of black and white film lighting is that of *Citizen Kane*, with its highly dramatic portraiture and extremely imaginative use of shadows and highlights. The advent of colour film, with its lower contrast range, meant that the lighting cameramen had to control the lights to a narrower band of illumination, using colour more imaginatively to obtain contrast.

Differences in techniques

The major difference between the techniques for theatre and pop and those for film and television, is that within the pop and theatre world lights are focused onto the scene of action at much steeper vertical angles than for the film and television studio. Why is this? At a pop concert or in the theatre, the stage area is relatively confined and as well as the need to suspend lights above the production, there is also the need for many items of scenery to be flown in and out. Consequently, space is at a premium. As we have already noted, we are attempting to make the audience concentrate on certain areas of the stage to highlight the enjoyment. Invariably, this is accomplished by lighting small areas which create the mood and atmosphere for the viewing audience. In general, for drama, realistic approaches are generally adopted, where colouring is generally natural and the use of filtered lights is restricted to scenery and effects. Lighting for music, opera and ballet will be accomplished by much broader sweeps of lighting, as the action takes place over a larger area than drama. It is probably due to the needs previously discussed that the theatre and pop lighting designers use small, fairly hard spotlights together with flood luminaires capable of giving broad washes of illumination. On the whole, the performers will always be lit by profile lights of some description with fill light supplied by luminaires of a similar type, thus hard lighting is used the majority of time on the artists. On the stage, the light levels used are those that are comfortable for viewing by human beings, therefore there is not the need for high light levels, as there is in the film and television industry; and in fact, light levels might not be necessarily much higher than those in some homes, although some modern theatre tends to be lit to fairly high light levels. The pop world and the theatre have an immense advantage over the film and television industry when using lighting effects, because the eye can distinguish between very minor changes and accommodate very high contrast where the camera cannot.

Whereas the theatre and the concert arena have to be lit for the entire viewed scene, the film and television industry is lit 'piecemeal'. Traditionally, the film industry has always shot for one camera position at any one time, therefore the lighting is only adjusted for that camera position. When the camera position is moved, the lighting is re-adjusted to suit the new position. This has two distinct advantages, one of which is that you only need one camera and, secondly, not too many lights. This technique is also used in television these days, particularly on location. Obviously, this is much more applicable to drama than it would be to musicals which would have to be lit at the same time, irrespective of the varying camera positions. A problem that exists with this technique is that continuity has to be watched very carefully, thus sunlight, if not accurately noted, could vary in its direction within a room. Higher light levels were required in the film industry, dictated by the sensitivity of the film stock in use at the time. The areas involved with productions could be quite large, and it was necessary to use luminaires which, when the beams overlapped, produced a much more natural effect than the spotlights used in the theatre. The use of the close-up occasioned the need for much better lighting on the artists and parts of the setting. The mere fact that the close-up can dwell on an area for quite considerable periods of time, necessitates a greater attention to detail. The best example of this would be the joins on sets when they are built or assembled in the studio and where the scenery flats overlap.

Lighting styles

The usual primary lighting for actors on the stage is two lights, one from either side of the actor's face, and both predominantly from a front position, so that reasonable modelling is achieved. As in television and film techniques, a back light enhances the look of the scene. A problem that exists in the theatre much more than in television and film, due to the slightly more confined space, is the need to watch where the shadows are projected from the artists and for that matter from the scenery. In television the area viewed by the camera often dictates where the shadows are projected. Pop lighting has to accentuate the artists concerned and although the technique is very similar to the theatre the result may be achieved with more light sources. Other than the modelling keys there is a need for dynamic lighting to give the production the impact required by the performance of the particular piece of music. A particularly interesting type of lighting is that for ballet and sometimes for effect where lights are focused from either side of the stage very low down and straight across. For ballet it enhances the legs of the dancers, in drama it has a dramatic effect when people walk in and out of the light beam. Strong side light also brings out the subject from the background, giving them a white outline and a 'cartoon' like clarity. This latter technique has been used most successfully on the European stage with the use of discharge lamps as the sources, but it must be noted that very few light sources were used during some of these productions.

2.1   Basic lighting

We have to remember that luminaires work in three dimensional space; they can move in two directions in the horizontal plane and be adjusted vertically. Additionally, we are concerned with the direction of light, the texture of light, the colour of light and the intensity of light.

Whereas lighting for theatre and pop concerts relies upon the skill of a lighting designer visually balancing the intensity of light and colour, in the film and television industries there is a requirement to achieve certain light levels, and an understanding of the problems with the factors that have an influence on incident light, is useful subject matter for this book. The floodlighting fraternity generally use horizontal plane measurements for their lighting. In the film and television industry, we are concerned with vertical planes such as actors and sets. This is not to say that the designer in the theatre or pop world should not have an interest in the physics of the light beam. In general, most people know that light falls off with the square of the distance. However, many people are unaware that the angle of the incident light falling on the subject also has an effect on the light level on the subject and consequently influences the reflected light which stimulates our eye, the film stock and the CCDs in the TV camera.

LIGHT IN THE VERTICAL PLANE

Most measurements assume that the light is directly on axis and that if, at a set distance from the source, the incident light level will be I/D^2, but in the examples that follow, it will be seen that the angle of incidence (cosine law) also affects the light level.

Throw $(T) = \sqrt{[d^2 + (H - x \text{ or } y)^2]}$

where: d is the horizontal distance in metres
H is the height of the luminaire above floor level
x or y is the subject height (1.3 m seated and 1.8 m standing)

Cosine $\phi = \dfrac{d}{T}$

Incident light level is given by:

$$\frac{I \text{ (candelas)}}{\text{Throw}^2 \ (T^2)} \times \frac{\text{distance } (d)}{\text{Throw } (T)} = \frac{Id}{T^3}$$

The luminaires used in the examples that follow are all Fresnel lens type in the flood position.

Basic lighting has very similar fundamental requirements, and the main forms of illumination used are outlined in the remainder of Section 2.1.

Figure 2.3 Incident light

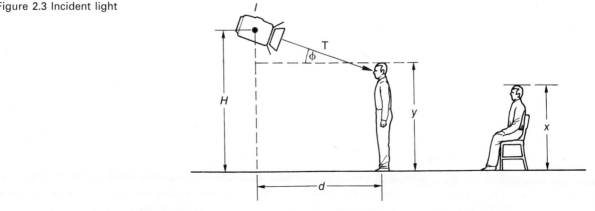

Figure 2.4 Lighting the subject: light in the vertical plane

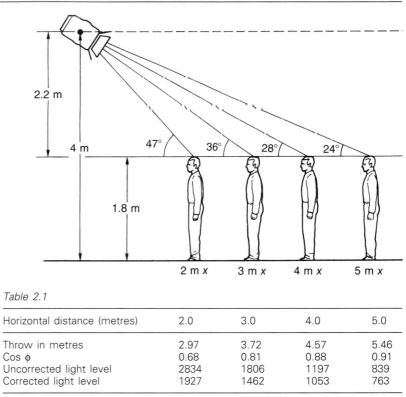

Table 2.1

Horizontal distance (metres)	2.0	3.0	4.0	5.0
Throw in metres	2.97	3.72	4.57	5.46
Cos ϕ	0.68	0.81	0.88	0.91
Uncorrected light level	2834	1806	1197	839
Corrected light level	1927	1462	1053	763

It will be noted that the differences in light level and incident angles are not very great except when close to the luminaire, e.g. 2 and 3 metres.

Table 2.2 Standing position (height 1.8 metres)

Luminaire	Light output (candelas)	Luminaire height (metres)	Distance (metres)	Throw (metres)	Angle (degrees)	Cosine of angle	Illumination In lux
1 kW tungsten	10 800	4	3	3.72	36	0.81	629
2 kW tungsten	25 000	4	4	4.57	29	0.88	1051
3 kW tungsten	45 000	5	5	5.94	33	0.84	1075
5 kW tungsten	75 000	5	6	6.80	28	0.88	1431
1.2 kW discharge	70 000	4	5	5.46	24	0.92	2147
2.5 kW discharge	100 000	4	6	6.39	20	0.94	2300
4.0 kW discharge	200 000	5	7	7.70	25	0.91	3070
6.0 kW discharge	300 000	5	8	8.62	22	0.93	3752

Table 2.3 Seated position (height 1.3 metres)

Luminaire	Light output (candelas)	Luminaire height (metres)	Distance (metres)	Throw (metres)	Angle (degrees)	Cosine of angle	Illumination In lux
1 kW tungsten	10 800	4	3	4.04	42	0.74	493
2 kW tungsten	25 000	4	4	4.83	34	0.83	890
3 kW tungsten	45 000	5	5	6.22	36	0.80	935
5 kW tungsten	75 000	5	6	7.05	32	0.85	1285
1.2 kW discharge	70 000	4	5	5.68	28	0.88	1908
2.5 kW discharge	100 000	4	6	6.58	24	0.91	2107
4.0 kW discharge	200 000	5	7	7.92	28	0.88	2820
6.0 kW discharge	300 000	5	8	8.81	25	0.91	3505

The key light

Why is it called the key? The luminaire used provides the principal light on the scene and tends to be the key to the whole picture. It establishes the mood and character and generally is capable of producing acceptable results when used on its own. However, it makes no contribution towards the depth of the picture. Key lights for film and TV tend to be used at a vertical angle of 30° to the subject but can be within the range of 20–45°, although the lower angle can produce disturbing glare to the actors. The key light can be used over a horizontal angle of incidence within 45° either side of the normal to the subject. As a general rule 30° vertical and 30° horizontal displacement gives extremely satisfactory results for visual close-ups. On the stage they are generally steeper due to the need to reduce projected shadows together with their greater suspended height.

The back light

The back light is needed so that the separation and depth are enhanced. The positioning of back lights is extremely critical and they should not be placed too steeply in the vertical plane because of the fact that they may spill over onto the subject's face and create rather disturbing effects. Back lights can be varied much more than a key light for their angle of incidence and in fact many good effects are produced by taking them to extremes. The back light usually is in a ratio of 1:1 with the key light, but if increased gives a much more dramatic effect. Single back lights can be effective on the subject but quite often twin back lights are to be advocated for any subject with long hair.

Fill light

Why do we require fill light? When viewed with the eye, a subject lit with a key and back light will look perfectly alright, however, due to the restrictive contrast ranges used for film and television, the results would look somewhat over-contrasted when viewed either on the cinema screen or the television screen; therefore fill light is used to reduce the contrast by diminishing the shadow areas. As a guide, the lighting level of the fill light is about 50% of that of the key. One point that should be noted is that having made a shadow with one light, there is no way that the shadow can be removed or diminished to any great degree by the addition of more and more fill light. Fill light is often a soft source because we are used to the sky being our fill light. However, if we use hard light in a controlled manner, which is the technique used by lighting designers, then we can still achieve a pleasing result. Whereas, in the theatre and at a concert, double shadows might not be quite so apparent on the human face, they are extremely apparent in close-up in the film and television media.

2.2   Choice of light sources and luminaires

Due to the merging of techniques throughout the lighting industry, it is very difficult to decide what type of source would be used in any one particular branch of the industry. However, we can generalize and say that in the film and television industries, Fresnel lens luminaires using both tungsten and discharge sources predominate. Recent times have seen the introduction of very high efficiency PAR discharge sources and these are being introduced very rapidly into both the TV and film industries. TV studios and the theatre favour tungsten as the predominant source, as it is easy to control and obtain extremely good lighting effects. The pop industry use Parcans and automated luminaires fitted with tungsten lamps which can be controlled by conventional dimmers, in addition to motorized luminaires using discharge sources where the light output is controlled by mechanical dimming systems. More recently 'low energy' lighting has been introduced into smaller studios, usually in the form of fluorescent lighting. Although not giving such good subject modelling, as the more focused sources would, low energy lighting does allow control of output light level by dimmers with consistently good colour.

Luminaire positions

All lighting must be positioned fairly accurately to give the correct effect that the lighting designer desires. The height of the lights is important in relation to the horizontal distance to the subject. In the film and television industry, flexibility in height and in the 'xy' axis, along and across the studio, is given by the various types of suspension systems on offer. This is also true for the theatre, although lights tend to be moved en masse and not individually as in film and television. With fixed suspension systems such as a grid in a small TV studio, or the larger truss members on a big pop rig, movement is generally achieved by pan and tilt – horizontal and vertical movement within the rig is very restricted. It is of course possible to provide local flexible suspension such as pantographs, which allow adjustment in the vertical plane. Due to the smaller size of luminaires used in the theatre and the large numbers used within the stage area, it is possible to precisely focus lights from an almost limitless set of positions. In television and film, the size of the luminaires prevents close proximity working and the type of suspension systems often do not allow such precise position in the horizontal plane. This is often circumvented by using cross bars, enabling lights to be positioned in a more precise way but often with a penalty of tying up two suspension points.

Soft sources

If we look in lighting manufacturers' catalogues, we will see a variety of soft sources on offer, and these go from fairly large to small luminaires. Therefore, it would appear that the larger ones are softer than the smaller ones, and this of course is true if they are set from the subject at the same distance. However, the small soft light near to the subject may provide a softer result than the larger one, at, say, twice the distance. This is due to the apparent area of soft light at the distance, due to perspective, and of course, the same effect applies to hard sources. It should always be remembered that a soft light looked at full on presents a large area source, but when viewed from the side, presents a very small source and this has often been

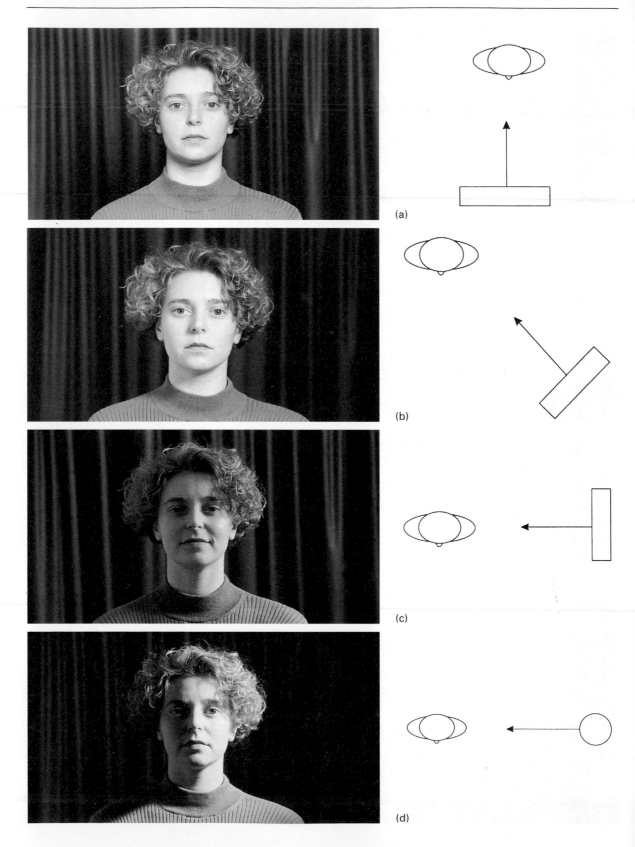

(a)

(b)

(c)

(d)

(e)

(f)

(g)

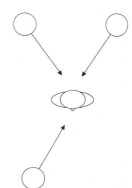

(h)

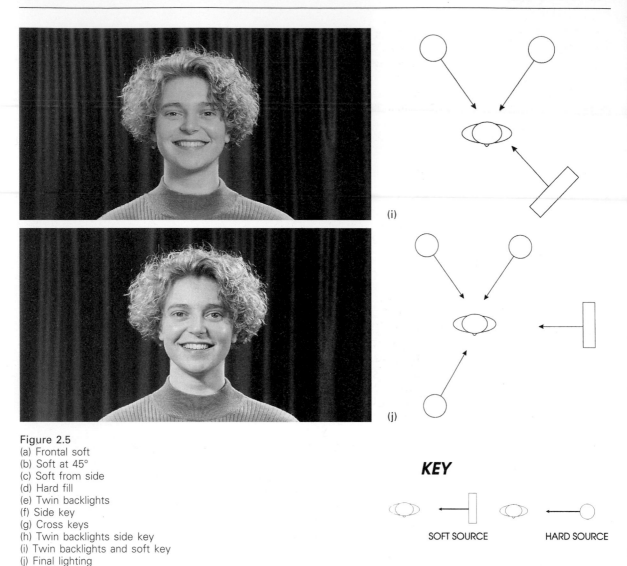

Figure 2.5
(a) Frontal soft
(b) Soft at 45°
(c) Soft from side
(d) Hard fill
(e) Twin backlights
(f) Side key
(g) Cross keys
(h) Twin backlights side key
(i) Twin backlights and soft key
(j) Final lighting

KEY

SOFT SOURCE　　　　　HARD SOURCE

the undoing of many a lighting designer in the television industry. It's a wonderful way of producing unwanted microphone boom shadows! (see Fig. 2.2).

Fresnel sources

In television and film, because of the need for broad lighting techniques, luminaires with much softer edges are employed, therefore the Fresnel spotlight becomes more useful with its soft edge to the light beam which allows an integration of light sources for a much smoother result. In the film studio, a 2 kW Fresnel is a relatively low powered luminaire, 5 kW and 10 kW tungsten luminaires are more the norm. The need of the film industry for extremely high light levels, particularly when colour was introduced with the old Technicolor process, etc., necessitated high intensity carbon arc sources, culminating in huge things like the 'Brute' with a power of 225 A. The arcs were often used on location to balance the shadow areas in scenes lit by sunlight. The carbon arc was superseded by discharge luminaires using HMI and MSR lamps and there is much to commend these lighting sources; they provide a very high quality light output which is about four times greater than their tungsten counterparts. However, they have the disadvantage that they can only be dimmed over a restricted range, and thus do not allow for complex lighting effects changes.

Fresnel control

In TV and film studios, the workhorse of the lighting director is the focusing Fresnel spot, whereas the same LD working outside on an OB or interview situation, will often use open faced luminaires. Normally, an LD who is given the choice will choose to work with the Fresnel spot because it offers many advantages over the open faced luminaire with a focal range from a 10° beam angle at spot to a 60° beam angle at full flood and a light output range of about 8:1. The light is very evenly distributed without striations in the beam and the barndoors provide a good soft edge cut off. The Fresnel luminaire, however, is most inefficient as a source with an efficiency of around 8% in spot and 26% in flood. When used in studios the lighting level from tungsten sources is quite acceptable because the cameras can be set to work at a much lower lighting level than is often possible on location where work is carried out in daylight and requires the artificial lighting to blend in with the high level of the ambient daylight and to match the same colour temperature.

Correction filters

Interior shots on locations may be lit with either tungsten or discharge lighting and it may be necessary to work with daylight coming through the windows. When using tungsten, this problem can be solved by either placing an orange filter on the windows and balance for 3200K, or balance for 5600K and use of a blue daylight correction filter in front of the luminaire which unfortunately reduces the light output by 50% at the very time that a high output is required to try to match the daylight intensity. Another solution is to use discharge lighting which offers a high light level, blends exceptionally well with daylight and is cooler in operation, but is more expensive than tungsten and requires a control ballast.

Open faced luminaires

The focusing open-faced luminaire, such as a 2 kW Blonde, has a much better efficiency than the Fresnel with up to five times more light in the spot mode; and nearly twice as much when in 'flood' compared to a 2 kW Fresnel. This variation in efficiency is due to the fact that in the 'spot' mode the lamp is relatively close to the reflector and the stray light is much reduced compared to the flood position. Redheads and Blondes are small, light and relatively inexpensive but the trade-off is a hard shadow produced from the direct light of the lamps' filament, with a second shadow produced from the reflector which is superimposed over the first shadow, giving harsh shadows. Light spill can be a problem and the barndoors are not very effective. The typical focusing range for a Blonde is from a beam angle of 23° in spot to a beam angle of 70° in flood with a light output range of 8:1. The Redhead goes from 42° in spot to 86° in flood with an output range of 6:1.

Rig positions

The methods of positioning lights varies quite considerably between the concert venue, the theatre and in film and television studios. There is obviously no need to hide the lights in the television studio or the film studio, and in a large pop rig the light sources are usually integrated into the overall design. However, in the theatre, the majority of lights have to be tucked out of the audience's viewing line so that they do not become distracting. The main lighting positions will be over the stage, at the front of house and to the sides of the stage. The stage lights will be suspended from bars, capable of being raised and lowered over the stage area and these bars will be interspersed between the scenery flying bars. These lights are the most important ones that have to be obscured from the audience as they would be directly in their sight line. Consequently the position of the lights in relation to people towards the front of the stalls is extremely critical and thus forces the lights generally upwards, vertically away from the stage area. The front of house lights which are above the audience are not so obvious and do not need to be obscured; however, from a consideration for the theatre decor, it is nice if they are not too noticeable.

To each side of the stage will be ladders or vertical bars for rigging selected luminaires for additional effect and use, particularly so for low angled cross lighting. Luminaires used for backings on stage productions include floodlights, which may be straightforward flood units, or special cyclorama lighting units for illuminating backcloths, etc. These units can be provided as single sources or in groups of 3 or 4 so that colour mixing could take place. Small Fresnel spotlights are used where a good smooth spread is desired and quite often used in theatres in the round; they are also useful as back lights on many productions, particularly with musicals. The profile spotlight is the most used luminaire in the theatre, because it enables precise control of the beam, the size of which is controlled by an iris diaphragm. Profile spots are also fitted with metal shutters for producing hard flat edges to the beam, and special shapes can be introduced into the projector gate of a profile spot. The edge of the light beam can be made either fairly soft or very hard by adjusting the lens. Many modern profile spots in use have zoom optics which allow a great deal of flexibility when rigging and lighting in the areas concerned. Recently the use of Parcans has become more normal; the only problem with the Parcan is that the beam width is dictated by the type of lamp used. With the correct choice of lamp and subsequently rotating the position of the lamp, it is possible to vary the beam shape quite successfully. It may also be advantageous to use a brushed silk filter in the luminaire to further modify the beam spread. Although the Parcan does not have the same flexibility as, say, a Fresnel spotlight or a profile spot, they do have advantages – they are cheap to purchase, fairly easy to maintain and allow a multiplicity of effects at not too high a cost.

Many productions in major theatres now use automated luminaires where functions such as focus, colour, pattern projection together with pan and tilt are controlled from a remote position; therefore a smaller number of luminaires may be required because of the ability to completely reset the output of a luminaire during the course of the production. The introduction of sophisticated colour changing mechanisms has also allowed the number of lights in the theatre to be reduced quite considerably. It goes without saying that remote controlled luminaires and colour changers have to be as silent as possible, otherwise they disrupt the audience's enjoyment of the play or musical.

Truss support

On rigs for concerts, pop shows, fashion shows and even for car launches a bewildering array of light sources will be found, all of which have to supported, usually from a truss system. Unlike the theatre and studio, where the support systems are part of a permanent installation and not always capable of modification, truss support systems are designed with the lighting of specific shows in mind. It is therefore possible to accommodate most of the lighting designer's luminaires and effects system without too much of a problem.

Theatre rig

In the theatre, the majority of luminaires tend to be suspended from the bars and around the edges of the acting area. In the film and television industry, other than using luminaires hanging from the grid or working from stands at floor level, there is a need to mount lights on the scenery flats themselves and to conceal luminaires within the sets for effect. On all these occasions, the size of the luminaire has a great bearing on rigging in the studio or theatre. Luckily, in the theatre, where many luminaires are used, they are relatively small, the only drawback being that the profile spot is rather a long device and therefore when panning around, requires quite a large operating circle. Although small, compact luminaires can be used for both film and television, the majority are fairly big in size and require a fairly large operating space. Therefore, rigging is often at a premium over a specified area.

Film rig

Lighting in the film industry tends generally to be from the floor upwards. Because of the rehearse/shoot techniques of the film industry, a production is generally filmed shot by shot, not necessarily in a logical sequence, and put together in the editing room. To make the lighting as flexible as possible, it is useful to have the luminaires mounted on adjustable stands which can be moved to new positions very quickly by the electricians on the set, rather then having the lights suspended from the ceiling, which tends to be rather fixed and time consuming when changes are required.

For the suspension of lighting units in film studios, the simplest form is to have a block and tackle with the capability of running along a steel RSJ mounted at roof level. Thus a single point suspension can be used which could be pulled across or along the studio. One drawback to this system is that to introduce any new light at any position often requires shifting other lights which causes further rigging problems. Another technique is to suspend long platforms with handrails either side, called 'boats', where several luminaires can be rigged on the rails and manipulated by electricians manually. Although access to the luminaires is obviously better, changing the position of the boats in the studio is a time consuming process, and probably only pays dividends when luminaires are set up for quite considerable periods of time on a major production.

Film lighting does not rely upon dimmers to balance the lights themselves. Lighting intensity is adjusted by spotting and flooding luminaires, by the careful selection of the power output of luminaires and, if necessary, scrims and neutral density filters can be used to achieve technical balance. The main reason for this technique being used is that film stock is generally balanced for 3200K or for 5600K daylight. Although the film stock concerned will have some small latitude of colour response to the lights concerned, the film industry has always gone along with the fact that the lights should be relatively fixed in relation to the 3200K or 5600K standards. When filming, it is necessary that the majority of the luminaires will be either tungsten or discharge sources; if not, there will be a requirement to colour correct some of the various light sources. For many years, tungsten was the main source of most illumination in the film studios, with carbon arcs being used when higher power was required. Nowadays, discharge lighting is normally used, due to its greater efficiency and cooler operation.

2.3   TV lighting systems

Television lighting, which evolved from film lighting, relied on the tried and tested methods used by the film makers for many years, and many of the original television studios were, in fact, converted film studios. As television became more and more sophisticated and the need for a greater productivity arose, the studios had to become more efficient with their output being raised so that the need for additional studios was avoided. During the 1960s it was possible that a day's filming would yield two minutes of finished material, whereas in television the need was to produce 30 minutes from each day of production. The basic luminaires used in television, after World War II, were the Fresnel spotlights in 1kW, 2kW, 5kW and 10kW versions together with a miscellany of soft lights such as Scoops, Tenlites, Hewitt Banks, etc.

Historical

In Europe during the 1950s, tremendous strides were made in modernizing television studios; the greatest of these was the adoption of motorized rigging systems such as the monopole and motorized barrel winch. This enabled a small team of electricians to service a studio rapidly and effectively and most important of all, safely. Subsequently the monopole system was generally employed where fairly accurate rigging was required, but not used on a saturated basis, working on the principle that lights could be moved to suit during the rigging periods. The solution reached by the BBC for monochrome TV during the 1960s, was to equip all its main production studios with motorized barrel winches utilizing 2kW Fresnel luminaires and Tenlites for soft sources.

Multi-purpose

The advent of colour saw a different technique evolve at the BBC. The single Fresnels and soft lights were replaced with the multi-purpose luminaire which is a combination of a soft light and a hard light. This tends to be something of a compromise as a soft source because of its small physical size and compact reflectors, but it was a fairly good Fresnel spot light. By having the complete area covered with the multi-purpose units, a saturated lighting system was evolved where the need to rig and de-rig luminaires was obviated to a large degree, and during the 1970s the BBC achieved extremely high productivity in its studios, based at that time on multi-camera shooting techniques. The multi-purpose luminaires were generally fitted with either dual wattage 2.5 kW or 5 kW lamps in the Fresnel half, and either 4 × 625 W linear lamps or 4 × 1250 W linear lamps in the soft half. This allowed the luminaires to be either in a 1.25 kW, 2.5 kW or 5 kW mode and enabled the operators to control the light level and colour temperature over various distances of 'throw' within the studio. A later development provided one filament at 1.25 kW with the other at 2.5 kW, thus enabling a range of one third, two thirds or full power, giving a much better control of light intensity within the limits of colour temperature, with the soft end of the luminaire fitted with four 625 W lamps capable of being switched between 1.25 kW and 2.5 kW only.

Camera line-up

With the spread of colour TV in the UK, experiments took place to ascertain the parameters that could be used to maintain good colour balance for the pictures, but allowing some form of control on the lighting itself, and it was found that a tolerance of 200K either side of 3000K was reasonable; thus the cameras were lined up for this colour of incident light. The light level requirement was given by the sensitivity of the colour cameras working between f2.8 and f4.0. The dimmers used in television studios normally have a square law light output, which means that the square of the fader setting from 1 to 10 gives the percentage light output, i.e. level 6 = 36%. It is normal when commencing operations in the studio to align the channel controllers to position '7' which means that the dimmer would supply current to operate the lamp at 49% of its light output; its colour temperature at this point is approximately 3000K. As we have an acceptable variation of ± 200K, it allows the fader lever to go down to '5' with a 25% light output and when faded up to 'full', to have 100% light output; thus we have 2 stops (4:1) variation in the light level. This system allows a wide variation in the intensity of light and allows a great deal of control so that we may balance the light sources. However, it requires that all luminaires are fed from

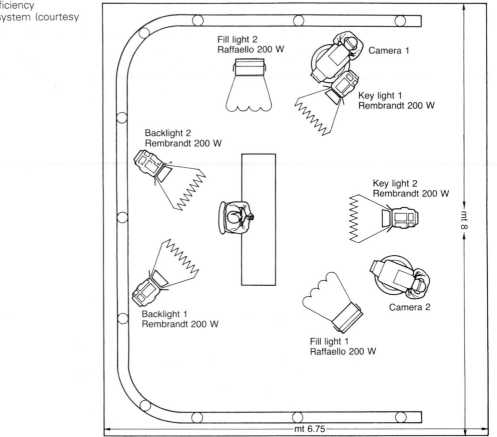

dimmers; thus there is a need for very large dimmer installations if saturated lighting systems are used.

It is possible to reduce the number of dimmers by using a power patching system, but this is often time consuming and not always convenient when in a rehearse/record situation. Also these days, a patch system costs almost the same as a dimmer installation.

Luminaire height

In both the film and television industries, if we adopt the principle that the key light has to be somewhere between 30° and 45° in the vertical angle to the subject, the luminaires' height above the studio floor will be dictated by the power output of any luminaire used and the intensity of light required on the subject; e.g. a low powered luminaire will be positioned closer to the subject and consequently will be lower in height to maintain the same incident angle. In television, with a 2.5 kW lamp at position 7 on the dimmer, this approximates to around 4 m above floor level. In the film studio it may be that the height above the floor is increased by using higher powered luminaires. In all branches of entertainment lighting the luminaire positions are greatly affected by their relationship to the scenery. On some occasions it will be impossible to get the preferred light source high enough and it may be necessary to use a smaller luminaire closer to the subject. On other occasions large pieces of scenery, as found on the opera stage or the double storey building on the film set, may force the luminaires to be unnaturally high, creating a requirement for much more powerful luminaires. Due to the decrease in lighting levels required in television studios, we have seen the introduction of 3 kW lamps to replace 5 kW lamps in 5 kW luminaires with a light output in the same ratio as the kilowatts i.e. 5:3.

Daylight control

Generally in television studios, there is no problem with large variations in light levels as they are well controlled within the studio area. On outside broadcasts, it is a vastly different situation where the light level may vary from almost nothing to light levels as high as 80 000 lux. There are occasions, however, where the controlled conditions of the studio and variations in light level of the outside world have to come together, and these are usually in studios where windows are provided to give a natural backing. It is relatively easy to raise the interior light level so that there is some approximation to the incoming daylight. However, this usually results in some form of discomfort glare to the artists and the generation of heat, caused by the high light levels. In these cases, of course, one invariably resorts to discharge lighting with its much more efficient light output efficiency. An important factor when designing for studios such as this, is the direction of the light through the windows. It's rather unfortunate if you are facing south west in the northern hemisphere and getting the rays of the dying sun. One method that was used at the BBC to control the incident light from the outside world was to use Polaroid sheet applied to the windows, with a rotating Polaroid filter in front of the studio camera. The rotational Polaroid only caused a 50% reduction in the reflected light from the subject to camera. However, the combination of the rotating and fixed Polaroid allowed the windows to be controlled from 50% transmission down to virtually 0% transmission. With the addition of an electronic exposure sensing circuit it was possible to have the rotating Polaroid filter automatically adjust according to the incident daylight. This method is only useful if the window has small areas of glass, as Polaroid sheet is only obtainable in fairly small sizes. Incidentally, the luminaire employed as the frontal key was a 1.2 kW Fresnel spot discharge source in 'flood', with two 75 watt low voltage PAR lamps used as backlights.

Outside source selection

Outside television studios used on large sporting events will require several levels of lighting being used to match the daylight, and it may be that the daylight keylights are 4 kW Fresnel discharge sources in full spot to give sufficient light level, whereas the night time lighting may be down to quite small discharge sources such as the 575 W in full flood. The natural light will vary in relation to the artificial light; but by using a selection of luminaires with various power outputs and switching between them it is possible to balance for the incident daylight. Of course, it is possible to balance for the maximum incident light level and just let the background slowly diminish over a period of time but with presenters using prompters and the danger of a high glare factor it is preferable to adjust the lighting to create more comfortable conditions. As the natural light diminishes changes are made between the various sources and it is hoped that these go relatively unnoticed by the viewer.

Conclusion

Light sources and luminaires come in a variety of shapes and sizes and whether tungsten, discharge, fluorescent or any other type of lighting is used, the final result will depend upon the intensity, colour, quality of light and incident angle to the subject. Lights are only a means to an end and even the most modern lighting devices will not correct for bad lighting practices.

To put the whole subject in perspective, a famous British lighting director once said of one of his colleagues 'that man could obtain good pictures using candles mounted in milk bottles'.

3
Theory of light

3.1 The eye

It is an incredible fact that we take for granted one of the most sophisticated pieces of the anatomy. Even with the wonders of modern technology scientists cannot come up with a piece of equipment that has to include the following:

Three dimensional optical system
High definition
Highly sophisticated colour sensitivity system
Auto focus
Auto iris
Automatic sensitivity
No signal to noise problems – no grain!
High overload factor
Virtually no maintenance

Luckily nature did, and from the time of our arrival on earth, eyes were essential for survival and, even more importantly for the advance of civilization, for communication. Before the telegraphic, wireless and TV systems were introduced in the late nineteenth and early twentieth centuries, we could only communicate directly through speech and additionally by symbols, drawings and script.

A major problem with the human eye is that it can be fooled; it is not an absolute measuring instrument such as a colour meter, but relies mainly on comparative measurements to assess information. If we show a human being, in a darkened room, a succession of similarly coloured lights with intervals of darkness between, the subject is totally unaware of a change over quite a wide range, e.g. from pale blue to a mid blue. However, two colours when shown side by side have only to vary by a small amount and the difference is noticeable. As we can process much visual information using our superior intelligence, the human eye does not have to be as good as that of many birds and animals.

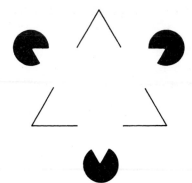

Figure 3.1 The figure has many possible triangles although no triangles have been drawn. The V shaped figures can be 'closed' by your brain to form one large triangle, or 'closed' opposite the apex to form three. The eye can use the portion of the V triangle 'underneath' the large white one to close off three smaller white triangles with an apex in each circle. You can also see a six pointed star by combining the large white triangle and the one formed by the Vs. These illusory triangles are called *Kanizsa triangles* after Professor Gaetano Kanizsa of the University of Trieste who first introduced them (Kanizsa, 1976).

Photopic vision

The most important aspect of lighting is photopic vision. Not every individual has the same sensitivity, therefore the CIE adopted an internationally agreed response, which is called the CIE standard observer. This gives the standard sensitivity for the eye for wavelengths from 380 nanometers to 760 nanometers. The peak sensitivity is at 555 nm, whereas the sensitivity at 400 nm is about 1/1000th of the highest level. In practice, this means that one watt of radiation in the green part of the spectrum has an effect 1000 times greater than one watt of radiation at the blue end of the spectrum.

Rods and cones

When light enters the lens of the eye, it is received by the retina which consists of millions of photoreceptors, packed into an area about 1.5 cm². Human beings have two types of receptors, called 'rods' and 'cones', because we live in two distinct worlds – night and day. The cones, which number approximately seven million, are for the detailed full colour examination of objects in bright light; the rods, which number approximately one hundred and thirty million, are for the examination of objects in low light conditions. Rods and cones are not dissimilar in their individual sensitivity; but to achieve a higher sensitivity several rods are coupled together, and this accounts for the loss of sharpness of vision at night.

The eye can accept intensity levels that vary by a factor of more than 10^{12} (a million million) but our eyes' iris can only control over a range of 16:1, how is this?

In 1877 Franz Boll, a German biologist, examined a frog's eye taken from a dark closet in the laboratory. At the back of the eye he saw a reddish substance that quickly faded upon exposure to light. This phenomenon had been noticed by other scientists who generally dismissed it as a blood clot. Boll was dissatisfied with this theory and upon examination discovered that if the eye was returned to the dark and the experiment repeated, the reddish substance re-appeared. Boll had discovered that a chemical change takes place in the eye when light enters it. In 1959 at the Johns Hopkins University, two scientists inserted a microscopic electrode into the brain of a cat and recorded the activity of a single nerve cell in the vision system of the brain. When the cat viewed a light flashing, electrical signals were emitted from the nerve cell. The connection between these two experiments is that light when passing into the eye creates a chemical reaction, and subsequently the chemical reaction is transferred into electrical energy.

Visual purple

Shortly after Boll had realized the significance of the reddish substance, Wilhelm Kühne managed to extract some of the chemical from the rods in the frog's eye. This substance was called *Sehpurpur* – a German word meaning visual scarlet, but was incorrectly translated into English as *visual purple* and even today is known as that. The chemical's correct name is rhodopsin. A rhodopsin molecule consists of two parts; a simple molecule called retinal and a protein molecule called opsin. Opsin is built from amino acids and its complex structure has not yet been fully catalogued. Different proteins are found in the cones and these determine the colour response. Incidentally the rhodopsin pigment is a close relative to the vitamin A of carrots. Earlier in the present century researchers had found that vision in humans was harmed by vitamin A deficiency, and to some people this meant that by eating large quantities of carrots they would improve their vision. However, this is not the case and people on a good balanced diet will not have any problems. The excess vitamin A taken by an overdose of carrots is simply passed through the body. The greatest danger is turning a shade of red by consuming large quantities of the 'carotene' present in the humble carrot.

Rhodopsin absorbs all wavelengths of light and when it is subjected to high light input levels it bleaches out and thus loses some of its absorbency. The reduction of sensitivity in the rods means that the cone receptors will be used. These being less sensitive will pass lower signals to the brain thus producing a form of automatic gain control.

Figure 3.2 (a) Eyeball

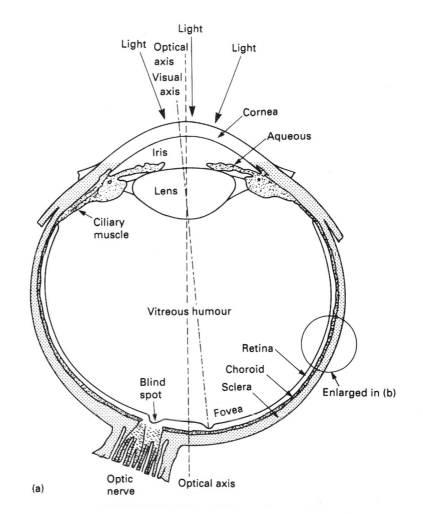

(a)

Figure 3.2 (b) and (c) Rods and
cones

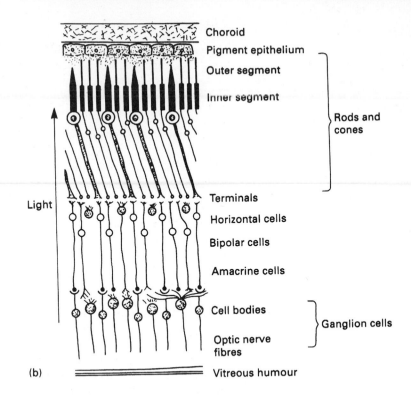

Choroid

Pigment epithelium

Outer segment

Inner segment

Rods and cones

Light

Terminals

Horizontal cells

Bipolar cells

Amacrine cells

Cell bodies

Optic nerve fibres

Ganglion cells

(b)

Vitreous humour

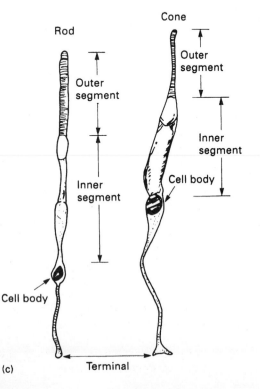

Rod

Cone

Outer segment

Inner segment

Cell body

Outer segment

Inner segment

Cell body

Cell body

(c)

Terminal

The optic nerve

Owing to the complexity of connections between the rods and cones and the optic nerve, there are 150 million photoreceptors connected to about 1 million fibres in the optic nerve, with a much higher number of rods in relation to the cones. As several rods work together into one nerve to increase low light sensitivity, our low light acuity of vision is poor. The cones with their lower density means signals are passed with higher resolution. Due to the cones' lower sensitivity, we all feel better doing fine work in high light levels when the cones are working efficiently (see Figure 3.2a–c).

In 1825, Jan Evangelista Purkinje noticed that at twilight the flowers in his garden apparently changed colours in relation to each other as the illumination changed. As it became darker, red flowers became black, although at this point the green leaves were relatively unaffected. Purkinje had experienced the change from 'cone' vision during daylight to 'rod' vision at night. The 'rod' light receptors, although generally more sensitive than 'cones', have a lower response to light at long wavelengths, thus reds diminish rapidly at dark. The Purkinje effect states that there is a shift of maximum sensitivity towards blue at low light levels.

Lightness constancy

If we view a mosaic made up of areas of white, black and several shades of grey under various levels of illumination, we do not see any significant changes to the mosaic. It appears the level of illumination does not seem to affect how we perceive the areas of white, grey or black. Even if the illumination is not even on the mosaic, our perception of the lightness or darkness of the black, grey and white areas of the mosaic remains the same. For example, it may be that a dark grey area is actually reflecting more light back than a white area, yet we will still see the grey area as dark grey and the white area will still look white.

Colour constancy

As we go about our daily lives, the world is viewed under many different sources of illumination. The colour of noon daylight is much bluer than the incandescent lights used in our homes. Fluorescent lighting, as well as street lighting, does not always provide good colour rendering. However, an apple held in our hand when we stand in any of these light sources appears to be the same colour *irrespective* of the light source. It is as though our brain is programmed to recognize the object for the colour differences, and therefore our colour vision may not be totally dependent upon the input to the brain (see Figure 3.3).

The effect just described is known as 'colour constancy' and holds true for single sources of general illumination. What happens when we are able to see contrasting areas of coloured light at the same time?

If we project a beam of white light onto a screen and encircle it with blue light the original beam will become yellow in appearance. Likewise if we encircle the beam with a red surround it will appear cyan. The original beam colour has not changed but we see it differently. Our eyes have seemingly adapted to the surround more than the reference white beam.

Figure 3.3 Sensitivity of eye receptors

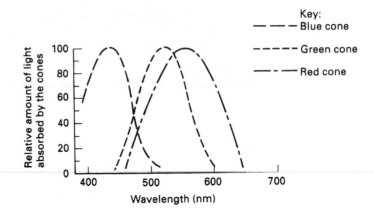

Image retention

We can also have problems with image retention; possibly the most well known demonstration of this effect is that of staring at a 'green heart shape' surrounded by a yellow border for about 20 seconds and then looking at a plain white surface. The after image is that of a magenta heart in a blue border. The theory here is that the green of the heart is bleached out and what is left are the 'red' and 'blue' receptors, hence magenta. However, image retention is the phenomenon which allows us to perceive the rapidly changing image on a television screen or cinema screen as one smoothly moving picture.

There have been so many theories over the centuries as to how the eyes' colour system works. Isaac Newton when he published the first edition of his famous book *Opticks* in 1704, speculated about colour vision. One statement was incredibly accurate with a view to the future.

> May not the harmony and discord of Colours arise from the proportions of the Vibrations propagated through the fibres of the optic Nerves into the Brain as the harmony and discord of Sounds arise from the proportions of the Vibrations of the Air? For some colours, if they be view'd together are agreeable to one another, as those of Gold and Indigo, and others disagree.

In 1801 Thomas Young suggested that the eye contained three colour receptors. It was also reasoned that to provide the correct colour information signals, the range of wavelengths for the red, green and blue receptors would have to overlap each other to some degree and it was only during the twentieth century that scientists discovered the true response of the rods and cones to the colour of light.

A point worth making here, as it is relevant, is that the photo-receptors can only respond by changing their voltage, which gives no absolute information as to the colour of the stimulus that caused the change. For the eye to assess accurately the colour and pass the information to the brain, nerve cells from differing colour receptors must be stimulated so that the relative amounts of colour energy in the viewed scene can be assessed.

Thus a stimulation of a red receptor and a green receptor will give a result between pale yellow and deep orange, depending upon the balance of the two receptors.

Coding systems

In more recent times evidence has emerged that in addition to the red, green and blue visual receptors, cells exist within the nervous system that respond to red, yellow, green and blue either in combination or opposition. This discovery tends to substantiate the theories of the nineteenth century physiologist Ewald Hering who proposed four fundamental colours: red, yellow, green and blue. The 'opponent colour theory' suggests that the four colours act in pairs – red/green and yellow/blue.

Colour after-images – staring at our green heart is a good example – can be explained by the bleaching of photo pigments coupled with some insensitivity in the eye's complex nervous system. However, it is difficult to explain simultaneous contrast effects such as our circle of light surrounded by another colour, particularly when we think of a white light beam turning yellow when viewed with a blue surround, without considering Hering's theory.

The process of seeing

Information from our eyes travels to the primary visual cortex at the back of the brain and the information it requires is as follows:

- Motion
- Form
- Depth
- Colour

We perceive motion as a primary signal to the brain, due to the fact that nature taught us to take evasive action when anything moves near to us, and this is generally processed in black and white. Form or shape, which gives us the information describing what we are looking at, is generally required with colour. Finally, our two eyes give us depth and the three dimensional image that gives us our dimensions of objects, etc. We can however, be tricked by perspective so we need additional information. Generally this is produced by shading. For example, old silent movies illuminated largely in flat lighting, do not have the depth that the later monochrome studio films had in the 1940s and 1950s, and in fact, it was this shading process that enabled black and white television to have some depth, due to the use of light and shade.

Information and meaning

The images presenting themselves to the brain give little or no meaning. What we require is perception, which gives us meaning from the image entering the eye. 'Meaning' is using memory stored from pervious encounters and checking that the image entering the brain corresponds to the stored information. For example, when you see an apple, your memory tells you that it contains seeds, you do not actually need to see them to produce this information. Recognizing a person's face requires both the image to the brain and the memory stored of the information regarding the face. For example, the eyes can be functioning perfectly correctly and give the correct image to the brain, but if the memory system has a fault such as may have occurred in a person who has suffered a stroke, recognition is faulty and almost impossible. Recent experiments suggest that the back of the brain is like a miniature television screen and that when we use our imagination we produce an image in this area, thus 'seeing' gives the same result to the brain as imagination. Whilst seeing we are receiving visual information and preparing the images from the memory system which is filling in additional information about the perceived scene which we do not see but what our memory says must be there (see Fig. 3.1).

Finally, as human beings, we can synthesize two memories together to create in the brain, an entirely new visualization. For example, your mother on roller skates: you know your mother and another memory tells you the information about the roller skates.

ADAPTATION AND GLARE

The light sensitivity of the eye usually adapts itself to the illumination we are observing. A good example of this is coming from a fairly dark room into very bright sunlight and it doesn't take very long for us to adjust to the new conditions, although the light levels are incredibly different.

Adaptation

Adaptation requires a period of time to work and in fact requires a long time to get used to dark after light – more than 30 minutes – but on the other hand it does not take long to be accustomed to light after dark. There are limits to adaptation and this can be when luminance is so great that glare can occur. We have all had the problem of reading from white paper in full summer sunlight, where the luminance value may be as high as 25 000 candela per square metre, and although it may be possible to read under these circumstances it is very uncomfortable. Why do we suffer from this problem? In fact, it is caused because the eye is not a perfect optical instrument and we can be affected by the scattering of the light rays which causes a high intensity source to be seen as if it were surrounded by haze. Where part of the retina is suddenly illuminated, the whole retina drops very rapidly in sensitivity (within 0.1 of a second). A good example of this is looking at a window which occupies part of the viewed scene which causes the eye to decrease in sensitivity and although the window may be reasonably clear, the remainder of the environment has become rather dark. Both of the above effects are very well known to the average motorist, either driving during the day when the road surface may reflect very bright areas, or indeed at night, from the headlights of the oncoming vehicles. Unfortunately, as we all know, it takes some time for our eyes to re-adjust to normal after we have received sources which give us glare problems. There are thus two forms of glare; the first which impairs the visual performance is called 'disability glare' and the second, which can cause visual discomfort, is called 'discomfort glare'.

Disability glare is caused by a bright source in the field of view, whereas discomfort glare is caused by excessively bright areas in the field of view and is usually caused by too high a difference between the dark areas and the bright areas being viewed. Generally, the luminance differences in the field of vision should not exceed 10:1. A good example of **discomfort glare** is looking at a bright sky to see what type of aeroplane is going over with the sun just out of the field of view. Generally we need to put our hand to shield our eyes from the glare of the sun.

We have tried to show in this section that although the eye is a marvellous instrument, it is not perfect. There is much that we do not know about its operation although the evidence so far shows that there is much in common between the eye, TV cameras and film cameras. In fact, it has been suggested that the coding system for passing colour information in the human brain is very similar to that used in the vision chain of any TV station. What we are aware of as we go about our daily lives is an abundance of wonderful pictures in 3-D and colour that enrich the human spirit.

3.2 Electromagnetic spectrum

The narrow band of electromagnetic radiation which lies between ultraviolet and infrared with wavelengths from 0.0004 mm (400 nm) to 0.0007 mm (700 nm) is detectable by the human eye and is known as light (see Figure 3.4).

Historical

Heinrich Hertz in 1888 experimented with the transmission of electromagnetic waves at a frequency of approximately 100 MHz generated by a spark-gap transmitter. Hertz was able to calculate the speed at which the electromagnetic waves travelled and found them to be exactly the same as the speed of light. He also, in the course of his experiments, observed wave reflection, wave refraction and wave interference. All of these are also well known optical phenom-

Figure 3.4 Electromagnetic spectrum

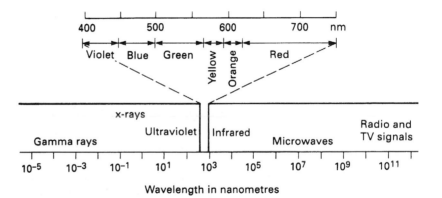

ena and thus Hertz concluded that lightwaves were another form of electromagnetic waves.

Hertz believed that his discovery of the properties of electromagnetic waves would not find any practical applications. He tragically died of cancer at the age of 37, approximately one year before Marconi demonstrated the first wireless transmission in 1895.

Radiant energy

When an object is heated it radiates energy in the form of electromagnetic waves. These waves go from the radio wave end of the electromagnetic spectrum through the infrared, the visible, the ultraviolet, X-ray and gamma ray. Ultraviolet (UV) is invisible to human beings, but unfortunately, in significant amounts is extremely harmful. Infrared is also invisible and produces a sensation of heat, but fortunately with no adverse side effects. For most of the hot objects that we encounter on Earth the energy lies mainly in the infrared region. A cooker hot plate may show no visible signs of heat, but when a hand is held over it, it feels warm; we are experiencing infrared at about 500K. When the hot plate is turned up and reaches 1000K we see a slight glow coming from the element which is the onset of visible radiation. The plate also becomes noticeably hotter, showing that there is a increase in the amount of radiated energy. A good example of infrared radiation is that from the black luminaires that are used in the entertainment industry. There is no visible sign of heat from the body of the luminaire, although we get a nasty burn if we touch it.

The tungsten filament in the lamps that we use radiates a white light around 3000K. To produce ultraviolet radiation in significant amounts, temperatures of 3500K and higher are required and most solid objects on earth melt by the time they reach this temperature. We generally produce temperatures around the 6000K mark by mercury vapour lamps, such as fluorescents, xenons and professional lighting discharge lamps and they all emit large amounts of ultraviolet radiation. When using discharge light sources, we have to be very much aware of the dangers connected with this type of illumination.

Ultraviolet radiation

Ultraviolet radiation covers the range 4–400 nm and it begins at the short wavelength limit of visibility (violet) and extends to X-rays. It is divided into near (400–300 nm), far (300–200 nm) and extreme (below 200 nm). The near ultraviolet energy is known generally as blacklight. The UV emitted is used to excite fluorescent pigments used in dyes, paints and materials to produce effects for advertising and more importantly to us, in the theatre and sometimes on television. The ultraviolet radiation in sunlight on the surface of the Earth extends from about 300 to 390 nm and is generally our source of getting a sun tan, with very long exposures causing cancer of the skin. At wavelengths shorter than this, UV becomes exceedingly dangerous to the human being. The reasons for this are that the radiation between 300 and 390 nm is little absorbed and is not so active on organisms. The radiation between 200 and 300 nm is well absorbed, produces damage to cells and the effect is nearly always permanent.

For the purposes of this book, we are mainly concerned with the visible part of the spectrum and to a large extent the infrared. The visible gives us the light by which we can illuminate for the purposes of entertainment, the infrared gives us problems with heating and subsequently the ventilation, which will be discussed later in the book.

3.3   Colour perception

If we read any book on physics concerning light, it will inevitably discuss the principle of waves and particles. At the turn of the twentieth century there was much discussion as to the physical properties of light, and in 1905 when Einstein demonstrated that light travelled quite happily in a vacuum, he proposed that light behaved like a wave and also like a particle. Most of the debate at that time centred around the theory of black bodies and their radiation; the problem being that the observed experiments did not conform to the scientific predictions. Although the world owes Einstein and his colleagues an enormous debt for showing us the way with most of modern physics, we are ourselves, for the purposes of this book, not concerned with the basic physical theory of light itself – only the effects it has and how we can use those effects.

Historical

The early philosophers, such as Pythagoras and Euclid, debated the nature of light and how the eye responded to a viewed scene. Theories went from a projected image from the viewed object which entered the eye, to the possibility that sensing rays went from the eye to the subject, rather like radar, and that these rays would pass information back to the eye. We now know that most objects do not radiate any lightwaves whatsoever, and only convert the incident light on them into the shape, colour and appearance that we see. The two sensations we are most concerned with are the objects brightness and colour. It was probably very fortunate for most scholars of today that Isaac Newton, to escape the effects of the great plague of London during 1665 and 1666, retreated to the family farm in the countryside. It was during this period of time that he focused his attention on the nature of light and subsequently produced his classic book *Opticks*.

Newton and the prism

Newton's experiments with colour were conducted by allowing sunlight to pass through a small hole in a darkened window. This beam of white light was passed through a glass prism and the emerging light spread out in a 'spectrum' of colours. The colours were red, orange, yellow, green, blue, indigo and violet. History tends to give Newton the credit for discovering the prism for this effect but this was not the case; it had been observed by scholars for many years. What Newton did was to take the original idea of splitting light with

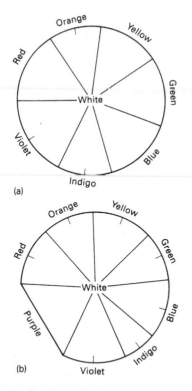

Figure 3.5 (a) Newton wheel (b) Modified by Harris

a prism and then use this to examine the colours coming through. By selecting one colour from the first prism and passing that colour through a second prism, he discovered that the second prism had no effect at all on the colour of the original light. He therefore concluded that colours were not the result of the prism changing the light but the fact that all normal white light contained the observed colours and the prism only acted to separate the colours. Having separated the colours out, Newton thought he should be able to return them back to the original white light source and by using an inverted prism after the first prism, he was able to re-create a white beam of light.

Newton had experimented with coloured objects under the various sources of illumination and from these experiments discovered most of the concepts that enabled modern colour theory to evolve. For instance, he found that a red object would efficiently reflect red light but would appear very dark and nearly black when illuminated by lights of other colours. It was apparent to Newton that objects have colour because they reflect certain colours while absorbing the remainder of the spectrum. If we view the spectrum as split by a prism, as Newton did, we will notice that it does not contain all of the colours that we encounter in our everyday lives such as magenta or black and white.

Newton's theories caused a great stir in the world at large and one of the reasons for this was the fact the most human beings first learn about colour by painting. The lessons learnt from mixing the colours of paint are somewhat different to those for mixing the colours of light. It has to be realized that light is the source of all colour but pigments in paint are simply reflectors or absorbers of parts of the light that illuminates them. Most artists when asked for their primary colours will quote blue, yellow and red, whereas the scientists, on being asked the same question, will list red, green and blue. One interesting fact is that the scientist does not quote yellow as a primary colour. However, if a beam of red light and a beam of green light are superimposed the result is yellow. On the other hand, if we mix red and green paint we get rather a nasty looking browny black colour. When using light, all spectral colours can be created by adding various component parts of the red, green and blue light and the system used is called 'addition', ultimately creating white. Pigments derive their colours by subtracting parts of the spectrum, therefore the system with pigments is called 'subtraction' and ultimately creates black.

The light from the sun and incandescent sources is generally white by nature and contains all the colours of the spectrum. However, as we will discover in other sections of the book various sources produce light by exciting portions of the visible spectrum to gain a response from the eye; but because they do not contain all the colours of the spectrum some distortion of colour can take place.

Colour specification

If we ring a colleague in Australia from England and we describe a red dress, she does have some idea of what we're talking about: the problem arises when we require our colleague to reproduce exactly the colour of the dress. How can we specify colour and its brightness accurately? One of the first attempts to define colour precisely was by an American called Albert Munsell in 1915, and his three dimensional colour system is still in use today (Plate 2). The Munsell system enables three qualities to be quantified and these are:

- **Hue:** describes the basic colour such as red or blue.
- **Value (or brightness):** refers to how light or dark the colour appears (it is a measure of the amount of reflected light).
- **Chroma (or saturation):** refers to the intensity of colour; as a colour moves away from white it becomes more and more saturated.

However the Munsell system is only as good as the illumination it is viewed in. We have all come across the problem of the piece of material that we're buying in the shop or the suit that we have selected which looks much better when we go to the doorway of the shop and examine it under daylight. We are also aware of how bad our skin looks under sodium street lighting. Coloured objects reflect light, the problem is that they don't reflect the entire spectrum of the light that falls on them or the light that falls on them is deficient in some way. The effect that the source of light has on any object is known as the colour rendering. In general, under normal illumination such as daylight, incandescent light, etc., there will be no problems, however discharge lighting (which may be fluorescent, street lighting or the type that we would use in studios or on location) will cause colour distortion by not having continuous spectral outputs. For instance, a green sample of cloth will only look green if there is green energy in the incident light. When we look in the manufacturers' data on lamps, we will invariably find in the sections on fluorescent, discharge etc., reference to the colour rendering index.

Two approaches have been used to describe colour, the first uses standard colour samples such as the Munsell system against which materials can be compared. A second system is to analyse the light reflected from a surface and then assign a set of values which specify the colour. As we are now looking at reflected light we can use the primary colours of red, blue and green, giving a 'tri-stimulus' to the eye. The first system to try to define the colour by its spectral components was that of Newton, but Newton used seven basic primaries derived from his prism observations where from any mix of the seven it was possible to produce a range of colours towards white. One of the problems with the Newtonian system was that it didn't contain the entire range of colours, for instance it lacked any reference to purple (see Fig. 3.5).

To be able to compile a very accurate system of colour specification, it was necessary to have a deeper knowledge of colour mixing, which unfortunately Newton did not have. He was also incapable of measuring light with the great accuracies that are required for modern colour measurement.

CIE system

In 1931 it was decided by the Commission International de l'Eclairage (CIE) to develop a more accurate colorimetric system. To compre-

Figure 3.6 Spectral distribution

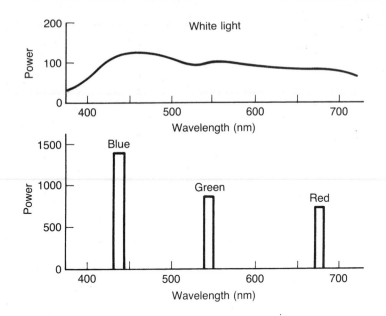

hend the system that the CIE adopted, we have to understand how metamerism works. The spectral difference between sources can be quite considerable, as shown in Figure 3.6 where a stimulus consisting of continuous power throughout the visible spectrum is matched by three narrow bands of energy in the red, green and blue only. If we choose three primary sources of light which are derived from standard white light filtered by a red, a green and a blue filter, we can use these as standard sources for colour mixing. The CIE system is based upon using a standard observer who is seated in front of a white screen. On one half of the screen is projected some arbitrary light source, on the other half of the screen is projected a combination of our three primaries. The observer has to adjust the intensity of the three primaries until both sides of the screen match exactly in colour and brightness. Although the two halves of the screen now look the same, they do not necessarily have the same spectral composition. The amounts of the red, blue and green sources specify the colour that we are viewing but not the light itself. Those three numbers are unique to the colour observed.

The theory of colour matching is quite complex and the CIE set out to create a system that was relatively easy to use and understand. Figure 3.7 shows the three primaries chosen by the CIE and these are called $\bar{x}$, $\bar{y}$ and $\bar{z}$, where $\bar{x}$ corresponds to the red primary, $\bar{y}$ to the green primary and $\bar{z}$ to the blue primary. The green primary curve ($\bar{y}$) shows the sensitivity of the human eye to light of different wavelengths and, as can be seen, the eye's sensitivity is at a maximum of around 550 nm but very poor towards the blue and red ends of the spectrum. By using the 'photopic curve', as it is known, as a 'multiplier' for any spectrum which is being analysed, we can calculate the apparent brightness. Usually, the source has much more energy than we are able to absorb.

The X, Y and Z values are called the tri-stimulus values of the spectrum and the relative amounts of each give the colour and

Figure 3.7 CIE primary functions

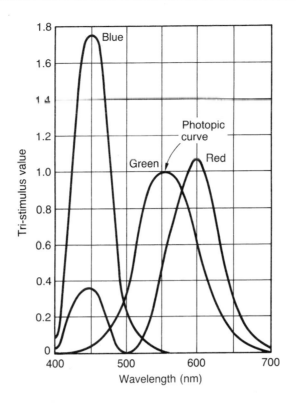

brightness of the viewed scene. To find X, we have to multiply the spectrum as measured, by the curve and the result gives the energy required for the stimulus. We would also have to do the same for the Y and Z values. The values of X, Y and Z are able to specify the colour accurately. The trouble is that it is very difficult when given these values to imagine what the colour actually looks like. We need a method by which we have an instant reference to the colour itself. The easiest way of looking anything up is to have a visual presentation, and in this case it is the CIE chromaticity diagram (Plate 3). The diagram is another version of Newton's colour wheel system, thus as we did with the Newton system we can use the chromaticity diagram to analyse colours. Newton's original colour circle didn't include purple which is of course a combination of red and blue, but as can be seen from Figure 3.5, we do have a purple line. What has happened is we have plotted the spectrum locus on a graph which has an x axis and a y axis. The colour co-ordinates are derived from the following formulae:

$$x = \frac{X}{X + Y + Z}$$

$$y = \frac{Y}{X + Y + Z}$$

$$z = \frac{Z}{X + Y + Z}$$

As the sum of x + y + z will always equal 1, we only need two variables as the third can be determined from the other two. By convention, we use the co-ordinates x and y to describe the colour. It must be noted however, that those co-ordinates only specify the hue and the saturation of the colour but *not* its brightness. To ascertain the brightness, we have to use the value of Y, the green tri-stimulus value (photopic curve). As we move from the periphery of the colour locus towards the centre of our diagram, saturation of colours diminishes until we reach white. The centre of the colour locus is positioned at the co-ordinates x = 0.33, y = 0.33, where the saturation has become zero. This point is known as *equal energy white* or reference white (colour temperature 9600K) (see Fig. 3.8).

In the laboratory we can do a spectral analysis of a source and then by using the CIE values compute the amount of X, Y, Z to give the tri-stimulus values. However, this is not always convenient in the studio, on the stage or in the middle of the sports field, and conveniently for us Minolta developed a hand held tri-stimulus meter which measures the values of the three primaries, does the computations for us and presents the figures for the co-ordinates and brightness very neatly on a little screen.

The CIE method enables us to do two things:

1. to analyse the colour of a surface,
2. to analyse the spectrum of a light source coming to a surface.

Most of our use of a colour meter is to measure the colour of the light source, be it normal or modified by filters, etc. If we are examining the colour of a surface, then we need to know the colour of the reference source to reduce the variables to manageable proportions. The CIE adopted three standard light sources and these are:

*   **Source A:** This is a source typical of an incandescent lamp operated at a colour temperature of 2856K.
*   **Source B:** This source is typical of noon sunlight and has a colour temperature of about 4870K.
*   **Source C:** This represents an overcast sky or average daylight and has a colour temperature of about 6700K.

Colour rendering index

In 1965, the CIE introduced a system to regulate the colour rendering index (Ra). The system measures eight colour samples taken from the Munsell system, illuminated with a test source and this is compared with a reference illumination. The reference source has a value of 100, and due to the deficiencies in spectral output, the test source can at best equal or generally be less than the reference source and thus the Ra can never be greater than 100, and in most cases will be 90 or less.

BLACK BODY RADIATION

The scientists studying black body radiation discovered the following facts:

Table 3.1

CIE general colour rendering index (Ra)	Typical application
Greater than 90	Where accurate colour matching is required, e.g. colour print inspection
80 to 90	Where accurate colour judgements are necessary and/or good colour rendering is required for reasons of appearance, e.g. shops and other commercial premises.
60 to 80	Where moderate colour rendering is required.
40 to 60	Where colour rendering is of little significance but marked distortion of colour is unacceptable.
20 to 40	Where colour rendering is of no importance and marked distortion of colour is acceptable.

Note: For film or TV use we would need an Ra index of at least 80.

1. The spectrum is continuous, just like that of the sun and includes all the visible colours together with the infrared and ultraviolet spectra.
2. When a graph is plotted of intensity versus wavelength, there is always a maximum intensity at only one wavelength.
3. As the object becomes hotter, the wavelengths of maximum radiation become shorter.
4. The hotter the object becomes the greater the total amount of radiation from a given area.

Lacking the knowledge of today's scientists, their predecessors postulated the theory of a body absorbing all the radiation falling on it and to do that effectively, it would have to be black and hence the world was introduced to the term 'black body'. What the scientists didn't know was that the black body was capable of radiation and although not commonly realized, every object radiates some light. The chair we sit on appears quite cool but in a room at 20°C, it is still 293° above zero Kelvin and according to the known laws of physics will radiate energy. Many modern surveillance systems actually look for radiated energy of low intensity. One good thing about black body radiation is that it starts in the very deep reds and goes to the very deep blues, passing through white in the process which, as human beings we happily accept. When we depart from the black body curve and approach green or magenta we are psychologically disturbed.

Figure 3.9 shows black bodies at 2000K, 3200K, 5600K and 6500K. In addition to the visible spectrum, many other wavelengths are also radiated; the more the temperature is raised, the more energy and subsequently light is radiated. The curves also show a shift towards the blue end of the spectrum as the energy becomes greater. Modern incandescent lamps are very close to the black body radiation curve and in general are given a colour temperature to signify the colour of their light output. Incandescent lamps that we deal with have a colour temperature around the 3000K mark. The sun is around 5000K and light from the blue sky is generally from about 6000K upwards.

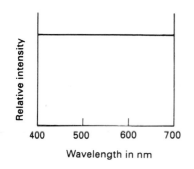

Figure 3.8 The equal energy spectrum

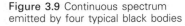

Figure 3.9 Continuous spectrum
emitted by four typical black bodies

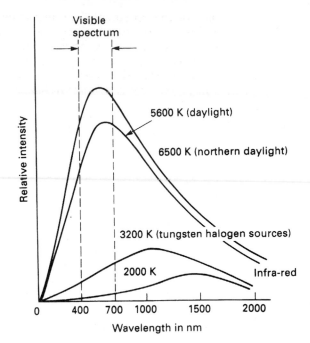

If we wish to measure purely colour temperature, we measure the relative amounts of red and blue of the black body curve of the source in question. When the source deviates from the black body curve we would have to use a tri-stimulus meter so we can measure the green component.

Discharge sources

Why is it that the discharge source is so different from that of the incandescent? Probably at some time in our lives, we have thrown an object into a fire and then been amazed at the magnificent colours produced when it burns. The colours are unique to the substance. In 1752 a Scotsman, Thomas Melvill, studied the light from a flame through a prism and discovered that the spectrum was not continuous. Some parts of the observed spectrum were bright and other parts were dark. When Melvill experimented with different chemicals burning in the flame, he found the locations of the bright and dark areas changed. From the early nineteenth century onwards the spectroscope was developed to enable researchers to examine the various colours generated within light sources.

Spectral lines

Each chemical element has a unique set of wavelengths and thus bright lines within its spectrum, and these can be used just like 'fingerprints'. With the advent of electricity research was carried out on the effect of voltage when applied to gasses. During the latter part of the nineteenth century many different gasses were studied and their element lines were plotted, and it was discovered that some gases have thousands of lines and some have very few. Sodium in particular has only two lines in the yellow part of the spectrum, so close together they appear as one, and this is the characteristic of many street lights that are in use today. Neon on the other hand, has very strong lines in the red and orange.

Observing these bright line spectra was one thing, but to actually understand their generation was another. Ernest Rutherford, of atomic energy fame, was the first to postulate the theory of the planetary atomic structure. This theory suggests that the atom is mostly empty space, rather like our solar system, and that the individual parts of an atom orbit a nucleus. The scientific theory of the time however, did not explain the existence of bright line spectra. In 1913, Niels Bohr, a Danish physicist, set out to explain how the bright line spectra evolved. His theory was that the electrons occupied defined orbits around the nucleus; these orbits were governed by the amount of energy an electron had as it orbited the nucleus. If the electron was given additional energy by some means, the electron could be made to move to one of the higher levels within the atom. As well as moving, the excited electron had also become unstable. To regain stability, the excited electron would have to fall back to the lower level from whence it came and in the process lose the energy again, in the form of light.

Phosphors

Bohr's experiments were generally confined to the energy levels of the relatively simple hydrogen atom, and thus provided details of the hydrogen spectrum. These experiments laid down some of the ground rules for further research, which in modern times has revealed more and more complexities of the atom. When we view sources made up of several lines of energy we do not see the individual lines because our eyes integrate all the energy and tend to mix the colours together. However, it may be that the energy is not in the visible spectrum at all and is produced in the ultraviolet region. This energy, while not directly visible, is able to produce visible light by exciting certain chemicals and a good example of this is the fluorescent light.

Fluorescent tubes are a glass tube coated internally with a phosphor. Phosphors are similar to atoms in their response to energy but produce bands of colours rather than individual line spectrum. An electric current flows through the vaporized mercury in the fluorescent tube and in so doing excites the electrons. When the electrons fall back to the lower levels they release energy. Some of the energy generated is in the visible region of the spectrum but mostly it is in the ultraviolet region and it is this ultraviolet energy that causes the phosphors to glow. It should be noted that higher energy sources can excite phosphors but lower energy sources are incapable, thus ultraviolet will cause the production of light but infrared energy cannot. Fluorescent tubes tend to have much energy at the blue end of the spectrum as well as nasty spikes in the green, and to balance their colour, combinations of phosphors are used so that the integrated light output approaches that of normal incandescent lamps. Thus we hear terms like 'daylight', 'warm white' etc. which are descriptions of their inherent colour, but not always of their colour rendering properties.

Discharge sources

The modern discharge sources such as the HMI, MSR and CSI, operate from the principles discussed, usually with an electric arc exciting mercury vapour and rare earth gases in various forms to give blends of colour. If we observe from its cold state a discharge lamp slowly warming up to its final operating temperature, we will see the discrete bands of energy joining in at various levels to form the colours that make up the composite output.

3.4   Spectral output of sources

Although the graphs in Fig. 3.10 are apparently very different to each other, the various light sources all produce a sensation of white in the human eye. When a light source produces light at every wavelength in the visible spectrum it is considered a continuous source. Although these sources appear white as far as we are concerned, when objects are viewed under the various types of illumination, we get different responses. As a yardstick, it would be nice to have a source that gave a perfect white, and such a source wouldn't show any imbalance towards the red, the blue or the green of the spectrum, and would contain equal amounts of each. This source is called an 'equal energy source' and has been discussed in reference to the CIE system (see Figure 3.8).

All black body sources are continuous radiation sources and although biased heavily either to the red or the blue according to the temperature of the radiator, the colour distortion is at a minimum. The interesting thing about continuous sources is the fact that nature has

Figure 3.10 Spectral distribution curves of four common sources

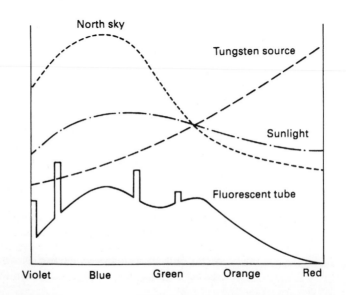

provided sources of this type from time immemorial and all the light derived from hot objects, such as candles, oil lamp, wood and coal fires, obey the laws of the black body radiator. It is only in recent times that sources of a different type have been developed for use by mankind; the reason is that more light is produced for the power consumed and this is usually a consumer-led development by lamp manufacturers. Probably the most well known of these is the fluorescent tube. One advantage of using mercury discharge sources was that they provided high efficiencies of light output. In the earlier days of discharge lamps however, quantity was put very much before quality. In the basic mercury discharge lamp, radiation is mainly found in the blue, green and yellow sections in very narrow band spikes and obviously does not give a good colour response. Typical examples of basic discharge lamps are those used in street lighting and some forms of crude floodlighting, which tend to be either rather blue or predominantly yellow.

Discharge halides

To improve the colour of the light source, it is necessary to introduce elements such as tin, indium, sodium, lithium and scandium. One of the problems with using some of these elements is the fact that they could react with the silica envelope and rapidly destroy the lamp. In practice, by using metals in the form of their halide salts (hence the name metal halide lamps) most of the problem is overcome. The list below gives examples of the radiation that can be produced with the various elements:

Tin	orange/red radiation
Scandium	blue and green radiation
Sodium	yellow radiation
Thallium	green radiation
Lithium	red radiation

By selecting the various metals and metal halides that can be used, we can introduce more spectral spikes into the characteristic and eventually end up with colour rendering of a very high order, such as those in HMI lamps and MSR lamps.

3.5 Filters

We have discussed in other sections the need for the almost apparent perfection of the white light that we use either for daylight matching or for incandescent source matching. In this section we shall talk mainly about distorting the colour of light.

The choice of colour to create the required effect or mood in theatre was established from very early days by placing a coloured glass or silk in front of the light source. In 1858 Covent Garden introduced overhead gas battens running the width of the stage, and providing colour change by stitching together two foot wide lengths of gauze coloured red, green and blue which could be pulled around the gas batten to produce the required colour. Alternative materials were silk, calico or tammy. A high price was paid for early experiments with lighting and the attempts to provide colour. Theatres caught fire and many people died, it is therefore no wonder that the fire officers of today insist that all materials used as colour filter must pass the appropriate safety tests.

Historical

Early colour filter material was made of gelatine dyed to the required colour. This offered an enormous range, but suffered the problem of handling. As it dried out, it would become very brittle and virtually shatter and fall to pieces and of course, presented a fire hazard. However, the use of gelatine filter persisted into the 1960s. The advent of electric lamps in the late 1890s provided another possibility for colouring the light by dipping the lamps into coloured lacquer. This provided an excellent choice of colours but, of course, it could not be changed once the lamp had been coated. With the introduction of the incandescent tungsten filament lamp in the early 1900s, the heat was to prove too much for the lacquer coating for anything other than low wattage sources. This led in the early 1930s, to the introduction of a new colour material made from cellulose acetate by a complicated method of shaving thin sheets from a large block of the dyed material and polishing the sheet until it became a transparent colour filter. This type of filter has persisted until today but has lost popularity to the alternative plastic materials that can be coated with the appropriate colours on a continuous production method of manufacture. The main problem with cellulose acetate filter is that it becomes very soft when used with tungsten halogen lamps with their more efficient light output. These lamps will also burn a hole at the centre of the filter, bleach the colour out or turn it dark, depending on the pigments used in its manufacture.

Glass filters

Glass filters have always been used and are still in use today. However, after the initial euphoria over the fact that the glass filter does not fade or burn out, one soon finds that they are so restrictive that they are not a very practical solution. The colour restriction is caused by the glass manufacturer requiring the lighting filter stockist to order what is known in the glass industry as a 'melt' which could be about one tonne, but of course, it is all one colour which will supply his customers for years. Unfortunately, any one particular melt cannot be guaranteed to match the next melt, therefore some permanent applications such as cyclorama backings that were thought to be ideal for glass filters, were faced with changing all of the filters when replacements were required, because the new colours stood out from the rest. An additional problem with glass filters is that they can shatter if they are unevenly heated, causing a safety problem when used in overhead luminaires.

The two main colour filters in use today are plastics, known as polyester and polycarbonate. Both are suitable for tungsten halogen luminaires and both have their attractions. Polyester is normally cheaper but does not last so long, and the polycarbonate tends to justify its price by the reduction in replacement costs and the time involved. Both materials are available in over 100 colours and hues and can even be used by adding colours in the same luminaire to create your own special shade for the lighting director (LD) who can't find the one he wants in the swatch book.

Many books have been written on the subject of the use of colour to create the right mood and setting from joy to sadness, from shock to restful security. However tempting it is to pursue this course, we must confine our studies to producing the colours for the LD to use, and the simple physics involved to achieve the desired effect. The LD has two variables to consider:

(a) the colour of the light, and
(b) the colour of the subject.

He has total control of the first variable but the second is completely beyond his control and must be determined at an early stage of planning if he is to achieve the desired artistic effect. The correct colour of costumes and scenery must be used during the rehearsals when the colour filters are being chosen or disaster will result.

As human beings we tend to associate reds and yellows with bright and breezy situations and blue with much more sombre occasions, red is also associated with daylight and blue with night. One only has to look at any old Hollywood movie or for that matter British movie to see the use of unfiltered carbon arcs giving extremely blue night time lighting for effect.

Colour filters

Originally very few filters were produced for effects purposes, but over the years manufacturers have come to produce vast ranges of subtle colour filters. Most of these, we suggest, are required by the individual foibles of the lighting practitioners and not necessarily by the requirements of the viewer.

Other types of filter required in the lighting industry are the kind that either change the colour of the light source itself, or change the colour of the viewed image as seen by television, film or photographic cameras. It must be said at this time that any filter which changes the nature of the light cannot necessarily be designated as a particular colour filter, a colour temperature changing filter or any other type. A filter essentially changes the colour of a light source and therefore could be used for any purpose where the resultant colour may be required. What is extremely important, for the purposes of this book, is how do we achieve good filtering, and at the same time keep a high transmission level so we do not waste large amounts of light. It also has to be remembered that a filter called 'Bright Rose' looks decidedly not 'Bright Rose' when put in front of a predominantly blue source. Most publications, and for that matter filter manufacturers, go into great realms of detail about *mired shifts*. It is our experience that most practitioners of the art of lighting tend to do things on a trial and error basis. The point is that mired values are only as good as the light sources themselves allow; in other words mired values applied to a known shift such as 5600K down to 3200K are somewhat changed if the source is not at 5600k to start with.

A good filter should only be interested in the visual energy, i.e. that from 400 to 700 nm. A perfect filter would only remove that portion of energy in which we are interested in a very precise way. However, filters cannot be made to this sort of tolerance and generally have some form of overlap and thus remove other bits of energy from the light beam. When light falls on any material, three things occur, some light will be reflected, if the material is translucent enough some light will pass through the material and some of the light will be absorbed within the material. The absorbed light will be converted to heat energy. When the majority of the light is either reflected or transmitted or a combination of the two effects, the smaller quantity will be the heating effect. To illustrate this effect, white and other pale coloured materials usually reflect most of the incident light. For example most people will wear lightly coloured clothing in the summer which reflects most of the energy in the sunlight but we generally wear dark coloured clothing in the winter to keep us warm. The black telephone sitting in the sunlight on our desks has an extremely low reflectance and it also transmits little or no light. Consequently the telephone gets rather hot, which may be good news for the telephone company's replacement programme, but is not so good for the user.

Colour transmission

When we wish to change the colour of a light source for effect or colour correction, we will invariably put some form of coloured filter in the light path. We cannot introduce a colour that is not present in the source. The colour of the emerging light from the filter depends upon the spectrum of the incident light striking the filter and on the characteristics of transmission of the filter itself. As well as the **colour** of the emergent light from a filter we will also be very much concerned with the **quantity of light** the filter lets through, otherwise known as the **transmission**. A filter works by subtracting selected portions of the spectrum away from the light source. If we start with the same amounts of red, green and blue light in the light source, and our filter takes away the green component, we are left with the red and blue, which when mixed together gives **magenta**. Thus our magenta filter can also be called a **minus green** filter. A yellow filter would allow the red and green portions of the spectrum through, taking away the blue, thus it can be called a **yellow** filter or a **minus blue**. A cyan filter allows the blue and green light through and stops the red portion of the spectrum, therefore a **cyan** filter is also a **minus red**.

So far, we have looked at removing one colour, if we remove two colours we can then produce our three primary **additive** mixing colours used for lighting, i.e. if we remove the red and blue components we are left with **green**. The removal of red and green gives **blue**; finally if we take away the blue and green we are left with **red**.

As will be realized, the filters we have just given as examples have the ability to subtract light *away from a portion of the visible spectrum,* it will also be obvious that we are looking at a subtractive light process. The amount of light transmitted by any of these filters will be determined by the density of colour of the filters which is determined by the thickness of the colour layer. By using combinations of the basic magenta, yellow and cyan filters, which are often used in photographic processes, in various thicknesses, almost any colour can be produced.

The alternatives given in Table 3.2 for red, green and blue show the two methods of achieving the same result.

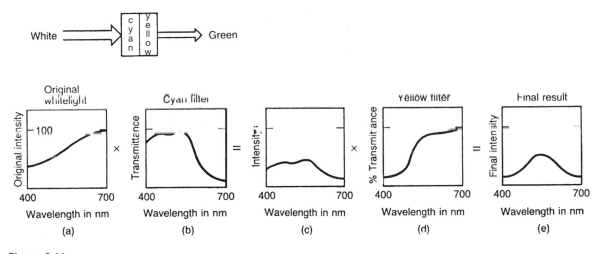

Figure 3.11

Table 3.2

Desired effect	Filters required
White	None
Black	*Yellow, cyan, magenta
Red	Yellow, magenta or (− blue, − green)
Green	Yellow, cyan or (− blue, − red)
Blue	Cyan, magenta or (− red, − green)

Note: * In other words removing all the light from the source

Effects

A fine example of the two principles of additive and subtractive colour was demonstrated by Adrian Samoiloff in the 1920s when he had a stage act of illusions created with coloured light and selectively coloured subjects; one of these was to make the actor up in red cosmetics and wearing a coat of black and blue/green stripes. The actor would first be illuminated using a red filter when he would appear to be a white man in a black coat, and then illuminated with a blue/green filter, he appeared to be a black man in a striped coat. This effect can be very interesting by design but quite a disaster if created by accident.

When we use two filters to produce a result, what has happened is that the original incident light has been modified by the characteristics of the first filter and consequently the emergent light from the filter is modified by the characteristics of the second filter. The transmission has also been affected and working this out is relatively simple, because if half the light was removed by the first filter and half of this light passed through the second filter, we would have ended up with a quarter of the original light. By this simple example it can be seen that the transmission can be down to quite low percentages on some colours; particularly when we are using primary transmission colours. Colour filters for light sources are usually produced with specified colours in various densities to meet the needs of the LDs. Some luminaires used for colour effects, which have a single light source, have to use combinations of yellow, magenta and cyan filters to achieve their results. A close examination of some manufacturers' filters, particularly in the yellow range, will reveal that a medium yellow filter could be made up from two or more sheets of less dense yellow filters. Other than the need to remove portions of the visible spectrum for effects purposes, there is on occasions a need to remove the ultraviolet and infrared energy from the spectrum. For example, when filming in museums, special precautions have to be taken to remove much of the infrared and UV portions of the spectrum from the light sources to avoid contaminating the colours on valuable paintings and objets d'art.

Dichroic filters

In general, the filters used for television, film and stage are essentially types of plastic with dyes in them. Other specialist filters can be produced and these are dichroic layers on sheets of glass. Dichroic filters work by having a very thin layer of a chemical deposited on a piece of glass. The thickness of the surface coating will be one quarter of the wavelength of the light concerned and is obviously extremely thin. The filter works by reflecting a selected wavelength within the spectrum and if a blue dichroic filter, such as the type used with small luminaires, is examined, it will be found that one surface reflects yellow in large amounts. Dichroic filters rely upon the light being perpendicular to the surface of the glass because of the need to keep a precise quarter wavelength for the selection of the colour to be reflected. Light incident from other angles will be affected in different ways, thus it is possible in practice to see a slight variation in colour over the width of a light beam when using dichroic filters. This problem could be solved by curving the filter surface so that all rays are normal to it.

When dichroic filters are mounted on toughened glass, they generally are much better able to withstand heat than conventional type filters. Manufacturers of dichroic filters are able to tailor the surface coatings very precisely to select portions of the electromagnetic spectrum, particularly with infrared and UV where the division between the visible light and the harmful rays is very narrow. A good example of dichroics is the infrared reflectors used on cold lamp sources in projector systems and in many of the low voltage sources used in shop displays and architectural lighting.

Colour correction

Colour temperature correction filters are those that change the balance between the red and blue portions of the spectrum only. To change a source from 3200K to 5600K means that the red end of the spectrum has to be diminished; therefore there is a higher balance of blue to red in the filter. To change a 5600K source to 3200K, an orange correction filter removes part of the blue from the light beam to achieve a correct red/blue balance.

Mireds

We need to use coloured filters to correct the output of light sources in one of two ways. It may be that we have a 3200K source that requires to be raised to 5600K to be used with daylight sources. It could be that we are using a source of 5600K and this requires correction down to 3200K. A problem that exists with filters is the fact that they cause a definite change and are dependent upon the light source for the resultant colour output. A blue filter placed in front of a 3200K lamp would create much less change than if it were used to filter a discharge source. As this is the case, we can hardly label a filter as a 2000K correction filter. Luckily for us, there is a way around the problem and we do this by using 'micro reciprocal degrees'. Suffice it say that a filter will cause a constant shift in the reciprocal value of the colour temperature of the source. To make the maths easier, the reciprocal value is multiplied by one million, and thus mired stands for 'MIcro REciprocal Degrees' Thus a colour temperature of 2000K is equivalent to 500 mireds and 4000K equates to 250 mireds. A filter which changed the light from the source from 2000K to 4000K would thus produce a change of –250 mireds. This filter can be designed so that it always produces the change of –250 mireds, irrespective of the original source. Note that filters which decrease the colour temperature of sources have positive values, but filters which increase the colour temperature have minus mired shifts.

If we look at some examples, they give a good idea how this system can be used in practice.

	Mireds
1. 5600K source	178
Filter value	+ 72
Final mired value	250

Therefore Colour temperature $= \dfrac{1 \times 10^6}{250} = \mathbf{4000K}$

2. 3200K source	312
Filter value	–72
Final mired value	240

Therefore Colour temperature $= \dfrac{1 \times 10^6}{240} = \mathbf{4167K}$

3. 4000K source	250
Filter value	–72
Final mired value	178

Therefore Colour temperature $= \dfrac{1 \times 10^6}{178} = \mathbf{5600K}$

Note that although the same filter has been used in examples (2) and (3), the colour temperature change in (2) is **967K** and in (3) **1600K.**

One type of filter that we require which would fail in its task if it changed the colour of the light in any way, is the neutral density filter. Its very name indicates its purpose: it has to be absolutely neutral and diminishes only the quantity of light and not the colour of light. It generally has two purposes, one of which is to diminish the amount of light entering the camera lens or it can be used to filter the light coming through windows and other apertures to allow a balance between a mixture of natural light and artificial light on any scene.

All the foregoing comments have been made with regard to light that was basically white in content on entering the filter. If the light entering a filter was essentially magenta in colour and filtered by a green filter, the result would be no light, as the green light has already been removed and the green filter would just remove the red and blue components of the magenta. This is obviously an extreme case but can serve to illustrate the need to be careful when filtering light sources.

COLOUR FILTER COMPARISON TABLES

One common request amongst filter users in film, TV and theatre, has been for a comparison table of various brands of filter to show that a filter is the same colour as another, or that it is a shade lighter or darker. The main reasons given for this request are:

(a) to select a filter of a different make;
(b) to select a filter of a lighter or darker tint;
(c) to reproduce an LD's lighting plot faithfully, anywhere in the world;
(d) to purchase replacements on the road;
(e) for rental companies, to provide the colours requested from their stock;
(f) manufacturers' comparison tables do not show colours that they do not make.

Colour filters

All colours offered by the brands are represented in Plate 1 in the colour plate section, irrespective of the fact that they are offered as an effects filter, or a colour correction filter thus making most colours available for effects use. The exceptions are a few odd colours that will not fit into the bands represented by the 70 colour references, and additionally colours such as chocolate, and, of course, the neutral density filters.

The authors have made all filter comparisons by using a 1000W 3200K light source and reading the xy colour co-ordinates on a tristimulus meter and the transmission at the same time. The filters were then mounted in order of colour and moved by eye for density, so the results can be considered as a subjective opinion of the authors. Cinemoid (a product of Strand Lighting UK) has been included; although it was discontinued in 1987, it had been in use since early 1930s and appears on many old lighting plots.

Reading the table

From the centre line of each of the 70 colour references, two lines have been drawn horizontally, representing the mid-position of that particular reference colour. Therefore all filter numbers that fall between these two lines are the same colour and density. Numbers that appear above the lines are lighter than the reference, and those that fall below the line are darker. Although the colour references

Colour filter conversion chart. The bottom row "Number series" shows five reference colour swatches spanning the data columns. Data columns (1–24) are unlabelled grid positions; each value is placed according to its horizontal position in the chart.

Brand	Product	No. series	1	2	3	4	5	6	7	8	9	10	11	12	13	14	15	16	17	18	19	20	21	22	23	24
	Gelatran effects	100									72															65	69
Arri	effects	300																								
Arri	correction	200	218	203		202									201											
Arri	effects	100															174	196						161		
Gamcolor	Cinefilter correction	3000	585	539									1536		573											
Gamcolor	Gamcolor effects	1000	870	885					830	820	842		860	888	880	882			840	815						
Strand	Strand effects	400															474							461		
Strand	Strand correction	200	218	203		202									201											
Strand	Chromoid effects	001/100					167										161			145						
Strand	Chromagel effects	001/100/300					61										64			65						
Rosco	E. Colour	100/200/300	218			202	203								201		174					196	161			
Rosco	Cinegal correction	3000	3216	3208	3206	3204								3202												
Rosco	Roscolene effects	800																								
Rosco	Cinecolor effects	600				649	648					647	650				651		655	654						
Rosco	Supergel effects	001/100/300	373			372		61			63						64			65				367		
Rosco	Roscolux effects	001/100/300			360	62	60	61			63						64			65				367		
Chris James	effects	300																								
Chris James	correction	200	218	203		202									201											
Chris James	Effects	100															174				196			161		
Chris James	L.P. Effects	001/100/200/300								061	063															
Lee	Cinemoid effects	100	67																					61		
Lee	effects	HT 001/HT 100/HT 300								061	063															
Lee	correction	200	218			202	203								201			201								
Lee	effects	001/100/300								061	063						174				196			161		

Manufacturer	Type	Series														
Arri	Gelatran effects	100		71			66	64					60		61	
Arri	effects	300				357	361						363		385	
Arri	correction	200														
Arri	effects	100		165			132	197		119			195		120	181
Gamcolor	Cinefilter correction	3000														
Gamcolor	Gamcolor effects	1000	847 848	810				910	835	845			850	890 915	905	
Strand	Strand effects	400		465			432			419					420	481
Strand	Strand correction	200														
Strand	Chromoid effects	001 100				91	86	92	119	163	93		140			
Strand	Chromagel effects	001 100 300				68	78	81	79	82	85		74			
Rosco	E. Colour	100 200 300		165			132	197	119	363			195		120	181
Rosco	Cinegal correction	3000														
Rosco	Roscolene effects	800		851		856			857 861			862	863		866	
Rosco	Cinecolor effects	600			656			653	657				661			
Rosco	Supergel effects	001 100 300		67		68	78	81 84	79	82	83		74	85	383	385
Rosco	Roscolux effects	001 100 300		67		68	78	81 84	80 79	82			74 83	85	383	385
Chris James	effects	300				357	361 384						363		385	
Chris James	correction	200														
Chris James	Effects	100		165			132	197		119			195		120	181
Chris James	L.P. Effects	001 100 200 300				132		197	079			195 363		055		181
Chris James	Cinemoid effects	100		32				63		19					20	
Lee	effects	HT 001 HT 100 HT 300					132	197	079	119		363	195	085	120	181
Lee	correction	200														
Lee	effects	001 100 300		165		068	132	197	079	119		363	195	085	120 198	181

Number series

Manufacturer	Product	Number series																
Arri	Gelatran effects	100									76						
Arri	effects	300		349			350	353						360				
Arri	correction	200																
Arri	effects	100		117				144			143	118		183	141			
Gamcolor	Cinefilter correction	3000																
Gamcolor	Gamcolor effects	1000	790			780	730		770	760		740		750				
Strand	Strand effects	400		417				444			443	418		483	441			
Strand	Strand correction	200																
Strand	Chromoid effects	001 100		117												141	162	
Strand	Chromagel effects	001 100 300		66												69	76	
Rosco	E. Colour	100 200 300		117			353	144				118		183	141			
Rosco	Cinegal correction	3000																
Rosco	Roscolene effects	800	848					853	850									859
Rosco	Cinecolor effects	600												658				659
Rosco	Supergel effects	001 100 300	363	66												69	76	
Rosco	Roscolux effects	001 100 300	363	66												69	76	77
Chris James	effects	300		349			350	353					383	360				
Chris James	correction	200																
Chris James	Effects	100		117				144			143	118		183	141			
Chris James	L.P. Effects	001 100 200 300													141			
Chris James	Cinemoid effects	100	45	17	40	86					43	18			41	62		
Lee	effects	HT 001 HT 100 HT 300							172			118		183	141			
Lee	correction	200																
Lee	effects	001 100 300		117			140 353	144	172		143	118		014	141			

Filter manufacturer cross-reference chart (colour correction and effects number series).

Manufacturer	Product	Number series	1	2	3	4	5	6	7	8	9	10	11	12	13	14	15	16	17	18	19	20
Arri	Gelatran effects	100															36					
Arri	effects	300														354						
Arri	correction	200			219																	
Arri	effects	100															115				116	
Gamcolor	Cinefilter correction	3000																				
Gamcolor	Gamcolor effects	1000	680	685					720				725						710	690		
Strand	Strand effects	400														415					416	
Strand	Strand correction	200			219																	
Strand	Chromoid effects	001 100								87	144			115								116
Strand	Chromagel effects	001 100 300								70	72			73								95
Rosco	E. Colour	100 200 300				219											115	354			116	
Rosco	Cinegal correction	3000																				
Rosco	Roscolene effects	800								849	855	854										877
Rosco	Cinecolor effects	600	673				677	676	675	652											613	
Rosco	Supergel effects	001 100 300					93			70	72	71		73		370						95
Rosco	Roscolux effects	001 100 300	92			93				70	72	71		73		370	15	354			16	95
Chris James	effects	300														354						
Chris James	correction	200			219																	
Chris James	Effects	100															115				116	
Chris James	L.P. Effects	001 100 200 300												115								116
Lee	Cinemoid effects	100																				
Lee	effects	HT 001 HT 100 HT 300															115				116	
Lee	correction	200			242		219		241													
Lee	effects	001 100 300													131	354	115				116	

Brand	Product	No. series													
	Gelatran effects	100						47							
Arri	effects	300								378		371			
	correction	200	278 246 213 245 244												
	effects	100				138		121		122		124		39	
Gamcolor	Cinefilter correction	3000		·587 ·585											
	Gamcolor effects	1000		520 535		540		570		660				655	650
Strand	Strand effects	400				438		421		422		424		439	
	Strand correction	200		213											
	Chromoid effects	001 100		151				121		122		123	94	124	
	Chromagel effects	001 100 300		96				86		89		389	94	90	
Rosco	E. Colour	100 200 300		213	244	138		121		122			124	139	
	Cinegal correction	3000	3317 3316 3315			3304									
	Roscolene effects	800						878				871		874	
	Cinecolor effects	600		669	671	642				672					674
	Supergel effects	001 100 300		96			388	86		89		389	94	90	
	Roscolux effects	001 100 300		87 96 88		51	388	86		89		389	94	90	91
Chris James	effects	300								378		371			
	correction	200	278 246 213 245 244												
	Effects	100				138		121		122		124		139	
	L.P. Effects	001 100 200 300							121		089				090
	Cinemoid effects	100	77			38		21		22	23	24		39	
Lee	effects	HT 001 HT 100 HT 300						121		122	089	124		139	090
	correction	200	278 246 213 245 244			243									
	effects	001 100 300				138	088	121		122	089	124		139	090

Number series

Brand	Product	Number series	1	2	3	4	5	6	7	8	9	10	11	12	13	14	15
Arri	Gelatran effects	100														81	
Arri	effects	300					340								339	381	382
Arri	correction	200															
Arri	effects	100							136		170					126	
Gamcolor	Cinefilter correction	3000															
Gamcolor	Gamcolor effects	1000				980				970		990				995	
Strand	Strand effects	400							436	470					469	426	
Strand	Strand correction	200								·							
Strand	Chromoid effects	001 100						172		136					126	96	
Strand	Chromagel effects	001 100 300						54		52					48	49	
Rosco	E. Colour	100 200 300							136		170					126	
Rosco	Cinegal correction	3000															
Rosco	Roscolene effects	800								840				838	839		
Rosco	Cinecolor effects	600				642						638					
Rosco	Supergel effects	001 100 300		351				54		52					48	49	
Rosco	Roscolux effects	001 100 300						54		52			47	48		49	
Chris James	effects	300					340						381		339		382
Chris James	correction	200															
Chris James	Effects	100							136		170					126	
Chris James	L.P. Effects	001 100 200 300															
Lee	Cinemoid effects	100							36							26	
Lee	effects	HT 001 HT 100 HT 300															
Lee	correction	200															
Lee	effects	001 100 300	003		169				136		170				048	126	

Manufacturer	Type	Series	Number series (color swatches)
Arri	Gelatran effects	100	88 62
Arri	effects	300	342 344 343
Arri	correction	200	
Arri	effects	100	137 142 194 180
Gamcolor	Cinefilter correction	3000	
Gamcolor	Gamcolor effects	1000	920 940 960 950 948 925 945 930
Strand	Strand effects	400	437 442 480
Strand	Strand correction	200	
Strand	Chromoid effects	001 100	89 171 137 88 170
Strand	Chromagel effects	001 100 300	53 55 57 58 56
Rosco	E. Colour	100 200 300	137 344 142 194 343 180
Rosco	Cinegal correction	3000	
Rosco	Roscolene effects	800	841 844 842 843 846
Rosco	Cinecolor effects	600	641 639 644 645
Rosco	Supergel effects	001 100 300	53 55 355 356 57 58 357 358 56 359 382 59
Rosco	Roscolux effects	001 100 300	53 55 355 356 57 58 357 358 56 359 382 59
Chris James	effects	300	342 344 343
Chris James	correction	200	
Chris James	Effects	100	137 142 194 180
Chris James	L.P. Effects	001 100 200 300	053 052 058
Chris James	Cinemoid effects	100	71 42 58 25
Lee	effects	HT 001 HT 100 HT 300	053 052 058
Lee	correction	200	
Lee	effects	001 100 300	053 137 344 142 052 194 058 180 343
		Number series	

Brand	Product	Number series													
Arri	Gelatran effects	100			15		08						09			
	effects	300														
	correction	200														
	effects	100	154	153	109		107				166		148		113	
Gamcolor	Cinefilter correction	3000														
	Gamcolor effects	1000			190		195					180			220	
Strand	Strand effects	400	454	453	409		407				466		448		413	
	Strand correction	200														
	Chromoid effects	001 100			110		106									
	Chromagel effects	001 100 300			36		26									
Rosco	E. Colour	100 200 300	154	153	109		107				166		148		113	
	Cinegal correction	3000														
	Roscolene effects	800			825	826		834						832		
	Cinecolor effects	600			626		621								620	
	Supergel effects	001 100 300			36		26		31	332			342			
	Roscolux effects	001 100 300			36	34	26		31	332			342		42	
Chris James	effects	300														
	correction	200														
	Effects	100	154	153	109		107				166		148		113	
	L.P. Effects	001 100 200 300														046
	Cinemoid effects	100	53		9		7						48		13	
Lee	effects	HT 001 HT 100 HT 300					026									046
	correction	200														
	effects	001 100 300	154	153	109		107				166		148		113	046

Number series

Color filter cross-reference chart. Values are listed left-to-right across the chart columns for each row.

Manufacturer	Type	Number series	Filter numbers (left → right)
Arri	Gelatran effects	100	05, 04, 63, 13
Arri	effects	300	328, 332
Arri	correction	200	249, 248, 247
Arri	effects	100	110, 192, 111, 128
Gamcolor	Cinefilter correction	3000	584, 583, 552, 580
Gamcolor	Gamcolor effects	1000	138, 137, 106, 155, 105, 160, 170, 150, 130, 110, 120, 140
Strand	Strand effects	400	410, 411, 412, 428, 449
Strand	Strand correction	200	
Strand	Chromoid effects	001 / 100	108, 90, 112, 111, 113
Strand	Chromagel effects	001 / 100 / 300	38, 35, 43, 45, 46
Rosco	E. Colour	100 / 200 / 300	249, 248, 247, 110, 192, 111, 328, 128, 332
Rosco	Cinegal correction	3000	3318, 3314, 3313, 3308
Rosco	Roscolene effects	800	827, 828, 837, 836
Rosco	Cinecolor effects	600	622, 624, 625, 627, 631
Rosco	Supergel effects	001 / 100 / 300	33, 38, 337, 35, 343, 43, 344, 339, 45, 349, 46
Rosco	Roscolux effects	001 / 100 / 300	333, 33, 38, 37, 337, 35, 343, 43, 44, 344, 339, 39, 45, 349, 46
Chris James	effects	300	328, 332
Chris James	correction	200	249, 248, 247
Chris James	Effects	100	110, 192, 111, 128
Chris James	L.P. Effects	001 / 100 / 200 / 300	035, 036
Lee	Cinemoid effects	100	10, 11, 12
Lee	effects	HT 001 / HT 100 / HT 300	035, 036
Lee	correction	200	249, 248, 247
Lee	effects	001 / 100 / 300	035, 110, 036, 192, 111, 002, 328, 128, 332

Number series

Manufacturer	Product	Number series														
Arri	Gelatran effects	100	17										08			
Arri	effects	300												321		
Arri	correction	200														
Arri	effects	100	157	193					164		182		106			
Gamcolor	Cinefilter correction	3000														
Gamcolor	Gamcolor effects	1000							280		270	235	245	250		
Strand	Strand effects	400	457						464		482		406			
Strand	Strand correction	200														
Strand	Chromoid effects	001 / 100			157	178		95	164	135					114	
Strand	Chromagel effects	001 / 100 / 300			32	40		24	25	19					27	
Rosco	E. Colour	100 / 200 / 300	157	193					164		182		106			
Rosco	Cinegal correction	3000														
Rosco	Roscolene effects	800						819	818					821		823
Rosco	Cinecolor effects	600					632									
Rosco	Supergel effects	001 / 100 / 300			32	40		24	25	19					27	
Rosco	Roscolux effects	001 / 100 / 300			32	40	41	24	25	19					27	
Chris James	effects	300												321		
Chris James	correction	200														
Chris James	Effects	100	157	193					164		182		106			
Chris James	L.P. Effects	001 / 100 / 200 / 300							019	024			026		027	
Chris James	Cinemoid effects	100	57		66				64				6	14		
Lee	effects	HT 001 / HT 100 / HT 300							019	024			026		027	
Lee	correction	200														
Lee	effects	001 / 100 / 300	157	193				019	164	024	182	026	106		027	

Number series

Manufacturer	Type	Number series	1	2	3	4	5	6	7	8	9	10	11	12
Arri	Gelatran effects	100												
Arri	effects	300								308				
Arri	correction	200	223	206							205			204
Arri	effects	100			159			103						
Gamcolor	Cinefilter correction	3000									1549		1570	
Gamcolor	Gamcolor effects	1000	353			440				365	360	385		
Strand	Strand effects	400			459			403						
Strand	Strand correction	200	223	206							205			204
Strand	Chromoid effects	001/100						103				98		
Strand	Chromagel effects	001/100/300							13			09		
Rosco	E. Colour	100/200/300	223	206	159		212	103		205			285	204
Rosco	Cinegal correction	3000	3410	3409						3408			3407	
Rosco	Roscolene effects	800					805							
Rosco	Cinecolor effects	600						605		608			613	
Rosco	Supergel effects	001/100/300							13			09		
Rosco	Roscolux effects	001/100/300						08	13			09	16	
Chris James	effects	300								308				
Chris James	correction	200	223	206							205			204
Chris James	Effects	100			159			103						
Chris James	L.P. Effects	001/100/200/300							013	009				
Chris James	Cinemoid effects	100	73						3					
Lee	effects	HT 001/HT 100/HT 300							013	009				
Lee	correction	200	223	206			212			205				204
Lee	effects	001/100/300			159			103	013	009				

Number series

Manufacturer	Product	Number series																		
Arri	Gelatran effects	100								41									36		
Arri	effects	300											306	309							315
Arri	correction	200			212																
Arri	effects	100	156							101		104	102				179			105
Gamcolor	Cinefilter correction	3000			1560															
Gamcolor	Gamcolor effects	1000			510	470	460	480	450						420					350
Strand	Strand effects	400	456							401		404	402				479			405
Strand	Strand correction	200			212															
Strand	Chromoid effects	001 100		159	150			101				146	149			102			97	
Strand	Chromagel effects	001 100 300		06	07			10				15	11			14			20	
Rosco	E. Colour	100 200 300								101	102	104						179		105
Rosco	Cinegal correction	3000																		
Rosco	Roscolene effects	800		804							806	810	809	807						
Rosco	Cinecolor effects	600		604					609											
Rosco	Supergel effects	001 100 300		06	07			10		312		15	11			14			20	
Rosco	Roscolux effects	001 100 300		06	07	310		12	10	312		15	11			14			20	
Chris James	effects	300										306	309							315
Chris James	correction	200			212															
Chris James	Effects	100	156							101		104	102				179			105
Chris James	L.P. Effects	001 100 200 300					007	010								015			020	
Lee	Cinemoid effects	100			50					1		4	49	2		46			33	
Lee	effects	HT 001 HT 100 HT 300					007	010								015			020	
Lee	correction	200																		
Lee	effects	001 100 300					007	010		101		104	102			015	179		020	105

Manufacturer	Product	Number series																	
Arri	Gelatran effects	100													18	06				
Arri	effects	300							303	386										
Arri	correction	200																237		
Arri	effects	100					162		52				151			176				
Gamcolor	Cinefilter correction	3000	555	552	575															
Gamcolor	Gamcolor effects	1000		364		340					325		305					260		320
Strand	Strand effects	400					462		452				451			476				
Strand	Strand correction	200																237		
Strand	Chromoid effects	001 / 100							154						152	175	176			
Strand	Chromagel effects	001 / 100 / 300							05						03	01	30			
Rosco	E. Colour	100 / 200 / 300						162	152				151			176				
Rosco	Cinegal correction	3000																		
Rosco	Roscolene effects	800														802				
Rosco	Cinecolor effects	600					602								603				617	
Rosco	Supergel effects	001 / 100 / 300							304	05		305		04	03	01	30			
Rosco	Roscolux effects	001 / 100 / 300					02		304	05		305		04	03	01	30			
Chris James	effects	300							303		386									
Chris James	correction	200																237		
Chris James	Effects	100					162		152				151			176				
Chris James	L.P. Effects	001 / 100 / 200 / 300									004									
Lee	Cinemoid effects	100							52		51		75			78				
Lee	effects	HT 001 / HT 100 / HT 300									004									
Lee	correction	200																		
Lee	effects	001 / 100 / 300					162		152		004		151			176				

This chart cross-references lighting gel / filter number series across manufacturers (Arri, Gamcolor, Strand, Rosco, Chris James, Cinemoid, Lee). Columns represent the "Number series" colour bands shown along the bottom.

Manufacturer	Product	Series	1	2	3	4	5	6	7	8	9	10	11	12	13	14	15	16	17	18
Arri	Gelatran effects	100						30							20				22	
Arri	effects	300						311			313				380	317				
Arri	correction	200		236																
Arri	effects	100						147				134				158			135	
Gamcolor	Cinefilter correction	3000		1545	1543	1565							1540							
Gamcolor	Gamcolor effects	1000					375	343					335			345		315		290
Strand	Strand effects	400						447				434				458			135	
Strand	Strand correction	200		236																
Strand	Chromoid effects	001 100													134	158				
Strand	Chromagel effects	001 100 300													21	23				
Rosco	E. Colour	100 200 300		236				147				134				158			135	
Rosco	Cinegal correction	3000			3401															
Rosco	Roscolene effects	800				811				813					815	817				
Rosco	Cinecolor effects	600				614	612	610					611	615			618			619
Rosco	Supergel effects	001 100 300													21	23			22	
Rosco	Roscolux effects	001 100 300		316			18		318	317	17	321			21	23			22	
Chris James	effects	300						311			313				380	317				
Chris James	correction	200	285	236																
Chris James	Effects	100						147				134				158			135	
Chris James	L.P. Effects	001 100 200 300														021			022	
	Cinemoid effects	100			47							34	5	58					35	
Lee	effects	HT 001 HT 100 HT 300														021			022	
Lee	correction	200	285	236																
Lee	effects	001 100 300						147				134			021	158		025	022 135	
	Number series																			

Plate 2 Munsell system

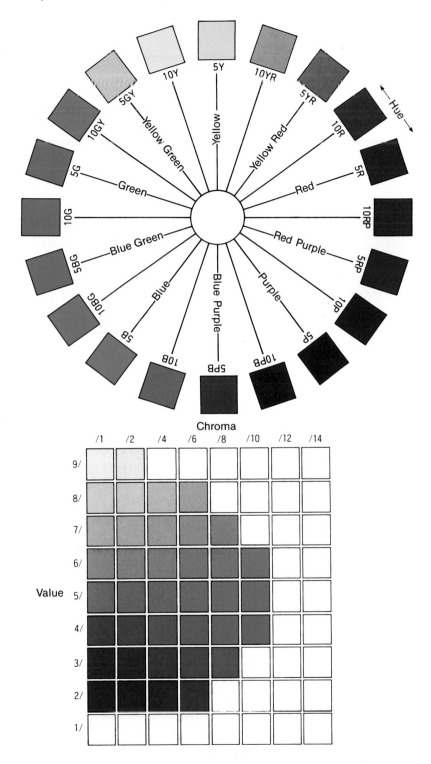

Plate 3 CIE chromaticity diagram

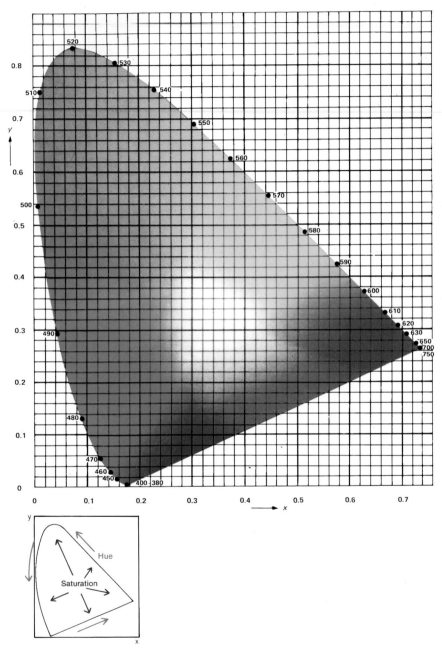

are actual photographs of the colour filters, they will not portray an exact representation of that colour, because of the colour shift inherent in the photographic and printing processes.

However, if a colour swatch book of any of the filter stockists mentioned is available, it is quite simple to look up any particular colour in the tables and then make comparisons with all of the other types.

Example: If Cinemoid No. 32, which is a medium blue, is called up on an old lighting plot, the alternative filters that are a direct comparison are:

Lee	165
Chris James	165
Rosco	67 and 851
Gamcolor	810
Arri	165
Strand	465
Gelatran	71

All of the following filter stockists provide colour swatch books with information on each filter, giving it a name, its light transmission and a spectral distribution curve. The colour filter comparison tables in Plate 1 only quote the manufacturer and their reference number. The range of filters covered are as shown in Table 3.3.

Table 3.3 Colour filter suppliers

Stockist	Name and intended use	Number series	Material
Lee Filters	Effects	001	Polyester
	Effects	100	Polyester
	Correction	200	Polyester
	Effects	HT001	Polycarbonate
	Effects	HT100	Polycarbonate
	Effects	HT300	Polycarbonate
Cinemoid	Effects	100	Cellulose acetate
Chris James	Effects	100	Polyester
	Correction	200	Polyester
	Effects	300	Polyester
	Effects	001/100/200/300	Polycarbonate
Roscolab	Roscolux effects	001/100/300	Polycarbonate/ polyester
	Supergel effects	001/100/300	Polycarbonate
	Cinecolor effects	600	Polyester
	Roscolene effects	800	Cellulose acetate
	Cinegel correction	3000	Polyester
	E.Colour	001/100/300	Polyester
Great American Market	Gamcolor effects	1000	Polyester
	Cinefilter correction	3000	Polyester
Colortran Inc.	Gelatran effects	100	Mylar
Strand Lighting	Chromagel effects	001/100/300	Polycarbonate
	Strand filter correction	200	Polyester
	Strand filter effects	400	Polyester
	Chromoid effects	001/100	Polycarbonate
Arri (GB)	Effects	100	Polyester
	Correction	200	Polyester
	Effects	300	Polyester

3.6 Conversion of light in film and television cameras

One only has to go to various television viewers' homes and see the adjustments made to individual receivers to realize that opinions on what constitutes good colour vary quite considerably, therefore before we progress any further, perhaps it would be wise to declare the main objective in the reproduction of colour in any system of image transferance. This objective must be that if we were able to look at the reproduced scene, side by side with the original, there would be very little difference between the two.

Whether light is a wave or a particle, there is no escaping the fact that light is a form of energy, similar to heat, electrical, mechanical and nuclear. In nature energy changes from one form to another. The energy conversion we are most interested in is the conversion of light, either into chemical energy, such as in the eye or in the process of filming, or by the photons that are guided by a lens to the electronic receptors in our television cameras.

Film sensitivity

Modern 35mm film emulsion can withstand enormous exposure latitudes and, to some extent, colour distortion. We as professionals in the entertainment field, must have standards to adhere to and, boring as it may seem, these usually involve a scientific measurement or some form of discipline in operational procedures. Whether we are going to produce negative film or reversal film the basic system is the exposure of three layers of emulsion to red, green and blue light. Those layers are inherently superimposed within the emulsion itself. It is of course possible to individually process the red, green and blue light arriving at the film by using three separate film stocks, and this was the basis of the old Technicolor system used from 1932 to 1955.

One of the problems with using three different stocks for the red, green and blue components is that although it is easy to separate the constituent colours, the superimposition of the three images to reproduce the final image is somewhat difficult and requires a high degree of precision. Even with the Technicolor process, the final copy of film sent to the cinemas for projection was multi-layer film stock. Although cameras have an iris exactly the same as the eye, we can only reduce the amount of light hitting the film; we cannot increase the light level above the largest opening in the iris of the lens. If we wish to have greater sensitivity, we have to change to a different type of film. As a general rule, the more sensitive film becomes, the greater is the granular structure. The reason for using larger grains in the film is that they stand a higher chance of being struck by the photons. This use of a larger grain structure is similar to the grouping of the rods in the human eye. In the case of the eye, and in the film, the sharpness of the image reduces with the need for greater sensitivity.

The exposure of film to light causes the photons to strike the silver halide crystals in the film emulsion and these will change according to the intensity of the light. Photographic emulsion is naturally sensitive to the blue part of the spectrum; to increase the sensitivity to

Figure 3.12 Film comparison.
Courtesy of Fuji Film Co. Ltd.

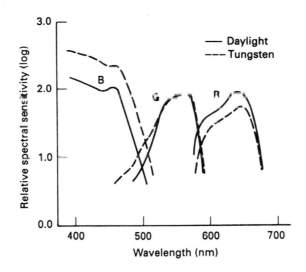

the green and red layers sensitizing dyes have to be added to the emulsion. If we use the basic emulsion as the top layer in our system, it will be sensitive to the blue part of the spectrum and because of this fact we need no filter for the blue input from the lens. Because of the sensitivity of the other two layers to the blue, we reduce the blue going through the film by having a yellow filter immediately beneath the top layer. If the bottom layer is made sensitive only to red light we will not need a red filter. Between the yellow filter and the red emulsion is the green emulsion. As the blue light has been prevented from reaching this emulsion, which is sensitive only to the green part of the spectrum, we do not need a green filter. By constructing the film this way, we have effectively had three single exposures for the red, green and blue but all taken at the same time and in perfect register. Also by allowing the longest wavelengths to travel the furthest through the layers, we reduce the tendency to scatter, which causes lack of resolution.

The film is now processed so that cyan, magenta and yellow images are formed in the three layers. This is typical of negative film stock. To produce the positive from this stock, it is basically only necessary to photograph it with a similar type of negative, although in practice very sophisticated films can be used for the reversal process. Films can be balanced for artificial light or daylight and this is accomplished by the balance between the red and blue emulsion sensitivity. Figure 3.12 shows the difference between negative film for daylight and negative film for artificial light.

As can be seen, this film is composed of three emulsion layers being sensitive to red, green and blue light along with a protective layer, a yellow filter layer, an anti-halation layer and other layers, all coated on a clear safety base. The other side of the base is coated with a black resin backing to provide such properties as antiscratch and antistatic. It also provides for lubrication so that its passage through the mechanical system is made easier. Different couplers are incorporated in the various emulsion layers and through post exposure processing, colour dyes and mask images are formed in the emulsion (see Fig. 3.13). The film contains an orange coloured mask

Figure 3.13 Negative film layers. Courtesy of Fuji Film Co. Ltd.

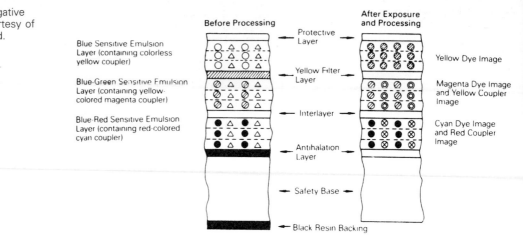

Blue Sensitive Emulsion Layer (containing colorless yellow coupler)

Blue-Green Sensitive Emulsion Layer (containing yellow-colored magenta coupler)

Blue-Red Sensitive Emulsion Layer (containing red-colored cyan coupler)

Before Processing

After Exposure and Processing

Protective Layer

Yellow Filter Layer

Interlayer

Antihalation Layer

Safety Base

Black Resin Backing

Yellow Dye Image

Magenta Dye Image and Yellow Coupler Image

Cyan Dye Image and Red Coupler Image

which allows for correct colour rendition when prints are made through this negative material on a positive film.

TV camera sensitivity

Television cameras have to analyse the light from a scene and the method is somewhat different to that used with film. The pickup devices themselves have the same colour sensitivity, and are therefore not adjusted for the individual red, green and blue components of the light. Secondly, there are no commercially available pickup sensors capable of producing the red, green and blue signals in a single device as required for the process of high quality broadcast colour television. A fundamental requirement for broadcast television standards is that three individual sensors have to be used together with colour filtering systems. Thus, the use of the three colour sensors and the consequent splitting of light that has to occur makes the colour camera optically very complex. Light falling on the three sensors must have a common entrance, i.e. each sensor must see exactly the same scene in order to avoid optical distortion. When processing the light through the optical system this has to be done with minimum loss, avoiding either excessive lighting levels in the studio, or producing noisy pictures by not having sufficient light to satisfy the sensitivity of the camera sensors. Most of the optical requirements with the systems for colour cameras can be met by using zoom lenses to create a single path from the viewed scene to the camera electronics.

Older style television cameras always used pickup tubes, which were mainly the lead oxide type and somewhat deficient at the red end of the spectrum, creating in the earlier days of colour television, noise in the 'reds', ultimately improved by clever electronic circuits that boosted the red signal. Eventually pickup tubes improved so that the red response was slightly better. Because tube systems use magnetic focusing, it was possible, quite often, when aberrations occurred, to correct these by adjusting the magnetic focusing system. The system still required that the red, green and blue images were in registration but this was relatively easy to accomplish in 'line up' by the use of the electronic system. Figure 3.14 shows a typical beam splitting system to derive the red, green and blue components.

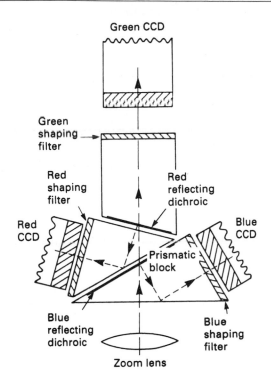

Figure 3.14 Splitter block

Charge coupled devices

The introduction of 'charge coupled devices' (CCDs) has somewhat changed the pickup system. CCDs have been introduced for several reasons and the main ones are that they are more *robust, free from shock and vibration and have much better geometry* than the old tube cameras. CCDs are also immune to the influence of external magnetic fields. In some older type cameras, it was possible when the camera panned to see slight variations in the vision output caused by stray local magnetic fields or even the Earth's magnetic field.

A major advantage of CCD systems is the fact that they are more sensitive than tube systems and this has allowed the incident light level to be reduced from 1600 lux to between 500 and 800 lux with a consequent use of about half the electrical power.

What is a CCD? A charge coupled device is a solid state chip covered in several hundred thousand photosensitive cells, all of this built onto a device roughly a centimetre square. Each photosensitive cell represents one piece of picture information (pixel). Like camera tubes, CCDs have the same colour sensitivity, therefore three devices and filters for the red, green and blue components have to be used. As the CCDs are built to an absolute, almost perfect matrix, there is a lack of geometric distortion in pictures. The three chips have to be positioned extremely accurately so that the individual elements are aligned to an error of about half a pixel. If a registration accuracy of 0.05% is required, this means the alignment must be accurate to two thousandths of a millimetre which can only be accomplished by the camera manufacturer. If we are aligning the chips on the prism block to this degree, it is not difficult to imagine that heat can pose a problem.

Geometric distortion

Temperature differences within the optical block will obviously cause misregistration, due to different co-efficients of thermal expansion. One advantage of this system is that having been aligned in the factory, the system will not drift out of tolerance. A further tremendous advantage of CCDs is that they have a superb colour response although a problem is that the peak sensitivity is in the infrared region. This has to be corrected, otherwise we would have problems with the reds in the system, and an infrared 'cut off filter' is fitted to the optical path to do just this. However, having looked at the two types of input system, either tube or CCD, at the end of the day all they do is produce small electrical signals which represent the red, green and blue components of the viewed scene. These signals are then processed within the camera control units and ultimately arrive in our homes as colour television.

4
Light measurements

4.1   Units, terminology and calculations

Historical

Human beings have always been dependent on light for their very existence but through ingenuity, we discovered how to extend the hours of daylight for our own purposes. The first artificial light was fire, so it was a natural progression into burning oil in a container with a lighted wick. In various parts of the world oil was extracted from available supplies of fish, nuts or vegetables, depending on the locality. Even the storm petrel was used because of their high content of oil by threading a wick through them to make a primitive type of candle. One wonders if this discovery came about by a barbecue that got out of control but there is no record of how many lux would be equal to one storm petrel! The more practical development of this idea was the rush candle, made by peeling all but the last layer of the outside leaves so that the soft absorbent centre could be dipped in tallow and dried. Obviously this was the prototype of the tallow candle as we know it but not so in the hot countries, because tallow melts at 52°C. Eventually, to measure and record light a unit was required that could be understood and repeated experimentally. This was of course the candle – but not any old candle. It had to be well defined so that it was repeatable (well, almost repeatable). It is quite laughable today to think of a world wide standard measurement of light being dependent on the repeatability of a burning candle, but it is a fact and the specification for the standard candle defined the type of wick and the tallow mixture to be used and the dimensions were an ⅛ inch wick and a candle with a diameter of 1⅛ inches.

Owing to the unreliability of a wax candle, it was replaced by a lamp burning vapourized pentane with an intensity equal to about ten of the original candles. Eventually, even this was considered inaccurate and in 1909 a filament lamp was adopted as the standard, which continued until 1948. To enable very accurate measurements to be made, it was decided, at this time, to create a standard based upon the light emitted from a platinum radiator at 1773°C contained within a special vessel.

The candela

The unit of luminous intensity, the candela, is defined as 'the luminous intensity, in the perpendicular direction, of a surface of 1/600 000 square metres of a black body, at the temperature of freezing platinum, under standard atmospheric pressure'.

Radiant flux

The **radiant flux** is the amount of light energy that is given off by an object each second and is measured in 'joules per second' (the physical unit of measurement is known as a watt). A 100 watt lamp therefore, radiates a total of 100 joules of light energy each second. However, a 100 watt tungsten lamp only radiates approximately 5 watts of visible light, the remainder being radiated as non-visible infrared. The more we compress the energy from the light source into the visible spectrum, so we raise the amount of useful watts of light output. As the eye varies in sensitivity with the wavelength of light, it is impractical to use the watt as a measure of the light output. The eye's peak sensitivity is at 555 nanometers (green) whereas as at 400 nanometers the sensitivity is 1000 times less. Thus, 1 watt of radiation in the green part of the spectrum is 1000 times more effective than 1 watt in the blue. Low pressure sodium lamps emit practically all their light at around 590 nanometers, as this is very close to the peak sensitivity of the eye, it is highly efficient in terms of the number of lumens per watt. Thus, by concentrating the energy into narrow bands, it may be possible to produce light sources with outputs as high as 160 lumens per watt and, in fact, it is this type of light generation that is employed in modern high energy light sources such as the HMI, MSR lamps.

Luminous flux

Luminous flux measures the total light output of a source and its unit of measurement is the **lumen**. However, in the entertainment business we are interested in luminaires that focus the light sources in a specific direction and **light emitted in a specific direction is measured in candelas**, and is called the luminous intensity.

Incident and reflected light

The incident light striking a unit area is called the illuminance and is measured in lumens/m^2 (lux) As well as incident light, we are very much concerned with reflected light. The **light emitted from a unit area in a specific direction is called 'luminance'** and is measured in candelas per cm^2, which indicates how bright an object actually appears, and this may be an illuminated area or the area of a source of light. The luminance of a surface determines how bright that surface actually appears. One candela per cm^2 equals 2920 foot Lamberts.

Table 4.1 Luminance values

Source	Luminance (in cd/m^2)
Sun	1600 $\times$ 10^6
Crater of carbon arc	200 $\times$ 10^6
Tungsten lamp (100W clear)	0.5 $\times$ 10^6
Tungsten lamp (100W pearl)	8 $\times$ 10^4
High pressure mercury lamp (400W clear)	120 $\times$ 10^4
Fluorescent lamp (80W)	0.9 $\times$ 10^4
Low pressure sodium lamp (140W clear)	8 $\times$ 10^4
Clear blue sky	0.4 $\times$ 10^4
White paper (reflection factor 80%) illumination 400 lux	100
Grey paper (reflection factor 40%) illumination 400 lux	50
Black paper (reflection factor 4%) illumination 400 lux	5

Note: For practical purposes the figures are given in cd/m^2 as cd/cm^2 is a very small unit.

Table 4.1 gives the values of luminance for typical sources.

As an example of how we may apply these units in practice, let us consider the light being emitted in Figure 4.1 which shows a candle burning with a luminous intensity of one candela. The light is assumed to be distributed evenly in all directions, and the two areas shown are representing parts of the inner wall of two spheres, one at one foot from the source and the other at one metre from the source.

Foot candle

It can be seen that the smaller area closest to the source will be brighter than the larger area further away from the source. By definition, one foot candle is the amount of light falling on an area of one square foot at a distance of one foot from a source of one candela. The principle is the same for one lux being defined as the amount of light falling on an area of one square metre at a distance of one metre from a source of one candela.

To find the relationship between foot candles and lux, it is necessary to relate the areas being illuminated in Figure 4.1. By converting the area of one square foot to square millimetres, we have 92 903 mm^2 and of course, one square metre is 1 000 000 mm^2. If we now divide the larger area by the smaller area we get a factor of 10.76 which is the conversion factor to use when relating foot candles to lux in Figure 4.2.

We explain the fall off of light as the distance is increased in Section 4.2 and the cosine relationship in Section 4.4 with the trigonometry involved to determine the light distribution at various distances. However the examples in Fig. 4.2 bring together all of these calculations in one place as a convenient reference.

4.2 Laws: inverse square and cosine

Although there are many ways of reducing the light output of a luminaire, there is not one way of increasing it, therefore our only interest is the reduction of light and the laws that it obeys.

Figure 4.1 Candela/lux/foot candle
relationship

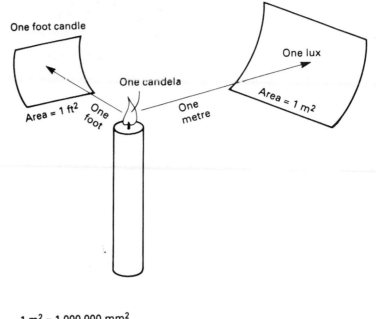

Figure 4.2 Relationship of lux to
foot candles

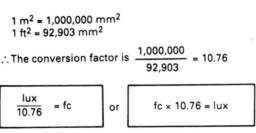

$1 \text{ m}^2 = 1,000,000 \text{ mm}^2$
$1 \text{ ft}^2 = 92,903 \text{ mm}^2$

$\therefore$ The conversion factor is $\dfrac{1,000,000}{92,903} = 10.76$

$$\boxed{\dfrac{\text{lux}}{10.76} = \text{fc}}$$ or $$\boxed{\text{fc} \times 10.76 = \text{lux}}$$

Light output examples
A 1000W 3200K tungsten source produces 26 000 lumens.
A 1000W Fresnel tungsten spotlight produces 74 000 candela.
A 1000W PAR tungsten source produces 270 000 candela.

Inverse square law

If a diffusion filter or wire gauze is placed in front of a light source, one would expect it to reduce the light output and it is equally obvious that if the material restricts half of the light, then the level will fall by 50%. It would appear by similar rationale, that the light from a luminaire would fall off with distance and a common misunderstanding is that at double the distance one would expect to get half the light. This is not so. The light is governed by a simple formula called the 'inverse square law' which states that the light is falling off as the distance is squared. Therefore if the distance from the light is doubled, the light will fall to one quarter. It must be said at this point that normal point light sources conform to the inverse square law when calculating illuminance. However, if we look at a larger source area, such as a fluorescent fitting, this needs to be dealt with in a different way. In situations such as this, the inverse square

Figure 4.3 Examples of applied laws

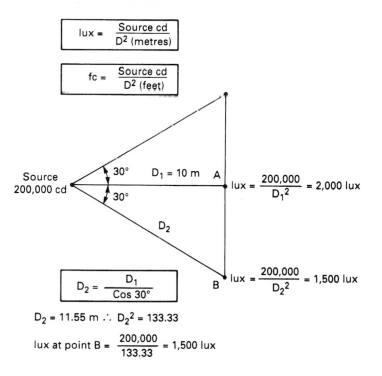

$$\text{lux} = \frac{\text{Source cd}}{D^2 \text{ (metres)}}$$

$$\text{fc} = \frac{\text{Source cd}}{D^2 \text{ (feet)}}$$

Source 200,000 cd

$30°$ $30°$ $D_1 = 10 \text{ m}$ A D_2 B

$$\text{lux} = \frac{200,000}{D_1{}^2} = 2,000 \text{ lux}$$

$$\text{lux} = \frac{200,000}{D_2{}^2} = 1,500 \text{ lux}$$

$$D_2 = \frac{D_1}{\text{Cos } 30°}$$

$D_2 = 11.55 \text{ m} \therefore D_2{}^2 = 133.33$

$$\text{lux at point B} = \frac{200,000}{133.33} = 1,500 \text{ lux}$$

law can be used only if the distance of the light source from the subject is five times the maximum dimension of the source itself. For example, if the source is half a metre across, the inverse square law will be accurate from 2.5 metres and above.

Let us consider more difficult distances other than the convenient ones mentioned. If the light reading is taken at a given distance, say 10 m, and has a value of 1000 lux, we can determine the light intensity from the luminaire by simply multiplying the lux reading by the distance squared, i.e. 1000 lux $\times$ 10^2 = 100 000 candelas. We now have a constant value for the intensity of the luminaire and it is expressed in candelas. As we arrived at the candela value by multiplying a lux reading by the distance squared, it is equally true that we can divide the candela value by any distance squared and obtain the lux reading at the new distance.

Cosine law

When the incident light falling on a cell is normal (at 90°) to the plane of the cell, the light cell will correctly measure the incident light. If however, the light reaches the cell at any angle other than normal, the amount of light to be measured will change. This variation in light is in direct relation to the angle the light enters the cell, and the light diminishes as the cosine of the angle to the normal and this is known as 'Lambert's cosine law'. Thus, in theory, light that enters the cell from the side, in other words 90° to the normal, would be 'zero' on a cosine corrected meter. This variation comes about by the fact that the light has to cover a greater area when striking from any angle other than normal.

Figure 4.4

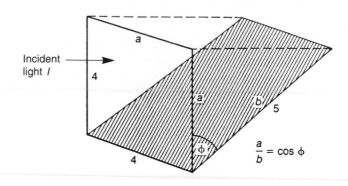

$$\frac{a}{b} = \cos \phi$$

Clearly *b* is longer, therefore the hatched area is larger,
e.g.   Original area = a^2 = 4 × 4 = 16
         New area = $a \times b$ = 4 × 5 = 20
         Also 16/20 = 0.8 = cos Ø

The best example of the spread of light is to consider the follow
spot used in a theatre. When normal to a surface it produces a round
beam of light. When pointed at an angle to the stage, to cover the
artist, the beam is now spread in an elongated shape. The amount
of light in the beam has not changed, but the area covered has
increased; thus the illumination per unit area has diminished.
Obviously, if the beam is elongated more and more as the light
approaches from the side, the area covered by the light beam
becomes infinite. Thus the amount of light per unit area becomes
less and less and approaches zero.

With very shallow angles to normal, the variations are not significant, but as the angles become greater and approach anything from
45° to 90° quite large variations in light level can occur. This is particularly so when considering outside broadcast lighting, and the floodlighting industry has had problems with this phenomenon for many
years. Just to give an example, the cosine of 30° = 0.866, the cosine

Figure 4.5

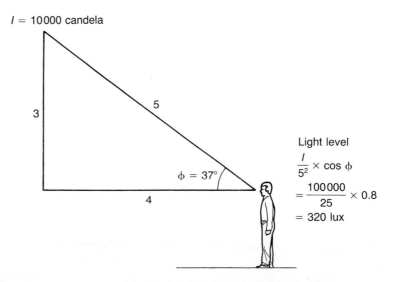

I = 10000 candela

3

5

4

$\phi = 37°$

Light level

$\dfrac{I}{5^2} \times \cos \phi$

$= \dfrac{100000}{25} \times 0.8$

= 320 lux

of 45° = 0.77, the cosine of 60° = 0.5, the cosine of 75° = 0.259, the cosine of 90° = zero.

As well as changing in one plane, the light can change in two planes at the same time. The light in the horizontal plane can come in at an angle as well as from the vertical plane, so both our x and y co-ordinates can vary. If this is the case, we have variations of the cosine law from two directions and this is normally called the 'cosine cubed law'.

4.3   Polar diagrams and their interpretation

Polar plot

We can determine two main important facts about the light output of a luminaire from its polar plot – the intensity of the light and its coverage. All lighting manufacturers use the same system to produce their catalogue information, so it is worth investigating the method of the test to help to understand the results. Whilst light meters are used to read the light arriving at the subject and so provide us with the actual information to work with, it is quite impossible to assess a luminaire against the manufacturer's catalogue information in the same way, because of the variables that must be catered for before a light output comparison can be made.

Calibrated lamp

The supply voltage must be stabilized at the design voltage of the lamp; a 5% reduction at 240 V will result in an approximate light loss of 15%. The lamp used for the test will have been calibrated by the manufacturer, who will also supply a laboratory report, showing

Figure 4.6 Method of producing a polar diagram

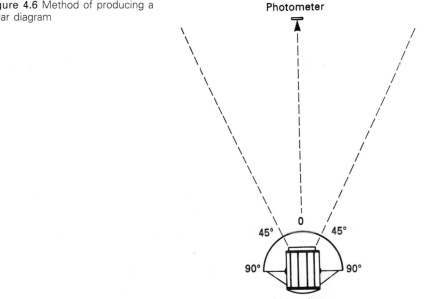

Figure 4.7 Fresnel polar distribution

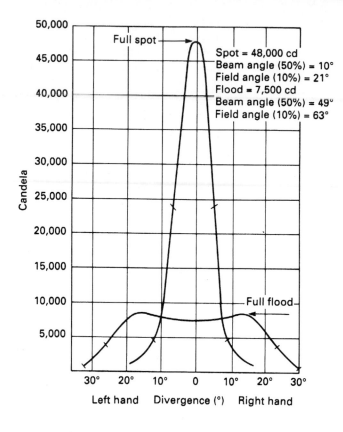

the exact voltage to run the lamp at to achieve the stated wattage and colour temperature. This sample lamp is kept by the luminaire manufacturer as the standard for all tests (see Figures 4.6 and 4.7).

Polar test

When assessing a polar diagram, determine if the manufacturer's light readings were taken without a wire guard in place; because a 25mm wire guard will reduce the total light by about 8% – a ploy often used to enhance a product's specification. When making a polar curve, the luminaire must be checked to see that the reflector is centralized and that the lamp filament is in line with the centre of the reflector. Assuming that lenses and reflectors are clean, then a meaningful test can be made. With the light cell set at the same height as the centre of the luminaire, two methods of test are available to us: a polar test or a flat wall test.

Flat wall test

The flat wall test is made by moving the cell of the light meter across a screen at a set distance from the light and recording readings at regular intervals. However, this method is far from accurate because of the distance measurements and the angle of the cell to the light, so the accepted method is a polar test, where the light is rotated and the cell remains stationary. Then, if flat wall information is required, it can be produced mathematically by simple trigonometry and the inverse square law.

Plotting a polar diagram

The tests are conducted in a darkened room and care must be taken to see that no reflected light from the walls or ceiling reach the light cell. The readings can be taken at any distance; however, a very short distance will require very accurate measurements to be made, because any error in the distance will be magnified by the effect of the inverse square law, so that a slight change in distance can produce a large change in the light level.

Typically, luminaires up to 1 kW are measured at 5 m, 1–5 kW at 8 m and 10 kW at 10 m, but this is only a guide because the test can be made at any chosen distance. The polar plotter is made up of a stand or platform that will allow the luminaire to rotate. A semicircular scale is placed under the luminaire, equally divided in degrees, and this scale is locked off to the luminaire, so that it rotates with it. A pointer is fixed to the bottom of the support structure so that it remains static. The test can now be made by aligning the centre of the scale with the pointer, and positioning the centre of the light output beam onto the cell. This setting up procedure is usually easier to achieve by first setting the focus to the spot position. The luminaire can now be rotated and readings taken at regular intervals.

Test method

A typical method is to take readings at every degree for the spot position, and every 2.5 degrees for the full flood position. The centre reading starts at zero degrees and the readings are taken left and right of centre. Having taken the readings and plotted them on a graph, similar to the one illustrated by the Fresnel polar diagram (Figure 4.7), it is normal to place a mark at the point on the curve that corresponds to 50% of the centre brightness and another mark at 10%. These are known as the 'beam angle' and the 'field angle' respectively. The significance of the 50% beam angle is that if two lights are required to overlap and provide an even reading across the two distributions they must overlap at the 50% mark to produce 100% to match the centre reading. The 10% mark is normally considered to be the total angle of the light, in view of the fact that any light outside of this reading is of little use.

The readings are taken in lux at a given distance, but are normally quoted in candelas. This is arrived at by multiplying the lux reading by the distance squared from the light to the cell. It is more useful to display the information in candelas because the light level in lux at any distance can be easily calculated by dividing the candela reading by the required distance squared. In this way the manufacturer makes up the typical light output readings in lux at various distances that are used in the catalogue data sheets. Then with a little trigonometry, the diameter can be predicted, given the output angle of the light and the distance. The shape of the flood position in the Fresnel distribution illustrated will produce an even reading across a line 90° to the source. Because the readings are higher either side of the centre this will compensate for the greater distance that the light is projected to reach that part of the distribution.

4.4   Types of meter

LUMINANCE (REFLECTED) LIGHT METERS

Photographic meters, either the built in type as with most modern 35mm cameras, or a hand held meter, measure the reflected light from the scene which is going to reach the film. As the film has a certain sensitivity, either the stop and/or the speed of the shutter have to be adjusted so that the correct quantity of light reaches the emulsion, so that well exposed pictures are produced. Of course, nowadays, most cameras do everything automatically. The basis of reflected light measurements is an 18% reflectance value which produces an average brightness standard of measurements for film and TV cameras. At this point it must be stated that we are only measuring the amount of light, not the colour of the source, as long as the meter responds faithfully to all visible wavelengths. If we have a red card that reflects 18% of the light striking it or we have a green card with the same reflectance, they will appear to be the equivalent as far as a camera is concerned because we haven't taken any account of the colour involved. We have all been caught out by taking pictures of snow scenes or pictures in very dark areas when the average brightness cannot equate the scenic values very accurately to the 18% reflectance.

Luminance meters are used for the measurement of a light source or surface brightness. Two of the most important factors with a luminance meter is the angle of acceptance so it can cover very small areas at a distance and secondly, to ensure that there is no light entering the cell outside the angle of acceptance, which would give false readings. For average use, an acceptance angle of one degree is acceptable, however for very accurate luminous measurements on small areas one third of a degree is possible in some meters. A normal luminance meter will be calibrated in candelas per metre squared and alternatively foot Lamberts. Photographic luminance meters will have systems where film speed and other parameters can be entered so that an exposure value can be obtained from the meter readings.

Spot meter

In addition to a standard luminance meter, it is now possible to obtain chromameters where the measurements of the colour tristimulus values are made in addition to the candela per metre squared units or Foot Lamberts. These meters would be used where the light sources are too small to be measured with standard colorimeters, for example, LEDs and small lamps. They are also useful to measure light sources when they are operating and obviously very hot. Further use is for inaccessible or distant light sources, the Minolta chromameter CS 100 (Figure 4.8) allows the accurate metering of areas as small as 1.3 mm in diameter.

Figure 4.8 Courtesy Minolta UK

Figure 4.9 Incident light meter. Courtesy of Minolta (UK) Ltd.

ILLUMINANCE (INCIDENT) LIGHT METERS

A better way of measuring the amount of light is by taking incident light readings which are not influenced by the subject matter itself. If we measure incident light, it is then up to the operator to adjust the equipment being used to give a balanced exposure on the scene itself. A good modern incident light meter should be capable of measuring the luminance in either lux or foot candles (Figure 4.9). In addition, it is much better if the meter has a digital readout so the figures are accurately displayed. The spectral response must match within fairly close limits the CIE photopic luminosity curve which gives the correct assessment of colour balance for incident light readings (see Figure 4.10a and b).

In our measurement of incident light, it is essential that we use a cosine corrected cell which gives readings which are correct and take into account the angle of the light incident on the meter. It is also important that the meter would be facing the direction of the most interest visually, i.e. along the path that the camera would look at the scene.

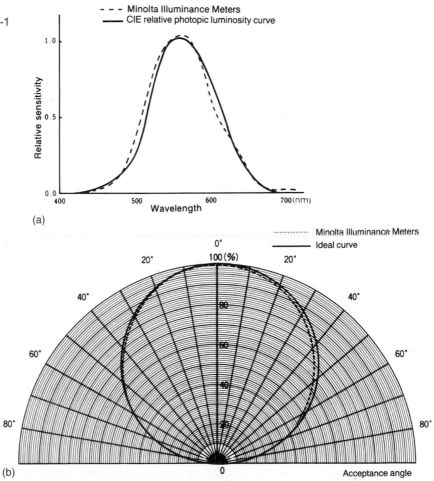

Figure 4.10 (a) Incident light meter – spectral response. (b) Incident light meter – acceptance angle characteristics. Courtesy of Minolta (UK) Ltd.

THE MEASUREMENT OF COLOUR TEMPERATURE

Kelvin units

William Thomson (later to become Lord Kelvin) was an eminent physicist of his day (1824–1907), and was responsible for establishing the Kelvin scale used for colour temperature measurement. Kelvin was faced, when experimenting, with two scales on which temperature could be measured – the Fahrenheit system and the Celsius or, as it is more commonly called, the Centigrade system.

The Fahrenheit system was developed by Daniel Gabriel Fahrenheit (1686–1736), a German physicist who worked in The Netherlands and also invented the alcohol and mercury thermometers. The Fahrenheit scale is based on 32° which represents the freezing point of water and 212° which is the boiling point of water, the interval between these two points being divided into 180 parts or degrees.

The Centigrade system was developed by Anders Celsius (1701–1744), a Swedish professor of astronomy who proposed a temperature scale of 0 to 100 degrees be adopted with **0° as the boiling point** of water and **100° as the freezing point**.

It was not until after the death of Celsius that Carolus Linnaeus (1707–1778), a professor of medicine in Sweden, reversed the scale to make the 0° the freezing point and 100° the boiling point. The conversion between the two systems is $F = ((9/5) \times C°) + 32$.

Both of these systems were in use for standard temperature readings and both suffered the same problem, namely that the scale did not start at the lowest point of a temperature range and produced negative values.

In their time the scales might have seemed adequate and to represent the Centigrade scale starting at zero, this being the freezing point of water, seemed a good idea. Unfortunately, water freezes at different temperatures at different altitudes and various degrees of purity and quite frankly, has no relevance at all, it could just as easily have been any other substance.

Kelvin decided that both temperature scales were unsuitable for scientific measurements. He had no argument with the Centigrade scale, it was its starting point that caused the problem. Being not only a prominent physicist but a brilliant mathematician, he calculated the theoretical point of absolute zero as being –273° on the Centigrade scale. At this point no material can be further lowered in temperature. This then was his starting point: to set zero on the Kelvin scale at –273° Centigrade, thus from zero upwards getting only positive values.

Since the Kelvin scale is a Centigrade scale displaced from its zero by 273 degrees, a tungsten filament which is glowing and radiating a colour that is 3000 Kelvin, is burning at a temperature of 2727° Centigrade (see Table 4.2).

The Kelvin colour temperature scale can only be used when measuring a source that emits energy in a continuous spectrum and approximates to a blackbody radiator such as a tungsten filament, or the ultimate in light sources, the sun.

What this means is that a lamp with a 2700K colour temperature produces approximately the same spectrum of light as a blackbody

Table 4.2 Kelvin colour temperature of typical light sources

Kelvins	Light sources
9000–11000	Bright sunlight with blue sky
6000	Electronic flash
5800	HI carbon arc and average daylight
5600	Film and TV discharge lamp (correlated colour temperature)
3400	Tungsten halogen film lamp and photofloods
3200	Tungsten halogen film and TV lamp
3000	Tungsten halogen theatre lamp
2600	100W household lamp
1925	Candle light
770	The eye starts to see the darkest reds
660	The eye starts to percieve a filament changing colour
0	Absolute zero

at 2700K. (Most hot objects do not follow Planck's blackbody radiation law: only perfectly black objects do.) If we examine the visible spectrum portion of the blackbody curves given it will be seen that the curves are continuous over the visible wavelengths. As the object becomes hotter, it is noticeable that the amounts of red energy and blue energy are varying in relation to each other. If we could have a meter which measured the ratio of the red/blue balance, we would then have a reasonably close approximation to blackbody temperatures. In fact, the older style of colour temperature meters made throughout the world generally worked on the fact that they employed a red and blue filter to measure the relative amounts of each and thus find the corresponding colour temperature.

Spectral output

The colour of light emitted from a discharge lamp cannot be expressed in Kelvins because the spectral output in the lamp is not continuous but dependent on the gases and rare earths used in its manufacture to introduce the required additional colours which help to create the colour of the source (see Figure 4.11), and the compounds used emit colours in only comparatively narrow bands.

Figure 4.11 Comparison of discharge and incandescent sources

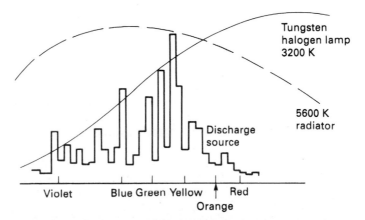

Tungsten halogen lamp 3200 K

5600 K radiator

Discharge source

Violet   Blue Green Yellow ↑ Red
Orange

Figure 4.12 Tri-stimulus colour meter. Courtesy of Minolta (UK) Ltd.

In photographic and television cameras the film stock and the colour receptors are responsive to the amounts of red, green and blue in the light, but unfortunately due to the spiky nature of the colour distribution from a discharge lamp a standard colour meter that measures only the red/blue balance of a source will give erroneous readings because it is not measuring the total spectral output.

TRI-STIMULUS COLOUR METER

The world of the theatre will rely upon the LDs setting the lights to give the maximum visual effect and although a meter might be useful, we strongly suspect it would be extraneous to the emotional feelings conveyed by the lighting to the audience and would ignore the fact that the eye is self-adjusting and has a built-in time lag in its response. Therefore a meter cannot take into account the previous light level which will influence the **apparent brightness** of the scene. In film and television however, we do need accurate measurements of incident light onto subjects, we need an accurate measure of colour temperature if we are using sources that approximate to the blackbody curve and we also need to be able to measure colour accurately of any type so that errors are avoided when operating discharge sources in either film or television.

A tri stimulus meter (Figure 4.12) is really a clever little hand-held computer. It contains three photo cells which are filtered to detect the primary stimulus values of blue, green and red light under a special opal diffuser. This diffuser is specially made to take account of the direction of light and therefore inherently calculates the cosine angle of incident light. The incident light level can be derived from the output of the green photo cell as this relates to the photopic curve. It would appear that only the blue and red photo cells would be required to give a colour temperature reading; however, meters of this type will compute a point on the spectrum locus from an analysis of the red, blue and green receptors.

5
Light sources

Light can be produced from electricity in several ways and the most important for the purposes of this book are:

- **Incandescence:** Light and infrared energy are produced by raising the temperature of a substance (e.g. tungsten) until it is incandescent.
- **Electrical discharge:** Light is produced by electricity passing through a gas or vapour, agitating or exciting the atoms of the filling to produce light, ultraviolet energy and infrared energy.
- **Fluorescence and phosphorescence:** This is the process by which ultraviolet energy is converted into visible light by phosphors.

Figure 5.1 and Table 5.1 show the relative light outputs for these sources:

5.1 Incandescent sources

Historic

In 1816 a development was taking place with experiments by Thomas Drummond, when he demonstrated a bright white light by

Figure 5.1

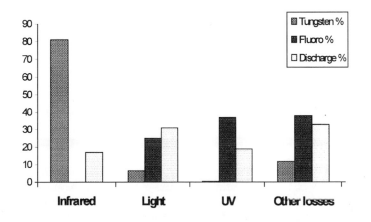

Table 5.1 Distribution of power

Incandescent lamp	
Lead wire conduction loss	2%
Gas conduction and convection loss	10%
Ultraviolet	0.5%
Infrared	81%
Visible light	6.5%
Fluorescent lamp	
Electrode loss	15%
Gas conduction loss	23%
Ultraviolet (phosphor conversion loss)	37%
Visible light from phosphor	23%
Visible light from discharge	2%
Metal halide discharge lamps	
Electrode loss	12%
Gas conduction loss	21%
Ultraviolet	19%
Infrared	17%
Visible light	31%

directing jets of burning oxygen and hydrogen onto a block of calcium (quicklime) thus heating it to incandescence. However, this form of lighting had to wait until 1837 before it was first used in the theatre and it was in widespread use by 1860. Because the light was difficult to operate, requiring a person in constant attendance, adjusting the block of calcium as it burned, and to adjust the flow of gas from the two cylinders of oxygen and hydrogen, the lights were used mainly from the auditorium as open-faced lanterns and were immediately named 'limelights'. Hence the expression 'in the limelight' means being at the focal point on the stage.

In those days, a follow spot operator most likely had the same instructions as today – 'when in doubt, follow the money!'

Lamp development

The incandescent filament lamp was the original backbone of the electrical manufacturing industry as we know it today. In the 1930s all of the large electrical companies owed their existence to the common household bulb because it was domestic lighting that created the demand for generators to supply the electricity to homes which had no other use for an electrical supply system. Following this, the motors in domestic appliances became the slaves of the generators. More importantly, the bulb sales provided the money for all of the electrical development in the early days. The original bulbs were very expensive. From 1883 to 1900 the price was 5 shillings (25p) while an engineer's salary was 30 shillings (£1.50) per week, so in today's terms, 16% of an engineer's weekly salary would seem extortionate for a common household bulb. In 1840 Joseph Wilson Swan showed an experiment of burning a thin filament made of carbon in the open air. It lasted a few seconds and was the first of his experiments.

In 1845 Mr Starr patented an idea in England of producing light by causing a carbon filament to glow in a vacuum. However, this idea could not be pursued for the time being and had to wait for Hermann Sprengel to invent an efficient vacuum pump to enable the bulbs to be exhausted of air. The development of the incandescent filament lamp was long and tedious, Swan finally completed his design and was able to demonstrate it in Newcastle in 1879.

Also during 1879 Thomas Edison was working along the same lines in America and was astute enough to take out a British patent for a carbon filament burning in a vacuum. The following four years were largely taken up by a legal battle between Edison and Swan over the rights to the idea with the only winners being the patent lawyers, for in 1883 they called off the fight and joined forces, registering the Edison and Swan United Electric Light Company. The manufacture of the carbon filament, which incidentally has the reverse characteristic to tungsten inasmuch as its resistance decreases as it heats, was manufactured until 1906, when the tungsten filament was first produced for domestic sales. This enabled the bulb manufacturers to greatly increase the light output from the filament by lacing it around supports and coiling it back upon itself to maintain a high temperature by the close proximity of the filament coils to each other. The filament could also run at comparatively high colour temperatures in view of the fact that the melting point of tungsten is 3410°C.

A common household 240V 100W bulb has 1147 mm of wire in the filament. Therefore the next development was the coiled coil filament where the wire is returned and coiled again on itself; this was a great advance in reducing the size of the source. Various improvements were introduced in the following years, one of which was the use of nitrogen and argon in the lamp to retard evaporation of the filament and thereby prolong its life.

Tungsten halogen development

The next significant development in lamps occurred during the late 1950s and when it became commercially available in 1960 it was known as the quartz iodine lamp, later to be renamed tungsten halogen with its benefit of the tungsten halogen cycle. Other advances were made by including internal reflectors inside the envelope of the lamp and in some instances a dichroic coating which not only reflected the light forwards but permitted the infrared end of the spectrum to pass through the reflector, thereby reducing the heat in the beam.

Tungsten halogen lamps can be divided into two groups of manufacture: synthetic silica quartz and hard glass (see Figure 5.2). In the case of the synthetic silica quartz, the walls are extremely strong and have a high melting point thus allowing a small envelope which permits a comparatively high internal pressure. This has the effect of doubling the life in comparison with hard glass. Therefore the hard glass envelope is thinner and much larger but still maintains the tungsten halogen cycle. At half the life one is not disappointed to find that it is approximately half the price, thus the cost per hour of life is approximately the same. Therefore the choice is purely a high initial capital investment with the synthetic silica quartz lamps with reduced maintenance replacements against the low initial cost of the hard glass (see Figure 5.3).

Figure 5.2 Tungsten halogen lamps

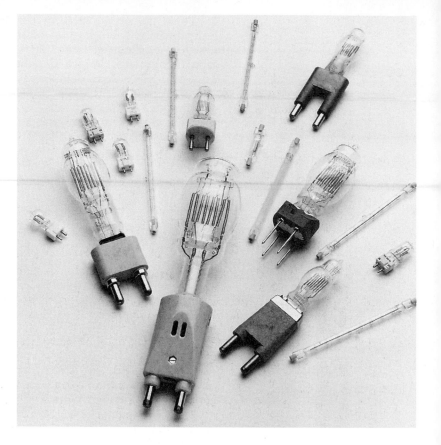

Figure 5.3 Silica quartz tungsten halogen lamps

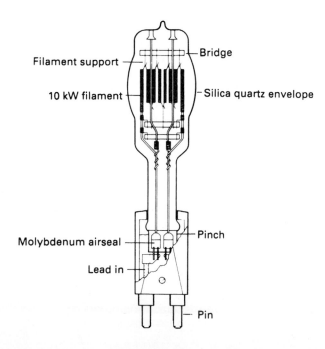

Filament support — Bridge

10 kW filament — Silica quartz envelope

Molybdenum airseal — Pinch

Lead in —

— Pin

Figure 5.4 Energy–wavelength curve of a 500W incandescent lamp

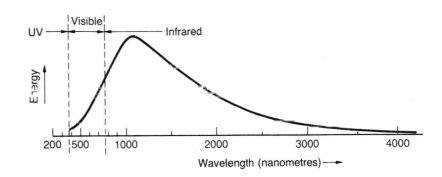

Lamp efficacy

The electric lamp is a heat generator from which we can get a little light. This would appear to be an odd statement until one compares the efficiency. The conversion of total electrical energy produces 6.5% light and 93.5% waste. The light energy is transmitted through the air which is also absorbing heat from the beam and the remainder of the heat is absorbed by the subject being illuminated – a very important fact when considering ventilation requirements for a building (see Figure 5.4).

The temperature of the lamp is one of the manufacturers main design considerations, with the need to operate at relatively high temperatures, bearing in mind the melting point of tungsten which is 3410°C. The high efficiency 3400K (3127°C) lamps are obviously burning very near their melting point and therefore only give approximately 20 hours life.

Figure 5.5 Filament designations. Courtesy of General Electric

Planar (MP) C13
Monoplane

Biplanar (BP) C13d
Biplane

C2V

C7A

C9

2C8
2CC8

C6 Oval

CC6
(Reflector)

CC8
(Reflector)

C6
CC6

C8
CC8

The lamp designer must be concerned not only with the correct temperatures to keep the tungsten halogen cycle working, but also the filament design to achieve the exact colour temperatures required (see Figure 5.5).

Pinch temperatures

There is also the problem of maintaining the lamp's seal temperature within the manufacturer's stated maximum. This is because the leadout of the filament through the silicon quartz envelope is made by a thin foil of molybdenum. The expansion of molybdenum and quartz are not quite the same, therefore as the temperature increases the difference increases and at very high temperatures the seal between them would become porous and the molybdenum would oxidize.

Typically, the maximum temperature of molybdenum seals fall into three categories:

(a) long life lamps with a maximum temperature of 350°C;
(b) short life lamps 400°C;
(c) special lamps designed to work with a maximum seal temperature of 500°C.

However, caution should be taken with the high temperature seal lamps because some of them have a shorter light centre length than the standard lamps and cannot be interchanged, because of misalignment within the optical system. However, when used in a purpose designed luminaire, the higher seal temperature lamps permit the manufacturer to design much smaller lamp housings. When lamps are used in a design with inadequate ventilation, the end of life can be seal failure rather than filament failure. At the other end of the scale, if the source is force cooled by a fan, reducing its wall temperature to 250°C, the tungsten halogen cycle is affected.

Filament noise

Filament vibration can sometimes cause an acoustic problem. With a sinusoidal voltage applied to the lamp, the current produces a shock on the filament every half cycle. The vibration of the filament can set up a sympathetic vibration in the luminaire and particularly in the case of scoops – the sound as well as the light is beamed down on the microphone. The lamp manufacturers tried to reduce this effect by clamping the filament supports onto the filament in a positive manner using non-magnetic wires and calculating the spacing of the supports to try to dampen the vibration. This problem was slight in the case of auto transformers and resistance dimmers; however, with the chopped waveform principle of dimming, the situation is much worse. This is because the current is rapidly switched on every half cycle and does not increase slowly as it would in a sinusoidal waveform. The worse position for vibration is at half power when the dimmer is firing at a 90° angle. Manufacturers of high quality dimmers use a choke in the output to dampen this effect. It is an interesting experiment to observe the filament movement with various firing angles by taking a standard lens and positioning

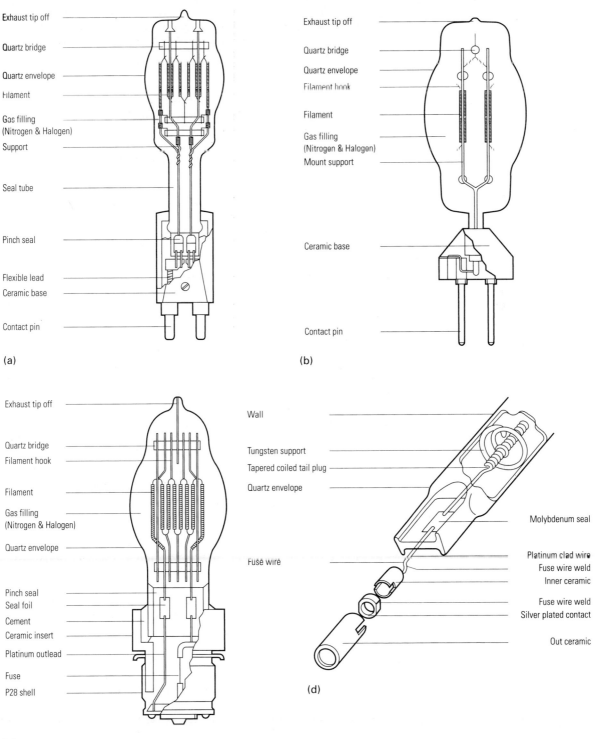

Figure 5.6 (a) A typical high wattage studio lamp. (b) A typical 4-pin twin filament studio lamp. (c) A typical low wattage theatre class tungsten halogen lamp. (d) End section of a typical quartz linear tungsten halogen lamp. Courtesy of General Electric.

it at its focal length from the filament projecting the image onto a screen, focusing the filament and observing the movement.

Inrush current

The cause of the inrush current on the initial switch on of a cold filament is that tungsten has a comparatively low resistance in its cold state. The current initially reaches a very high value but as soon as the filament heats, its resistance increases and the current soon falls. To generalize, the inrush current can be from 10 to 17 times the normal running current, depending on the filament size and the impedance of the circuit, but only lasts for approximately 0.2 to 0.8 seconds. This can become a problem in determining the type of fuse for a circuit and the current rating of miniature circuit breakers (see Section 12.6).

The effect of varying voltage

All lamps are designed for one specific voltage; the manufacturer decides the following criteria: operating voltage, colour temperature, life, current and the wattage, which is a product of the current and voltage. The performance of a light source is tested in a integrating sphere, where the total luminous efficacy is measured and then expressed in the manufacturer's data as 'lumens per watt'. The higher the lumens per watt, the higher the lamp temperature and consequently the colour temperature.

If any parameters are changed, all the other values must change because they are all inter-related. The easiest way to understand that is to take the case of varying the voltage to the lamp. If the voltage is reduced, the flow of current will reduce, and as the wattage is a function of volts × amps, the wattage will reduce. Because the filament is now burning at a lower temperature, the colour of the light will change and will move towards the red end of the spectrum and the good news is that the life will be extended.

It is apparent by now that it is very difficult to calculate the outcome of a voltage change because all of the values that could be used for a formula are variables with no constant to latch onto. Even the resistance of the filaments increases when it is heated, therefore, when we reduce the voltage and thus the heat of the filament, the resistance will decrease.

It is, however, possible by the use of the graph in Figure 5.7 to read off all the changes that take place with varying voltage by starting with a complete set of known values. Fortunately, every lamp manufacturer provides the relevant information which is peculiar to his product so it is necessary to first determine the make and type number of the lamp. A typical example would be type: CP-40 (ANSI code FKJ) 240V, 1000W, 3200K, 26 lumens per watt, thus giving a total of 26 000 lumens and a life of 200 hours.

It will be seen that the horizontal scale of Figure 5.7 refers to percentage change of the applied voltage and the vertical scale shows the resultant change by percentage of the manufacturers stated values.

Do remember to convert any value into a percentage of the manufacturer's stated value. For example, taking the CP-40 1000W

Figure 5.7 characteristics of tungsten halogen lamps

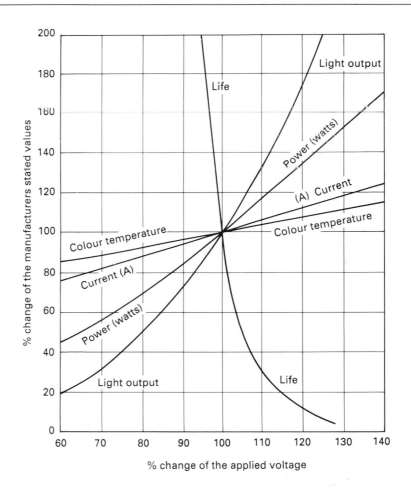

lamp quoted earlier, we have a rated voltage of 240. If the voltage is reduced, to say 205V, a reduction of 35 in 240 equals 14.6% (say 15%). Referring to the horizontal scale of the graph, percentage change of the applied voltage, a reduction of 15% gives a value of 85% voltage. Move vertically up the 85% line and read off the following values:

Light output	60% of 26 000 lumens	= 15 600 lumens
Watts	77% of 1000 watts	= 770 watts
Current (A)	92% of 4.17 amps	= 3.84 amps
Colour temperature	94% of 3200K	= 3008K
Life (est.)	300% of 200 hours	= 600 hours

In the case of life, it was necessary to project the life curve above the graph and estimate that it would meet the vertical line at approximately 300%. When the life value is changed considerably, it cannot be estimated with great accuracy, however the principle gives a good indication of the life that one would expect. The example quoted is in fact the result of running the lamp at position 7.5 on the lighting control console, if it has a square law fader characteristic (refer to Chapter 8).

The electrical supply system in the United Kingdom is normally very good. However, the supply authorities are very generous with themselves in allowing a maximum variation of +10% and –6% about 400 volts for three phase supplies and +10% and –6% for 230 volt supplies which **represents 253 V to 216.2 V.** Referring to the graph, 253 V equals 106% voltage for a 240 volt lamp which would result in a life of 50%, so don't always blame the lamp manufacturer for poor life performance – it might not be their fault.

As a matter of interest, the change to a stated value of 230 volts for the mains supply (for European harmonization) will not cause too many problems in practice as most systems in the UK will still operate at about 240 volts and therefore most lamps will be supplied as 240 volt versions for the UK.

The tungsten halogen cycle

When a tungsten filament is burning at a comparatively high temperature, tungsten atoms leave the filament and normally attach themselves to the inside surface of the lamp envelope. This is most noticeable in the household bulb, which becomes quite black by the end of its life. Theatre and studio lamps, before tungsten halogen designs became available, had the same problem, resulting in the reduction of both light and colour temperature throughout their life. The chemical principle of including a halogen gas in the lamp to reduce blackening was well known for many years before it became practical to produce a lamp to accommodate it.

The first lamps to appear on the market in the early 1960s used a quartz envelope and an iodine filling. This had the desired effect but unfortunately the iodine had a slight pink colour when hot and changed the colour of the light. The new development was called **quartz iodine** but in fact most of the halogen gases would work in the same way. Unfortunately, most of these gases radiate a colour when heated or were quite aggressive towards the tungsten filament, eating it away before it reached old age. Some halogens would even attack the filament when it was on the shelf, resulting in a very short life instead of an extended one. Over the next five years, the manufacturing techniques improved, enabling the lamp manufacturers to use a bromine in place of iodine and a synthetic hard glass in place of pure quartz. In general, the more reactive the halide, the more effective is the halogen cycle. So in theory, fluorine, the most reactive, should be the best, but it is so reactive that it even attacks the glass or quartz. Therefore iodine, bromine and chlorine are the only ones in use for halogen lamps.

Although this was a great technological breakthrough because the bromine did not add an obvious colour to the light, and the new material for the envelope was cheaper than pure quartz, it produced havoc with the lamp manufacturers' marketing departments, which had spent years promoting quartz iodine only to have the name changed because the product no longer used quartz or iodine. The safe way out was apparent, because all lamps would use a tungsten filament and a halogen gas filling, the name **tungsten halogen** was agreed upon, resulting in years' more publicity and a confused public.

The tungsten halogen cycle is simple in principle. Atoms of tungsten evaporate from the filament and combine with atoms of bromine which then circulate together, eventually returning to the filament and separating, leaving the tungsten atoms on the filament and releasing the bromine atoms to circulate and repeat the procedure. In principle, it is an everlasting lamp – but fortunately for lamp manufacturers, it doesn't work quite like that, because the tungsten emits uniformly along the filament, but the returning atoms prefer to select the cooler parts of the filament, therefore the thinner parts of the filament, which are also the hottest, get thinner and the thicker parts get thicker. However, the advantages are enormous:

1. A greatly extended life.
2. A constant light output throughout life.
3. A constant colour temperature throughout life.
4. A smaller envelope means that compact luminaires can be designed.
5. Reduced maintenance costs in time spent replacing lamps.
6. In general, a higher light output is achieved (higher lumens/watt).

To simply explain the tungsten halogen cycle, a lamp is designed so that the wall of the envelope is moved close to the filament to maintain it at a high temperature. The evaporating tungsten atoms leaving the filament soon cool down below 1400°C. In this state, they can combine with the halogen atoms and circulate until they find the temperature that is below 250°C that would enable them to separate. This eventuality has been designed out of the lamp by moving the envelope close to the filament to maintain it at a high temperature, say 350°C, at which temperature the compound will not separate. So the tungsten and halogen atoms circulate until they find a temperature above 1400°C (which is obviously the filament) permitting the compound to separate and deposit the tungsten atoms back onto the filament (Figure 5.8).

It would appear that because the tungsten halogen compound separates at temperatures above 1400°C and below 250°C, a problem would occur when dimming a lamp to a low light level, subsequently reducing the wall temperature to below 250°C. This, however, does not cause a problem in practice, because the evaporation from the filament is substantially reduced at lower temperatures and the small amount of deposit that does occur is rapidly removed when the lamp is restored to full voltage.

UV radiation

One aspect of the tungsten halogen sources to be considered is that of ultraviolet radiation. Synthetic quartz will pass ultraviolet rays and can cause a slight sunburn. For instance, if the skin is exposed continuously for 4–5 hours with a light level of 2000 lux, a slight reddening of the skin will take place with a 3200K lamp. At half this level, 1000 lux, the time would be double. The problem applies particularly to lamps running in open reflector luminaires. If however, the lamps are operating behind a lens which is normally manufactured from borosilicate glass, the problem does not exist because borosilicate glass is a good UV filter.

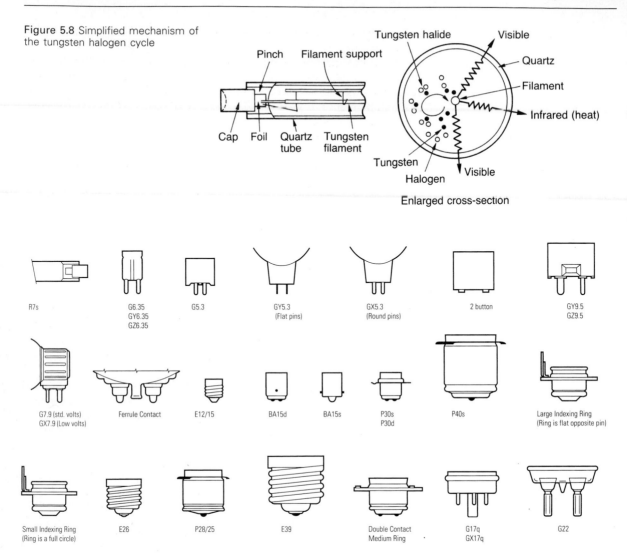

Figure 5.8 Simplified mechanism of the tungsten halogen cycle

Figure 5.9 Some photographic lamps with their IED codes and normal names or common abbreviations. Note that the illustrations are not to scale. Courtesy of General Electric.

Filament construction

Lamps for entertainment, in the main, have compact filaments to produce the smallest size source for the optical systems employed, with the exception of floods and soft lights, where an elongated filament is a distinct advantage when trying to evenly illuminate a large reflector (see Figure 5.8).

5.2 Discharge sources

Historical

If we accept that the sun was the first light source with a nuclear fusion reaction in its core, which is approximately 14 000 000K, and an outer surface temperature of 5800K, then an electrical discharge was certainly the second.

Benjamin Franklin, the American statesman and scientist who helped in the forming of the American Constitution, also found time to invent the Franklin stove and bifocal spectacles. In 1745 or thereabouts, he demonstrated how to electrocute oneself by flying a kite in a thunderstorm. That part of the experiment did not work; however, the real object of the experiment did. Franklin was so convinced that lightning was caused by an electrical discharge that he submitted himself to the risk of electrocution by pointing his finger at a metal ring attached to the end of a silk line that was holding the kite and demonstrated that a spark jumped from the metal ring to his finger. This experiment proved that light was generated from an electrical discharge and established Benjamin Franklin as the inventor of the lightning rod.

The same type of discharge phenomena could be seen on the tall masted sailing ships of the day when in a storm a greenish glow appeared around the top of the mast and was known by sailors as 'St Elmo's fire'.

We now know that the electrical discharge in the form of lightning is caused when the changing temperature within a cloud produces raindrops, hail and ice particles, which collide causing friction that produces a negative charge in the falling particles whilst the smaller rising particles within the cloud gain a positive charge. In this way, charges of up to one million volts can be produced in the clouds and cause sheet lightning if the discharge takes place between clouds, and fork lightning if the discharge is conducted to earth with a power estimated to be between 20 000 and 40 000 A.

Carbon arc

Sir Humphrey Davey (the inventor of the miners' safety lamp), demonstrated an electrical arc between two rods of carbon in 1810. To maintain an arc the two rods were continuously adjusted at the same rate as they were being burnt away, a hot, dirty job, bearing in mind that carbon vaporises at 3382°C. These experiments employed Alessandro Volta's type of battery that used alternate plates of zinc and silver. This demonstration took place at the Royal Institution in London and required 2000 battery cells to provide the voltage and current required to maintain the arc.

Battery operated carbon arc lights first appeared for entertainment when they were used at the Paris Opera. They were also used for floodlighting in the Place de la Concorde in 1830 and later at the Royal Exchange in London.

Arc lights for the film industry

The early work by Humphrey Davey in his experiments with carbon arcs laid the ground for the film industry to develop a succession of arc lights from 1900 through to 1965. In the early 1900s the film industry blossomed in Hollywood and the studios all had their own generators to run the lighting. Because carbons arcs require a direct

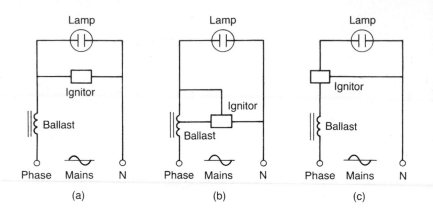

current (dc) to maintain an arc and a voltage in the range 40 to 85 V between the carbons, the generators were made to produce 115 V dc so that a resistance ballast could be conveniently connected in series with the supply to limit the current flow and maintain the arc volts.

The size of the luminaires were rated by the current that was drawn by the carbons, e.g. 40 A, 60 A, 150 A, 225 A and 300 A. For comparison, today's discharge lamps have a range which includes 125 W, 200 W, 270 W, 400 W, 575 W, 1.2 kW, 2.5 kW, 4 kW, 6 kW, 12 kW and 18 kW.

The 'Brute', an extremely powerful 225 A Fresnel spotlight, was developed in 1950 with geared drive to feed the carbons as they burnt away and to rotate the positive carbon at the same time. The 'Brutes', which were regarded with great affection, have today been replaced by discharge sources but comparisons are still being made between the old and the new. The light readings published by Mole Richardson (England) when they introduced the 'Brute' in 1953 make interesting reading:

> At full flood, over a throw of 35 ft (10.67 m) the light level was 1000 footcandles (10 760 lux) with a beam width of 25 ft (7.62 m)
> or
> At full flood over the longer distance of 60 ft (18.29 m) the light level was 340 footcandles (3661 lux) with a beam width of 43 ft (13.1 m).

which rather proves that trying to balance the shadow areas in daylight shooting requires a lot of light!

A 300 A water cooled follow spot was developed for the film Red Shoes and was used in the rental department of Mole Richardson for many years. However, the 300 A 'Super Brute' developed in 1963 was not successful because the extra light did not warrant the increased current, i.e. only three 'Super Brutes' could run from a 1000 A generator, whereas four standard 'Brutes' could be supplied.

Like many inventions, discharge lighting could not be used commercially to any great extent until the electric dynamo was invented by Michael Faraday in 1831 to provide a continuous source of electricity. The first commercial generator was produced by Woolrich of Birmingham and was used for electro-plating in 1844.

Figure 5.11 Run-top curves for a cold discharge lamp

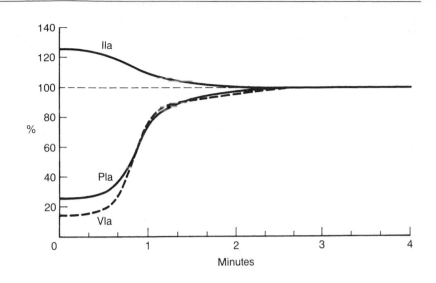

Cold cathode discharge

The first practical discharge lamps were the cold cathode carbon dioxide 'Moore' tubes of 1895. Light is produced by the activity caused when fast moving electrons collide with molecules of gas. In order to accelerate electrons in the early lamps, the applied voltage was in the order of 2000–10 000V at high frequency. Cold cathode tubes contain gas at low pressure, about 1/100 of an atmosphere. The colour of the light is dependent on the gases used. Carbon dioxide emits a very white light of very low intensity. Neon, first isolated in 1898, produces a red light and was used extensively in advertising displays from 1922.

Hot cathode discharge

The hot cathode lamp was a much better commercial proposition because it could operate at mains voltage. This was made possible by using metallic substances such as 'thoriated tungsten', which when heated to incandescence, produces a high level of electronic activity in the tube. By 1932 the hot cathode lamp led to the development of the high pressure sodium and mercury lamps with their much higher efficiency and these lamps are still in use in today's street lighting.

Discharge lamps: basic operation

In all types of discharge lamps an arc is struck between two electrodes in an envelope containing an inert gas or vapour. A choke or electronic ballast is used in the ac supply to limit the flow of current after the arc has been established. Striking the arc is usually achieved by applying a high voltage (see Figure 5.10) across the electrodes to break down the resistance between them so that the gases or vapours inside the lamp may start conducting. Typical starting voltages are between 2000 and 10 000 V. At this point, the ballast

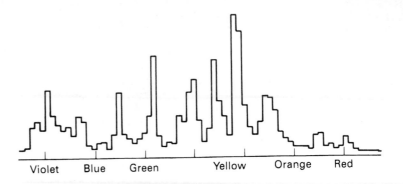

Figure 5.12 spectral distribution of a discharge source

Violet Blue Green Yellow Orange Red

takes over and regulates the flow of current. This starting up procedure normally takes from 1 to 2 minutes until the heat in the lamp
vaporizes the metallic elements which emit their characteristic
colours, but if the lamp is switched off it will need to cool down
before it can be restruck. The cooling time can take from 2 to 5
minutes to allow the internal pressure of the lamp to reduce to a
level where conduction can occur. Alternatively, lamps are designed
for 'hot restrike', in which case a voltage between 20 000 and 70 000
is applied to overcome the high internal pressure and provide instantaneous starting when the lamp is hot.

Metal halide lamps

Discharge lamps are made using mercury, halides, rare earths and
gases; often containing a mixture of many types of chemicals. There
are some 40 metal halides to choose from and each manufacturer
has its own 'brew'. Iodides of sodium produce mainly yellow light,
mercury emits blue/green light in the visible parts of the spectrum
and a great quantity of invisible radiation in the ultraviolet
wavelengths. Thallium is used because it emits mainly green light
(Figure 5.12).

Lamp types

There are many types of discharge lamps, each with its own reference code, although many have similar characteristics. We will only
consider here the lamps that will be useful in entertainment, being
those that approximate to daylight or have a correlated colour
temperature approaching 3400K. As the lamp manufacturing companies develop a new design of lamp, they register the reference as a
trade name so other manufacturers are obliged to make up their
reference for a similar development.

Correlated colour temperature

Although lamp manufacturers quote a colour temperature of the
light in Kelvins, this is only an approximation to the nearest point
on the black body curve.
    The total output from a lamp is made up of many separate colours
from any number of the halides and gases employed to achieve the

Table 5.2 Lamp types

Note: the following sources require an ac supply

HMI	Hydrargyrum (Latin for mercury) Medium arc length Iodides
	95 lumens per watt, 5600K
	Made by Osram
HMI/SE	Single Ended version of the HMI
	95 lumens per watt, 5600K
	Made by Osram
MSR	Medium Source Rare earth, single ended
	95 lumens per watt, 5600K
	Made by Philips
MEI	Metal Earth Iodide
	95 lumens per watt, 5600K
	Made by Osram
GEMI	General Electric Metal Iodide
	95 lumens per watt, 5600K
	Made by GE Lighting
CID	Compact Iodide Daylight
	70-80 lumens per watt, 5500K
	Made by GE Lighting
CSI	Compact Source Iodide
	90 lumens per watt, 4000K
	Made by GE Lighting
SN	Tin halide
	60 lumens per watt, 5500K
	Made by Philips
DAYMAX	Mercury Halide source
	95 lumens per watt, 5600K
	Made by ICL, USA
BRITE ARC	Mercury halide source
	95 lumens per watt
	Made by Sylvania, USA

Note: the following sources are fed from dc supplies

EMI	Xenon
	40 lumens per watt, 6000K
	Made by GE Lighting
XBO	Xenon
	40 lumens per watt, 6000K
	Made by Osram

correct colour balance in the red, green and blue parts of the spectrum to match the response requirements for colour films and TV cameras.

Lamp care

Discharge lamps are generally made of a synthetic quartz material which permits very high operating pressures within the lamp when it is hot, therefore care must be taken when relamping to ensure that the lamp has cooled down before the luminaire is opened. The operator must avoid handling the envelope even when the lamp is cool to prevent grease from the skin contaminating the quartz

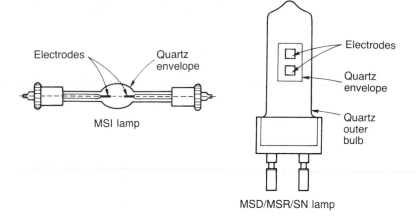

envelope. Care has to be taken when inserting a lamp into its holder because exerting pressure on the envelope can cause a fracture at its joint to the base (Figure 5.14).

UV radiation

The discharge lamp emits large quantities of radiation in the ultra-violet wavelengths which pass straight through the quartz envelope; it is therefore most dangerous to be directly exposed to the lamp. It must always be housed or have a lens or protective glass in front of it. It is fortunate that all standard borosilicate Fresnel lenses have the characteristic of absorbing UV, but if the luminaire is open faced the safety glass provided must also be capable of absorbing the UV radiation. Because of the UV radiation, safety standards require that a switch is fitted to the lens door or safety glass to automatically extinguish the lamp to prevent hazards to the operators and artists

Figure 5.14

by opening the luminaire while the lamp is on. Alternatively the lens door or glass must be securely fastened by fixing screws or bolts.

End of life

The end of life of an incandescent lamp is very obvious, however this is not the case with a discharge lamp. Normally the end of life will be caused by the electrodes burning back during their life, creating a larger gap. The effect of this is a poor starting characteristic requiring many attempts to get the lamp to run continuously after the initial high voltage spark is applied. Therefore inconsistent starting is an indication of the end of life.

Source size

Discharge lamps provide a comparatively small light source. This is certainly welcomed by luminaire manufacturers enabling them to make efficient optical systems. Another bonus is that the total light output of a discharge lamp is comparatively constant throughout its life. However, many lamps suffer devitrification of the quartz during life which is not visible to the eye but has the effect when the lamp is running hot of diffusing the inside surface making the apparent source size that of its envelope. This is most noticeable in ellipsoidal spotlights and follow spots where the initial light output can be **double** that of the light performance halfway through the lamp's life. The effect of the apparently enlarged source size due to devitrification does not significantly affect focusing Fresnels.

Lamp efficacy

Most of the modern developments in daylight balanced lamps have an efficacy of about 95 lumens per watt. It is useful at this point to make comparisons with the studio incandescent tungsten halogen lamp of 3200K that has an efficacy of 26 lumens per watt. This means that the discharge lamp has approximately four times the light output of the tungsten halogen lamp for the same wattage, or an alternative comparison is that for the same light output the discharge lamp is running at 25% of the tungsten halogen 'lamp watts' – an important fact when considering the heating effect in the luminaire and the air conditioning installation in a studio.

Power factor

We make the point of saying 'lamp watts' because the current drawn from the mains may be much higher than would be expected. This is because the current and voltage are not always in phase and can have a 'power factor' as low as 0.5. If a choke ballast is used it is the copper winding on an iron core which makes the current lag behind the voltage, whereas an electronic square wave ballast can make the current lead the voltage by about the same amount.

A typical example is a 2.5 kW discharge lamp compared with a 2.5 kW incandescent lamp. From a 240 V supply, the tungsten halogen lamp would draw 10.42 A, in the case of a discharge lamp supplied from an inductive ballast with a power factor of 0.6, the

Figure 5.15 (a) An inductive current
limitation. (b) Simple vector diagram
of a lamp circuit. (c) Current and
voltages as a function of time.

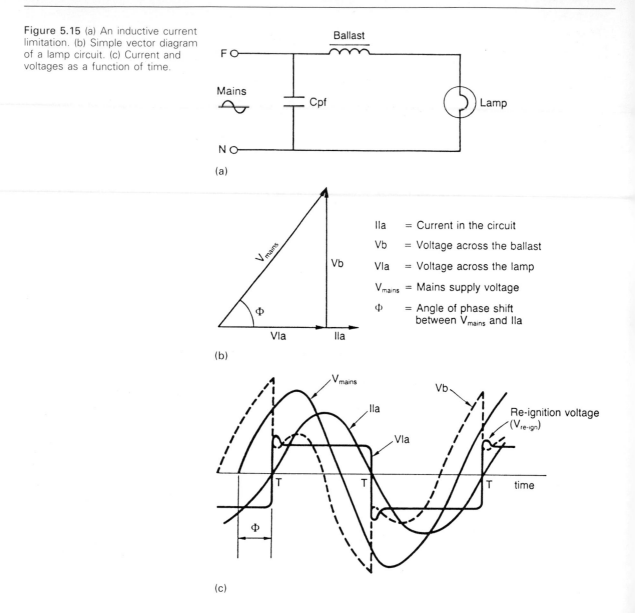

(a)

(b)

Ila   = Current in the circuit

Vb   = Voltage across the ballast

Vla   = Voltage across the lamp

V_{mains} = Mains supply voltage

ϕ = Angle of phase shift
          between V_{mains} and Ila

(c)

current drawn from the supply is 17.36 A, (W = VI cos ϕ, where cos
ϕ is the cosine of the angle of lead or lag of the current). This is
obviously an important consideration in supply requirements. The
current apparently lost between the resistive load and the inductive
load is known as the 'wattless' current. Manufacturers usually add
components to the ballast circuit to improve the power factor so that
it approaches 'unity'.

Flicker problems

Light flicker is caused by the light following the mains frequency
from zero to a maximum value and back down to zero again. This

Figure 5.16 Contours of safe lamp supply frequencies for one ripple ratio value. (a) 24 FPS. (b) 25 FPS

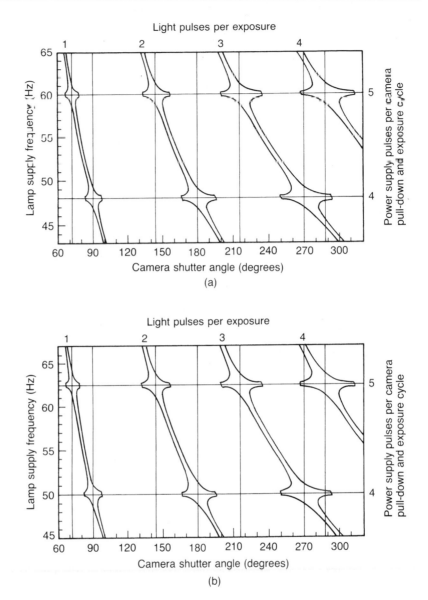

causes a flicker at twice mains frequency when the source is current regulated by a choke and a film camera set to certain shutter speeds or shutter angles will 'see' this fluctuation and produce reduced exposure frames at repetitive intervals. This effect will render conventional ballast equipment useless at high shutter speeds. However, the problems can be overcome by the use of an electronic square wave ballast. By using very fast switching times between the positive and negative half cycles the current 'off' period is very small compared with the current 'on' period; consequently the light output appears to be constant, and the user does not have to worry about any synchronization for the various shutter angles of film cameras and the time-bases of TV systems (see Figure 5.16).

Discharge lamp voltages

Gas discharge lamps generate light from an electrical discharge with a fixed characteristic voltage which may be 70 V for low wattage lamps rising to 225 V for high wattage lamps. The resistance of the lamp falls rapidly above this voltage to a very low value and any attempt to simply connect a lamp to the supply would result in an uncontrolled power output and the bulb would simply explode. The gas behaves as a resistor to the current but has a negative characteristic, therefore to prevent the current increasing to very high levels and possibly destroying the lamp we must control the flow of current.

Current control

With ac operated devices, there are three ways in which we can control the flow of current, namely by using:

1. a resistor,
2. a capacitor, or
3. an inductor.

The main disadvantage of using a resistor is the high losses (I^2R) which result in very low efficiency and the generation of a lot of heat. A capacitor has the lowest inherent losses but unfortunately the waveform produced can damage lamp electrodes. Thus, these disadvantages of the resistor and capacitor has led to the inductor being the most commonly used type of ballast for discharge sources.

Power factor

These ballasts are composed of copper coils wound around an iron core. In order to limit the losses in the ballast and to ensure that the lamp current is stabilized for various conditions, it is important to have the correct combination of the sizes of wire used, the type of magnetic core and the air gap. Due to an inductance being used in circuit, the power factor (cos ϕ) of the system is very low and a typical value is 0.5. To conform to the requirements of the supply authorities means that the power factor has to be raised to a certain minimum value. This is usually accomplished by placing a capacitor across the mains input in front of the ballast. The inductance is chosen to have the right level of reactance to be able to support the difference between the lamp voltage and supply voltage at the rated current. Figure 5.15a shows a very simple inductive ballast used with a lamp and Figure 5.15b,c shows the vector diagram of the voltage and current in the circuit.

Choke ballasts

A complication is the tendency of the higher wattage lamps to have high operating voltages, say 225 V, and therefore only a small difference from the normal single phase supply voltage. The answer to this is not simply to use a smaller choke to support the voltage difference because after ignition a cold lamp will run at a voltage of only 30 or 40 volts. If a small choke were used the starting current would

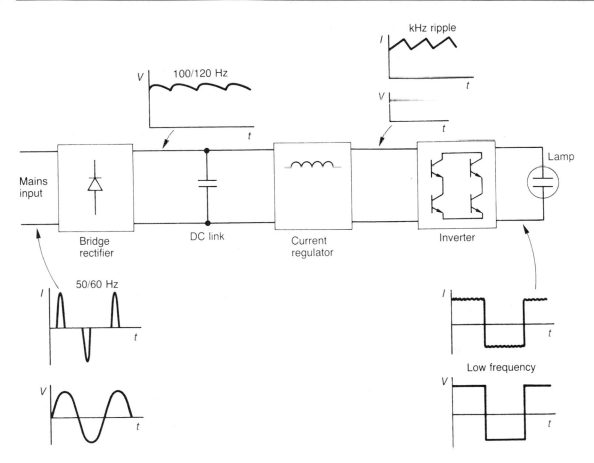

kHz ripple

100/120 Hz

Mains input

Bridge rectifier

DC link

Current regulator

Inverter

Lamp

50/60 Hz

Low frequency

(a)

Figure 5.17 (a) Electronic ballast (non-PFC). (b) Electronic ballast (power factor corrected).

be very large and would damage the lamp. The result is that many ballast chokes of 4 kW and above have a boost transformer connected to the input to ensure that the supply is always high enough above the lamp voltage. All this makes the choke very heavy and almost always fitted with wheels.

Electronic ballasts

Electronic ballasts overcome the weight problems associated with conventional ballasts by using switching regulators to control the output current feeding the lamp circuit, thus avoiding the need for a current limiting choke. The switching regulators will be running at a set frequency in the range 20 to 50 kHz according to the manufacturer's circuit design.

The essential components of an electronic ballast are (see Fig. 5.17a):

1. A rectifier to convert the input supply to dc.
2. A reservoir capacitor to convert the raw dc to smooth dc.
3. A switching current regulator to limit the output current.
4. A dc to ac converter circuit to produce the actual square wave.

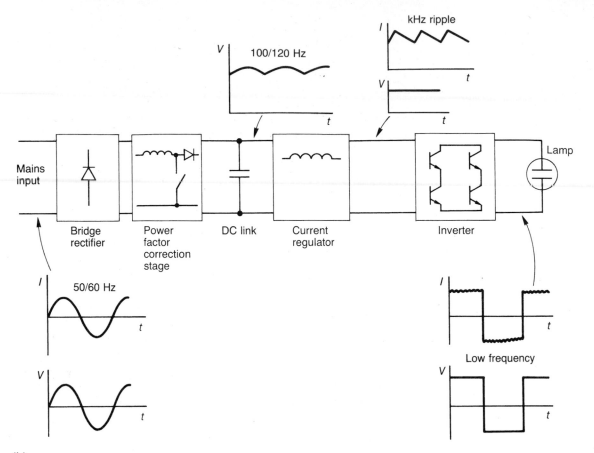

(b)

Discharge lamps, in practice, vary slightly in their operating performance due to the manual manufacturing methods which are generally employed. Even from the same manufacturer there are slight variations in the arc voltage and, if on the low side, this means that the lamp output will be lower in wattage than the stated output. Some may, of course, have high voltage and this means that the power is above the stated value of the lamp, thus overheating the arc and causing short life in the lamp. The lamp voltage is also variable with age. Other than the variations of voltage from a manufactured batch, there are also reasonable voltage differences between similar lamps produced by various manufacturers. To get around this problem, it is preferable that the electronic flicker free ballast system can sense the volts and the current and automatically adjust one to the other to give 'power control' so that the wattage output of the lamp is kept consistent with the manufacturer's stated values. The frequencies of the square waves used with flicker free ballasts are between 40 and 400 Hz.

Square wave operation

It is essential that the output of the switching regulator is filtered so that high frequency components between 25 and 50 kHz are not superimposed on the square wave output.

One of the foremost electronic ballast suppliers, Power Gems of Manchester, England use a 100 Hz square wave output with a switching frequency for the current regulator of 25.6 kHz. The units they produce are equipped with *active power factor correction circuits* (see Fig. 5.17(b)) giving a power factor close to 'unity' and also have a microprocessor management system to give messages on a LCD display for system status and information on any fault condition. Typical fault conditions may be 'over or under voltage', 'output over current', 'over temperature', etc. In all these conditions the output will shut down, a message will be displayed and a fault code stored in the internal logging system.

Many of the electronic ballasts of today have various outputs which can be selected according to the mode required e.g. 'flicker free', 'silent' 50 Hz, 'silent' 60 Hz, etc. When used in modes other than 'flicker free' the appropriate square wave output has the square edges of its waveform 'rounded off' by circuits in the ballast unit, so that it approximates to a sinusoidal waveform.

Dimming and colour shift

An advantage of the electronic ballast is that it is possible with the correct selection of the discharge lamp to obtain a degree of dimming. However, dimming can only be performed over a comparatively small range typically 50% of the light output before the arc becomes unstable. One major problem that can exist during dimming is a colour shift so it is wise therefore to do tests before relying on dimming a discharge lamp.

IGNITION SYSTEM

Ignition voltage

To enable a discharge lamp to ignite, high voltage peaks have to be applied to the lamp, and the peaks are proportional to the gas pressure in the lamp envelope. Thus there is a difference between the ignition of a cold lamp which is at relatively low pressure and of a hot lamp which is at high pressure. The ignition voltage will be generally at least 2000 V and anywhere up to 10 kV with cold lamps. Some special discharge lamps which have a higher filling pressure in the cold state require higher voltages. When the lamp is hot, the pressure has increased by at least 10 times and to re-ignite lamps when hot voltages of between 20 and 70 kV are required depending upon the type of lamp. Figure 5.10 shows three types of igniters used with discharge sources. In order to keep the igniter unit to a small size, the components are small, and consequently this means that to avoid abusing the circuit the starting time must remain for very short periods (0.5–3 seconds). There is also a requirement to limit the number of starts per minute and this is generally specified by the lamp manufacturer. On the other hand, the lamp requires a minimum period of energization to ensure that it starts reliably and again these times are given by the lamp manufacturer. Control of the ignition period is usually accomplished by means of an electronic time switch placed in the power supply or the lamphead.

PROBLEMS IN PRACTICE

If a magnetic ballast is used to regulate the current to the lamp and the unit does not have a good power factor, the only problem that ensues is that the voltage and current are out of phase to some degree but their waveforms are essentially sinusoidal in shape. If an electronic ballast is used with a poor power factor there will be a substantial distortion of the electrical supply waveform, due to the nature of the circuits employed. This distortion, caused by a high harmonic content, can give problems with a generator. The generator may become confused as to what are the correct circuit volts, and the automatic voltage regulator (AVR) will take corrective action, usually raising the voltage, which results in the connected equipment being over-volted.

Neutral current

With a balanced load on each leg of a three phase supply there is virtually no neutral current when using loads with a high power factor; but balanced loads with high harmonic content will produce very high neutral currents. In practice this means that the neutral conductor has to be rated much higher than would normally be expected.

In the case of both magnetic and electronic ballasts a poor power factor means that some energy is wasted; only the 'in phase' current and voltage components of the supply qualify as watts! The wattless component means that losses in the generator will be higher, thus to supply the useful and wasted electrical energy the generator will have to be larger than would appear at face value. Power factors of around 0.7 will mean that a generator needs to be about 30% higher in output. This reflects in the cost of generation and the overheating in the system will result in increased maintenance.

Lamp acoustics

The lamp envelope surrounding the arc acts rather like a miniature sound chamber and its shape affects the acoustic output of the arc. Although not usually a problem when using magnetic ballasts with a sine wave output; a square wave presented to the electrodes can induce an audible noise in the arc as well as in the ballast. Additionally, if there is too much ripple on the square wave supply (see Fig. 5.17) there can also be quite high frequency noise coming from the lamp. These high frequency components are often the cause of lamp instability.

A very important factor with regard to the operation of solid state ballast units is the ambient temperature in which they will operate so that the solid state devices within the units do not overheat and fail. It is possible to fan cool all the devices within the unit but this has to be carefully engineered as the units may be used in all types of conditions where there could be an ingress of either dust or water vapour. In the Arizona desert, just to make things worse, there is a high proportion of copper dust – which is a good recipe for a high voltage flash-over.

Ballast and fan noise

The noise from the fans and the electronics in the ballast unit, although very low, can be troublesome when the units are close to the acting area. Whilst the noise in the ballast can be isolated by running it in a remote position, care should be taken when positioning luminaires to determine if any noise is being directed towards any microphones in use. The noise from the luminaires is more of a problem when using the smaller sources from 200 W to 1.2 kW. Above these wattages the lights are generally working further away and the problem becomes less.

Electro-magnetic interference

Other types of interference can be present in an electronic ballast. The output from the ballast can produce:

(a) Voltage spikes which can be sent back down the supply line and hence onto the mains, which in turn can effect other electronic equipment connected to the same supply.
(b) Radio interference transmitted down the supply cable to the luminaire which is picked up by microphone cables in close proximity, causing audible hum on the sound output.

The introduction of the EMC Directive requires that these problems are reduced significantly by the manufacturers, probably by the addition of high quality filters in the ballast unit.

Although, in the past, electronic ballasts had a poor reputation for reliability, today's 'state of the art' devices probably have a comparable life to that of any modern washing machine, say 7–10 years. Usually any problems are caused by damage by the users themselves.

XENON DISCHARGE LAMP

The xenon discharge lamp is very similar in appearance to other discharge lamps and has the same type of quartz envelope that should not be handled without gloves, because if oil from the fingers is left on the envelope, it will cause devitrification of the quartz when it is heated and produce a grey mark on the envelope that will overheat and can cause the quartz to blister. If a lamp has been handled it should be cleaned with alcohol before it is used.

Xenon lamp characteristics

The lamp also requires a very high voltage of approximately 40000 V to restrike it when it is hot and it produces large quantities of ultraviolet radiation, but here the similarity with other discharge lamps ends. Xenons have been used for many years in film projectors and follow spots with great success, mainly due to the following advantages:

(a) DC operation means that the arc does not flicker.

(b) The lamps have a very good daylight colour rendering 5600–6000 K correlated colour temperature, with a colour rendering index (R_a) approaching 95.

(c) A small source size with all of the useful light concentrated at the point on the cathode known as the 'cathode spot' which is near to the negative electrode. This means that the source can be positioned very accurately in a mirror optical system to redirect most of the light to the first lens in the system.

(d) When the lamp is switched on there is instant constant light with no warm up time required. The lamps can be switched on and off without the problem of waiting for them to cool before being restruck.

(e) A wide range of lamps is available from 75 W through to 10 kW.

With so many advantages over other discharge lamps, why hasn't the xenon lamp been more widely used in TV and film studios? Mainly, because the disadvantages and problems encountered with xenon lamps outweigh the advantages.

Xenon supply requirements

To run the lamp on DC from an AC mains supply, a transformer/rectifier unit is required in the supply line, which, by necessity of the high current, low voltage requirements of the lamp, is very large – a typical example is for a 2 kW xenon lamp, where the arc characteristics are 2000 W at 25 V dc, drawing 80 A and producing 80 000 lumens, which is 40 lumens per watt, approximately half the value of other discharge lamps, with a typical life of 2000 hours.

The main problem here is the high lamp current of 80 A, which implies a cable of considerable cross sectional area to carry the current from the transformer/rectifier unit to the luminaire.

Safety considerations

Finally, the main problem is one of safety, because of the extremely high internal pressure of the xenon lamp's filling, which can be from 6 to 8 atmospheres when cold and 15 to 20 atmospheres when hot. This means that special precautions must be taken to prevent access to the housing for a considerable period after switch off to allow the internal pressure to drop and when cold the manufacturers recommend that protective gloves and goggles are worn when handling the xenon lamp and special precautions are taken when transporting it. So it would appear that the use of xenon lamps will be restricted to follow spots for some time to come.

FLUORESCENT LAMPS

A fluorescent lamp produces light by the effect of phosphorescence (Figure 5.18). The arc discharges through low pressure mercury vapour and generates ultraviolet with a small amount of blue light. The phosphor coating on the inner surface of the glass tube converts this ultraviolet energy into visible light; the colour from the fluorescence tube we perceive depends upon the type of phosphors used in the coating. When light sources which use phosphorescence are

Figure 5.18 Low pressure mercury vapour fluorescent lamp

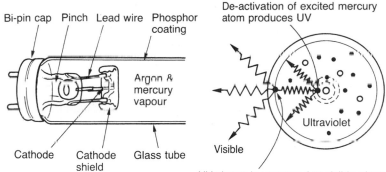

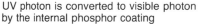

switched off, there is a short 'afterglow'. The use of phosphors therefore smoothes out some of the variations in the light output.

The light output is affected by the temperature of the lamp, due to varying the internal vapour pressure of the gas in the tube. Lamps are usually designed to operate in an ambient temperature of around 20°C and if the lamp runs hot, or indeed cold, a lower light output results.

Fluorescent operating characteristics

Fluorescents normally run from 50 or 60 Hz supplies, but there are great advantages in increasing the frequency of operation. The efficacy (lumens per watt) of fluorescent lamps is increased by about 10% if we change the frequency from the normal mains to between 20 and 100 kHz. However the increase in efficacy is less at frequencies in excess of 30 kHz, therefore this is the normal region for high frequency operation. A benefit of using frequencies around 30 kHz gives the advantage that it is outside the audible range and below frequencies at which losses in the electronic ballast system would become noticeable. Due to a reduced power consumption in a high frequency system, the temperature in luminaires will be lower than those at normal mains frequencies. By using high frequency electronic ballasts it is possible to reduce the amount of flicker which is normally noticeable in mains operated ballasts. This has the advantage of overcoming the stroboscopic problems with moving machinery or fast moving subjects, and obviously can be a great advantage when using film or TV cameras.

Fluorescent efficacy

Originally, fluorescent lamps were approximately 25 mm in diameter and about 1.5 m long, but in more recent times, the diameter of tubes has decreased and also lamps have been moulded into shapes, such as a circle and U-tube. Nowadays, a whole range of compact fluorescent lamps is produced, with each lamp folded in half, with the ends connected to a single lamp cap. Various phosphors are used to give good colour rendering with a choice of colours. By using high frequency ballasts, it is possible to achieve very high efficacies.

Figure 5.19 (a) Standard
fluorescent tubes; (b) tri-phosphor
tubes

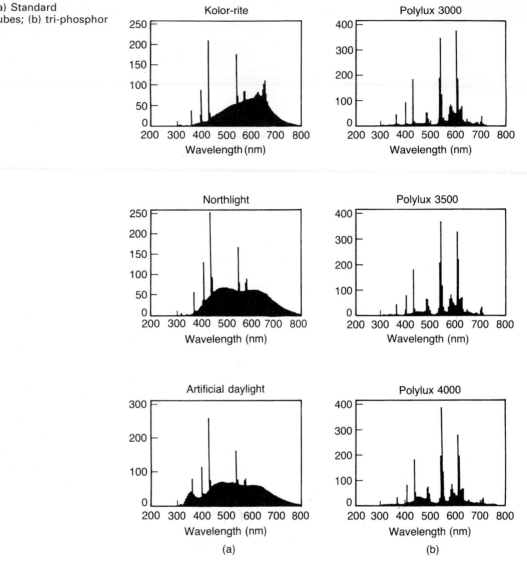

(a)   (b)

Typical efficacies are as follows:

40W tubular range	100 lumens per watt
55W compact bi-axial	85 lumens per watt
36W compact bi-axial	80 lumens per watt
26W compact quad	70 lumens per watt

6
Luminaires

6.1 Optical design theory

THE FRESNEL AND PLANO-CONVEX LENSES

Historical

In 1748 George Louis Leclerc de Buffon originated the idea of dividing a plano-convex lens into separate concentric rings in order to significantly reduce the weight. In 1820 the idea was adopted by Augustin Jean Fresnel (pronounced 'Frenel') to overcome a real problem in lighthouses. Before this date the only way of controlling the light distribution from a lighthouse was with mirrors.

At that time it was impossible to mould large conventional lenses of the size required for a lighthouse because the glass could not be gathered in sufficiently large 'gobs' quickly enough to fill a mould of the size required. The problem was that the method of handling the molten glass during this period, was by using a rod which collected relatively small 'gobs' of glass which were cut off and dropped into the mould.

It would also have been quite useless, even if the process had succeeded, because the lens would have been so thick that its weight would have prevented its use in a lighthouse optical system.

Fresnel lens

Fresnel adapted de Buffon's idea to make a one piece moulding of the separate concentric rings which could be pressed in a mould of large diameter but maintaining a thin cross section to reduce its weight. In this way, very short focal length lenses could be produced which would normally require a very thick cross section. Therefore, a Fresnel lens can be considered to be equivalent to a standard plano-convex lens of the same focal length.

Plano-convex lens

In Figure 6.1 the plano-convex lens is superimposed on the equivalent Fresnel lens showing that the same curvature of the plano-

Figure 6.1 Fresnel/plano-convex lens comparison

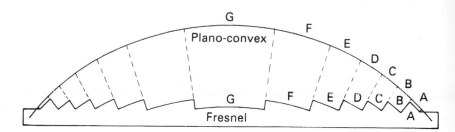

convex lens can be achieved by moving sections of the surface down to the same plane. The sketch is an over simplification of a Fresnel lens design, but it is sufficient to show the principle.

The focal length of either lens is the point behind the lens where an object in front of the lens will be focused. The focal point can be found by focusing a bright object such as the sun onto a surface and measuring the distance from the lens to the image when it is in sharp focus, in the same way that children ignite a piece of paper by focusing the sun's rays onto it with a lens.

If a light source is placed at the focal point of a lens, the reverse procedure would be expected, thereby producing an image of the filament when it is projected onto a screen. This is the position of the source when a Fresnel or plano-convex luminaire is focused to the full spot position. The sharpness of the filament image is smeared over by adding a slight diffusion to the rear surface of the lens. As the source is moved forward the beam will increase in angle and achieve full flood in its most forward position. The two luminaires that employ the above lenses are obviously the Fresnel and the plano-convex. Other luminaires that employ the plano-convex lens are the profile projector (ellipsoidal as it is known in the USA) follow spots and effects projectors.

6.2 Reflection and refraction

We are so accustomed to the reflection of light that we would not normally stop to consider that our very existence depends upon it. Every item that we see is reflecting light to our eyes so that we can form an image of it. When we think of a reflector, we visualize a bright shiny surface. However, every solid that is exposed to light is a reflector, otherwise we could not see it. The laws of reflection (Figure 6.2) are the same for all bright plane surfaces, that is, if the surface is not diffused, which would have the effect of scattering the light.

If we consider a bright, shiny surface with a light ray falling onto it we can see that the ray is reflected off the surface at the same angle as it approaches it. That is, if the angle is measured from a line drawn at a tangent to that part of the reflector. This rule remains true for any shape of reflector and as the angle of reflection becomes less as the ray approaches 90° to the surface, (at which point the angle onto to the reflector is the same as the angle off the surface) so that the light ray is returned to its place of origin, which explains why a flash from a camera will over expose any part of the subject

Figure 6.2 Reflection

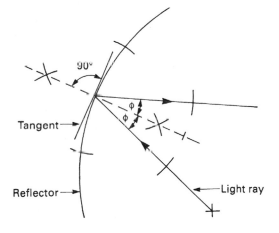

that is at exactly 90° to the camera. A simple analogy can be applied to estimate where the reflected light will be directed, because it behaves in the same manner as a billiard ball striking a cushion where the angle off the cushion is the same as the approach angle.

Refraction

The most obvious demonstration of refraction is shown in Figure 6.3 where a stick is placed into the water at an angle. If this is viewed from the side the stick appears to change direction. This displacement of the image accounts for the difficulty in trying to pinpoint the position of an object under water, such as a fish. We can therefore say that refraction causes a light beam to change direction when striking or leaving a surface of a transparent material.

Figure 6.3 Refraction in water

Figure 6.4 Refraction in glass

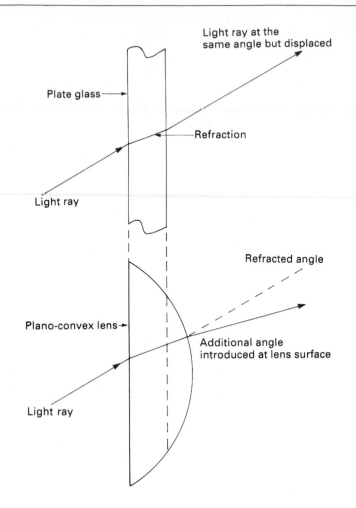

Figure 6.4 shows a piece of glass with a light ray entering from the left hand side. At the point of entry, the ray is refracted down towards the norm, this being a line at 90° to the surface. The ray does not change direction through the glass, no matter how thick it might be, but it does change direction on leaving the surface of the glass on the right hand side, adopting the same angle of refraction as it had when approaching the other side, but now it is displaced.

Figure 6.4 also shows an overlay of the refraction in the sheet of glass with a front surface of a lens superimposed onto it. The dotted line shows the original refraction of the light ray, which is now also influenced by the curvature of the lens. So, it can be stated that the direction of a light beam passing through a plano-convex lens is changed, firstly by the refraction and secondly, by the angle of the surface at the point of departure. The reason for refraction occurring in the first place comes about by the difference in optical density of the two substances; in this case that of air and glass. Each has assigned a refractive index which relates to the speed with which light can pass through it. The refractive index of a vacuum is 1.0, at which light travels at 300 000 kilometres per second, so all other transparent substances have a refractive index greater than 1.0. Glass

Figure 6.5 Sections of a cone

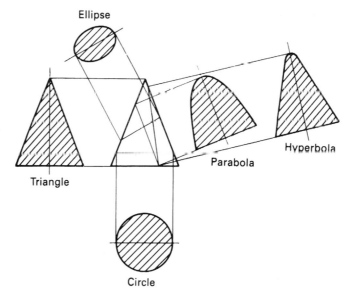

Figure 6.5 Sections of a cone

is typically 1.5 to 1.9, showing its higher optical density, with the resultant lowering of the speed of light through it, and a refractive index of 2.0 would halve the speed of light.

Air is so near to the value of a vacuum that we can ignore the difference and treat air as having a refractive index of 1.0. Given the wavelength of the ray of light, the refractive index of the glass, and the angle of approach, the resultant displacement of the light ray can be calculated.

6.3   Reflector designs

Figure 6.5 shows a simple solid cone which is responsible for all the reflector shapes that would be required for any type of luminaire. It can be seen that by cutting through the cone, along the lines indicated, that five basic shapes are generated. We will employ some of them in the following reflector designs.

Circular true radius reflector

The circular true radius reflector is used extensively in luminaires such as Fresnels and PCs and in fact, any design that requires a single small source of light. It can be seen from Figure 6.6a and b that all the light falling onto the reflector is returned to its place of origin where it joins the rest of the light. Although this reflector provides the single source requirement, it is very inefficient because it is quite useless to extend the reflector to collect more light if the resultant redirected rays cannot be directed onto the lens. The reflector is therefore designed with the source in the full flood position which is nearest to the lens by drawing the two outer extremes of collection from the lens through the source and then projecting them to determine the maximum diameter that is

Figure 6.6 (a) Fresnel system. (b)
PC system

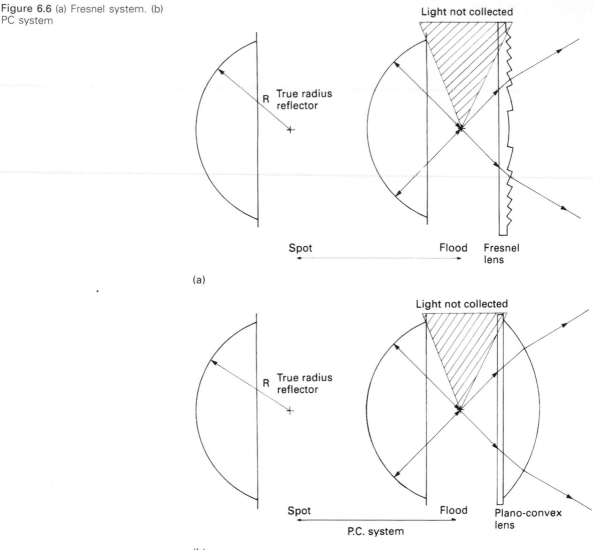

(a)

(b)

required for the reflector. Any true radius reflector with its centre
at the source will suit the design so the resultant size and radius can
be determined by the luminaire size and the cooling requirements.
Figure 6.6 also shows the gross inefficiency of this type of reflector
which does not collect the light shown in the shaded areas. This
system is even more wasteful in the spot position which is rather
ironic because most lighting technicians think that the high intensity spot is the more efficient position of focus, but it is obvious from
the figure that a lot more light goes through the lens in the flood
position. A good point to remember when using colour filters is that
the most arduous position for the filter is when the luminaire is in
full flood with the added heat of the lamp being very close to the
lens and therefore close to the filter.

Figure 6.7 Elliptical reflector used in a profile projector

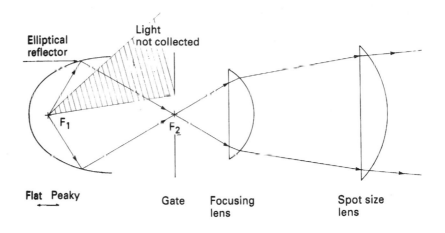

Elliptical reflector

Figure 6.7 shows an elliptical reflector in its most common application in a profile projector. With the source placed at F_1 the reflected light is directed to F_2. This reflector system is comparatively efficient compared with the true radius reflector but it still suffers the losses shown in the shadowed areas. It is pointless making the reflector larger to collect more light if the resultant increase in collection cannot be directed onto the first lens at an angle that can be redirected by the lens. Some designers have used an annular reflector to redirect the wasted light back through the gate. However the steep angle of collection and redirection normally provides only 15% more efficiency at a much higher cost. A much better refinement is to use condenser lenses placed between the gate and the light source: this has the effect of directing the diverging rays of light through the gate and is normally a standard high temperature plano-convex lens. The first design requirement must be the light output angles. Once these have been fixed, the correct lens combinations can be determined and their relative positions drawn in. The gate diameter can now be positioned and the light ray lines drawn from the lenses to the reflector. Having satisfied these design requirements, any size of elliptical reflector can be used, with the choice varying from a long thin shape to one that appears to be almost a circle. They will all obey the same reflective law. This can be easily demonstrated with a piece of string and two drawing pins where the pins will be F_1 and F_2 and the string will represent the light ray. This form of design provides a wonderful range of ellipsoidal sizes to be considered but would no doubt cause great hilarity in the tool room where the finished reflector tool is made. We would therefore recommend the method of construction shown in Figure 6.8.

Parabolic reflector

The parabolic reflector is normally used as the name implies, in applications where a near parallel beam of light is required. The searchlight is a good example where the discharge source is mounted along the optical centre line facing the reflector. In this way a very

Figure 6.8 Construction of an ellipse

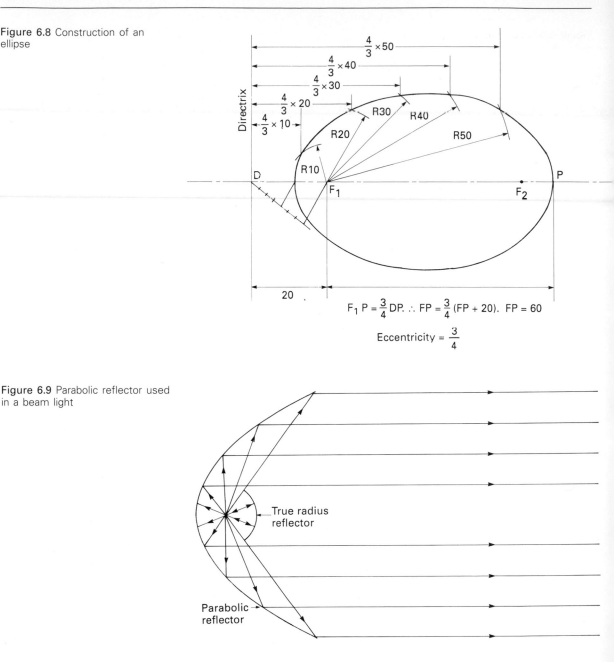

$$F_1 P = \frac{3}{4} DP. \therefore FP = \frac{3}{4}(FP + 20). \ FP = 60$$

$$\text{Eccentricity} = \frac{3}{4}$$

Figure 6.9 Parabolic reflector used in a beam light

efficient collection is achieved because all the light from the source is reflected in the output beam.

Figure 6.9 shows a typical design for a beam light where the forward light from the source is redirected back through the source by a true radius reflector which can be part of the lamp's envelope, which has been silvered, or a separate reflector mounted in front of the source. Greater efficiency can be gained by the use of low voltage lamps that provide higher lumens per watt and a small source size – typically 12/24/48V lamps are used. The only problem is, of

Figure 6.10 Construction of a parabola

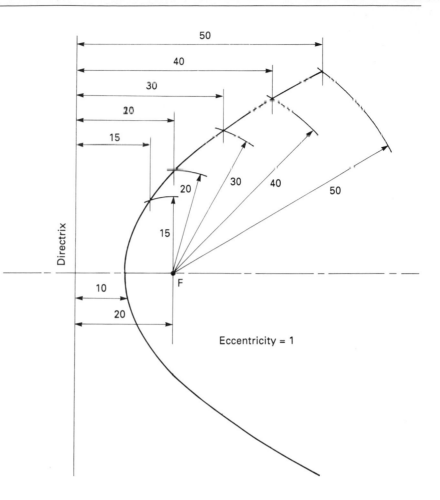

course, that the mains electricity must be reduced by some form of either transformer or power supply circuit.

Focusing open-faced luminaire

The type of open-faced luminaire shown in Figure 6.11, achieves a degree of focusing by moving the source along the optical centre line of the reflector. The direct light from the source will not change, but the reflected light can be superimposed onto the centre of the distribution, producing a higher lighting level. This reflector design is arrived at by tracing the required rays back to the reflector where a tangent can be drawn between the angle from the source and the required ray. In this way a series of tangents can be formed into an approximation of the required curve. A good example of this type of reflector is the 'Redhead'.

Soft light

The reflector shown in Figure 6.12 is constructed in the same manner as the open-faced reflector by ray tracing. However, if the light output is to render a soft shadow the small source must be covered

Figure 6.11 Focusing open-faced reflector

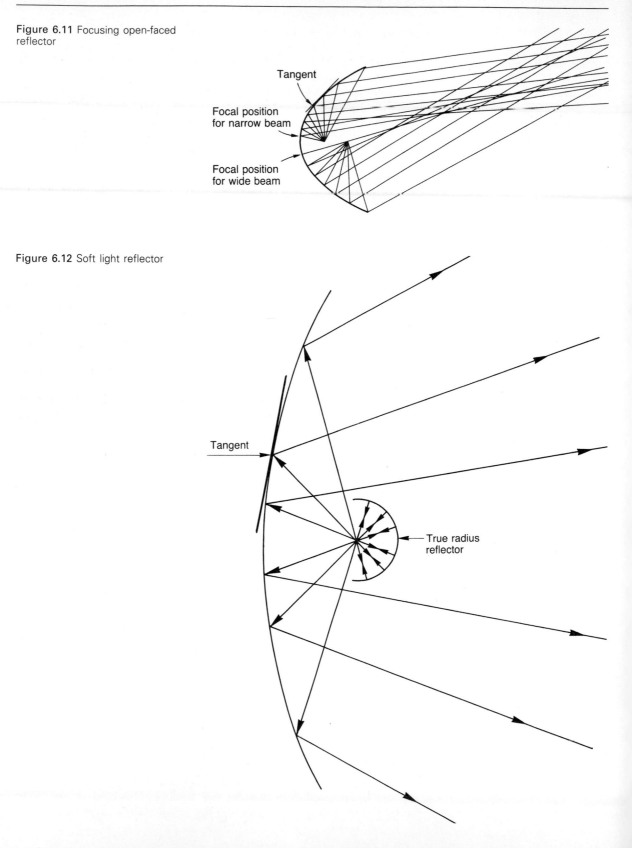

Tangent

Focal position
for narrow beam

Focal position
for wide beam

Figure 6.12 Soft light reflector

Tangent

True radius
reflector

up so that it does not produce a conflicting shadow which would appear as a well defined hard shadow from the source, followed by a secondary soft shadow from the larger reflector. As the softness of shadow is a direct function of the size of the reflector and the distance of the luminaire from the subject, it is desirable to have the largest reflector surface area that can be achieved. Additionally, a light stippling of the reflector will help to diffuse the light. Sometimes matt white paint is used; however, this deteriorates with age and becomes yellow, resulting in a reduction in the colour temperature. The reflector placed in front of the source is normally a true radius reflector so that the light rays from it can be ignored because they will be incorporated with the other rays produced by the source.

Cyclorama reflector

The cyclorama reflector shown in Figure 6.13 is made by ray tracing in the same manner as the open faced reflector, but in this case an asymmetric distribution is required to provide as much light as possible to the top of the cyclorama. It is quite common with this design to make the bottom of the reflector a true radius drawn around to the point of cut off at the bottom of the cyclorama. In this way, the only light falling on the bottom of the cyclorama is the direct light from the source. The amount of reflected light is increased as the distribution extends up the cyclorama in an attempt to cancel out the fall off of the light through the inverse square law. It is not, however, practical to achieve a constant lux reading up the cyclorama because

Figure 6.13 Cyclorama light reflector

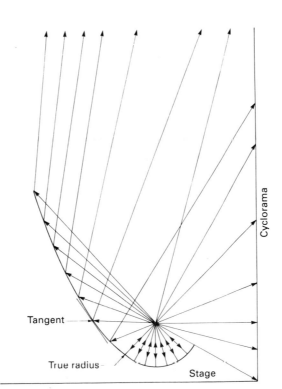

the light level at the bottom of the cyc will always be determined by the direct light from the source leaving insufficient reflected light available to match it, so the next best type of distribution is one that falls off evenly at a constant rate without dark or light bands which would draw attention to the change.

When lighting a large cyclorama from the top only, if an even distribution is required in the vertical plane, the cyc lights will need to be mounted 3 m or more from the cyc cloth and level with its top. A more common method is to use top and bottom mounted cyc lights to achieve this even distribution on the cloth. The reflector design is the same in principle for both top and bottom cyc units; a top unit is basically a 'bottom' unit turned upside down to achieve an asymmetric light distribution.

6.4   Luminaire types

Historical

The entertainment lighting industry should have its own dictionary of names and descriptions to guide the potential user through their catalogues. Every manufacturer has contributed to the proliferation of pet names for their products, so what is basically the same luminaire can have many names. Originally, no doubt, it was fun to build up a vocabulary that could only be understood by the lighting fraternity, thus adding mystique to the art. Some examples are shown in Figure 6.14:

- **'Brute':** an enormous 225A arc (Figure 6.14a).
- **'Basher':** a 500W bulb in a reinforced pudding basin (Figure 6.14b).
- **'Skypan':** an enormous dustbin lid with a 5kW lamp at its centre (Figure 6.14c).
- **'Northlight':** a bounced softlight from a corrugated reflector(Figure 6.14d).
- **'Pup':** a small focusing Fresnel (Figure 6.14e).
- **'Inkie Dinkie':** a miniature focusing Fresnel (Figure 6.14f).
- **'Scoop':** in essence a loud hailer megaphone with a 1kW lamp at its centre. (Figure 6.14g).

Note: The photographs of these very old designs are included for their historic value, so that we do not lose sight of the originals that were given these names by Mole Richardson.

TYPES OF LUMINAIRE

The list is endless and not one of the names describes the use of the luminaire and each manufacturer uses a different name for a similar type. To expose the mystique we will place every luminaire in the entertainment business into only eleven groups, each group can be subdivided when reading a lighting catalogue into wattage, voltage, beam angle, incandescent or discharge source, manual or pole operated controls followed by the finer points which separate one make from another. The eleven basic types are:

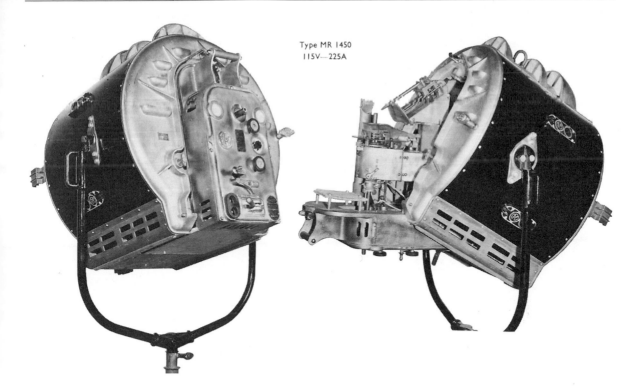

Type MR 1450
115V—225A

Figure 6.14
(a) 225A Brute
(b) Basher

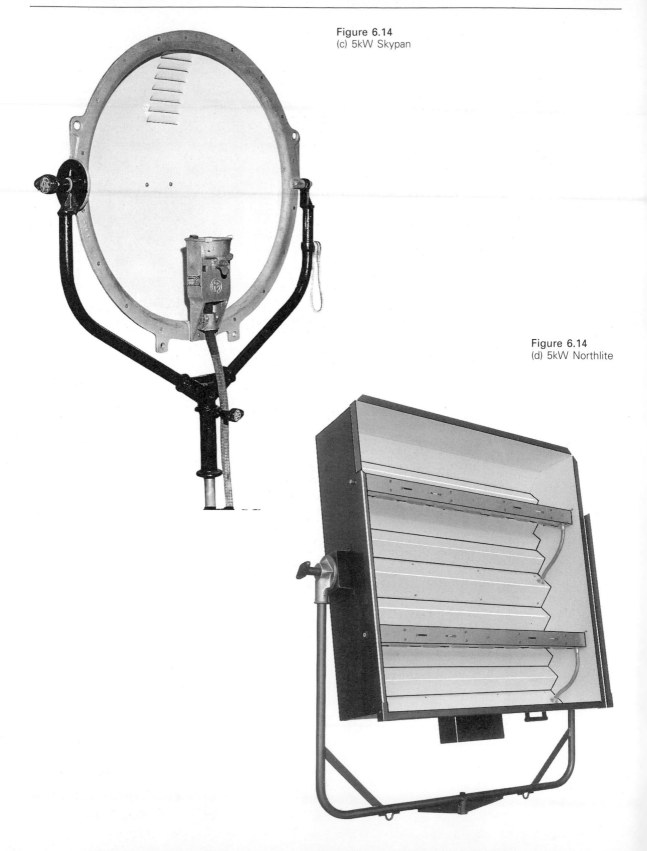

Figure 6.14
(c) 5kW Skypan

Figure 6.14
(d) 5kW Northlite

Figure 6.14
(e) 1kW Fresnel (Pup)

Figure 6.14
(f) Inkie Dinkie

Figure 6.14
(g) 1kW Scoop

1. Fresnel
2. PC
3. Profile
4. Follow spots
5. Floodlight
6. Softlight
7. Focusing reflector light
8. Beam light
9. Sealed beam
10. Cyclorama/backing light
11. Effects

We will now break down the eleven groups, describing their use and optical systems.

1. Fresnel

This luminaire employs a Fresnel lens and circular reflector with the source placed at the centre of radius of the reflector (Figure 6.15). To focus, the light the source and reflector are moved together. The spot position of focus is when the source is at the focal point of the lens and maximum flood is achieved is when the source is nearest to the lens. The variable beam is typically 8–65° and provides a soft edge keylight used as the main illumination on the artist or subject in TV, film and photography and for large area illumination in theatre. One disturbing fault with the Fresnel is that light is scattered from the top of the risers on each zone of the lens which can cause a problem of spill light.

Figure 6.15 (a) Fresnel luminaire. (b) Discharge features. (c) Tungsten features (courtesy De Siski lighting)

(a)

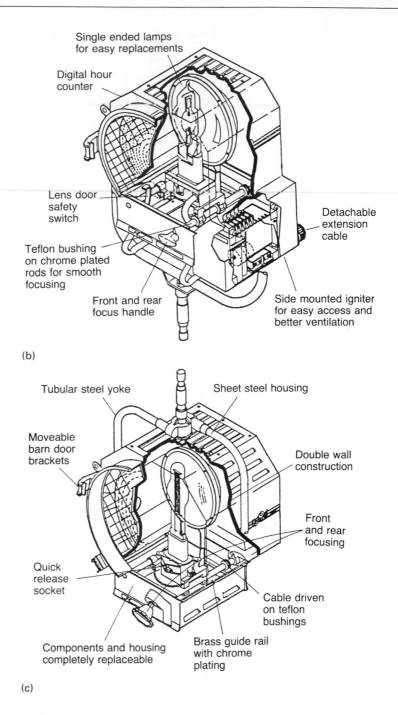

Single ended lamps
for easy replacements

Digital hour
counter

Lens door
safety
switch

Teflon bushing
on chrome plated
rods for smooth
focusing

Front and rear
focus handle

Detachable
extension
cable

Side mounted igniter
for easy access and
better ventilation

(b)

Tubular steel yoke

Sheet steel housing

Moveable
barn door
brackets

Double wall
construction

Front
and rear
focusing

Quick
release
socket

Cable driven
on teflon
bushings

Components and housing
completely replaceable

Brass guide rail
with chrome
plating

(c)

2. Plano-convex

The PC uses a plano-convex lens and circular reflector and is similar
to the Fresnel in construction and performance (Figure 6.16). It is
used mainly in theatre and has a beam appearance of an out of focus
profile. In performing a similar role to the Fresnel the question is
often asked 'Why do we require both types?' The main reason is that

Figure 6.16 PC luminaire

it has a well defined soft edge to the beam and does not produce spill light that would otherwise fall onto parts of the set or backing and cause problems. The disadvantages, however, are that the filament tends to image itself in full spot and any plano-convex lens has the problem of producing a dark hole in the centre of the beam between the full flood and the full spot positions. Some manufacturers provide a diffusion on the rear surface of the lens to reduce both problems.

3. Profile (ellipsoidal USA)

Europeans refer to this luminaire (Figure 6.17) as a 'profile', describing its ability to project an outline of a cut-out image placed in the gate; whereas in the USA it is referred to as an 'ellipsoidal' which

Figure 6.17 Profile spot

describes the type of reflector employed. The unit uses one or more plano-convex lenses and an ellipsoidal reflector, with the option of having condenser lenses to improve the light output. The light source is positioned at the first point of focus of the reflector. The beam size and focus of a zoom type can be varied by moving the inter-relationship of the two lenses and the beam can be modified to provide a hot centre or an even field by fore and aft movement of the source in the reflector. Normally the most rear position of the source in the reflector provides the most even beam and produces the sharpest images of the gate, shutter blades and gobos. To obtain an efficient zoom, the beam angles are normally restricted to 2:1, i.e. 16 to 32° or thereabouts. One luminaire can be designed to cover all of the beam angles but it would be very inefficient in terms of light output and would be as long as the narrowest beam luminaire and as wide as the largest lens – thus very heavy – instead of a thoroughbred a 'luminaire camel'. On wide angle, the edge of the beam is often ringed in a halo of blue halation which can be removed by placing a reducing cut-out circle between the lenses at the expense of the luminance efficiency. Typical beam angles are 5 to 45°. The beam shape can be modified by four beam shaping shutters or an iris diaphragm which can be focused from a sharp definition to a soft edge. This luminaire is the workhorse of the theatre and is used mainly as a keylight for the artist, or as a silhouette projector. For TV and photography it is used as a gobo projector for backgrounds. The beam is a clear cut, well defined illumination that can be focused to provide a sharp image or the focus can be backed off to provide a soft edge without emitting spill light. The main disadvantage is that the housing is very long, particularly on narrow angle units and can prove a problem in restricted rigging space and adjacent flying scenery can sway and knock them out of position.

4.   Follow spots

The optics for the follow spot (Figure 6.18) are the same as the profile projector and the unit only varies from the profile by the

Figure 6.18 CSI follow spot

following characteristics. The gate area is much more elaborate than the profile, it omits the four beam shaping shutters and replaces them by two horizontal blades; one in the top of the gate and one underneath the gate. A single lever operates both blades in unison producing a variable parallel slot of light known as 'Chinese'. The blades can close the gate completely, giving a blackout known as a 'dowser'. In addition to the iris diaphragm for spot size and gobo projection, a dimmer iris is often provided by placing it in the light path but keeping it well out of focus. This has the effect of dimming the light without changing the colour temperature or the shape of the spot – a desirable feature for normal control and very useful when balancing the light on stage from two spots at different distances. A cruder, simple way of achieving this effect in profiles, as well as follow spots, is to put a barndoor from a Fresnel into the colour runners and move all four blades inwards to dim the output. Some follow spots provide a mechanical coupling between the two lenses to produce a zoom effect of automatically maintaining focus when changing distance. The main advantage of a follow spot is the ability to focus constant attention onto a moving artist, however, the disadvantage of a low angle follow spot without other illumination is a complete lack of modelling and atmosphere for anything other than the 'sock it to them' approach.

5. *Floodlight*

From Figure 6.19 it can be seen that the floodlight produces a very wide angle illumination which is unfortunately totally uncontrollable. The beam will not provide a cut off if a barndoor is used because of the large area of the source and reflected light, and therefore spills onto everything in front of it. It is hardly ever used in television, except for house or working lights, and in the theatre it is limited in

Figure 6.19 Floodlight

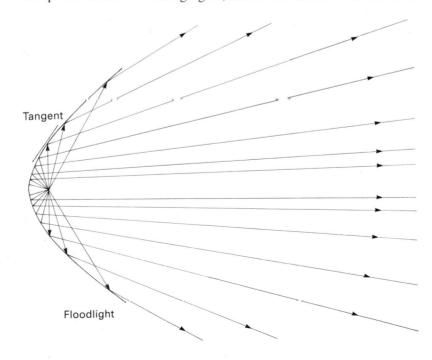

Tangent

Floodlight

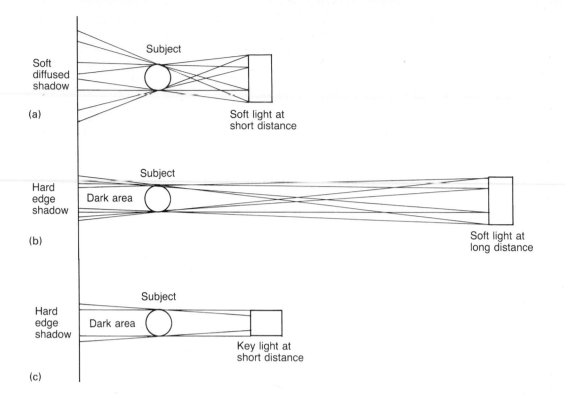

Figure 6.20 (a) Soft light. (b) Discharge features. (c) Tungsten features (b,c courtesy of De Siski lighting)

use to large areas of colour wash. Other disadvantages are that the shadows cast from this type of luminaire give a confused rendering. The shadow from the filament is very hard in the vertical plane and softer in the horizontal if a linear lamp is used. Add to this the secondary shadow of the light from the reflector which appears softer than the shadow from the source and the resultant illumination is beyond control. The advantages are a very wide angle and high efficiency because most of the light is projected out of the housing. The units are usually low cost. The same principle of an open faced reflector is used in the portable 'Redhead', refined by moving the lamp to give spot and flood focusing. The disadvantages of poor barndoor control are tolerated in favour of the high light output, small size and weight.

6.   Soft light

The name soft light refers to the shadow definition and implies that the edge of the shadow bleeds away without a defined edge to it. The ultimate soft light is the bounced light from the northern sky which is so large in comparison to man that the light approaches from a very large angle so that we appear to have no shadow at all. There is therefore no such thing as a small soft light and the term is open to abuse. We do know, however, that the larger the reflector the softer the shadow so the design of a soft light is always a compromise between the largest that can be reasonably achieved and the size that can be tolerated. Soft lights are mainly used in photography and television as a fill light to lift the shadow areas created by the key light to an acceptable level for the film stock or television camera. It is desirable

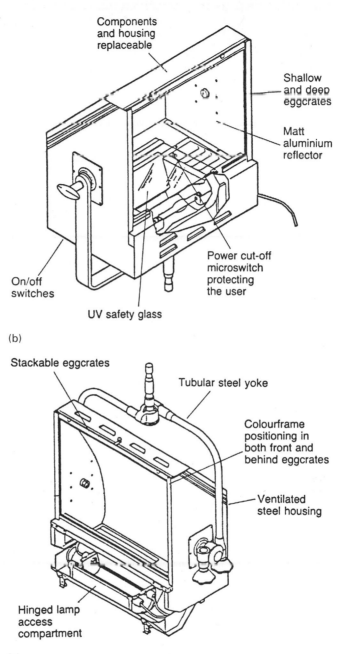

Components
and housing
replaceable

Shallow
and deep
eggcrates

Matt
aluminium
reflector

Power cut-off
microswitch
protecting
the user

On/off
switches

UV safety glass

(b)

Stackable eggcrates

Tubular steel yoke

Colourframe
positioning in
both front and
behind eggcrates

Ventilated
steel housing

Hinged lamp
access
compartment

(c)

to achieve this without creating more shadows on the subject. The
main disadvantage is light spilling onto backings or cycloramas – this
can be partly controlled by an egg crate louvre placed in the front of
the luminaire which restricts the light output to an angle of 90° vertical, 120° horizontal. The term 'soft' and 'hard' are comparative and
do not define the shadow created by the light. Charles Neenan
tackled the problem by defining the shadow and produced a test

whereby a cross is placed in front of a backing and the light is measured in the shadow area and the lit area. The two are expressed as a ratio, known as 'the Neenan factor'. Whilst this method of test works, the industry has not adopted it, still preferring to put up a hand in front of a backing, and, after much consideration, declaring the shadow to be good, bad or indifferent (see Fig. 6.2).

7.   Focusing reflector light

There are many types and wattage of focusing reflector lights but the most famous is the 'Redhead' (Figure 6.21). The name describes the colour of the housing, but of course the French have their own way of expressing themselves and call it a 'Mandarin', referring to its segmented shape. The unit is mainly used in television and photography and is particularly useful in interview situations because of its comparatively high light output from a small unit and the ability to focus the beam. This focusing is achieved by moving the lamp fore and aft in the reflector which provides two superimposed beams, one from the direct output of the source, and the other from the reflector. When the lamp is moved into the spot position the reflector provides the increased intensity in the centre of the beam while the overall total light output angle remains practically the same because of the direct illumination from the filament. Two problems with all open faced lights are hard shadows and the need to provide a safety glass or mesh to catch the quartz from the envelope in the event of the lamp shattering. The standards require that particles of quartz 3 mm or more in size are arrested.

8.   Beam light

This luminaire employs a parabolic reflector with the source placed at its centre of focus. With an ideal point source, the optical system would produce a parallel beam of light, the same diameter as that of the reflector. However, if a true radius reflector is placed in front of the source, it prevents the light from the source leaving the housing in a direct line, thus reflecting all the light that falls onto it back to the source and hence through the filament to the parabolic reflector. In real life, the size of the source has the effect of slightly spreading the beam and typical beam angles are 4 to 8°. A slight amount of focus can be achieved by moving the source fore and aft in the reflector and this will provide a few degrees' change in the beam. This optical system has been used for many years in lighthouses and searchlights, where in the old type of searchlight a positive carbon was mounted along the centre axis of the reflector with its light emitting crater facing the reflector. The beam light was originally used by necessity in large opera houses and the big 'Germanic type' theatres, because of its high efficiency and the narrow beam which is required when lights were positioned a long distance from the stage.

The main disadvantages of a beam light are that the beam angle cannot be increased to any great extent by focusing and that the most efficient luminaires will use a low voltage lamp to make use of its small source size and high light output (lumens per watt) therefore requiring a transformer in the mains supply line. The main advan-

Figure 6.21 Redhead focusing
reflector light

Figure 6.22 Beam light

tages are a very narrow beam for long throw applications, a high efficiency and very little spill light (see Fig. 6.22).

9. Sealed beam

The sealed beam lamp (see Fig. 6.23) employs the same optics as the beam light but replaces the front reflector with a moulded lens which

Figure 6.23 (a) Sealed beam optics. (b) Discharge PAR features (courtesy of De Siski Lighting)

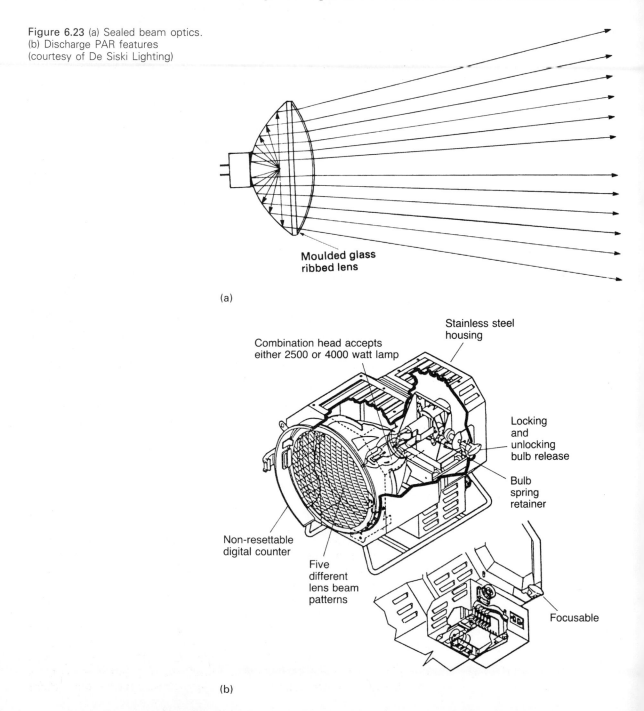

Moulded glass ribbed lens

(a)

Combination head accepts either 2500 or 4000 watt lamp

Stainless steel housing

Locking and unlocking bulb release

Bulb spring retainer

Non-resettable digital counter

Five different lens beam patterns

Focusable

(b)

has the effect of controlling the beam to a predetermined angle. Because the lamp is completely sealed, it can be run at a high pressure and consequently provides a high efficiency. The lamp manufacturers offer a choice of five beam angles by lamp selection; each lamp has a different lens moulded onto the front in quite the same manner as the car headlamp. The most popular lamp in entertainment is the PAR 64 and as with all PAR lamps, the number is the diameter expressed in eighths of an inch, therefore a PAR 64 is eight inches in diameter or 204 mm. The beam is usually oval and typical beam angles are 9°H 12°W, 10°H 14°W, 11°H 24°W, 21°H 57°W and 70°H 70°W for 240V lamps. Alternatively, separate front lenses are available which can be mounted in the front of the luminaire to change the beam angle. The manufacturers make a clear lamp with plain glass for use with separate lenses. Beam angles and efficiency vary with voltage, particularly when comparing 240V lamps with 120V versions because of the small filament in the low voltage lamps. The most common application of this lamp is the Parcan generally used on 'pop' rigs for its high light output, small size, low cost and light weight. It is the only luminaire that comes to mind that costs less than the lamp that is used in it. Increasingly the sealed beam lamps are being used in theatre and television supporting the argument that lighting for theatre, TV and film are coming closer together.

10.   Cyclorama/backing light

By following the ray diagram (see Figure 6.13) it can be seen that the lower part of the reflector is a true radius about the source. This has the effect of returning all of the light that falls onto it back to the filament and through the envelope to the main part of the reflector. The main part of the reflector is designed to direct as much light as it can towards the top of the distribution and to only light the bottom part of the cyclorama with direct light from the filament. With the inverse square law working against the designer, it is always a problem to get enough light to the top of the cyclorama, so it should be realized that a cyclorama or backing cannot be evenly lit from either the top or bottom either when the units are placed relatively close (i.e. 1 m). It is necessary to light from both positions if an even effect is required. If only top or bottom lighting is used, then the fall off of the light should be designed to be a continuous reduction without any dark or bright bars. In this way, the change is not exaggerated.

The choice of linear tungsten halogen lamps is important because of the ring supports that hold the filament in the centre of the envelope. These cause shadows which will appear as five or six fanned out dark bars, projecting up the cyc, and can be overcome with the use of frosted lamps. When assessing the light distribution of cyclorama lights, it is not possible to get a true result by observing only one unit, because the lights are designed to have a wide horizontal angle of distribution, typically 45° each side of centre. It is necessary to use at least three units spaced at the recommended distance from the cyclorama and positioned at the correct distance apart; this being when the overlapping lighting gives an even horizontal coverage. Under these conditions it is possible to assess the vertical distribution on either side of the centre unit. Polar

Figure 6.24 Cyclorama lights

figures are not normally produced for cyc lights because they have no practical application, so it is normal for manufacturers to set up three lights as described above, and take readings progressively up the cyclorama and to show this information graphically. When setting cyc lights, it is a good guide to remember that it is the horizontal distance of the units from the cyclorama that determines the coverage; a small change in the horizontal distance will create a large change in light level opposite the luminaire and almost no change in the light level at the furthest point on the cyc because the length of throw in the vertical direction has hardly changed.

A starting point to set up cyc lights is to place the ground row 1.2 m from the cyc to the back of the fixture and to have each recurring colour at 1.2 m centres, this being the average design criteria. However, having said that this is a good starting point, you will always be compromised by the demands of the set and often return to the action to find that your cyc lights have been pushed so close to the backing that the lighting result looks like a series of bright blobs – nothing like the dawn you visualized. Top cyc units are rigged approximately 3 metres away from the cyc at 2.5 m centres.

Cyclorama lights are made in the following configurations:

- single and double units,
- four lights in line and the same configuration with hinges between each compartment for bending around corners, and
- four-way unit mounted in domino formation.

All types of unit allow for up to four colours before the first colour is repeated to provide colour mixing or four particular choices of colour, but don't forget to include a clear compartment if you are using a red/green/blue colour mix to desaturate the colours. Also remember that the dimmer setting is just as important as the colour that has been chosen.

The design of colour frame can have 'tiger teeth' along the edge to break up the shadows created by the linear lamp filament being in line with the inside edge of the colour frame. This can be important in television when lighting the cyclorama from the top and allowing it to spill out onto the floor. The main disadvantages of cyclorama lighting systems is that they eat up dimmer circuits at an alarming rate, so it is necessary to investigate distribution systems that can be patched from acting area lights to the cyclorama when required, and the possibility of using a 9-way plug and socket system (see Fig. 12.6) at $4 \times 5\,kW$ per circuit; the cyc lights can then be daisy-chained to work in parallel. The space taken by the luminaire is always difficult to find in operation, and the TV lighting barrel system presents a particular problem of trying to rig the lights on the side of the cyclorama that is presented with the ends of the barrels without tying up every barrel for this purpose – a point often overlooked when designing a studio lighting barrel system (see Fig. 6.24).

11. Effects light

Effects projectors normally employ a true radius reflector or an elliptical design similar to the reflector used in a profile projector. Figure 6.25 shows an elliptical reflector with its increased efficiency when compared with a true radius type. The first element is normally a heat absorbing glass that has the effect of reducing the heat passing through it by about 80%, with a light loss of approximately 20%. This special glass requires an airflow over its surface to dissipate the heat collected. An alternative heat filter is a glass with a dichroic coating which reflects the heat from the surface of the coating back into the luminaire. This type of filter is slightly more efficient than heat absorbing glass but care must be taken to ensure that the source is not overheated.

The condenser lens, as the name implies, helps to direct diverging rays of light through the gate and can be a conventional plano-convex lens, or to provide a slightly diffused output and a weight saving, a Fresnel lens is often employed. The gate is designed to accept a conventional photographic slide or a large piece of glass with the scene to be projected painted onto it. It is therefore possible to make a photographic slide of the actual backing required from the correct position to give the correct perspective and then project it onto a white backing. In the same way, an effects projector can be used to project a scene onto a backing for the scenic artist to sketch in the outline with the correct perspective before painting it. An alternative accessory is a rotating disk positioned on the front of the

Figure 6.25 Effects optics

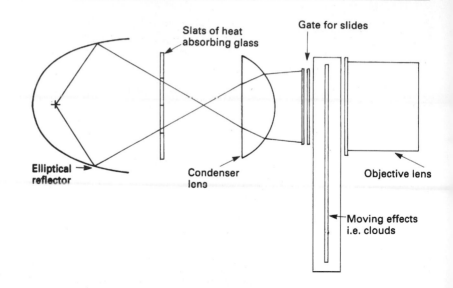

projector with the appropriate effect painted onto the rotating glass,
e.g. rain, fire, snow, etc. In this way a moving effect can be created
at variable speed. A choice of objective lenses are made available
to give the coverage required at the appropriate distance.
Disadvantages are the high cost of the projectors and high effects

(a)   (b)

Figure 6.26 (a) Multi-purpose luminaire. (b) Twister

Figure 6.27 Four-pin twin-filament lamp

costs and comparatively low light output levels that cannot compete with high lighting levels on the TV and film set. A very steady mount is required, as any vibration will produce judder in the output beam and ruin the effect.

6.5 Special designs

Multi-purpose luminaire

This is basically a focusing Fresnel mounted back to back with a soft light and was developed for television in 1961 (see Figure 6.26a).

The reason for the development was a requirement to mount luminaires at regular intervals all over the studio at approximately 2m centres, known as a saturated lighting system, where in this way a light can be found somewhere near the required place, pulled along its barrel and positioned. The luminaire is then rotated, offering the choice of Fresnel key light or Softlight. A switch is then selected to divert the electrical supply to the chosen light, and a second switch selected to provide a choice of power. This is achieved by using four tungsten halogen linear lamps in the soft end, and a twin filament, 4-pin lamp in the Fresnel end (see Figure 6.27).

This arrangement is intended to cover 80% of the requirements of the LD, with the remainder being mounted for each show. The additions include 1kW Fresnels, profiles or specials as required. To add more flexibility to the system, the multi-purpose luminaires are mounted onto pantographs to provide a degree of independent height adjustment. The BBC adopted this form of luminaire in all their major studios, claiming very fast turn round time, increasing the output from the studio. Leaving the lights permanently rigged substantially reduced the damage normally caused when lights are continuously rigged and de-rigged.

6.6 Fluorescent lighting

Fluorescent light sources have been used in television over quite a number of years but generally in situations where they were used more for effect rather than for their intrinsic lighting values. Quite often, chroma-key backings were huge banks of fluorescent light sources. The New York studios of CBS devised a colour mixing fluorescent ground row cyc lighting unit over 20 years ago and this was tested at the BBC Television Centre in London. The unit, which comprised four tubes filtered by coloured gels, had a smooth light output and the red (two), green and blue tubes could be dimmed with a reasonable degree of success giving quite a good range of colours. The drawback was that, in addition to the large physical size of the unit, its light output was half that of filtered Strand tungsten halogen ground row units giving the same colour effect. It is an interesting thought that given the light levels of today the unit probably might have become a standard tool in the lighting designer's armoury.

Efficacy

In more recent times, with the advent of smaller fluorescent tubes and high frequency operation, it has been possible to design luminaires not too large in physical size for use in studios and on location. The claimed benefits of using fluorescent light sources is that they are much more efficient than tungsten with three to four times the efficacy (lumens per watt). Although they have a high efficacy they do not lend themselves as a focusing source, and for example they have an efficiency (usable light divided by total light output) of around 40% which is comparable to the 49% of an open faced luminaire in flood. The fluorescent luminaires only gain by the tubes producing more visible light and less infrared than the equivalent tungsten source and therefore, per watt, have a light output which is about twice that of tungsten. A good example is that a 300W fluorescent produces 630 lux at 4 m, and a 650W 'Pulsar' in flood produces 517 lux at the same distance. The fluorescent luminaires tend to be a cooler source of light and they produce less glare to the artiste.

Operating frequencies

Fluorescent units designed for television usually operate on frequencies between 28 and 39 kHz, giving an improved efficacy of output and virtually flicker free light. Modern phosphors allow for colour rendering indices of better than 70 and can be as high as 90 but this usually means a reduction in the efficacy of the fluorescent tube.

Tri-phosphors

The fluorescent lamps selected for this type of lighting have the normal phosphor coating inside the tube together with a coating of various rare-earth, high-output phosphors, similar to those used for the production of coloured TV tubes. By varying the combination of the red, green and blue phosphors, different shades of white can be produced and these lamps are referred to as tri-phosphor lamps (see Figure 5.19b). This type of lamp can provide high light output with good colour rendering with a reduction of around 7–10% in input power compared with more conventional phosphor coated fluorescents.

Early applications for fluorescent lighting in television were broad sources such as fill lights and for back lighting large diffuse panels used for Chroma Key. One special use was in the design of fittings used over snooker tables for tournaments which required a soft source which was also cool. The main use of fluorescent lighting is usually in news and current affairs studios where the set ups are fairly static and it is reasonably easy to control the light.

One of the problems with fluorescent lighting for television is that it is not focused light but tends to be a broad source of illumination and therefore only controlled by the use of louvres (eggcrates). Although the louvres can reduce the amount of light emanating from the side of the beam, the sources are very wide angle in application, thus their adoption into normal production television studios would probably not be advantageous because of their physical size and control of light. Fluorescent fittings can now produce outputs of around 600 lux at a

Table 6.1 Light output comparison (at 3 metres)

Luminaire type	Power rating	Mode	Beam width	Light output
Vid-lite (fluorescent)	375 watts	n/a	60°	830 lux
Quasar (fluorescent)	416 watts	n/a	76°	700 lux
Mizar (tungsten)	600 watts	Flood	46°	900 lux
Pulsar (tungsten)	650 watts	Flood	72°	920 lux
Redhead (tungsten)	800 watts	Flood	86°	720 lux
Piccolo (discharge)	200 watts	Flood	48°	1150 lux
Piccolo (discharge)	575 watts	Flood	46°	2000 lux

Note: Manufacturers' published figures

distance of 3 m from the subject with unit dimensions of 500 mm × 400 mm and in excess of 900 lux at 3 m from units approximately 700 mm across by 700 mm high. These light outputs do mean that fluorescent lighting has to be used nearer than conventional tungsten or discharge lighting which can be focused and by being nearer also has to be lower to maintain the necessary incident lighting angles. Obviously, by being lower the physical size of the units could be a problem in highly mobile studios. Although generally the lighting is acceptable for fairly static newsreaders, the lack of definite modelling shadows does reduce the three dimensional effect on camera.

Recent developments have produced units where the tubes are bunched very close together in a small circular formation in ellipsoidal reflectors; and although the light is still generally soft, it does have a more focused look than some of the broad sources in the past.

Fluorescent luminaires for television, film and photography, particularly digital imaging photography, come in power sizes from around 100 watts to about 1000 watts.

6.7   Battery hand lamps

These are mainly used for news gathering on outside locations, so they are completely self powered from their own battery (Figure 6.28). The most popular batteries for size to weight ratio are nickel-cadmium. A typical luminaire has an open-faced reflector, containing a tungsten halogen or discharge lamp. The largest tungsten halogen lamp is 250 W at 30 V and the range of daylight discharge lamps include 125 W, 200 W, 275 W and 400 W. The battery unit will also be complete with a high frequency converter for the discharge lamp. A degree of focusing is obtained by moving the lamp in the reflector.

General care of ni-cad batteries

Ni-cad batteries retain their capacity better if the discharge cycle is completed to the point where the knee of the discharge curve is reached. To discharge batteries beyond this point may push some cells into deep discharge from which they may not recover, thus potentially rendering the battery useless. Overcharging a battery is not good practice and **if a battery has been left charged for some time or is partially discharged, it should not be recharged before it**

Figure 6.28 Hand lamp and battery

is discharged fully. Chargers should not be plugged into fully or partially charged batteries as most chargers will initially charge at a high current for a period before they reduce to a low charge rate.

Batteries charged slower than 1/10 of the ampere/hour rating of the battery (trickle charge) can be left on charge for long periods without damage to the battery.

Ni-cad batteries do drain slowly when left charged (approximately 10% per week). Battery manufacturers recommend that ni-cad batteries should be stored in a discharged state. However, they may be left on trickle charge for 'stand-by' use for urgent work.

Routine checks of ni-cad batteries

In order to check the capacity of a 30 V battery, a typical procedure is shown below:

1. Discharge the battery to 25 volts using a battery capacity meter (see Fig. 6.29).
2. Recharge the battery.
3. Re-connect the battery to the battery capacity meter.
4. Adjust the discharge voltage to 27 V.
5. Switch the discharge current to 8.5 amps.
6. Zero the digital timer and press the red 'discharge' button.
7. When the battery has discharged to 27 volts the timer will register the discharge time.

If the discharge time is in excess of 20 minutes, the capacity of the battery is satisfactory. If the discharge time is less than 20 minutes, the battery should be recharged using a charger in the recovery mode. After the charging is complete repeat the test procedure. Any battery that discharges in less than 20 minutes for a second time should be referred to the appropriate maintenance department or supplier for remedial action.

Charging batteries

A typical charger of the fast type will charge a fully discharged 7Ah battery in approximately 2 hours, or a 4Ah battery in approximately one hour and then drop to a trickle charge state.

There is no common connector standard for many of the proprietary battery packs and belts used in the lighting industry; therefore, it is important to have the necessary adapter leads for the various items of equipment.

6.8 Assessment of luminaires

The LD's assessment of a luminaire is how well can he achieve his lighting requirements with this instrument, which is quite understandable from his point of view. The electrician that has to rig and set it has quite different criteria and the maintenance engineer has his own particular problems to keep it in good repair. The LD's assessment is quite straightforward and can be seen by demonstration; it is also well documented by the lighting manufacturer with polar figures for the light output.

We shall therefore turn our attention to the mechanical assessment that will affect the reliability and practical needs of the user. It is most interesting to watch the experienced practical user at any exhibition. He will walk up to a luminaire and in minutes run through a set routine of things to try, gained by years of disappointment and annoyance with things that can go wrong and just don't work in the way that they should. His checklist leaves the manufacturer in no doubt that he is demonstrating his product to a discerning user.

LUMINAIRE CHECKLIST

Mechanical construction

Check on the general mechanical construction, particularly with a view to maintaining the luminaire in the future. Examine the quality of the finish on the body of the luminaire together with the paintwork involved.

Electrical construction

Ensure that all wiring used on the luminaire is adequate for the working temperatures to be encountered. Check that all metal parts are adequately earthed to the main earth terminal. Ensure that the switches and wiring are adequately rated for the current to be used

Figure 6.29 Battery capacity meter

within the device. Check that the input cables are adequately terminated and accessible for test purposes or for replacement and maintenance.

Dimensions and weight

Examine the overall dimensions in all planes with particular reference to the space occupied by the luminaire when panning and tilting. Check the weight of the basic luminaire plus the weight of any accessories to be used.

Pan and tilt

Unlock the tilt lock knob and see if the unit is in the centre of gravity. Not only does the luminaire take charge and trap your fingers, if it is not in balance, but it will also put a pressure on the locking mechanism that can result in the luminaire drooping after it has been set; so the second test is to lock the tilt mechanism and try to force the luminaire downwards, making it slip in the yoke. If the unit is pole operated, try the tilt and pan for backplay in the drive mechanism. In the case of the tilt, an out of balance luminaire will result in a jerky movement in one direction and a heavy load in the opposite direction; this is caused by the load alternately taking charge and then being arrested by the gears. Backplay in the pan movement will result in a horizontal wandering movement after the light has been set. Check that the carcass rotates in the yoke assembly correctly, particularly with open barn doors. When pan and tilt pole operation is fitted, ensure that they can be over-ridden by manual adjustments.

Focus

Here we are looking for a smooth movement, best tested with the luminaire pointing 45° down from the horizontal. This will show up judder, if it exists, or sticking, followed by a sudden movement, both of which cause lamp failure due to the fact that the lamp must be lit to focus it when the vibration on the hot filament can cause it to rupture. Check for 'end stops' on lamp holder movement within the luminaire body.

Note: Check the amount of torque required for operating the focus and the pan and tilt controls because if it is too stiff this will cause problems in practice, particularly with pole operation.

Optical tests

Check the polar light diagram and note the peak intensity of the luminaire. Check the beam angles, both vertical and horizontal at the extremes of focus. Check the quality of the light, both vertically and horizontally at the extremes of focusing, thus ensuring a subjective check for striations and evenness. Ensure there are no light leaks from the luminaire so that light emits outside the main beam and can cause problems in operation. Check for evenness of colour distribution in the light output beam, particularly with discharge sources. Check for the efficiency of the luminaire to convert the power into useful light output.

Temperatures

In the luminaire's normal working mode, e.g. with the luminaire pointing 45° down from the horizontal, check that the pinch temperatures on the lamps are not in excess of the lamp manufacturers stated values. Check the cable gland input working temperatures to ensure cables are not getting too hot. Check all external surfaces to ensure that the luminaire is not going to be too hot in practice.

Shutter blades

Profile shutters have always been a problem, mainly because they are in the hottest part of the beam and will normally run at a temperature that makes them glow red, so adequate insulation on the operating handle is essential. The most common complaint however, is the shutter blades that slide down in the guides when they get hot, so try it after the other tests have been done to make sure that you maintain a positive movement on the blade at high temperature.

Profile edge focus

Most manufacturers demonstrate a profile projector in a sharp focus position, demonstrating its ability to project a well defined image. Adjust the lens movement to the minimum and maximum angles to determine if the edge is sharp over the whole range and at the same time observe the edge for colour fringing. It is most important with the profile that it can be soft focused, so determine there is sufficient lens movement at both ends of travel to achieve a soft edge.

Barndoors

The main points to observe are that the flaps stay put with sufficient friction to sustain the top flap when it is hot. A floppy barndoor flap

Figure 6.30 Barndoor

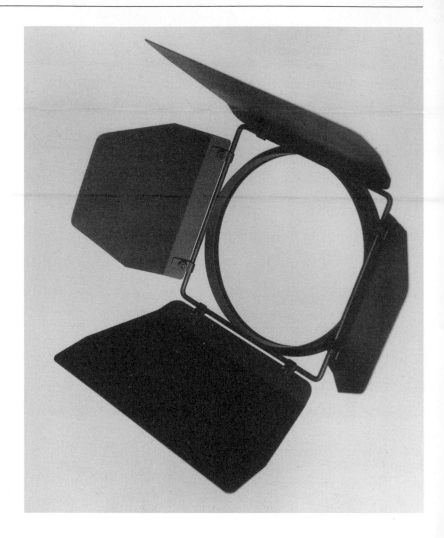

is the lighting technicians' cross. Check that smooth rotation can be
achieved by poking it with a pole (quite a common practice). Light
leaks can be assessed by half closing the two small flaps and then
bringing the large flaps in to touch them. A well defined 'letter box'
shape should be produced at this point; observe any spill light that
comes out of any slot between the sides of the short flap and the
large flap. This is a good time to see if spill light comes out between
the back of the barndoor and the front of the housing. One easy way
to check for spill light is to pass your hand around the area of
concern, which will soon pick up any unwanted light.

Safety requirements

The following items should be checked. Has the luminaire had a
drop test done, and if so, was a certificate issued. If so this should
be provided. Luminaires are also generally supplied with safety
bonds or chains and these should come with certificates or specifications indicating their suitability for use with the item of equipment.

Have adequate safety precautions been taken against an exploding lamp and the loss of minute pieces of glass? Secondly, have precautions been taken with regard to lens breakage and the possibility of large pieces of glass leaving the luminaire? Ensure that the most important bolts and screws which attach items that may become dislodged from the luminaires are adequate for the purpose intended. Are supplementary safety bonds or clips provided for any detachable accessories, such as colour frames, barndoors, etc., or how are the barndoors retained in normal practice? Check for any sharp edges or dangerous protrusions which in practice may give problems for the operators.

Burning angle

It is a requirement to state the permitted burning angle of the luminaire. This is normally found on the product label and will give the permitted angles above and below the horizontal. This limitation can be imposed by either the luminaire's cooling system or the lamp manufacturer.

Spares

Ask to see the spares list. Some manufacturers do not automatically provide one; this could save a lot of trouble identifying spare parts in the future. Check on the availability of spares and what components are used and where are they sourced.

Lamps

Determine if the type of lamp used is made by more than one manufacturer or if not, is it going to be readily available in your area. One common problem with lamps is arcing at the pins. Check the clamping arrangements for any lamps in use. In addition check for the ease of operation when fastening and unfastening lamps in their holders.

General

A general inspection should examine the ease of stacking for storage purposes. Where is the attached luminaire cable stored when not in use?
Check for ease of handling when being carried and rigged.

6.9   Centre of gravity design considerations

Every luminaire is suspended by a yoke, stirrup or fork. All are names describing the same support that are used in film, TV and theatre; the function remains the same, that is to provide a means of support that will enable the luminaire to rotate (pan) and to tilt. It is the tilt movement that needs to be mounted in the C of G of the luminaire. Whilst every luminaire has a means of locking the tilt movement, or in the case of a pole operated unit, gears are provided to hold it steady in tilt, it is necessary to position the yoke at the

Figure 6.31 How to find the centre of gravity

C of G to prevent judder. In the case of pole operation if the luminaire is out of balance it will be difficult to rotate the pole in one direction and judder will result in the other direction caused by the gears alternately releasing the load and stopping it again. In the case of the manually operated luminaire, an out of balance unit causes two main problems: one, when the tilt lock is released the out of balance weight takes charge and rotates the luminaire very quickly, normally trapping your fingers between the housing and the yoke. The annoyance caused by an out of balance luminaire is seen when rigging lights onto a bar in a theatre which has already been fully rigged and all beams directed and set. Then an additional unit is added – the worst case being an out of balance profile. The influence of the weight of the large lenses mounted at some distance from the C of G produces a moment about the mounting hook clamp which tends to rotate the bar causing all of the other lights that have been previously set to tilt downwards, much to the annoyance of the electrician that has to reset them all.

Having established the desirability of having luminaires in balance, sometimes a compromise is required because the C of G might come in line with the gate or some other obstruction. However, the first step for the manufacturers is to find the C of G, which can be simply achieved by experiment.

First of all one must position the variables that can occur to represent mid position when in operation. In the case of the Fresnel, the barndoors should be open, the lamp must be inserted in the lampholder and the focus in the mid position. In the case of a profile, the lenses should be placed in a mid position. From Figure 6.31 it can be seen that the luminaire is being suspended from two corners on opposite sides with a plumb bob weight positioned in the centre of the support bar mounted in line with the two support strings. Two marks are made behind the plumb line and a straight line is drawn between them. The luminaire is now rotated approximately 90° to the next two corners and the experiment is repeated. Where the two lines cross is the C of G.

6.10 Ventilation

The importance of adequate ventilation in a luminaire cannot be overstated. An overheated lamp will give a short life, the internal electrical system and lampholder will deteriorate and the housing will become dangerously hot. The rules to achieve good ventilation are simple but are so often ignored. A common mistake is to believe that lots of holes in the housing will introduce a lot of airflow through it. In fact, the opposite may be true. A splendid example is

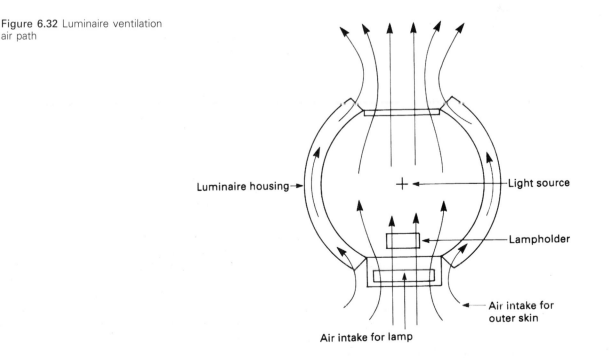

Figure 6.32 Luminaire ventilation air path

a kiln, where a chimney is erected with hot air rising through it, creating a partial vacuum behind it, sucking the air into the kiln at the place where it is required to fuel the fire. The same it true for luminaires and an air path is worked out bearing in mind the working angles of the unit to determine the inlet and outlet path. One system is to have an inlet – scoop or mouth – positioned so that internal baffles can direct the air across the base of the lamp and then between the lamp and reflector and ultimately through an escape chimney. The chimney has to be designed so that water or foreign objects cannot directly enter, electrical safety has to be checked by using 'British Standard Finger' tests.

This system works well to maintain the correct lamp temperature; however, other means are required to cool the housing. If a wall cavity is provided by placing internal baffles in the housing, a separate ventilating system can be adopted to keep the outer skin cool. By providing separate inlet vent holes between the two skins, the air can be accelerated through the cavity by positioning the outlet slots adjacent to the chimney outlet, the hot air rising through the chimney creates an air rush around it, sucking the air up through the two skins. A third ventilating system will be required around the lens and colour filter (see Figure 6.32).

6.11   The carbon arc

Most high efficiency carbons produce about 46 lumens per watt, which is double the efficacy of a tungsten halogen lamp and half the efficacy of a discharge lamp. All of the light is emitted from the centre of the positive carbon. The positive is constructed by an outer shell made from compressed carbon with a core injected under high pressure made of various rare earths and carbon. This enables the manufacturer to create the correct mix for maximum efficiency and the required colour temperature. This construction also provides a hollow in the centre of the core which contains the crater – that is the centre of the light output. It is necessary with most carbon arc luminaires to have an operator present to keep a constant distance between the two carbons and this is known as trimming the carbons. The correct burning position can be seen from Figure 6.33 where the tail flame is held in the vertical at the correct angle. If the positive or negative carbons are allowed to overfeed and become out of alignment, the tail flame will become unstable and create a flicker and ultimately the carbons will set up a squealing noise. One simple method of setting up a carbon arc when cold is to take a spent end of a positive carbon and use it as a gauge by placing it between the tip of the negative and the front edge of the positive carbon. In this way a reasonable running condition will result when the carbon is struck – that is the negative is raised up until it touches the positive and then allowed to drop immediately an arc is struck. As soon as the arc has been established the gap can be adjusted by eye through the coloured glass of the viewing port. The running speeds are normally adjusted by a motor drive which feeds the positive and negative carbons towards each other at a predetermined rate which can be varied by a potentiometer. The negative carbon does not rotate; however, the positive carbon is rotated continuously to

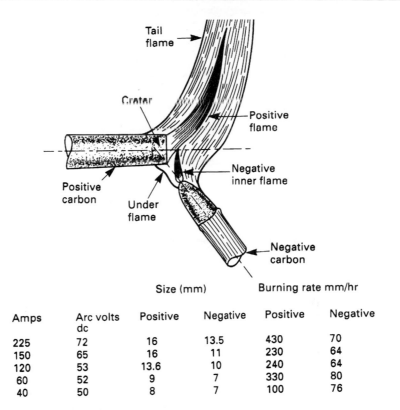

Figure 6.33 Carbon burning characteristics

Amps	Arc volts dc	Size (mm) Positive	Negative	Burning rate mm/hr Positive	Negative
225	72	16	13.5	430	70
150	65	16	11	230	64
120	53	13.6	10	240	64
60	52	9	7	330	80
40	50	8	7	100	76

prevent the outer shell of the carbon burning away at the top and allowing the crater to spill out. Carbons always operate from a direct current which can be derived from generators or from a transformer rectifier unit working from ac mains.

If carbons are used in a confined space, adequate ventilation must be provided to extract the fumes and the large quantities of ozone which are produced. Arcs normally work with a controlling ballast in series with the supply to them, the ballast will provide high voltage to initiate the arc and then become self regulating as the arc starts to draw current through the ballast increasing its resistance and reducing the voltage. Arcs have mainly been replaced by the higher efficiency discharge sources which do not require adjustment during operation and can therefore be remotely controlled. However, the arc still lives on and is still used in some rental departments throughout the world, due to the dramatic quality of light and by those practitioners who tend to use them for nostalgic reasons.

7
Lighting suspension systems

7.1 Suspension and why it is needed

In theatres and studios, the majority of lighting is placed at a reasonable height above the acting area. The reasons for this are quite simply that we do not wish the acting area to be full of equipment, additionally in a TV studio the floor is also cluttered with cameras and booms. In this section we will look at the various ways that operators can suspend equipment above the acting area accurately and quickly, together with a high degree of safety.

Historical

In 1803 Frederick Winsor demonstrated on stage a coal burning apparatus for the generation of coal gas. The light consisted of a Cupid holding a lighted torch in one hand whilst holding onto the gas pipe that was suspended from the ceiling with the other hand. Of course, a lighting suspension system for candles and later for oil lamps had been used on the stage for many years. Winsor went on to greater things and was responsible for the installation of gas lights for the King's birthday in 1807 on the walls at St James's Park and Carlton House. You might well ask what relevance this anecdote has to lighting suspension in view of the fact that the lights were fixed to the walls. Winsor ran a supply pipe from his house in Pall Mall, where he had installed coal gas generating equipment, several hundred yards over gardens and along the walls. The relevance is that he chose 1.5 inch bore pipe for his supply system. He could hardly know that this size of pipe would become the standard size to be used in theatres, because the gas supply system for London was not introduced until 1812 with the forming of the Gas Light and Coke Company, and the first gas street lighting was installed on Westminster Bridge in 1813. Theatre followed in 1817 when the London Lyceum introduced gas lighting over the whole stage but the overhead gas batten had to wait in design until 1865 when it was introduced and consisted of a 1.5 inch bore gas pipe with rat tail

Figure 7.1 Film studio 'boats'

burners mounted along its length every few inches across the whole width of the stage. The pipe was suspended from steel ropes and fed by flexible hoses from the sides of the stage.

Barrels

As far as we can research, this was the introduction of the 1.5 inch gas pipe for lighting suspension which has remained the standard for the industry to this day. We are no longer concerned with the nominal bore of the pipe, but only its outside diameter when we are suspending lights. It is interesting to note that 48 mm is the outside diameter of a 1.5 inch gas pipe (1 29/32 inches), and this was adopted as the standard for the industry. It is obvious by now that theatres used the redundant gas pipes that they had to hang their new found electric lanterns when electricity was introduced at the London Savoy Theatre in 1881.

The film industry, which had progressed from glasshouses that tracked in a circle so that the sun provided a constant key light, to studios that were lit by electricity, tended to use single lights suspended by hemp ropes from blocks and tackles mounted on steel beams in the roof. On occasions, a platform with hand rails (called a 'boat') was suspended from two or more blocks and tackles above the studio so that the additional lights attached to its side rails (arcs or luminaires which required adjustment due to the absence of pole operation) could be attended by the studio electricians (see Figure 7.1). In some film studios the use of long barrels to suspend lights was being introduced. It is worthwhile stating here that the film and photographic industry tend to work from the studio floor 'up', as opposed to the theatre and TV industries which work from the ceiling 'down'.

In 1936 when the BBC started television transmission, all the lighting equipment came from theatre and film manufacturers, mainly using the rigging techniques of the film industry, such as hemp ropes and blocks and tackles.

Hoists

By 1956 the BBC had introduced a motorized hoisting system for lighting, comprising a unit with a motorized gearbox and wire ropes to suspend a 2.4m long, 48mm diameter barrel (Figure 7.2).

Telescopes

With the introduction of commercial television in 1955, a new type of suspension system had been designed, which consisted of an overhead walkover grid at high level with slots, running the length of the studio into which telescopic suspension units were placed and winched down to the required height from the grid (Figure 7.3a and b).

Starting from this date, an argument ensued and persists until today of the merits and disadvantages of motorized barrels versus single point suspension. The motorized barrel protagonist will insist that the saturated lighting rig with two or three lights on each barrel provides enough choice of lighting positions and can be rigged from the studio floor at the same time as other trades are working on the set in comparative safety, whereas a single point suspension installation requires people to be above the grid for rigging. The lighting director, working in a single point suspension studio, will argue that

Figure 7.3 (a) Monopole grid, viewed from above. (b) Monopole grid, viewed from below

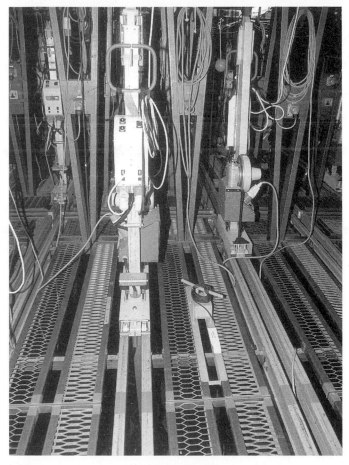

(a)

(b)

he can be more precise and can place the luminaire of his choice at the point in space where he wants it, with independent height control of every luminaire. No doubt the argument will continue.

Before we get immersed in the detail of each system, it would be useful to have an idea of what each type of suspension offers.

7.2   Grids

The dictionary defines a 'grid' as a grating, a gridiron, a framework. It is also described as the 'framework above a theatre stage from which scenery and lights may be suspended'. The original theatre grids were usually wooden platforms suspended from the roof structure, providing a working level for men to walk over. The floor, which was slatted, provided a means by which ropes or scenery could be suspended. Additionally, the lighting bars were suspended from this platform.

In television, the term 'grid' usually describes the roof structure that supports the lighting systems installed and these can be from the very simple fixed barrel rigs, down to the highly sophisticated monopole grids. The television industry tended to follow the example of the theatre, due to the need to suspend lights and scenery. The film industry has traditionally always built scenery from the studio floor upwards and any rigging is done by using ropes and blocks and tackles, suspended from RSJs at high level.

Figure 7.4 Theatre grid. Courtesy of A.S. Green and Company (Lancashire) Limited

Grid walkways

In a television studio where motorized units are installed, the basic need to walk to the units installed at high level can be met by walkways adjacent to the units. However, some organizations have made the entire area at high level completely free to walk over, thus allowing unrestricted access to almost any point above the acting area. Monopole grids do require access by staff to move the units.

Grid safety

One of the problems associated with walkover grids is that of safety. Obviously, no object must fall from the grid with personnel working on the studio floor and to this end, either pocketless overalls are worn by staff or any items that can be used at high level are usually attached to devices to prevent them falling through the grid slots. Arguments ensue all the time as to the viability of walkover grids, bearing in mind modern safety legislation, and most studios installed these days, generally provide maintenance access only.

The alternative to this safety problem is to allow only those staff working at high level to remain in the studio, having cleared the acting area of all other staff. Unfortunately this is time consuming and raises the operational costs.

Basic grid

The most basic design of grid from which we can hang a light consists of 48mm diameter metal barrels suspended above the acting area. The height will generally be fixed although the use of spring pantographs or drop arms can be advantageous. When the lighting requires adjustment, steps or ladders have to be used to provide access to rig and de-rig the luminaires. If the position of the luminaires is correct then pole operated controls enable adjustments to be made quickly without much disturbance to the rehearsals. Power sockets are usually distributed in a uniform manner just above the fixed barrels.

Roller barrels

To give more flexibility, at a low installation cost, a **roller barrel** system is often used (Figure 7.5). This allows barrels, about 2 m long to run along a set of parallel tracks mounted at high level in the studio. It is usually the practice with this type of installation, to mount the trunking with the power sockets attached, between the trackways. As this requires the minimum of space, the trackways can be installed very close to each other, subsequently allowing the luminaires to be positioned with a high degree of accuracy. It is essential that the moving barrel units are provided with trolleys designed so that they run smoothly along the trackways when pushed or pulled at any point on the barrel unit. There is nothing more annoying to the operator than pushing a roller barrel along the track-way only to see it jam and then having to waste time and effort in moving the unit once again. It is often advantageous to fit a brake to the barrels so that they maintain their set positions in the studio.

Figure 7.5 Roller barrel system

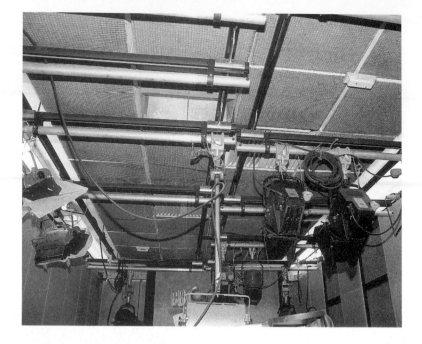

The barrels must be installed so that they cannot be removed from the trackways without the use of tools; otherwise a hazardous situation can occur. This system, which allows very good positioning in the horizontal plane, still suffers the drawback that unless additional equipment is provided, the height of the luminaires is fixed. Also, when the barrels move over a reasonable distance, some plugging and unplugging of the feeder cables would have to take place due to the fixed socket arrangement. It is normal practice with the roller barrel system to suspend each luminaire from the barrels by a roller trolley, therefore movement in two planes is achieved. To make the system even more flexible, the luminaire can be suspended by a variable pantograph from the barrel trolley, giving a high degree of flexibility in three planes.

Moving pantographs

A system of suspension that has achieved a reasonable degree of success, is the use of pantographs, mounted on roller trolleys and moving along long single trackways. This gives extremely good height flexibility and when the trackways are positioned as near to each other as possible, also offers a very good coverage over the acting area; the spacing between the trackways are dictated by the maximum size of luminaires used in the installation.

Spring pantographs

Generally, the system uses spring pantographs where the height can be easily adjusted (Figure 7.6). Horizontal movement is accomplished by dragging or pushing the pantograph top trolley unit along the trackway. The major drawback of the system is that special safety precautions have to be taken when changing luminaires on spring

Figure 7.6 Spring pantograph

pantographs. The power feeds to the individual pantograph units are often provided by a catenary cable system, rather like those used for overhead cranes.

Motorized pantographs

A modern advance, favoured by some large broadcasting organizations, is to use motorized pantographs where the height is adjusted by motor driven wire ropes and the horizontal movement accomplished by a motor drive onto the trackways (Figure 7.7).

Catenary feeder cables for both the control system and the power system are essential. The system can be easily adapted for remote control and has the great advantage of overcoming the safety problems connected with spring pantographs and is very quick and

Figure 7.7 Motorized pantograph

easy to use. The above systems have mainly allowed only one luminaire to move at a time. When we wish to move more lights at the same time, the systems become mechanically more complex.

Counterweight system

The most basic of these systems is to use a long barrel with the adjustment of height made by a counterweight system (Figure 7.8). In the theatre, these consist of very long barrels up to 10 m long, slung from several wire ropes. The lights are all at the same height and the weight on the barrel can be considerable when the power cables are attached. The counterweight system allows for the weight of the barrel, plus all the luminaires and cables mounted on it, to be balanced by a selection of special iron weights and provides an easy method of raising and lowering barrels with heavy loads. Counterweight barrels are mainly used in the theatre; although they have been used in some television studios, they cannot provide the flexibility of other systems for this application.

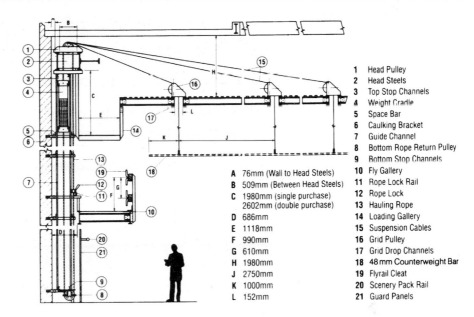

Figure 7.8
Counterweight system

1	Head Pulley
2	Head Steels
3	Top Stop Channels
4	Weight Cradle
5	Space Bar
6	Caulking Bracket
7	Guide Channel
8	Bottom Rope Return Pulley
9	Bottom Stop Channels
10	Fly Gallery
11	Rope Lock Rail
12	Rope Lock
13	Hauling Rope
14	Loading Gallery
15	Suspension Cables
16	Grid Pulley
17	Grid Drop Channels
18	48 mm Counterweight Bar
19	Flyrail Cleat
20	Scenery Pack Rail
21	Guard Panels

A	76mm (Wall to Head Steels)
B	509mm (Between Head Steels)
C	1980mm (single purchase)
	2602mm (double purchase)
D	686mm
E	1118mm
F	990mm
G	610mm
H	1980mm
J	2750mm
K	1000mm
L	152mm

Motorized barrels

An advance on the counterweight systems is the provision of motorized barrels. The motor unit can be separate from the barrel unit, or in the case of self-climbers, integral to the barrel unit.

Self-climbers

The barrel itself is over 2 m long and enables several luminaires to be placed side by side along the bar. Power is provided by fixed sockets, mounted on trunking along the barrel so that the luminaires can be easily plugged into the lighting supply. The adjustment of height is totally flexible and the system inherently safe by its design. It is very easy to operate from a remote control (Figure 7.9).

Finally, we come to probably the most accurate lighting positioning system of all. The monopole grid, although expensive to install, allows monopoles to be positioned about 600 mm from each other in adjacent tracks and to be individually placed anywhere along the trackways. The height of the monopoles is either adjusted by personnel at grid level, using portable drive tools, or by remotely controlled integral drive motors. The main drawback of monopoles is that a reduction in the number of units used in a studio for economic reasons means more physical movement of the units themselves and this requires riggers working over the acting area, which with modern safety legislation dictates that special arrangements have to be made. It is difficult to move the units in the grid area if they are permanently cabled so the electrical system has to be designed to cater for multi-positional use, allowing the units to be connected as necessary.

When discussing more sophisticated lighting suspension systems, there are certain items that are common to either monopoles, motorized barrels or motorized pantographs. If we cover the ground rules

Figure 7.9 Self-climbing barrel

for the component parts, the understanding of the complete pieces of equipment becomes easier.

It is difficult to state which items have the most importance due to the reliance upon one another for the satisfactory operation of particular items of equipment. However, to stick our necks out, we plump for the electric motors first as without these we have to resort to muscle power.

The motor unit

Most modern barrel winch units today employ three phase electric motors of about 1–1.5 kW rating. They also have a combined gearbox. The gearbox will have reduction gears so that the barrel unit moves up and down at a reasonable speed which is usually 8–10 m per minute. The gearbox is selected so that when maximum weight is applied to the barrel and the electrical system is 'off', the unit will not move, thus providing a self-sustaining system of gearing. To prevent the barrel unit over running when being raised or lowered, an integral electrical braking system is installed on the high speed side of the gearbox. This brake is normally applied and only released when the motor is activated. Monopole motor units may use three phase, single phase or dc drive motors. Because a monopole has a maximum lifting capacity of about 60 kg only, compared with a barrel of about 150 kg, the motors are generally smaller. It is easy to reverse a three phase motor but single phase motors have to have special drive circuits to allow forward and reverse operation. If dc motors are used, although they allow very easy control, they may present problems by becoming generators and supplying harmful voltage back into any control circuits. With any of the systems using motor drive units, it is essential that some form of manual drive is available in the event of electrical failure of the system.

Wire rope winding drums

There are two basic types of winding drum. The first being the scroll drum where the wire rope is wound on side by side in much the same way as a cotton reel. Due to the length of wire rope, together with the need to keep a low torque on the motor, the drums are usually reasonably small in diameter (200 mm approx.) and as only one turn of rope is used, around 250 mm wide. It is important that the drum width is held as small as possible so that the horizontal angle where the wire rope meets the drum is kept within certain limits. Usually a groove is formed in the winding drum so the rope follows the correct path. A big advantage of the scroll drum system is that the speed of the barrel unit remains constant when being raised and lowered.

The other type of winding drum is the pile wind and this works rather like a large yo-yo. The rope is piled singly, several layers thick upon itself between two substantial metal plates. This means that as the effective diameter of the drum is changing as the rope piles the barrel units speed of travel varies from its highest point to its lowest. A problem for the designers of pile drum systems is that the torque is not constant and the system has to cater for the worst case, which is when the barrel is at its highest point where the pile drum provides maximum speed with reduced lifting ability. This means that larger motors have to be used on pile wind winches than will be used on a scroll drum winch of similar lifting capacity. The system also suffers from the tendency for the ropes to be easily damaged if the mechanical design is not of the highest quality particularly if the retaining plates on the pile drum are weak. With both scroll and pile wind drums the wire ropes have to be very positively anchored to the drum and two clamps are used for each rope. To ensure a margin of safety, a minimum of two turns of rope must be left on either type of drum when the barrel is at its lowest operating point.

It is preferable on self-climbing winches to use scroll drums because, by keeping to a low torque, it will also enable the motor to be smaller – with obvious benefits. Obviously, with a self-climber, having the motor unit positioned approximately in the middle of the bar, with scroll drums either side, means that the unit will be wide and this might prove to be a problem. In practice, this does not appear to be the case. As an alternative it is possible to use scroll drums positioned so that they lay in the same direction as the barrel, but if this is used, precautions have to be taken to make certain that the unit, when winding up and down stays in the same vertical plane. Also, there is the danger that the motor unit sticks out to one side and causes an out of balance condition. It is very normal with self climbing winches to use four wire ropes to enable a better balance to be achieved and to meet current safety standards.

Diverter pulleys

Diverter pulleys (used to guide the wire rope to the correct plane) which are generally made from steel for strength and durability consist of a grooved wheel running on bearings. When the wire rope leaves the winding drum it has to be guided via the diverter pulleys to the correct position. The diverter pulleys are grooved and it is important that the wire rope fits snugly in that groove. The diameter of the pulley is also important due to the wire rope having a minimum quoted bending radius so that damage to the rope is avoided. Current regulations call for a diameter not less than 20 times the rope's thickness. The pulleys must run on properly lubricated bearings due to the high mechanical loads involved, and to keep noise to a minimum. As a general guide each diverter pulley in the system will reduce the lifting capacity by between 2 and 5% dependent on the type of bearings used.

Wire ropes

Barrel winches normally have two ropes, each capable of supporting at least six times the total applied load. Self-climbing winches generally have four wire ropes for suspension, however, the rules for the breaking strain of the ropes remains at *six* times total load for each rope.

Monopoles and motorized pantographs which could be operated by a single wire rope, have to be provided with twin lifting ropes for safety. Each single rope must support the total load of the monopole or pantograph in event of failure of either of the two ropes. The minimum breaking strength of each rope must be able to cope with at least *six* times the safe working load (SWL) plus the weight of the suspension tubes and electrical cables. In the event of a single rope failure, free fall via the rope length compensator system should be no greater than 12.7 mm. It is extremely important that in practice wire ropes do not become frayed and damaged. If a wire rope gets nicked or crushed it is vital that the rope is changed.

MOTOR CONTROL AND SAFETY SYSTEM

Various functions on the motor unit have to be made automatic to avoid either damaging the equipment, or more importantly, injuring staff. The functions are as follows:

Limit switches

Limit switches (Figure 7.10a and b) generally consist of a striker which is driven along a finely threaded shaft towards a microswitch which activates a relay and switches 'off' the power to the motor. Rotational movement of the strikers is prevented by a retaining bar which is placed in slots on the strikers themselves. To adjust the strikers, the bar is simply raised and the striker is screwed along the thread to the pre-set position desired and then the retaining bar is replaced. The threaded shaft which activates the strikers is driven from the main gearbox usually by a belt, chain or set of gears.

Top limit

A switch which will automatically disconnect the motor supply when the lifting assembly is raised to its highest set point. To avoid straining the motor gearbox, the diverters, wire ropes, etc., if the unit tries to drive itself to a dead stop, in the event of the top limit switch failing, current European standards require a second top limit switch

(a)

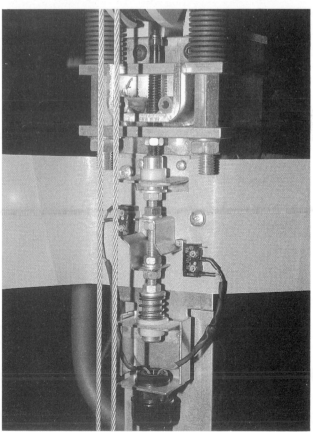

(b)

situated just after the normal top limit. This system is generally used where an automatic overload cut-out is not provided. If an automatic overload system is provided, another solution under the European standards is to have a mechanical buffer which the barrel unit will hit before it reaches its highest point just after top limit thus causing the automatic overload system to trip causing the unit to stop. Either of these solutions has to prevent an overload to the unit of more than 1.4 times thus ensuring no permanent mechanical damage.

Bottom limit

A switch which will automatically disconnect the motor supply when the lifting assembly is lowered to its lowest set point, which is usually 1 m above floor level. In the event of failure of the bottom limit switch, and if the ropes keep unwinding, the slack rope switch will operate.

Slack rope (underload)

If any of the wire ropes which suspend the units are allowed to slacken, usually by meeting an obstruction on the descent, a dangerous situation arises. If the unit does not automatically stop it may:
(a) tangle its own ropes causing permanent damage to them,
(b) suddenly fall free under its unbalanced weight.

Obviously (b) is the more hazardous and to prevent any danger sensors are usually fitted to each individual wire rope which operate rapidly as soon as any slackness occurs. Slack rope sensors usually consist of a striking mechanism attached to a spring under compression and a short distance away from a microswitch. When the ropes slacken, the spring expands and forces the microswitch to operate.

Overload

Although not specified under current European regulations, a sensing system should be provided so that if a load greater than the SWL is applied to the barrel unit, the motor supply will automatically shut off. The European tolerance for overload is 40% but some organizations ask for closer limits of about 20–25%. Overload rope sensors usually consist of spring biased pivoted diverter pulleys. Normally the spring keeps the diverter pulley assembly from striking the microswitch. On overload the spring compresses and the microswitch operates. Obviously the springs have to be selected to cater for the designated load of the particular unit.

In the case of standard winches or self-climbers, the overload condition is dependent on the position of the load applied to the barrel. Some units are designed to assess the overload as if it were positioned in the centre of the barrel. Thus 100 kg will present a load of 50 kg on each rope, in the case of a two rope system. If each rope were designed to sense a 100 kg overload, the system would not work; if however, the ropes were designed for 50 kg each, the system would work correctly. The main problem would arise when a load of 100 kg is off centre, thus presenting an overload condition to one rope most of the time. Most modern winch systems should attempt to use a design where the load is added, totalling the correct SWL irrespective of the load's position on the bar.

Both overload and slack rope systems are usually designed to automatically reset once the problem has been cured.

All of these sensors are fed to a purpose built electrical control box which contains the contactors for the raise and lower motor functions together with the control circuits for top and bottom limits, overload and slack wire rope sensors. Local control for raise and lower is usually provided for ease of maintenance. The system accepts remote control signals from elsewhere in the operational area.

Labels and warnings

Each unit has to be provided with labels to clearly indicate operational functions used by the staff. In addition, warning labels have to be provided to ensure staff safety. A reasonably comprehensive list is given below.

1. Unit number.
2. Lighting supply cable identification.
3. Lighting power socket identification.
4. Each control must be labelled, e.g. Raise, Lower, Local control, Remote control, Supply on/off.
5. Warning labels must be provided to indicate the mechanical loading and the electrical loading.
6. Any safety hazards connected with the operation of the equipment.

Barrel suspension unit

The length of the barrel is dictated by the needs of the installation. The unit, which would be capable of lifting loads up to 150 kg, is fitted with brackets so that the wire ropes from the winding drums may be attached. In line with the rest of the equipment connected with a winch the attachment brackets must have a sufficient safety factor and this is normally six times the applied SWL. The barrel, which may be steel or aluminium, will bend when loaded with lighting equipment and it is important that the barrel does not deflect more than recommended amounts. Therefore the barrel supports must also be capable of some deflection without permanent damage. The wire ropes must be attached to the brackets by correctly locked off shackles so that they will not loosen in operational use. The ends of the wire ropes where the shackles pass through must be permanently formed into eyelets by correctly splicing the ropes.

Power sockets

A trunking is usually fitted above the barrel itself for the termination of the power feeder cables and these cables usually go directly to sockets mounted on the front face of the trunking. The trunking is usually mounted approximately 300 mm above the barrel (see Fig. 7.11). Many configurations of sockets are used according to the electrical standards of the user country. In the UK most companies have now settled for 240V, 32A, BS 4343 sockets. This allows the connection of 5kW lights and falls in well with the practice of using

Figure 7.11 Electrical distribution

5kW dimmers. The BS 4343 16A socket is also used for lower powered luminaires and sub-circuits. Many British theatres still use the old 15A plugs and sockets.

Power cables and support systems

The power cables for the lighting socket outlets are fed from high level down to the trunking on the barrel unit. Over the years, many systems have been used but the two most popular are the '**curly cable**' and '**flip flop**'. The first system uses cables formed into a coil which is wrapped around the wire ropes. The cables which are suspended from the high level structure adjacent to the winch units, tend to act like elongated springs. Either one or more of the wire ropes can be used and the curly cables are generally multicore. Due to the weight of the cables, there is a tendency for the coils to compress immediately above the barrel unit. The flip flop system, on the other hand, allows the cable to fold in a uniform and controlled manner. Each section of the fold is about 1 m long; the cables can be unsupported, where each fold is determined by a mechanical clip or a device to form a radius. Although more costly, a system of lightweight support trays can be used as a definite route so that the cables fold almost perfectly. Plastic trays, although on the surface seemingly ideal for the job, will probably distort in the heat from luminaires hung from the barrel especially at the lower end of the flip flops, just above the luminaires. Precautions have to be taken so that the trays will pivot at grid level to avoid damage if a barrel assembly is moved sideways. The cable system should never be allowed to become straight in its maximum travel thereby avoiding the sections of cable tray from attempting to fold in the opposite direction to normal.

7.3 Pantographs

Pantographs allow luminaires to have their operating height adjusted over a specific range. Manual pantographs come as two distinct types, either spring balanced or manually wound with wire ropes. The ones most used in practice are those which are spring balanced. The reason for this is that once the springs are adjusted to balance the weight of the luminaire on the pantograph, very little effort is required to raise and lower the luminaire and this system is extremely quick in studio use. The main problem with spring pantographs is that adjusting the springs is extremely hazardous if not carried out by trained staff. Wind up pantographs, on the other hand, have little or no safety problems, but the disadvantage of this type is that they are slow in operational use due to the gearing via a pole operated system. Manual pantographs come with either two springs, four springs or six springs. The number of springs has some bearing on the adjustment range for the luminaires. Obviously with more springs, a finer range of adjustment can be achieved. Spring balanced pantographs generally have a range from approximately 1.8 to 4.5 m. The stabilizing framework for pantographs can either be twin cross armed devices or a single cross armed device. Spring pantographs are always twin cross armed devices. The pantographs are usually fitted with cable clips, either side along the cross armed devices, to allow for cable routeing from the trolley, where the unit is usually mounted on the barrel, down to a socket outlet at the base of the pantograph which can either be free, or permanently fixed adjacent to the luminaire spigot holder. As the weight of pantographs are an additional load for the grid, they are generally made from aluminium. Due to the range of springs that can be fitted to pantographs, units come in various weight ranges, therefore during the planning of the studio installation, it is important to know the weight of the luminaires to be used.

Pantograph motor units

The original motorized pantographs had one motor for lifting to ease the problems associated with spring and manually wound pantographs. However, without a traversing motor, it means that the operators had to drag quite heavy units along the trackways.

Modern motorized pantographs are usually fitted with two motor units, one for lifting and one for traversing on its associated trackways. All the electrical cables are terminated in a box at the top of the unit. A socket outlet is provided adjacent to the luminaire attachment point. The unit is generally designed to occupy as little height as possible when fully raised to the grid. The pantograph must be capable of operating with any load between zero and its SWL plus the weight of all permanently attached components such as the stabilizing framework, the electrical sockets, cables and cable supports.

The luminaires are usually attached to the bottom of the pantograph by means of a female 28.58 mm (1⅛ inch) spigot holder or a 'C' clamp over a mini barrel (Figure 7.12). Normally they are designed for a SWL of approximately 40 kg. The speed of operation is extremely important with the 'raise and lower' being approximately 8–10 m per minute.

Figure 7.12 Spigot holder

Speed of operation

The pantograph's traverse speed must be slower than 15 m per minute. At speeds faster than this the unit is inclined to jerk, and the luminaire may oscillate in travel. Bearing in mind that the pantograph unit should be as compact as possible, the usual operating height range is around 7 m due to the length of wire rope needed and the subsequent effect on the size of the winding drums. The two motors are normally powered from an ac single phase supply. The unit for raising and lowering the luminaire will be approximately 600 W and the unit for traversing will be about 100 W.

Brakes are required to stop the unit over running and these should operate on the high speed side of the motor gearbox units. The brake is automatically applied whenever the motor supply is switched off or interrupted and electromagnetically released when the motor supply is on. The gearbox, as usual, should be self-sustaining. For the purposes of maintenance the electric motors, gearboxes, brakes if fitted, wire rope winding drums, travel and load limit switches, must be accessible and easily replaced in the event of faults occurring. Provision must be made so that the units can be wound by hand in the event of failure of the electrical equipment or in order to facilitate maintenance. In a similar manner to monopoles, two wire ropes have to be fitted to meet current safety standards, and the twin drums will be either pile wind or scroll. The suspension system using the wire ropes on a pantograph is the same as that used on a monopole, and to compensate for the differential in rope lengths a toggle bar is used for the rope attachment at the base of the unit. The pantograph should be fitted with slack rope and overload sensing systems, it must also incorporate vertical travel limits to stop the pantograph at pre-set positions at the top and bottom of travel. The traversing system consists of an electric motor, a gearbox and generally a friction drive system formed as an integral unit. The pantograph would normally be propelled along the trackway by a friction wheel or similar drive. The drivewheel is normally permanently engaged but must have a method of easily uncoupling and manually traversing the pantograph in an emergency.

Control

These types of pantographs rely upon remote electrical control. A termination box has to be provided and fitted close to the motor unit assembly. This box will accept the remote control supply system, together with a main luminaire supply for the particular unit. All of these signals will be supplied through a catenary cable feeder system. The remote control system has to provide 'raise', 'lower', 'traverse left' and 'traverse right' signals. To keep the complexity of the electrical system on the pantograph system to a minimum, it is preferable to remote the control relays and use mains drives direct to the motors. The unit should also be provided with local electrical control where the traverse and vertical control of the unit is accomplished by standard pole operation cups pinned to the shafts of biased rotary switches. Pantograph movement is obtained by turning the switches either left or right. It is obviously impossible in practice to have a left and right traverse, as it is dependent on the position of the operator in the studio, so the directions are called 'red' and 'white' and appropriate marker boards are fitted to the studio walls. The indicators for red and white direction and raise and lower must be clearly visible from the studio floor.

7.4 Counterweight bars

The counterweight bar shown is the primary means of support for everything above stage in the theatre (see Figure 7.8). The bars are adapted to lift scenery, lighting, drapes and practicals. The only special adaptation for the lighting bar is the provision of a distribution system of sockets running along its length with a terminal box at one end of the barrel supplied from a hanging multi-core cable system known as 'tripe'. The support cables or ropes travel via diverter pulleys to the side of the stage where they are connected to a counterweight box. The box is loaded with cast iron weights until it balances the intended load. At this point very little effort is required to raise and lower the bar, a function carried out by the flyman on the fly gallery. When the bar has been adjusted to the required position, a clamping device is applied to the ropes to hold them firmly in place.

The rope brake is designed to hold with only a small out of balance load. This prevents a dangerous condition when either the barrel is overloaded or luminaires are removed by mistake, e.g. the rope starts to slip with about 25 kg out of balance load.

The counterweight bar appears to satisfy all of the rigging needs of the theatre, although it should be pointed out that the total weight load on the grid is double that of the lighting, i.e. the weight of the lighting plus the weight of the counterweight system. It does however, present a problem inasmuch as the counterweight box is normally 2 m high which represents a loss of height by the time it reaches stage level. To make maximum use of height in the fly tower, the scenery should go immediately next to the grid, when it clears the sight lines. However, to achieve this the roof would need to be 2 m higher or, as is more commonly the practice, the floor of the stage is cut away at the wall allowing the counterweight boxes to travel through the stage into the understage void. Whilst this system works very well for theatre, its adaptation into television studios does not permit the counterweight system to travel through the studio floor. Therefore, when contemplating such a rigging system for lighting in a television studio the height of the weight box and the ultimate height of the lighting bar must be considered. However, the main disadvantage of this suspension system in television studios is that even if the bars are made half the width of the studio with counterweights on both sides, the bars are still much too long to provide accurate lighting positions for other than one or two luminaires, in view of the fact that all of the rest of the lights on the bar are in a compromise height position. The exceptions to this statement are a row of top cyclorama lights at the side of the studio presenting a continuous length of barrel and banks of floodlights.

7.5   Motorized barrel winches

Standard barrel winch unit

The main drive unit which can be mounted at high level in the studio, on a side gallery or at floor level, consists of a substantial framework to which is attached the electrical motor drive unit, gearbox, wire rope winding drums and the wire rope diverter pulleys. When the units are mounted in the grid, the imposed weight load is that of the units plus the lighting. However, in the case of motor units attached to the side walls, most of the load on the grid is from the lighting only. The barrel unit, together with its associated lighting power sockets, mounted on an integral trunking system, is suspended from high level by wire ropes, which may be taken to the drive unit by additional diverter pulley systems. The associated electrical control box can be positioned adjacent to the unit or away from the unit in purpose made cabinets. However, a remote control unit would require more individual mains cables to connect it to the winch in the studio area.

The design of winches should provide for the lightest weight of support framework commensurate with minimum mechanical distortion. Any framework distortion may give problems with the mechanical sensing systems for 'slack rope' and 'overload'. It also may give problems with the pile or scroll drums. The physical size and weight of the unit is extremely important as this will have considerable impact on the support structure. A problem that always exists with conventional barrel winches is that of access to the motor units, usually solved by either walkways adjacent to the units or 'walkover' grids.

Self-climbing winch unit

In essence a self-climbing barrel winch is an upside down standard winch with the motor gear box mounted above the barrel on the same assembly. The main problem with self-climbing winches is that in addition to lifting the normal SWL, they have to lift their own weight. Bearing in mind that the weight of the unit is usually similar to that of the SWL, it would not be inconceivable that a self-climber would have to be rated to lift something like 250 kg from the studio floor. This means, in general, that the power of the motors will be more on self-climbing units, particularly so if pile wind drums are used, hence the motor gearbox becomes heavier, which poses a design problem. The self-contained unit consists of a motor and gearbox, wire rope winding drums, diverter pulleys and the sensing system for top and bottom limits, slack rope and overload. The unit is secured and suspended by the steel wire lifting ropes from the underside of a suitable ceiling or grid structure. All lighting and control circuits are fed from the ceiling or grid structure via flip flop or curly cables. The barrel, which is usually from 2 to 2.5 m long, and capable of lifting loads up to 120 kg, is suspended from the main housing which contains the motor gearbox unit, etc. With self-climbers it is generally normal to integrate the lighting power sockets into the main housing instead of supplying a separate trunking system.

A major advantage of self-climbers is that they do not require complex grid systems and are much less time consuming to install. Generally any maintenance can be carried out at studio floor level.

7.6 Monopoles

A monopole or 'a single suspension unit' (Figure 7.13) is a means by which a luminaire can be raised or lowered by a wire rope winding system with stability being maintained by metal tubes which are telescopic and slide within each other. Due to the self-sustaining gearboxes employed, it would be a very tiresome business to manually wind a luminaire from studio floor level to grid level. Therefore, the units are generally operated by powered drive systems.

Operation

A manual monopole will be normally operated by a portable tool which could be driven by compressed air or electricity. Alternatively, the unit may be operated by a purpose designed integral electric motor gearbox unit and is designated a 'motorized monopole'. Generally, both types of monopole are mechanically much the same.

Figure 7.13 Monopoles

The SWL of monopoles is approximately 45 kg with some specially designed units capable of loads up to 60 kg. Due to handling problems at high level, it is important that the weight of each unit does not exceed 80 kg and preferably should be a lot less.

Construction

Each monopole generally consists of seven or eight interlocking steel tubes and are usually manufactured for a working height range of 10 m and all the tubes used have to be made to close dimensional tolerances and straightness. The telescopic sections should be provided with interlocking retaining tabs, which prevent the monopole twisting too much in operational use. Each tube locks into the one above to restrict rotational movement of the individual tubes to within ± 2.5°. It should be noted that the telescopic sections are only to give stability and are not load carrying. The tube sets are always made longer than the wire ropes at their maximum extension and it is extremely important that the tubes do not stick at any point. If the tubes do stick at high level, and then suddenly become free, the energy transferred to the rope suspension system will probably be sufficient to cause considerable damage.

Due to safety considerations, each monopole must be fitted with twin wire ropes and these can be contained within twin scroll or wire rope pile drums. The twin cables must be independently terminated on the winding drum assemblies and to a compensator attachment (to allow for differential in the length of the ropes) which should be fitted to the base of the telescopic tube assembly. All the wire rope terminations must have provision for a visual inspection at regular intervals to meet current safety standards. The gearbox on both motorized monopoles and manual monopoles must be self-sustaining. Where integral electric drive motors are used, they are usually a special single phase type but dc motors are also used. Due to the lower SWL of monopoles together with their lower self weight, less powerful motors can be used.

In the case of monopoles with integral drive motors, electro-mechanically operated overload and slack wire rope devices should be incorporated into the units, together with top and bottom travel limit switches. In the case of manual monopoles, which employ drive tools, it is obviously important to have some form of torque limitation on the drive system, otherwise undue stress will be applied to the wire ropes and pile drums. The motor control units, which are generally mounted at the top of the monopole, normally require an ac supply. The control units should also provide a local or remote control facility which can be selected. Remote control circuits are usually by low voltage dc. The local control can either be an 'up' or 'down' button or a centre biased 'raise' and 'lower' switch. In an emergency, or in the event of system power failure, the gearbox should have a spindle drive facility for the unit to be operated by hand or by suitable portable drive tools.

Monopole trolley

The monopoles have to be provided with a trolley which is purpose made to suit the grid slot system in use and will have to meet such safety standards as required by the installation and to the operators' satisfaction. Normally these trolleys are fitted with eight wheels to mount on the grid slots. The trolley should be braked, and can be fitted additionally with lifting mechanism for ease of rotation for direction changes when using transfer slots.

Power feed

A spigot holder has to be provided at the lower end of monopole tube sets, generally to take a standard 28.58 mm (1⅛ inch) spigot as normally fitted to luminaires. For many years, the electrical supply cable to the luminaires suspended from monopoles was generally dropped from high level with a female socket attached so that the luminaire could be plugged in at low level. In recent years, some manufacturers have provided luminaire supply cables which are made in preformed coils and wrapped around the telescopic sections with a socket fixed adjacent to the spigot holder and, in this way, a much neater system has evolved. The supply socket would obviously need to meet the requirements of the particular studio and country where the installation occurs.

7.7 System controls

It's no good installing motorized units in a theatre or studio without having some form of control. The simplest form of control is two wires that go to a unit, and say, 'go up' and 'go down'. However, doing this one at a time is very time consuming. It is far better to have a certain number of units that could move up at the same time as another set could come down. In the case of the winch systems, the 'up/down' commands are the only ones needed. Unfortunately, if we are using motorized pantographs, or for that matter, motorized monopoles with a traversing system that requires control, then the system becomes more complex.

Let us now consider how we can control a fairly simple unit going up and down. It is obviously more economical if, from the control console to each unit, we use the minimum of copper wire, and to achieve this we use low power relays driving mains contactors. In the case of three phase drive motors, we use subsidiary relays to drive the 'up' and 'down' contactors. Today's systems usually employ 24V relays. The mains power for the motors can be derived from a ring main going from unit to unit; if the power requirements of each motor are fairly small, then a reasonable size ring main will allow several units to be used at once, and most studios aim to control 20 units at any one time. This avoids a surge on the electrical supply

Figure 7.14 Hoist control console

caused by the motors all starting at the same time and prevents a large dynamic mechanical load being applied to the grid. For either standard barrel winches or self-climbing winches where the installation is fixed, the electrical control system is relatively straightforward. If, however, there is a need to control monopoles from the studio floor, to reduce the amount of operational work at grid level, the monopoles would have to be provided with either extremely long electrical cables coming from the motors or a multiplicity of control points would have to be provided at grid level.

Console control

The most common consoles used today are equipped with a 'green' and 'amber' group control system, where each winch is capable of being routed to either the 'green' or 'amber' control (see Fig. 7.14). Therefore some units can be switched to green control, giving up/down commands, and other units can be switched to the amber, also giving up/down commands. The amber and green controls are completely independent of each other; therefore some winches can be going up while others are coming down. Where winch units are coupled together for operational reasons, some clear indication of this state must be made on the appropriate console. In the past this was often bits of sticky tape, or pieces of perspex coupling the switches together; in modern consoles this can be accomplished by electronically interlocking the system.

The limitations placed on the number of winches to be used at any one time is generally occasioned by the dynamic mechanical load applied to the grid structures when the motors start. Some recent advances in the control of suspension units in studios include using microprocessor control with alpha-numeric keyboards and VDUs to display the information. With some intelligence built into the system it is therefore possible to have sophisticated selection whereby units that are coupled together are easily recognized by the system and the studio should generally become more safe.

The large control consoles, which are mainly banks of switches, are usually positioned on a convenient wall in the operational area, but there are occasions when it is impossible to see what is happening when operating from the console, therefore remote control units are often used to allow the operator to walk to the area being lit and so have good sight lines to the equipment being moved. Originally these remote controls were wired back to a point adjacent to the main console. Recent developments include radio and infrared transmitted control systems.

Remote control of monopole systems has never been developed to any degree, whereas motorized pantograph systems have become quite complex. The motorized pantograph requires control of 'up' and 'down' and its traversing motion. Units in use at the BBC in their regional studios also control on/off information of the luminaires as well; control being accomplished by a small portable handheld radio controller that can be carried about in the studio and used by the LD or senior electrician. The system is used for a rigging aid and not for total control of the luminaires. It does have the advantage that one man can move and adjust lights with relative speed. Control of motorized pantograph units is generally done from a base system, which sends mains signals to the motorized pantograph units, thus avoiding too many relays and subsidiary circuits within the units mounted at high level.

7.8   How to rig monopoles and pantographs

Pantographs, both manually and electrically controlled, are normally mounted onto roller barrel trolleys or heavy duty 'C' section track. The method of mounting when using this track is to slide the pantograph unit into the track from one end making sure that the end stops are replaced in both ends of the track. When mounting pantographs onto a barrel roller trolley, the trolley is placed over the barrel so that the support wheels may traverse along the barrel. Safety bolts or plates are then fitted to the trolley to prevent it lifting off the barrel. Having mounted and secured the pantograph, the mains cable should be inspected to determine that none of the loops attached to the side of the pantograph can be trapped between the cross links which will act like a pair of scissors when the pantograph is opened and closed.

Pantograph spring adjustment

Load adjustment of spring pantographs is made by moving the position of the end of the spring up and down the outside rungs by use of hook plates attached to the end of each spring. This is a dangerous adjustment, and must be performed to the manufacturer's instructions to ensure that the spring is not released when it is moved from one rung to another.

When balancing the load it is a good practice to equalize the position of diagonally opposite springs to keep the pantograph from twisting. Extending the springs towards the base of the pantograph adjacent to the luminaire mounting point allows a greater load to be balanced. To load a luminaire onto a spring pantograph it is necessary to either climb up to the top position adjacent to the grid with the light, which makes it difficult to adjust the springs for the applied load. A much preferred practice is to tie a piece of rope to the base of the pantograph and pull it down to floor level, where a sandbag or other convenient weight can be attached whilst the luminaire is being fitted to the base. The springs may now be adjusted until a perfect balance is achieved and the rope can be released. Extreme caution must be taken when unloading a spring pantograph to make sure that the reverse procedure is adopted to that of the mounting procedure, preferably with the rope, so that the pantograph is allowed to slowly close as the rope is played out. We have seen the results of a pantograph being released at floor level, allowing it to fly up to the top without a load and the result is quite dramatic and very dangerous. Springs become detached and links are broken, showering debris on those below with a real danger of the whole pantograph frame structure falling on the person responsible for letting go of it.

Motorized pantographs

Motorized pantographs are much easier to mount in view of the fact that they are lowered by a motor and can be loaded at floor level, however, the same procedure is required as in the case of the spring pantograph with regards to mounting and the path of the cables. If electrical traverse is provided, extra care is needed to ensure sufficient length of trailing cable and its safe routing.

Monopoles

Monopoles, because of their weight, are difficult to handle, require at least two people and, in the case of the motorized monopole, with its mains cable, three people to rig them. If it is practical, it is a better proposition to use a small hoist or tackle to get them up to grid level and then the most simple monopole may be lowered into the appropriate slot from above, having made sure that the grid end stops are in position. With more sophisticated grids, a transfer trolley is provided so that the monopole can be loaded into the trolley from the top gallery, pushed along to the appropriate slot, and then positioned in the grid.

When the monopole has been placed in the grid slot, it is necessary to guide the mains cable through the cable guide ring that holds it in the centre of the slot. This is to prevent the cable being trapped by the wheels of the trolley. Monopoles are positioned in the vertical and lateral position by motor drives in the case of the fully motorized unit, but in the case of the manually operated monopole these functions can only be performed from above the grid. Under no circumstances should the monopole be pulled along the slot from below by pulling the tubes. This will damage or break the tubes or at least, distort them, causing them to stick and bind when being lowered.

Monopole supply

A good practice when installing monopoles is to determine the type of plug or connector being used at the luminaire end of the supply cable. Many types of 5 kW plug will not go through the standard grid slot of 2.5 inches (62.5 mm) and therefore must be fed through the end of the grid slot. This small observation before installation could save hours of shunting and moving monopoles around the grid when it comes to connecting up.

7.9 Loading barrel winches

Barrel winches come in a variety of types: they may be suspended by a counterweight system; they could be a standard winch unit where the motor is mounted at grid level or they may be a self-climber where the motor unit is integral to the barrel. Two features that are common to any type of barrel suspension is that they have well-defined safe working loads, and being fairly long devices, occupy a large space in the grid system.

In the theatre, where barrels may be around 5 m long, it is purely a matter for the electricians to rig luminaires as dictated by the LD on the particular production, bearing in mind the physical space required by each unit, and when all the units are hung, check that the SWL has not been exceeded.

Another aspect of rigging barrels in a theatre is to allow sufficient space for the scenery that has to be flown in and out during a production so that the lights miss scenery flats and cloths. The majority of luminaires rigged will be at the same height. If large effects lighting units are being used, note should be taken of the extra space required. It may be that the addition of some units to the normal rig, will exceed the SWL of the bar, therefore some compromise has to be reached with the final positions of the luminaires so the weight load is evenly distributed between the bars. With the advent of motorized lighting units which replace two or three standard luminaires, it may be the density of rig is not so high, giving more flexibility to the LD and the electricians concerned.

Generally with counterweight systems, it is almost impossible to overload them as the counterweight bucket usually only contains sufficient weights to balance the SWL on the bar. The overload warning system heard is probably the grunts and groans from the 'sparks' using the system.

Owing to the need to fly scenery between the lighting bar rows, cross barrel systems from one lighting bar to another are virtually unheard of in the theatre. Other than the fact they would impede the scenery, there would be no point in attempting to get the subtle variations in the angle of throw from the luminaires within a theatre as the distance between the suspension barrels is never very great.

Motorized barrel loading

Motorized barrel units, as used in television studios, pose different problems. Because of the larger lights used in television, the spacing between barrels is fairly wide and this, together with the end to end spacing of the barrels, poses problems for the positioning of the luminaires. The position of the lighting has to be reasonably accurate and is dictated by the layout of the sets within the production area and the requirements of the LD to cover the action correctly. Many studios use a standard rig of luminaires which may be fastened directly to the barrel unit, or attached via a short spring pantograph, so flexibility in height is provided. Where luminaires and pantographs are supplied as combinations, there is usually very little spare weight capacity on the bars, thus when additional equipment is required to be rigged to the bar, it may take the bar over its SWL limit. This poses real problems and the LD now has to decide whether to lose a luminaire or use another type of light. It may be possible to de-rig a pantograph leaving its luminaire in place, although with long barrel units it is preferable to keep the pantographs to allow flexibility between the luminaires attached to the bar. Another problem is that even if the bar was capable of taking the extra luminaire weight, it might be that the unit is too large to fit in the available space. At this point, the LD could use a short drop arm on the luminaire required so that it hangs just below the space occupied by the luminaires already present on the bar; although this may restrict the up/down movement of the luminaires on the pantographs.

Cross barrels

What happens in TV studios when the barrel units do not provide the LD with the desired position for the luminaire? The only thing

Figure 7.15 Cross barrels

to do is to provide a temporary barrel that bridges two of the normal barrels. The two major problems with using cross barrels is that they tether two units together, inhibiting flexibility and the ends of the cross barrel attached to the standard barrel units impose extra weight. This load will be in proportion to the length of the crossbar between the attachment points and the point loads on the cross bar. For example, 50 kg in the centre of a cross barrel between two standard barrel units, will present a load of 25 kg to each barrel unit. At the other end of the scale, if the point load of 50 kg was positioned at one of the attachment points most of the 50 kg would be present at that point. It can be seen, therefore, that as the load moves along the bar, it moves proportionately between the two attachment points on the barrels.

Cross barrel hazards

The above case illustrates that it is not just simply a matter of putting a cross bar between two units. When using crossbars what happens when only one bar is raised and the other bar does not move? The bar that is moving in an upward direction will eventually take the total weight of the crossbar and attempt to pull it with itself. Just after this point in travel the crossbar will attempt to start raising the other winch barrel. Unless very good overload sensors are provided, it might be that the whole cross barrel structure is raised and eventually becomes dangerous because the luminaires are not hanging normally by the barrel clamping arrangement provided but have rotational stress applied. It may be that these exceed the mechanical tolerances as designed.

Conversely, the lowering of one of the main bars eventually means that one end of the cross bar becomes lower and lower and then will start to drag the other supporting bar into the moving unit. Once again, additional torque may be introduced into mechanical sections of the units. This case highlights the need for good overload protection but it is quite possible in practice that none of the loads on either the two original bars, or the crossbar exceeded the system specifications, only when the units were moved. In practice, it is therefore extremely important that any crossbar is clearly marked so that the electricians operating the winch control console will not raise or lower one bar without the other. The situation cited above involved two bars, with one crossbar attached, but in long experience in studios, we have seen several crossbars across several barrel units all at the same time, together with crossbars on crossbars, and one shudders to think of the complications this causes in practice.

The same rules apply to studios that employ self-climbing units but unfortunately, an additional hazard exists. When using cross barrels in self-climbing studios, not only would the cross barrel attempt to lift the SWL, it ultimately starts to lift the entire load of the barrel unit, and although it might not progress to a great height, it might get sufficiently high to suddenly swing free and act like a giant pendulum, which would be extremely dangerous to say the least.

In recent times, broadcasting organizations using motorized barrel systems have examined more sophisticated control of their winch systems to prevent problems such as these occurring. Two methods can be employed; one of which is to *remove from any form of control* the two bar units with a cross barrel attached once they have been positioned; alternatively ensure that any movement of one of the normal bars will *guarantee the other bar moves in unison,* thus maintaining the status quo for the cross barrel, although as can be seen from Figure 7.16, tape works better!

Luminaires rigged directly on a bar require a safety bond that passes over the barrel as the second means of suspension in accordance with normal safety procedures. If however, a pantograph is used to support a luminaire a different technique must be employed. **If the pantograph is attached to the support system by a wheeled**

Figure 7.16

trolley which cannot be removed without a tool then a safety bond will not be required at the top of the pantograph. However, the luminaire still requires bonding to the base of the pantograph. **Bonds are required at the top of portable pantograph units and drop arms**, and this must pass over the main barrel. At the base of any pantograph, where the luminaire is attached, either by a spud directly into a spigot holder or by a 'C' clamp onto a spade fixing at the base of the pantograph, the luminaire safety bond must pass over the permanently attached bottom section of the pantograph unit.

When using bars that are say, 2.4 m long, it is important that the roller trolleys used for the luminaires' horizontal adjustment do not entangle the luminaire cables which are plugged into power sockets adjacent to the bar, supplying the luminaires. Various methods have been employed over the years to prevent this happening, one of the most successful is to have a small subsidiary bar, adjacent to the main bar, with small runners attached so that the power cable is conveyed along out of harm's way, rather like the power feeds used with gantry cranes. Another important point to watch when rigging bars is to ensure that the cable does not droop from the socket across the heat outlet at the top of the luminaire and thus get either too hot or melt completely. This may seem rather obvious, but unfortunately in practice happens too often and the cables do become very brittle and thus pose a safety hazard.

Raising and lowering barrels

Many modern winch systems are fitted with a local barrel switch which enables the electrician, when rigging, to move the barrel up and down by using the operating pole in the cup of the operating switch. This allows very fine adjustments which are only limited by the length of the pole used, and improves the productivity during the rigging period. The normal procedure for rigging bars in studios is to bring sections of the barrel system down to the studio floor level so the electricians can remove luminaires where necessary, introduce new luminaires, change filters and fit any other equipment as desired by the LD. This operation is usually done in groups of about 20 bars, this being the maximum amount that the winch system caters for at any one time and, by coincidence, is usually two rows across a production studio of about 800 m^2. While the rigging is taking place, it will usually involve a team of two electricians on the bars, one electrician fetching and carrying and another based near the winch console to move the bars up and down when requested. It is obviously extremely important that the communication between the team is good to ensure the correct weights are applied to bars, cross barrels are carefully noted and when the bars are moved they do not foul items of scenery and technical equipment. Additionally, on those occasions when a temporary circuit such as a 10 kW feeder is draped across several bars for convenience, that this is also noted as this fairly large cable acts like a **soft cross barrel**.

Technical facilities on suspension

Other than additional luminaires or positions for luminaires which require cross barrels, there is also a need to provide facilities for

slung video monitors and column loudspeakers in a standard lighting rig. In installations where permanent audience areas are
allocated, although the seating may not always be in situ, it is
customary to feed specified bars with sound and vision facilities.
Sometimes special bars are provided to be used only for vision and
sound audience facilities. However, if we have to rig a large video
monitor onto a barrel, we will invariably have to move some of the
existing equipment due to the weight of the monitor. If the equipment to be removed is a short spring pantograph, supporting a
luminaire, it is essential that the spring pantograph is collapsed
before removing the luminaire. Alternatively, it may be possible to
remove the pantograph and luminaire as one combined unit in
absolute safety.

**Having removed any lighting equipment it is essential that it is
transported safely to a secure area for storage thus ensuring no
damage occurs**.

7.10   Rigging luminaires

The first consideration when rigging luminaires must be safety. Any
light mounted above people is a potential hazard. Each suspension
device will have a maximum SWL. This must be observed. Further,
each luminaire is required to have its own safety bond around the
primary means of support and the luminaire to arrest it in the event
of it falling. The accessories such as barndoors and colour frames,
also require their own safety retention device to prevent them
becoming dislodged during movement. Having established that these
requirements have been met, the electricians can mount the
luminaire onto its support. In addition to the safety bond, a safety
pin is also provided and this should be inserted into the top of the
spigot when it has been passed through the spigot holder. The
electrician connecting the luminaire to the supply is responsible for
visually examining the cable and connector to establish that they are
electrically safe before plugging the luminaire into its socket. The
choice of luminaire is normally dictated by the lighting plot which
will show the electrician the type of unit, its wattage and the colour
of any filter to be used. A space is usually left on the lighting plot
for the electrician to complete the circuit number used, in the event
that one has not already been allocated. It is normal practice to open
the luminaire and determine that the correct size lamp has been
fitted and then switch the luminaire on, focus and direct it to the
approximate position as indicated on the lighting plot. These disciplines can save an enormous amount of time during rehearsals when
in all probability, to get to a luminaire over sets and obstacles, it will
be necessary to use tall steps or a portable tower. There will be
occasions when it will be impossible to reach the luminaire after
rigging is complete and rehearsals have commenced.

8
Dimming and control

Introduction

Why do we need dimmers? Why not just put the lights on as we do at home? In the average lounge where there may be wall lights as well as centre fittings, some degree of limited balance often has to be achieved, usually by the selection of various wattage lamps. When using a multiplicity of light sources, it is necessary to balance between all of them to achieve a pleasing result to the eye or for that matter a TV or film camera.

Reducing light level

Before the introduction of sophisticated electrical control of dimming, various methods of reducing the light level developed and many are still in use today. The main disadvantage of electrical dimming is that by lowering the voltage to a tungsten luminaire the colour of the light source changes. This has a two-fold effect; the source runs at a lower colour temperature, moving towards the red end of the spectrum, and secondly any colour filter that is placed in the luminaire will give a different result when the source is changed. The most exaggerated change will result with a heavy blue filter. When the source is running at full power it is producing light across the spectrum with some blue to penetrate the filter and provide blue light. When the source is dimmed down, the colour shifts towards the red end of the spectrum and produces very little blue, therefore the filter which restricts the red and green will pass little, if any, colour. This is an important fact that all LDs learn early on in their career that the dimmer setting is just as important as the selection of the colour filter when designing the lighting plot.

MECHANICAL DIMMING

Before we discuss the electrical methods of varying the voltage to the lamp, let us consider some mechanical solutions that have been used over the years that do not change the colour of the light from the luminaire.

Scrim

A scrim can be a piece of wire mesh placed in the colour runners of a luminaire and normally available in order of the amount of light that it will allow through the holes in the mesh: 25%, 50%, 75% etc. If the required effect is to reduce the lighting level and to produce a softer shadow, the scrim could be a piece of cloth or gauze or a frost plastic filter, held in a frame and mounted at some distance in front of the light.

Neutral density filter

Plastic neutral density filters are available that work in the same way as the scrim, but of course, suffer deterioration with light and heat causing a change in the light output.

Shutter blinds

A thin box shape containing lateral slats, rather like a venetian blind, can be mounted in the colour runners of the luminaire and the slats moved from the horizontal, where very little light will be obscured, to the vertical when the effect will be a total blackout. This movement can be a manual push/pull control or a more sophisticated control is obtained by gearing the blades to a motor gearbox device to provide remote control.

Iris

In profiles and follow spots the optical design provides an opportunity to place an iris in the optical path, normally between the objective lenses so that it will be well out of focus. In this position the iris will not affect the spot size and will produce an even dimming effect. The control can be a manual lever on the luminaire, or a motor gearbox will provide remote control.

Barndoor

Most of us associate a barndoor with a Fresnel spot. However, a little known fact is that a standard barndoor can be placed in the colour runners of a profile or follow spot, where it is out of focus, and used as a dimmer simply by bending in all four flaps to interrupt the light beam and adjust the intensity. This is a very useful ploy to balance the light output from follow spots that are mounted at different distances from the acting area. The barndoor will not affect the beam size and can be manually or remote control operated.

Gas lighting

A major advance for the illumination of indoor theatres was the introduction of gas lighting, which in its early days suffered from many problems, the major one being that of safety. As the gas systems became more advanced, control of portions of the lighting was achieved by small control taps and stopcocks placed in strategic pipework so that sections of the lighting could be switched off while other sections could be switched on. A major problem with gas lighting is that it requires ignition to achieve incandescence and it was very inconvenient to light each gas jet individually. Several methods were used to enable the gas jets to be controlled, the most favoured one ultimately was to have a system where either a pilot light was employed or the actual gas jet was never completely extinguished. As far as we can research, no form of intermediate light level was provided by gas lighting, purely the ability to fade up sections of lights and fade down sections of lights within the auditorium and in the stage area. To actually hold the light level at a point somewhere between 'zero' and 'full' to achieve a lighting balance, is a practice that only became normal with the advent of electricity.

Electrical history

The biggest step forward in the control of lighting in general was made by Richard D'Oyly Carte at the Savoy Theatre, which opened in 1881 and was to be used specifically for performances of Gilbert and Sullivan light operas. From the outset D'Oyly Carte was determined to have the new electric lighting in his theatre to give much better illumination for the performances. He was also shrewd enough in the earlier days to have a gas system installed in addition to the new electrical power. Due to teething troubles, the official premiere on 6 October had to be delayed until Saturday 8 October. At that performance the stage was lit with gas and it was not until Wednesday 28 December that the entire theatre was lit by electricity. We quote from a publication of the time and it is interesting to note that the idea of controlling light was first mentioned.

> An interesting experiment was made at a performance of *Patience* yesterday afternoon, when the stage was for the first time lit up by the electric light, which has been used in the auditorium ever since the opening of the Savoy Theatre. The success of the new mode of illumination was complete and its importance for the development of scenic art can scarcely be over rated. The light was perfectly steady throughout the performance and the effect was pictorially superior to gas, the colours of the dresses, an important element in the aesthetic opera, appearing as true and distinct as by daylight. The Swan incandescent lamps were used, the aid of gas light being entirely dispensed with. The ordinary electric apparatus has the great drawback for stage representations that the flames (sic) cannot be lowered or increased at will, there being no medium between full light and total darkness. This difficulty has here been successfully overcome by interpolating in the circuit . . . what in technical language is called a resistance. This resistance consists of open spiral coils of iron wire. . .

The above quote was from the *Daily News*, 29 December 1881.

A technical observer commented in *Engineering* in early 1882.

> The most interesting feature however, from a scientific point of view, of this most interesting installation, is the method by which the lights in all parts of the establishment are under control. For any series of lights can in an instant be turned up to their full power or gradually lowered to a dull red heat as easily as if they were gas by the simple turning of

a small handle. There are six of these regulating handles corresponding to the number of the machines and circuits arranged side by side against the wall of a *little room or rather closet* on the left side of the stage, and each of these handles is a six-way switch which by throwing into its corresponding magnet circuit greater or less resistance (increasing or decreasing it in six stages) the strength of the current passing through the lamps is lessened or increased by as many grades.

We find it interesting that the machinery for controlling the lights was placed 'in a little room or closet', which rather sets the scene for the subsequent years where we are often confronted with small dimmer rooms and control areas, be it in the theatre, television, film or any other entertainment media.

It is not that many years ago that most control from lighting consoles to dimmers was by a minimum of two wires for any individual dimmer, although by using a common return wire it is possible that 100 dimmers would have only required 101 wires.

DIGITAL CONTROL

From the beginning of the 1980s digital control, using a pair of conductors was introduced, which had two distinct advantages:

(a) the amount of wiring was reduced because it was possible to feed all the dimmer racks with a coded signal down one wire, and the dimmers would decode the signal that only applied to them;
(b) secondly, soft patching became extremely easy and dimmers could be grouped very readily, usually in real time, without having the need to resort to the pin patch panels provided in the 1960s and 1970s.

Recent times have seen digital control signals transmitted by radio and infrared across an area where direct cabling would have been difficult.

Dimmers on bars

Other developments include small groups of dimmers being integrated into lighting hoists and suspension systems. However, if a group of dimmers have a common ac supply and a fault develops, the device protecting the main supply wiring to the dimmers could fail, thus losing not just one but several dimmers. The electrical installation must ensure that there is suffcient discrimination between the individual dimmer fuses or mcbs. There is little difference in weight between one heavy cable feeding three dimmers, or three smaller individual cables. It is important that dimmers mounted on the suspension system are audibly noise free. One very practical problem is that, when maintenance is required, how difficult is it to actually maintain the dimmers. Any dimmer should be capable of being removed, taken to a workshop and a replacement easily fitted.

Multiplex digital signal

There have been some interesting developments with dimmers. In the past, a signal went from the lighting console to the dimmer rack and only by observing the luminaires, together with hard wired indicator warning systems did the operator know the state of the studio or stage. Although in recent years, multiplex digital control signals to the dimmer room were employed, they still had to be decoded and converted to local dc control signals within the dimmer racks. Today, dimmers have been introduced where the digital signals are taken directly to the dimmer modules. This now allows much greater control of the individual dimmers. It is now possible to stabilize the output voltage of the dimmers to a high degree of accuracy, e.g. 196 V which represents setting '7' on a square law system. However, it should be noted that we still can't make up volts, when the input voltage of the system falls below the set levels we can only go to the input voltage level, e.g. if the dimmer has been set for an output voltage of 240 and the input voltage falls to 230, we will still only get 230 volts. From the console we can programme the dimmer laws with great ease, in addition to built in 'square', 'S' and 'linear' laws, it is also possible for the user to programme his own curves. Rather than having to remember that a certain keylight is Channel 123, it's possible to use a 5-character alphanumeric name. The dimmers are clever enough to report back to the operator various problems. These are *no load present; no output volts present; there is an excess of dc in the system; there is no control available and the units have exceeded their normal temperatures.* Whether or not we need this intelligence is for the operators of the systems themselves to decide. The inescapable fact however, is that it is extremely easy for the manufacturers to design very elaborate controls for the entire system.

8.1   Theory of dimmers

Resistance

A dimming device is one that reduces the flow of energy from a source to a destination and the source we are concerned with is electricity. The original control of the flow of electricity was by resistance which consisted of varying the length of iron wire introduced into circuits.

Salt pot dimmer

Another form of resistance dimming was by varying the distance between two electrodes in a saline solution. The dimmers themselves looked rather like large portions of underground glazed drainage pipe, containing a solution of salt water, with a fixed electrode within the cylinder and a movable electrode usually lowered in and out of the solution, by a wire or piece of rope. It is interesting to note that 'salt pot' dimmer installations were in use in London, at the Garrick Theatre until 1958 and the Savoy Theatre until 1960. The major disadvantage of resistance dimmers is the fact that the introduction of the additional resistance causes power to be wasted.

Auto transformer dimmer

In an attempt to reduce the power wasting situation and to also give better control of systems, Strand Electric, during the 1950s, introduced the auto transformer dimmer. Whereas a normal transformer has a primary winding and a secondary winding to transform the voltage across it, the auto transformer is generally made with one winding where part of the winding is common to the primary and secondary circuit. By varying a tapping point on the secondary side of the transformer we can vary the voltage applied to the load. Auto transformers have a lower resistance loss in their windings, and the efficiency is generally higher than in a transformer with two windings. A big advantage of the auto transformer dimmer is that it has a superb output law for the smooth control of any lights connected to it. The law of a dimmer is the relationship between the input setting and the light output from the luminaire.

Saturable reactor dimmer

Other than auto transformer dimmers, saturable reactor dimmers were used to control lighting systems. These worked by having an iron cored coil in series with the ac fed lamp. By applying dc control signals the saturation of the coil can be adjusted and hence the impedance to the flow of current to the lamp is also adjusted. The main disadvantage of saturable reactor dimmers was that they were extremely heavy, which had major implications in dimmer rooms and the biggest problem of all was that the law of the dimmer varied considerably according to the wattage of the luminaires supplied. One big advantage of a saturable reactor dimmer was that the small dc control signals could be supplied from a remote point. Both the resistance dimming systems and auto transformer systems generally depended upon complex mechanical drive arrangements being provided to achieve any form of control.

Thyristor

The greatest advance in lighting control came about during the mid 1960s with the introduction of the **thyristor** (silicon controlled rectifier, SCR). Because the thyristor is a uni-directional device, two have to be used for the control of ac supplies for lighting systems so that we control the positive and negative half cycles of the ac supply. A close cousin of the thyristor is the 'triac'. Whereas the thyristor is uni-directional, the triac is a bi-directional device, and by applying a signal to the gate, we can obtain full wave control of ac power. There are several advantages by using solid state devices such as the SCR and triac, the power loss is exceedingly small, they are very easily controlled and the most important of all, that they are independent of the load across them. In the 'good old days' it was not unknown to connect, for example, two 1kW luminaires across the output of a 2kW auto transformer dimmer – one, the real load and the other a dummy so that the dimmer output was fully loaded, thus ensuring the law of the dimmer. The major drawback to solid state switching devices is the fact that the period of time from its 'off' state to its 'on' state is extremely small, in fact of the order of microseconds,

Figure 8.1 Thyristor waveform
diagrams

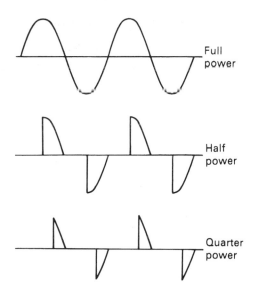

Full
power

Half
power

Quarter
power

and it is this switching cycle that gives problems in practice. All the
other types of dimmers that have been mentioned such as resistance,
auto-transformer and saturable reactor, work on the principle of
diminishing or increasing the sine wave with virtually no distortion.
The thyristor dimmer output, as can be seen from Figure 8.1, chops
the wave form into discrete quantities.

Controlling thyristors

The input control signal for a thyristor dimmer is varied at the
control console. The signal level reaching the dimmer is compared
internally on the dimmer control circuit and according to that
comparison, the dimmers are switched on at some time during the
positive and negative half cycles. Thyristors automatically switch off
when they pass through the zero point of the mains cycle; therefore
a signal has to be applied to the thyristors controlling the positive
and negative portions of the input mains every half cycle, to enable
them to conduct continuously. If for instance, we are working on a
linear system, and '5' on the fader literally means 50% power output
from the dimmer, the thyristors would conduct at the 90° point,
which is halfway between the start of the half cycle and the completion of the half cycle. Solid state devices such as the thyristor depend
on a flow of current to keep them activated, which is somewhat
similar to the action of the holding current in the coil of a magnetic
relay. Thyristors require a well defined minimum current to
maintain a conducting state. When the current drops below this
minimum level, which is known as the 'holding current', the thyristor will stop conduction and become effectively an open circuit. It is
therefore essential that a minimum current has to flow in the thyristor circuits so that they are stable. In the earlier days of thyristors,
it was felt practical that one short pulse applied at the nominated
switch on point in the half cycle would be sufficient to keep them
conducting for the remainder of the half cycle and in most practical
situations this was true. It was found in practice however, that

dimmers used for tungsten lighting became unstable with small resistive and inductive loads. Several methods were employed to overcome this problem, one of which was to keep a continual stream of pulses into the thyristor gate during the nominated conduction periods of the negative and positive half cycles, so that there was no tendency to switch off. Another method was by applying a switching signal which consisted of a constant dc signal to the thyristor gate during the nominated conduction period, so that during the half cycle there was always a voltage present to ensure that the thyristor fired for the selected period of time.

Cold inrush

When lamps switch on, the current flowing through a cold filament may be up to 15 times greater than the normal current. Thus a 5 kW studio Fresnel spotlight with a normal steady state current of around 21 A on a 240 V supply, would have a cold inrush current of anything up to 300 A. This obviously must have some effect on a thyristor being used as the dimmer. The main problem is that to cater for the short term high current, the thyristor has to be rated at a greater current level than would normally be expected.

Gate sensitivity

A problem associated with thyristors is that, as the output power of thyristors increases, the gate requires a higher current flow and to ensure high sensitivity of input for large current devices, a subsidiary thyristor may be used to fire the gate circuit. The reason for this is that the small primary thyristor will require a very low current at its gate to conduct and its output, which will be several times greater than the input current, will quite adequately fire a higher powered thyristor. Most of the discussion taking place here relates to the practice of using two 'back to back' thyristors, rather than any use of triacs, which only tend to be used in lower quality dimmers. In recent times, it has become possible to obtain solid state devices which incorporate the two thyristors and some of the associated firing circuitry, all in one encapsulated package.

8.2 Problems in practice

Since the inception of modern electronic dimmers using thyristors, etc., all manufacturers have been trying to solve the problem of the chopped waveform and the associated electromagnetic interference. Several ideas have emerged from manufacturers to reduce that interference to manageable levels, and recently devices other than the thyristor have been introduced as the power controllers. Unfortunately at the lower priced end of the dimmer market, the interference is only just contained to the general level set by the standards authority of the countries concerned, and is usually not good enough for professional installations where microphone cables and video cables are used. At the upper end of the market, manufacturers, at a cost, will make dimmers with very low interference levels from the point of view of audio and video circuits. The strict implementation of the EMC Directive by all manufacturers should ensure that dimmer interference is much lower in the future.

In practice, most thyristor dimmers are operated at about 80% of their full output and this is enough to guarantee that we will always have a rapidly rising current waveform which is the switch on point of the negative and positive half cycles. We hope our readers will appreciate, without going into complicated mathematics, that any waveform approaching a square wave is made up of a multiplicity of other waveforms, varying from waveforms at fairly low frequencies to those at extremely high frequencies and it is the generation of these high frequency waveforms that gives us the most problems.

Lamp sing

If we examine the effects of the lower frequency waveforms, we find that these can cause sympathetic vibrations to be set up in lamp filaments every half cycle and if these approach the resonance of the filament itself, we can have quite loud acoustic noises coming from the luminaires, which manifests itself in a high pitched buzzing, colloquially known as 'lamp sing'.

Dimmer chokes

It would seem on initial inspection that to get around the problem of the wave shape output of solid state dimmers is almost impossible. However, this is not the case in practice and a very simple trick can be employed. By introducing into the circuit a choke, which consists of a coil of wire wound on a fairly heavy iron core, the rise time of the leading edge of the waveform (the switch on point) is slowed down and if we effect a change from the normal two or three microseconds switch on time to around 500 microseconds, then we will have overcome most of the interference problems. More recent developments use controlled switching sequences for the power devices; thus instead of rapidly changing levels in a few microseconds a ramped switching is used to give much longer transitional period thus producing less interference.

Noise measurements

A method of measuring the amount of noise generated is required and the generally accepted standard for assessing interference from dimmers was that introduced by the BBC during the late 1960s which still holds true today. Various groups of people had experimented with measuring the amount of interference generated and the experiments included specific lengths of wire being laid adjacent to the dimmer power cables. Special coils were also used mounted adjacent to power carrying conductors, so to assess the electromagnetic radiation. One of the problems with these methods is that they are much too flexible and have too many variables, e.g. length of cables used, the position of the cables in relation to each other and how to equate the current flowing with the interference received. Before making any measurements or standards it was necessary to establish the levels of noise that would cause problems in practice. In general, within controlled studio conditions, very few problems occur with the vision circuits – only on the audio.

The basis for the measurements to avoid audio problems was as follows. On the assumption that when a microphone is working at –70 dB, its normal operating point, quite considerable amplification has to take place before the audio signal is processed. It was found at that time that sound desks had a signal to noise ratio of about 50 dB, so a figure in excess of this had to be aimed at to avoid deterioration in the quality of sound.

Star Quad cables

It is very easy to keep the dimmer power cables away from the audio and vision circuits in the permanent installation, but it is extremely difficult where many flexible cables are used. At the time these experiments were taking place, Star Quad microphone cable with very superior interference rejection properties came into use. This enabled quite reasonable levels of interference to be tolerated, and thus the dimmer manufacturers weren't presented with quite the problem they originally envisaged.

It should be noted that Star Quad cables have varied over the years, and the introduction of a thinner type of cable with lower rejection limits caused some concern during the early 1980s but does not seem to have proved to be a problem in practice.

To measure the interference accurately, it was decided that the best way would be to wire some form of measuring device into the circuit so that as many variables as possible were removed.

A solid state dimmer, which chops the waveform, when conducting at any level under maximum will generate on its output a string of interference pulses. These pulses are at a maximum amplitude when the dimmer is at 90° conduction. It was essential that the test circuit when placed into the power feeds disturbed these pulses as little as possible, so avoiding erroneous readings.

Ultimately the circuit as shown in Figure 8.2 was adopted as the most effective method of measuring the interference in dimmer circuits. Two main points have to be observed when making these measurements, and these are:

1. As any noise generated by a waveform is proportional to its energy content, a method of measuring the root mean square (rms) value has to be used.

Figure 8.2 Circuit diagram of dimmer test system

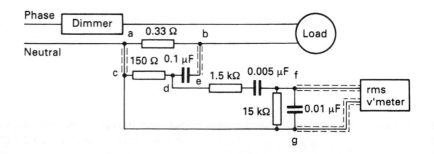

2.   As the test is to assess electrical interference which becomes audible, a method of weighting the reading to the ears' response has to be incorporated.

The measurement of rms is relatively straightforward as several test meters made by reputable manufacturers are available. Point 2 is covered by the circuit which electrically gives a similar response to the ear. Having decided upon a measuring technique, it was relatively easy to set the levels of permissible interference in the studio.

The measuring circuits have to be adequately encased within metal boxes so that external electric fields are minimized and no stray voltages are present on the meter readings. One other extremely important point is that the source impedance of the electrical supply to the test dimmer and load should be as low as possible because the interference readings may be artificially lowered on high impedance sources.

Having set up the test rig, the sequence to be followed is:

1.   Normal supply volts are applied to the dimmer.
2.   The control level and hence the 'switch on' point of the thyristors is varied to give a maximum reading on the meter, and this generally occurs at a firing angle of 90° with maximum rated load.

Test results

To meet acceptable levels, the rms meter readings must not exceed 15 millivolts rms for 2.5 kW, 3 kW or 5 kW dimmers, and must not exceed 30 millivolts rms for 6 kW and 10 kW dimmers.

The figures given are for the interference limits in 240 V dimmer circuits. Both 120 V and 240 V systems generate interference; the problem with 120 V supplies is that the current for any given wattage is double that of a 240 V system. As the interference is proportional to the amount of current this will mean taking extra precautions on 120 V installations.

Interference

If the power cables going from the dimmer room to any of the luminaires run very close to other cables, then electrical induction takes place, and the 'rubbish' voltage from the dimmers is transferred on to all other forms of wiring. This might not be so bad if the wiring is the normal mains system around the premises, but it is obviously extremely bad if it is the vision or audio circuits that are affected. Of course, one of the unfortunate side effects of using a large choke in the output is that the choke itself can cause acoustic interference, and dimmer rooms in this day and age can become quite noisy places, so much so that it causes problems in installation.

8.3   Dimmer types

Dimmers come in various shapes and sizes, the most popular being 2.5 kW, 3 kW, 5 kW, 6 kW and 10 kW. Smaller dimmers are avail-

Figure 8.3 Plug-in dimmer

able but these are generally used for the amateur stage and for small location lighting packs.

Dimmers are available in two distinct types; those which are 'wired in' and those which have 'plug in' dimmer modules (Figure 8.3). Wired in dimmers are usually permanently installed inside some form of container, be it a small portable crate or a reasonably large metal enclosure rather like a filing cabinet. The majority of dimmers in use are generally of the wired in type. Plug in dimmers are often used where failure of particular dimmer modules causes problems with regard to the progress of rehearsals, transmissions and any live performance.

Plug in dimmers

A plug in dimmer consists of a chassis, which these days may be metal or plastic, on which is mounted the control circuit, made as a removable pcb, the output power devices, which could be either individual thyristors or an integrated circuit power block. Filtering chokes are generally mounted on this chassis, although in some systems, the choke is mounted separately within the dimmer cabinet. When using plug in dimmers, it is important that some distinction is made electrically and/or mechanically in the inter-changeability of units within a dimmer rack. This is to avoid making the mistake of putting a low powered dimmer on a high powered source. One major problem that occurs with plug in dimmers is that of safety. It is obviously important when removing a dimmer module – which may be approximately the size of a shoe box – from a dimmer rack, that operator access to any live terminals is prevented, thus preventing any electrical shock hazards.

Wired in dimmers

This type of dimmer system is usually supplied with master printed circuit boards, with the control circuits on it for each of the individual dimmers. The power thyristors or integrated circuit power blocks are usually separate from the mother board. Although a dimmer

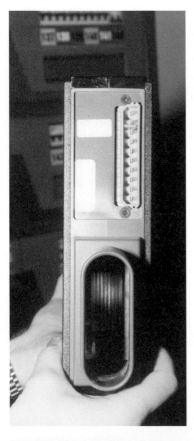

Figure 8.4 Plug-in dimmer connectors

Figure 8.5 Wired-in dimmers

rack may contain quite a large number of dimmers, it is important that the printed circuit boards control only small numbers of dimmers from the point of view of failure. One master control circuit board failing could be quite disastrous if it is controlling 30 or more dimmers. Control circuits that are common to about six dimmers are preferable.

High density wired in dimmers (Figure 8.5) are mounted in cabinets where access is only possible by the use of a key or tool to open the door so that safety is maintained. Small 6-way dimmer packs, which are very common in practice, usually have to be dismantled by removing screws and covers to gain access for maintenance.

DIMMER TECHNICAL PARAMETERS

Dimmer stability

To avoid fluctuations in the light output of the luminaires when controlled by dimmers, it is important that the dimmers are relatively independent of the input voltage variations. Most good quality dimmers made today are usually supplied with 'feed back loops' so that the dimmer output is maintained within certain limits (usually 10:1). However, it should be borne in mind that a dimmer only works from the nominated output mains voltage downwards. Unless supplied with special transformers and control circuitry, it is not practical to have a dimmer which boosts the output, e.g. if the dimmer is rated at 240 V output and the mains input is only 210 V it is impossible to make the output any higher than 210 V.

In practice dimmer loads vary considerably and any type of dimmer may be required to work with loads of small power (e.g. our old friend the 60W practical lamp). It is obviously essential that the dimmer should remain stable on such occasions and not go into any form of variation of output caused by say, internal oscillation. Dimmers are also somewhat abused by the operators and more than likely they will have isolating transformers plugged into them or many other inductive loads. On these occasions, it is essential that the dimmer does not lose its stability or for that matter, draw excessive current which might destroy the output thyristors.

DC component

If the output power thyristors or integrated circuit power pack does not have a balanced output, the imbalance will be seen as a small direct current component in the output. It is essential that this direct current is kept to an extremely low level so that it does not cause problems to any of the connected loads or for that matter on the mains supply to the dimmer room. The electricity supply authorities are not too happy with dc on their ac distribution system.

Interference suppression

All dimmers have to meet normal electromagnetic spectrum interference regulations in the country concerned. Additionally, the dimmers must reduce the high frequencies present in the output waveform which would cause problems with the sound and vision circuits in any installation. In Europe, on 1 January 1992, the EMC Directive came into force for the control of electromagnetic interference from all types of apparatus (see also Section 8.7).

Dimmer response

It is obviously important when controlling dimmers that the application of a control signal will produce a known response. In practice dimmers are required to respond instantly to any change of the control signal, the only limitation being the lag within the lamp filaments themselves.

A problem that exists with the larger light sources such as the 5kW and 10kW, is that of 'thermal shock', due to the large inrush currents. Modern digital techniques can vary the 'turn on' time to allow a build up of power over several cycles of the mains when the channel is switched to 'full' thus 'fading' the lamp up, although it appears to be 'instant'.

Control input

Until recently dimmers have always been controlled by analogue, dc control signals, e.g. the application of a small control voltage from 0–10 V dc will produce the changes within the dimmer itself. Several disadvantages exist with analogue control signals; first and foremost is that each dimmer has to have one input control wire, thus if a control system of 240 ways is driving 240 dimmers, 240 control wires would have to be used, together with one or more common wires. Today, the application of digital control signals to dimming systems has become the normal practice. Digital control inputs are generally decoded on special cards situated within the dimmer pack and the control signal is conveyed either by co-ax cables or twisted pairs. Thus all the dimmer control signals are fed down one cable, the usual limitation being the digital control system itself and this seems to settle at blocks of 512 channels, thus two cables are needed when we exceed this number of channels.

Dimmer law

A dimmer will obviously respond in some way to the control signal – that response will be dictated by the needs of the operators. It may be that a rapid fade up is required over the lower portion of the control channel with a slower progression over the upper portion of the control channel; or the operator required very little light change from the luminaire over the lower portion of the fader characteristic with a large variation when the channel is raised towards its maximum. Dimmers have been made with built in 'laws' to cater for various tastes in the entertainment industry for many years. However, in recent times, with the advent of more sophisticated control from modern lighting consoles, it is possible to use 'linear' dimmers where the law shaping is done by variations on the input control signals. With digital control, it is possible to set the 'law' of the dimmers precisely to the operator's requirements by adjusting the 'dimmer programme'.

Table 8.1 Square law dimmer control

Fader	Light Output %	CT (K)	%	Output volts 240	Output volts 120	Current %	Power %
10	100	3200	100	240	120	100	100
9	81	3120	93	224	112	96	89
8	64	3040	88	211	106	93	82
7	49	2960	81	194	97	88	72
6	36	2860	74	178	89	85	63
5	25	2750	66	158	79	78	52
4	16	2600	59	142	71	73	43
3	9	2400	51	122	61	67	34
2	4	2200	39	94	47	59	23
1	1	–	23	55	27	46	11
0	0	–	0	0	0	0	0

Square law dimming

The square of the fader setting gives the percentage light output, as shown in table 8.1, e.g. fader at '6' equals light output of 36%.

In practice if we fade on an American system at 120 V or a British system at 240 V, we see little or no difference to the operation of the lighting system. However, if we choose to do comparisons of the parameters concerned, it is important to remember that each volt of variation will produce a change of 10K degrees within a 120 volt dimming system, whereas at 240 V, each volt change produces a difference of 5K degrees. This is because of the relationship of Kelvin degrees to the current, and for the same wattage load a 120 V system will have twice the current of a 240 V system.

8.4　Fusing and sub-fusing

How do we protect our dimmers?

Fuse

The first thing that would come to mind is the good old fuse! The problem with fuses is that, believe it or not, they take a finite time to operate. If a solid state device is rated at say, 40 A, it quite happily carries a current of 40 A indefinitely, and over short periods of time, it will carry currents in excess of 40 A quite safely. However, a high current for long periods of time will be fatal for the device. The reason for failure of thyristors is that the semiconductor junctions within the device overheat and ultimately break down, thus if we overload the device well in excess of its normal current rating, for any period of time, we will destroy the thyristor. Therefore our first consideration when selecting a fuse is that it should adequately protect the thyristor circuitry. Additionally, the fuse must be capable of handling the cold current surge of the lamps without failing. Fuses operate extremely rapidly when a very high current is applied; or it might be a low current for a longer period of time. The time can be over the range from a few milliseconds to several thousands of seconds. It is therefore not possible to give the operating time for any specific fuse when the operating time is dependent on the value of the currents involved.

I^2t

Before we go any further it would perhaps be better to introduce a new friend and this is a term I^2t, which refers to the time/current characteristic and is a quantity consisting of the time period combined with the square of the instantaneous current passing through a fuse between the instant when the circuit fault commences and the instant of the fuse rupturing. I^2t is often described as the 'let through energy'. Both thyristor manufacturers and fuse manufacturers publish I^2t curves for their devices, and the manufacturers of dimmers simply have to compare these curves to select the correct type of fuse to protect the devices used. It is therefore essential to observe the manufacturer's choice of fuses for their equipment.

Thyristors and triacs will also be damaged if an over voltage is applied in the reverse direction to the normal current flow and in most cases will only tolerate twice the peak value of the steady state voltage.

Fuse rating

Fuses to protect thyristors and other solid state devices in dimmers should meet the requirements of IEC 269-4 and BS 88 part 4. Fuses for 2.5 kW, 240 V circuits usually are 10 A rating and those for 5 kW 240 V circuits are rated at 20 A. Any fuses used should be generally available and not specially made.

Practical lamps

One problem that can occur with dimmer installations is that a 5 kW dimmer may be used to feed a practical light on a set and this practical light may only be a 60 W lamp fed via some lighting flex. In this case, the 20 A fuse would be well over the approved rating for the flex feeding the individual lamp; therefore some form of sub-fusing must take place. This sub-fusing must be inserted at a point in the electric circuit so that it adequately protects the wiring concerned.

8.5   Dimmer rooms and switchgear

If we are designing from scratch, we can obviously make allowance for some area within an installation which would house the dimmers, their racks and the associated switchgear to control those racks. In practice however, any broom cupboard seems to be the solution to the dimmer room. What do we require from a well designed dimmer room?

Figure 8.6 Plug-in dimmer racks

First and foremost it is space. Secondly, the room has to be either self-ventilating or provided with proper means of ventilation. If we have a large area that can be used for the dimmers, it is possible to install dimmer racks containing a small number of dimmers per rack. As most areas allocated for dimmers are small, modern practice is to use high density racks, and these may be up to 192 dimmers per rack. The physical numbers in the rack does not necessarily create a problem, but the weight of the racks on the floor area does. The other possible source of concern is that by using one rack with many dimmers in it, controlled from only one piece of switchgear, any form of breakdown in the main supply would be quite disastrous on any transmissions, rehearsals or live performances. As a general rule, it is better to spread the eggs over more than one basket. Although this requires more pieces of switchgear, because each dimmer rack must be provided with a means of isolation, independent of all the other racks, it is obviously much more expedient from an operational point of view and also from a maintenance point of view.

Waste heat

Another snag that occurs with high density dimmer racks, is that all the output power cables going to the stage or studio area have to be terminated somewhere within the dimmer rack itself and the greater the density, usually the greater the problem of termination. If we allow for a waste heat generation of approximately 100 W per 5 kW of dimmer power, it can be appreciated that in a high density rack quite high heat loads are generated. Thus the dimmer racks usually have to be force cooled by fans mounted within the racks, and in fact in one installation seen by the authors in America, the degree of cooling required in a room with several high density racks was so great that it was difficult to close the dimmer room door against the gale!

Input phasing

Dimmer racks will be designed for either single phase input or three phase input and this could be either by cables or some form of busbars. The dimmer rack itself should preferably be no higher than 1.8 m so that access to the rack is feasible without the use of steps or with the operators having to over reach, which in itself is dangerous. It is obviously easier to make the control and power connections made when there is access from the front of the rack.

Rear access

If rear access is required, allowance must be made for additional space within a dimmer room as the rear access would no doubt have an opening door and a clearance of at least 600 mm must be provided. Many modern dimmer racks have front access only but the problem of front access is that all the input and output terminals must be accessible and this often involves the manufacturers in some conflicts of interests with regard to space within the rack. Where small dimmer racks such as 6-way packs are used, the problems are not so acute, although each of these racks would have to be provided with a small isolator adjacent to the racks for safety reasons. Dimmer racks have to be clearly marked because there will be several circuits within a rack, all with fuses or mcbs which must be clearly marked.

Indicators

The dimmer racks must also have indicators which show that power is supplied to the rack and each individual dimmer must have some form of indicator to show that it is live. It is important that any form of earth leakage should be detected, although this is not usually provided on small dimmer racks. It is preferable that some kind of overheat detection is supplied within larger racks and this can be for two purposes: to detect firstly the generation of fire, and secondly the generation of additional heat which may be caused by fan failure within the racks. Although not a large danger within the premises, it may be that the failure of the fans causes the individual dimmers to fail by becoming excessively hot subsequently causing the semiconductor devices to fail.

It goes without saying that all dimmer racks have to meet high electrical and mechanical safety standards. Any form of electrical apparatus built within a rack or chassis system has to meet the requirements of the country of manufacture and also the country in which it would be used.

Several years ago when one of the authors was working for a major British broadcasting organization, a problem occurred with safety in a studio. One of Britain's better loved lighting directors was leaning back on a microphone boom platform in a studio admiring his work, when at the same time he reached forward to adjust a Northlite from a well known equipment hire company. Unfortunately, the hired equipment had not been checked correctly and did not have an earth wire connected. At the same time a live wire had become dislodged and had touched the chassis of the offending piece of equipment, thus the luminaire had become live. The lighting director therefore received quite a severe shock between one arm adjusting the luminaire and the other arm resting on the microphone boom platform, which was connected to a very good earth. Fortunately, the resulting shock was not fatal. At that time, it was considered by the broadcasting organization concerned whether or not to introduce earth leakage circuit breakers on all forms of lighting equipment. Although this was ultimately done on distribution systems for outside broadcasts, it has not been adopted within studio premises.

Residual current device

On the surface it would seem a very good idea to employ a residual current device (RCD), formerly known as an earth leakage circuit breaker, with a very low sensitivity (30 mA/40 ms) on the output of each dimmer, which would ensure that any operator coming into contact with either of the live wires, i.e. the phase or the neutral, would be safe. Evidence exists that would indicate that any RCD must be carefully chosen so that it operates almost independently of the dimmer output voltage levels. A point to be watched is that RCD manufacturers don't necessarily endorse the use of their products when used with dimmed, chopped waveforms. To quote from a paper given by a member of Strand Lighting at a safety conference:

> finally there is a risk that increased use of RCDs may lead to complacency regarding the safe use of electricity. The use of RCDs is an additional safeguard and in no way forms a substitute for good electrical practice whether in the field of installation, operation or equipment maintenance.

Maintenance access

It is no good having a nice looking dimmer rack where, when faults occur, access for maintenance is a nightmare. It is particularly galling to any operator to find that to change the simplest of components requires minutes and sometimes hours removing screws, nuts, washers, panels, etc., often cutting one's hand in the process, accompanied by the usual quietly mouthed expletives. For ease of maintenance it is obviously essential to have good technical information which gives circuit diagrams, constructional details of the cabinets and a complete set of instructions of how to go about maintaining the equipment itself, and this must be totally unambiguous. Much modern equipment however, is quite sophisticated and any maintenance, other than first line, would probably have to be carried out by the manufacturer, but this usually entails extra expense when calling upon a service engineer from the manufacturer concerned.

8.6   Control systems

Historical

In the days of resistance and salt pot dimmers, control of lighting was slow and cumbersome. The cues were accomplished by the electricians on the stage or in the studio coupling sections of rope and levers and wires together to make several dimmers move in unison for effect and even to move one dimmer was a considerable task. The main problem being that the LD was not in control of the lighting system at all.

Eventually Strand Lighting introduced electrical controllers, driven from a rotating mechanical shaft system, that allowed the amount of current fed to the luminaires to be varied. The most famous of these were the auto transformer dimmers which were driven by an up/down clutching system driven by a variable speed shaft drive arrangement (see Fig. 8.7).

The system worked on the principle that when the fader lever on the console was adjusted it changed the electrical parameters of a 'Wheatstone bridge' circuit, thus engaging the appropriate up or down clutch to follow the direction of the fader lever. These systems were relatively slow in operation and produced good fades but not as swift as those accomplished today. These earlier systems generally were 'two pre-set' which allowed two states for each dimmer, according to which of the pre-set channel controllers were in use. The consoles were provided with master controls for over riding the pre-set states, so that fades could be accomplished with groups of lamps.

Figure 8.7 Shaft driven dimmers

One of the drawbacks with systems such as these, was the fact that there were no memory systems which memorized the on/off state of the channels – thus groups of channels could not be switched on and off at will. Strand Lighting came up with an ideal solution for the time by using the technology from the organ builders and pictures of old control boards which looked like the consoles of cinema organs. The system of memory was extremely simple inasmuch as a small flexible contact pin was allowed to engage in a movable bar with contacts arranged as small notches along the bar, thus offering low voltage control of the particular channel and upon selection of the appropriate notch bar, would bring into play the group of channels. As can be well imagined to have many memories meant that the system required a multiplicity of contact pins and several notch bars, thus this type of console was usually limited to about 40 memories on the red pre-set and 40 memories on the blue pre-set. It was not uncommon in the early days of memory systems that the operators had to re-plot major portions of the action to take advantage of the memory grouping facilities. One problem associated with memory control in those days was if you didn't release your foot at the correct moment off the 'pre-setter' pedal on the console, you were in great danger of having a random selection of pins in the notch bars which caused rather a lot of soul searching by the operator concerned.

One of the biggest steps forward was the introduction of solid state dimmers, which allowed voltage control of the dimmer directly from a console rather than control via the electromechanical system. These lighting consoles were hard wired systems where the voltage or current output of a fader was taken down one individual wire to control a dimmer, using a common return. As has already been noted, the saturable reactor system allowed direct control but unfortunately the memory systems were extremely primitive when using this system.

Thorn 'Q' file

Up to the late 1960s the majority of lighting control systems were based on a fader directly controlling a dimmer, be it a resistance, saturable reactor or auto transformer. In 1967, Tony Isaacs of Thorn Lighting devised a new type of control system, using logic circuits. These circuits were extremely crude compared with today's silicon chip devices and were constructed from germanium transistors, resistors and capacitors. The memory system was based on a ferrite bead matrix where a series of these beads carried the '0' and '1' magnetic information to give channel level and on/off instructions.

This console was capable of memorizing several levels from one channel. For the first time a control system worked by sequentially scanning each piece of channel control information, from a dedicated controller capable of controlling any channel number input from a numeric keyboard. Whereas systems before this relied upon the setting of a fader, the fader on the Thorn console could be used to set one channel level, which was stored and another channel selected and another level set. This also allowed a multiplicity of levels for any single channel. The faders were servo-coupled and always followed the selected channel level. The amount of group memories was limited purely by the fact that the ferrite bead matrix memories were expensive and difficult to construct. The original system comprised rather a neat control panel but tucked away in a little room adjacent were four bays of equipment. With the introduction of integrated circuits, the system reduced to two bays of equipment, but was very large when one looks at a system today where the actual electronics are no greater than those contained in a PC.

MMS console

The Thorn system had dedicated control panels and not long after its introduction Strand introduced the MMS (modular memory system) console, where individual components of a console could be blended to give different alternatives for the various customers. For instance, the theatre would require a different system to those requested by the BBC and other broadcasting users.

Changes between one lighting state and another can be incredibly complicated with variations of the speed of fade down or fade up of the lights all intermixed to provide a variety of effects, and all these can be programmed to be accomplished very quickly or very slowly. In the theatre, many changes are taken over a long period of time, whereas in television the changes are relatively quick. This is also the case with lighting for the pop world. Due to the advances in microprocessor design and the use of PCs, it is possible to make relatively cheap lighting systems with an incredible range of facilities. Modern memory systems now have to control the intensity and colour of the light, and additionally the position of the luminaire and all its beam pattern and shaping functions.

PC based console

Many consoles today are based on typical PC components such as the 486 and Pentium processors and these enable a lighting console to be fitted with the necessary hardware to cover all eventualities, and the software program in operation can be changed so that the desk operates in different ways. An important feature of consoles is that any operation should give a predictable result, therefore not confusing the operator. The ergonomics of design of the controls and their placement on a lighting console is extremely important; the physical size should be kept as small as possible so that one operator can get to all controls with relative ease. Due to the various operating philosophies adopted in different parts of the world, it is now possible for consoles to be programmed to take into account the customer preferences as to the way they wish the console to respond to their commands.

Network distribution

Even consoles have entered the magic world of 'the net'. By using network systems it is now possible to access the control signals from various points on the network. In the past, distributed signals around a production area probably involved several multiway cables, co-ax cables and various other types of cables to accommodate the data necessary to provide remote control and remote viewing of console outputs. By using a modern network system it is possible to use one high grade cable system with the necessary termination points fitted and all signals run through this system. Previously, a lighting director and possibly the assistant, would have to draw on a large-scale plan the lights that are required, the various gels that may be used and the positional data for all the luminaires. Having done all this preparation, it was then necessary to transfer all this information to the lighting console when in the production area.

Off-line programs

Today, by using off-line editor programs, which are capable of running on a fairly average PC, it is possible to prepare the production lighting and adjust all the necessary effects and balances, where this is possible, and to record them onto a disk which can then be used in the lighting console. Having recorded the necessary memories and any effects to be used, it is possible for them to be replayed in real-time on the PC and its associated VDU. It should be noted that the use of an editor does not necessarily give the positional information of the lights; this more than likely will still be prepared on a good old fashioned piece of paper.

Virtual lighting console

Some companies now produce Windows based programs which provide a virtual lighting console on a PC. To keep the screen information to manageable levels, it is possible to select on the VDU several different pages of pre-sets together with their master controls, e.g. channels 1–20, channels 21–40 etc. A drawback when using a 'mouse' is that you may be unable to independently move individual fader levels up and down at the same time. One advantage of this system is a small number of channels per page with the ability to change pages rapidly to gain access to other channels, although to simultaneously gain access to channels spread over several pages may be difficult and time consuming.

Console basic functions

Although many modern lighting consoles are rather daunting in appearance, they still have to provide the following basic functions.

1. To be able to set the channels and hence the dimmers anywhere from zero to full light output.
2. The ability to switch a channel on or off at any level of its fader setting.
3. To group channels together.
4. To mix either individual channels or groups of channels together.
5. The ability to over-ride channels by 'master' or 'group' faders and by master switching.
6. The ability to collect the channel information which would be its fader setting and/or its on/off condition; either as individual channels or in groups or combinations of groups and consequently store in some form of memory system.
7. To be able to rehearse complicated fade sequences involving groups of channels or memories in a timed sequence and subsequently record this information.
8. To be able to recall settings, change them and re-record the result.
9. To replay the information stored in memory either manually or automatically in a sequence to suit the action.

Lighting consoles come as three distinct varieties, the first being the manual system, where each channel is individually fed from a fader. The second system is that of an 'enhanced' manual system where several faders are employed together with a very simple memory control so that the channel settings can be memorized and replayed and some or all of the faders can be re-used for other purposes. The third type of system is the fully automated control system where channel selection is invariably by a keypad; there are

Figure 8.8 Manual control boards

only one or two channel faders employed and these may exist in the form of a wheel rather than the traditional lever. The control console will have a memory system where anything is possible, and effects systems are built in.

Manual control systems

Generally, in a manual system each channel is directly fed from a fader, thus a simple 60-way system uses 60 faders. If the system is two pre-set, this means that two faders are provided per channel with the ability using two pre-set master faders, to fade between either one of their preselected states, the highest of the selected states taking precedence when the two masters are fully on.

For example, channel X is set at '7' on the red pre-set and '5' on the green pre-set. With the red master 'up' and the green channel 'down', channel X is set to '7'; when the red master is 'down' and the green master is 'up', the channel is set at '5'. When the red master is at 'full', raising the green master to full will not change the state of the channel, as the red channel is the highest, the output will always be '7'. This gives simple twin-state (or pre-set) mixing. The state of each channel can be easily set on the lighting console and an over-riding master facility is available. For simple productions and the control of lighting of many types, this console is more than sufficient and generally is very fast in operation, as channels are very easily accessed. Most manual systems these days have a control where the cross fade is usually dipless, i.e. there is a small amount of electronic control which provides for a smooth fade progression between the two pre-sets.

Small installations will use consoles with 12, 24, 36 or 48 channels and these are usually fairly simple two preset manual consoles, with one channel fader dedicated to each dimmer. One of the drawbacks of manual systems is that you cannot have more than two states of each channel with two pre-set systems, because otherwise you have to reset the fader lever.

The next step up from a basic, manual console are those where a limited memory system is also available. The method of recording a lighting scene is usually to use a specified preset of channel faders to set the various levels and when the scene has been lit, the submaster is then memorized, and this then records the current lighting state, allowing the next scene to be set up using the same set of faders. Because of the enormous memory capability, it is now possible to set up several hundred cues which may be very subtle changes to the lighting states, but it enables the lighting designers and their assistants not to have to keep notes, as was the case in years gone by. The only thing needed now is an accurate cue sheet to ensure that the right lighting is selected at the right time during the production.

Automated control systems

We finally come to the all singing, all dancing, memory control systems that exist today (Fig. 8.9). Generally the system will have at least one or two channel controllers, each one of these having the ability to control any channel. It will also be quite possible that memories and groups may be introduced into the main system via the channel controller. Consoles of this type work on the principle that we select a channel on the controller, the level is set and is then stored away and we now move onto the next channel to be controlled. Thus systematically, one by one, we assign levels to the lights concerned, either on stage or in the studio. As the channels are switched on and the levels are set, we slowly build up the lighting within the scene. At the end of this period, it is possible, by using the memory system, to store all the channels at their various levels for future use. One advantage of this system that if the same lights are used for a further piece of action within the scene, the lighting director can set completely independent levels from those already memorized without ever considering the information stored away. The control system does it all for him. To replay the scenes that have been memorized, they are usually recalled from the memory system by the selection of the appropriate buttons and subsequently played back via the master controllers which enable either cuts or fades to progress. Memories may also be added or subtracted and multiple effects can be combined

Figure 8.9 TV memory control system

before being introduced into the lighting output. Additionally, consoles provide facilities for controlling automated luminaires.

Talking to most operators, we generally find that they prefer a fader per channel which gives instant access, particularly on live events. One big problem with us humans is that we like all the little frilly extras that exist on any pieces of equipment. One of the difficulties that exists with very sophisticated consoles is how fast can the operator respond when a problem occurs. Is it really necessary, or so it seems, for the operator to require a science degree to be able to understand and operate many modern lighting consoles?

There is a tendency by manufacturers, because of the competition within the industry, to provide every 'bell and whistle' possible within their control system, the main reason being that they do not want their product to look deficient in any way – quite often ending up with a console trying to be everything to everyone. There is a conflict of interests between the requirements of the television industry and those of the theatre industry and the 'pop' industry. It is very difficult to have a hybrid lighting console to bridge the gap, and invariably we end up with the horse so designed that it turns out to be a camel!

Advantages however, do exist with modern consoles, inasmuch that effects can be immediately accomplished, without much of a problem. Most modern consoles have integral soft patching systems, which allow the control of many dimmers usually via a smaller number of control channels. They also have the ability to shape the input control characteristic of the dimmers themselves, thus different shaped characteristics can be provided for lamps that respond rapidly when switched on, such as 1 kW profile spot luminaires, compared with the 5 kW and 10 kWs which have a much slower response time. It is now possible, within complicated fades, to tailor the curve of each individual light to gain a most harmonious result.

As an example of a 'state of the art' console, Plate 9 shows an Avolites Rolacue Pearl. This console although small in physical size, allows control of 512 channels, 60 channel faders, 450 memories and 15 active playbacks.

Channels can be allocated as highest takes precedence (HTP) or latest takes precedence (LTP). Using a personality system it is relatively straightforward to patch moving lights and colour changes. The console provides for:

- any channel to control multiple dimmers,
- individual response curves for each dimmer channel,
- patching of dimmer and colour changers by typing a DMX number.

It is possible to arrange the functions of automated luminaires so that they appear on certain faders in a defined sequence. The console is provided with a high resolution backlit LCD screen which shows:

- channel output in % and 0–255 steps,
- DMX 512 output levels,
- channel useage with instrument name (e.g. Superscan),
- patching information,
- preview of memories,
- preview of sequences and chases,
- chase speed and cross-fade settings,

- sequence information,
- fade progression, and
- and other items of information to help the operator.

All the console information is stored in solid state memory with memory retention of not less than five years (without mains power). The operating system is stored in flash memory which allows software upgrades to be loaded from the floppy disk. The floppy disk provides for 'saving' and 'loading' shows and provides a method of loading system software. The console also can run diagnostic tests on the various functions. In conjunction with the Pearl console, Avolites also provide a graphics tablet which is an interactive stage plan system (Plate 10).

This enables the LD to map out the stage and to 'focus' the luminaires as desired. Once set, lights can then be moved or tracked across the stage in real time by clicking on and moving a pen around the graphics tablet. The graphics tablet provides a full colour mixing control which allows rapid changes to be set for the colours of the light beams from the luminaires.

Interfaces

If we buy a console from a manufacturer together with that manufacturer's dimmers, no doubt they will nicely work together. However, this is not always the case when we would desire to buy dimmers from one source and a lighting console from another. It is absolutely essential that the console talks intelligently to the dimming system. In the days when systems used analogue dc control signals, this was more than likely possible, although over the years manufacturers all had their subtle variations, around a 10V dc theme. With the advent of digital control systems, it is important that the digital signal is recognized by the dimmer units and several different types of protocol have been used and been suggested by manufacturers, but no common standard seems to have been adopted for use throughout the lighting industry. It seems that manufacturers always 'do their own thing'.

Remote control

Although the lighting console is 'remote' from the dimmers in most installations, the term 'remote control' usually refers to additional methods of control other than the main console. Two types of remote control of dimmers are required. The first is a fairly simple type of remote control which generally consists of switching dimmers off and on only, which is used for rigging purposes by the electricians within the installation concerned. This might be a large panel mounted on the wall in a studio and often called 'an electricians panel' or it might be a small hand held controller. The BBC in one of their latest installations provide a 'mini console' adjacent to the studio winch control panel for use by the studio operatives.

The second, which is the LD's control, is required to be virtually an extension of a complete working console, thus enabling the LD to sit either in the stalls, or conveniently stand within the studio and plot his lights at first hand (see Fig. 8.11). Designers controls generally will give access to all the channels and memory system.

Figure 8.10 'Electricians' panel' and remote control

Backup systems

If the power input to the installation fails the dimmers will not work and of course we have lost the ability to control them. If, however, the main lighting console fails what would we expect to be able to do? In years gone by pin matrix systems were used, which allowed several channels to be control patched to master faders offering a fairly crude form of backup system in the event of the main console failing. The main problem was that it only permitted large numbers of channels to be grouped together and faded up and down, and was almost a return to the original control systems seen during the age of gas lighting for the theatre. Possibly the best form of backup system is where we virtually duplicate all the console facilities, and in fact, in some systems, this is actually done, although obviously at

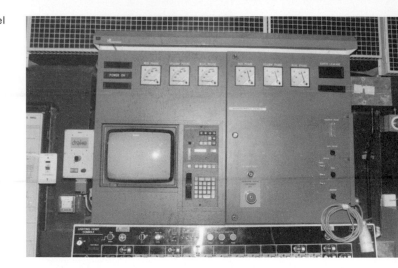

Figure 8.11 Remote control panel

some premium. The biggest loss of facilities is when the memory system itself fails, because of the reliance upon the memory system to store all the channel information. In general, backup systems are not really used with manual control and enhanced manual control systems, but are only used with the more sophisticated consoles. Obviously where a lever per channel is the operating method, the actual memory system is the fader itself. The most advanced backup systems in use today allow for a monitoring of the main system and recording constantly all the channel levels to update the system in event of failure. If the backup system allows for the selection of the memories together with some grouping and the ability to fade up and down from its master faders, then it is unlikely that the audience will notice any major differences.

DMX 512

DMX 512 is a world-wide standard signal which allows lighting consoles to send information to dimmers (Figure 8.12). The intensity level is sent as a digital code, using an 8-bit number with 8 bits providing 256 levels from zero to full intensity. In addition to controlling dimmers, it is also possible to control colour changers with DMX data sent to each unit. DMX signals are also used to control automated light sources and smoke machines. One DMX cable can transmit 512 individual levels, with each of these having a unique address number. Therefore, 512 addresses can control 512 dimmers. A motorized luminaire used for effect will probably have several attributes being controlled; if we use a channel of DMX for each attribute, we will obviously soon run out of control signals within DMX 512 control cable. Therefore a modern console will code the signals in such a way that one channel number in the system will be capable of controlling a number of individual attributes.

Typical attributes of an automated luminaire are as follows:

- intensity
- focus

- iris
- colour
- cyan dichroic
- magenta dichroic
- yellow dichroic
- gobo
- rotating gobo
- pan
- tilt
- speed
- reset

The MIDI system

MIDI (musical instrument digital interface) is a communications system by which a code is used to transmit and receive messages. MIDI was devised to connect electronic musical instruments together so that they can either be controlled from a central point or linked directly to each other. MIDI is now used in lighting control to execute remote fades, to control lighting effects and to synchronize the audio and lighting so they work together to enhance the production. If the lighting console is capable of receiving a MIDI signal, it can receive instructions and execute them in real time. For instance, it is possible that the MIDI system will instruct the lighting console to flash various lights at a nominated point in the programme timing. It is also possible to record the lighting cues via the MIDI system by running the sound tracks and the lighting console operator does his cues in real time, thus a parallel track is recorded, one for the music, or sound effects and the other for the lighting. On replay the MIDI system will output the necessary signals so that the sound and lighting is bi-synchronized. The MIDI system does have a limitation when it comes to controlling dimmers, caused by the fact that it can only record 128 different levels, whereas most

Figure 8.12 DMX connection system

modern consoles allow at least 256 levels. MIDI is extremely useful in its capability to link two small desks together to give a larger control system where one desk becomes a slave of the other and the master controls of one can control both desks at the same time. This is obviously a great advantage when say, there may be a 48 channel desk available and it requires expanding to a 72 channel system. In the past it would have been necessary to change to a 72 channel desk, which would have proved to be an expensive operation, but now the extra 24 channels can be provided by a small additional desk. If, by using MIDI, we can connect two consoles together it is also possible that the slave desk can copy the master desk and thus operates as a back up system. With the wider use of automated lighting units where there is a need to control intensity, colour, position and movement, as time is money, and rehearsals are often time consuming, it is more than likely that, these days, several operators will be used with several small consoles to set the lighting during the rehearsal sessions. Once the rehearsals are complete and the lighting cues finalized, they can be concentrated onto one master console and only one or two operators are required to operate the show.

8.7 Electromagnetic compatibility (EMC) Directive

If every piece of electrical apparatus in the world only used a sinusoidal waveform there would be no need for the EMC Directive. We are only too aware of the clicks generated by the refrigerator switching on and off affecting our radios; the buzzing noises from fluorescent chokes and the rather nasty noises which emanate from the loudspeaker if one takes a medium wave radio close to a PC. Although these manifestations of electromagnetic disturbance are annoying, they are not necessarily in themselves, dangerous. However, in a world that is now full of radio communications and telecommunications networks, it is important that any forms of interference do not affect the safe working of systems. For many years several standards have been applied in the United Kingdom for the reduction of radio disturbance from household electrical appliances, portable electric tools, fluorescent lamps and luminaires, broadcast receivers and associated equipment.

The EMC Directive seeks to ensure that any electrical/electronic equipment throughout Europe adopts certain standards to define the permissible electromagnetic disturbance levels that the equipment is liable to generate. The Directive is extremely important to the lighting industry mainly because of the dimmers we use, the consoles and the discharge lighting, all of which are quite complex electronic pieces of equipment and all capable of generating some form of electromagnetic interference. Additionally, mechanical equipment used in studios and on 'pop' rigs is also controlled by electronic systems and it would be dangerous if these control systems suffered interference in such a way as to affect its performance. It is obviously not practical to quote the entire contents of the Directive, but what follows are some of the highlights which should be understood by any practitioners in lighting systems and it is strongly recommended that any members of the lighting industry reads and fully understands the implications of the EMC Directive.

For the purposes of this Directive:

1. *'Apparatus' means all electrical and electronic appliances together with equipment and installations containing electrical and/or electronic components.*
2. *'Electromagnetic disturbance' means that any electromagnetic phenomenon which may degrade the performance of a device, unit of equipment or system. Any electromagnetic disturbance may be electromagnetic noise, an unwanted signal or a change in the propagation medium itself.*
3. *'Immunity' means the ability of a device, unit of equipment or system to perform without degradation of quality in the presence of an electromagnetic disturbance.*
4. *'electromagnetic compatibility' means the ability of a device, unit of equipment or system to function satisfactorily in its electromagnetic environment without introducing intolerable electromagnetic disturbances to anything in that environment.*

This Directive applies to:

'apparatus liable to cause electromagnetic disturbance or the performance of which is liable to be affected by such disturbance'

which is constructed so that:

a) *'the electromagnetic disturbance it generates does not exceed a level allowing radio and telecommunications equipment and other apparatus to operate as intended;*
b) *'the apparatus has an adequate level of intrinsic immunity of electromagnetic disturbance to enable it to operate as intended'*

Declaration of Conformity

'In the case of apparatus for which the manufacturer has applied the standards, the conformity of apparatus with this Directive shall be certified by an EC Declaration of Conformity, issued by the manufacturer or his authorized representative, established within the Community'

The Declaration of Conformity must contain the following:

a) *description of the apparatus to which it refers*
b) *reference to the specification under which conformity is declared and, where appropriate, to the national measures implemented to ensure the conformity of the apparatus with the provisions of the Directive*
c) *identification of the signatory empowered to bind the manufacturer or his authorised representative*
d) *where appropriate, reference to the EC type-examination issued by a notified body*

The CE conformity mark

'The manufacturer or his authorized representative shall also affix the CE mark to the apparatus or else to the packaging, instructions for use or guarantee certificate'.

The CE mark consists of the letters 'CE' and the figures of the year when the mark was affixed.

There is also a requirement for manufacturers to produce a technical construction file which describes the apparatus, and sets out the procedures used to ensure conformity of the apparatus with the necessary requirements.

9
Stage and studio technical design

Introduction

Historical

Before discussing modern installations, it is well worth glancing through the installation details of the Savoy Theatre in 1882 when Mr D'Oyly Carte revolutionized the illumination of entertainment.

> ... installation was entrusted to Messrs Siemens Brothers & Co., who appointed one of their electrical staff, Mr C Koppler, to carry out the work on their behalf. The theatre is lighted by no less than 1158 Swan lights of the improved form recently introduced by Mr CH Gimingham of the Swan Electric Light Company, who have adopted it as their most improved pattern. Of these 1158 electric lights, the auditorium is lighted by 114 lamps attached in groups of three, supported on very elegant three-fold brackets projecting from different tiers and balconies, each lamp being enclosed within a ground or opaloid shade, by which arrangement a most soft and pleasing light is produced.
>
> Two hundred and twenty lamps are employed for the illumination of the numerous dressing rooms, corridors and passages belonging to the theatre, while no less than 824 Swan lamps are employed for the lighting of the stage. The stage lights are distributed as follows:
>
> | | | | | | | | | |
> |---|---|---|---|---|---|---|---|---|
> | 6 rows of 100 lamps each above the stage | | | | | | | | 600 |
> | 1 " | " 60 | " | " | " | " | | | 60 |
> | 4 " | " 14 | " | " | fixed upright | | | | 56 |
> | 2 " | " 18 | " | " | above the stage | | | | 36 |
> | 5 " | " 10 | " | " | ground lights | | | | 50 |
> | 2 " | " 11 | " | " | above the stage | | | | 22 |
> | | | | | | | | | 824 |
>
> And in addition to the above-mentioned lights within the theatre, there are eight pilot lights within the engine-room, which serve the purpose of illuminating the machinery; and as they are in the same circuit

of the lights in the theatre, they indicate to the engineer in charge of the machines, by the changing of their illuminating power, when the lights on the stage are turned up or down.

The lamps are at present worked in parallel circuits in six groups, five of which comprise two hundred lamps each, and the fifth embraces one hundred and sixty-six lamps. The current of each group is produced by one of Messrs Siemens Brothers' W_1 alternate current machines, the field magnets of which are excited by a separate dynamo-electric machine of the Siemens type, known as D_7 and which is in general form similar to that shown. The machines and engines are fixed in a shed erected on a piece of waste land adjacent to the Victorian Embankment, the current being conveyed to the theatre by means of insulated cable laid beneath the soil.

The most interesting feature however, from a scientific point of view, of this most interesting installation is the method by which the lights in all parts of the establishment are under control, for any series of lights can in an instant be turned up to their full power or gradually lowered to a dull red heat as easily as if they were gas lamps, by the simple turning of a small handle. There are six of these regulating handles – corresponding to the number of the machines and circuits – arranged side by side against the wall of a little room or rather closet on the left of the stage, and each of these handles is a six-way switch which, by throwing into its corresponding magnet circuit greater or less resistance (increasing or decreasing it in six stages), the strength of the current passing through the lamps is lessened or increased by as many grades.

. . . we would also point out that it is part of the Swan system as is that of Mr Edison, to make use of little fusible safety shunts at various places in the circuits, so that if from any cause there occurs any liability for the conductors to become overheated the current is instantly interrupted. . .

Safety

The installation of lighting systems has a major impact on safety. It introduces large mechanical loads to structures. Heavyweight devices are hung over areas which may be populated by the public, artists or technicians. The lighting system introduces electricity to many areas and, particularly when this is on flexible leads feeding equipment, can be a source of danger. The majority of electrical wiring in areas concerned with the entertainment industry will be used for the lighting system and associated with it will be large power supplies. Most of the heat generated in the building will probably come from the lights being used. The electrical and mechanical systems installed can maim or even kill if we fool with them. Therefore, there is a necessity to install lighting systems as safely as is humanly possible.

Dimmers in luminaires

Generally, systems have luminaires in one place and the dimmers that control them in another. Over the years suggestions have been made for the controlling dimmer of a light source to be within the luminaire itself. In the case of the standard arrangement, all that is required from the dimmer to the luminaire, are two wires carrying the live and neutral or the positive and negative. In the case of motorized luminaires, signals in addition to the mains feeds have to be provided. If a luminaire is used with a dimmer mounted within its casing, the mains can be taken either from a radial supply system or from a ring main, but one has to remember that with a large number of luminaires, the ring main conductors become very large indeed, and the weight of the cables will be a problem. Conversely, dimmers traditionally are not the lightest of objects and we suspect that each luminaire would have a reasonable weight addition to its normal configuration. This would then mean the luminaires themselves are getting heavier, consequently they may impose additional loads on structures that are inadequate. By using dimmers within luminaires, a careful approach would have to be made to the protection of the wiring feeding these luminaires, either by the correct fusing or choice of mcbs.

Lighting systems for the theatre have to be integrated with the scenery flying system and there is also a fundamental requirement that from an aesthetic point of view, and for the comfort of the audience, lighting should be as unobtrusive as possible. The theatre hasn't really changed its method of lighting for many years, thus there is a recognizable pattern to the installation of lighting systems in the theatre and this is generally adhered to. This is not to say that the theatre is behind with new ideas, but most of these are in the types of luminaires used in the theatre. We therefore apologize, at this stage (if you'll pardon the pun), and state that this section of the book will mainly be about television studio installations.

May we make a plea to all architects and end users to contact a reliable lighting consultant before deciding on the shape and size of any place of entertainment. We have both experienced the problem of being called in at a late stage of construction and being presented with a *fait accompli*, having no regard for the technical requirements.

9.1   Project team

Before discussing the technical aspects of installing lighting systems we have to have a team of people who will be intimately involved with the planning and construction of such systems. Normally on large installations, a 'project team' would be formed consisting of senior key personnel. These would comprise the **architect** who will be responsible for the overall planning of the building installation and its associated services. The major concern will be the construction of a pleasing building or conversion of an existing building, together with the correct installation of any technical plant. The architect will be aided in his work by a **quantity surveyor,** who will cost the work and thus enable the architect to make decisions with regard to the budget. One of the main concerns of the architect will be the size of the structure required to support lighting systems together with the weights involved. To solve the structural problems that will arise, a **structural engineer** will work very closely with the architect, and it is their calculations that will decide the structure of the building. The lighting produces tremendous heat loads in a structure and obviously from the point of view of audience or artists' comfort, these loads have to be successfully dealt with. The person concerned with this aspect of the installation will be an **air conditioning engineer**. One of their main problems will be that to move the vast quantities of hot air requires large amounts of plant and these have to be housed somewhere in or on the building; the other problem is that the air conditioning itself can generate noise. This brings us to another valuable member of the team, the **acoustic engineer/architect** whose concern will be to ensure good acoustics for either the audience in the theatre or for the reception of sound in film and television studios. Major concerns here will be the shape of the building and the noise generated by equipment, such as air conditioning, etc., and how this can be adequately dealt with.

Finally, we have two people who will work extremely close together; one of these is the **lighting consultant or theatre consultant,** designing the lighting system and responsible for the technical aspects of lifting equipment such as the scenery flying systems, counterweight and motorized bars, cyclorama support systems, the dimmers and the provision of the luminaires. The other important member of this two person team will be the **electrical engineer** concerned with the installation. One of their prime functions will be to interpret the needs of the lighting consultant for the wiring, the lighting power sockets and the power supplies needed for the lighting in the building. In addition, the electrical engineer will be concerned with the electrical supply for the air conditioning system and the general lighting in the premises, together with normal power sockets around the building. They will also be concerned with fire detection and emergency lighting systems for either audience, technical staff or artists.

Items to be considered by the project team are as follows:

1. **Overall plan**
(a) What exactly is the requirement?
(b) Is it a new building or modifications to an existing premises?
(c) Is it a refurbishment?
(d) Is this the final scheme, or is any allowance to be made for future expansion or development?

2. **Building construction**
(a) Floor
(b) Walls
(c) Ceiling or roof structure
(d) Proscenium arch or open stage
(e) Access to working area
(f) Ancillary and control areas

3. **Studio/stage size**
(a) Length/depth
(b) Width
(c) Grid height
(d) Fly tower height
(e) Overall height

4. **Ventilation/air conditioning**
(a) Position in studio or on stage
(b) Capability
(c) Plant and ducting routes

5. **Power system**
(a) Method of supply, i.e. single or three phase, 'Star' or 'Delta'?
(b) Voltage and current capacity of incoming supply

6. **Lighting requirement**
TV/film studio
(a) Light levels required
(b) Saturated grid or minimum facilities
(c) Type of suspension
Stage
(a) Position of lighting bars in relation to the main stage area
(b) Position of 'front of house' luminaires

7. **Studio/stage requirements**
(a) Scenic suspension facilities
(b) Main lighting
(c) Effects lighting (cycs, projection systems and automated luminaires)
(d) Special facilities, e.g. remote control of lighting power

8. **Control and Dimming requirements**
(a) Type of lighting control console
(b) Location of lighting console
(c) Number of dimmers
(d) Location of dimmers
(e) Provision of power and switchgear for dimmers
(f) Provision of remote control consoles for scenic and lighting systems
(g) Switching of lighting in remote areas; or, remote control of the system from two or more points

9. **Special requirements**
(a) Orchestral pit
(b) Stage trap-doors and stage revolve system
(c) Provision for moving scenery
(d) Audience seating

10. **Provisions for safety**
(a) Smoke detectors/sprinklers
(b) Local authority requirements
(c) Users' requirements

9.2   Safety requirements

As the requirements of safety have become more onerous in the theatre, film and television industries with the introduction of the Health and Safety at Work Act and the Electricity at Work Act, these now have a major influence on the installation themselves. Therefore, it would probably be sensible to discuss this first, so that we can see how they influence the decisions ultimately made by the project team.

If we go back in the history of the theatre, which was the major area of entertainment for many years, we find that there have been several tragic accidents, and most of these were caused by fire. Fire in the entertainment industry, usually comes from the acting area itself. This is usually caused by the use of wooden scenery together with the close proximity of various types of light. In years gone by, naked flames were quite common, but in more recent times the use of small electronically driven candle effects has been introduced, thus reducing the amount the amount of naked flames in use. One shudders to think before the introduction of such devices, what the modern version of Phantom of the Opera would have looked like with all naked flames. On a stage, any fire usually within the area created by the proscenium arch and the rear of stage will funnel towards the fly tower itself, causing a *venturi* effect, which creates a powerful upward draught enhancing the heat generated.

If we have a standard stage, which has a proscenium arch, it is relatively easy to have a safety curtain to drop down at the front of the stage and this provides an immense barrier between the audience and the stage. Over the stage would be provided a water sprinkling system which would be activated by any heat over the normal design levels. Many modern theatres don't necessarily provide the standard proscenium arch, but they do have stages that protrude into the auditorium, and if this is the case, the safety standards on the stage area have to be much higher due to the close proximity of the public during a performance.

One of the problems in any premises with a fire, is that there is a tendency for people to panic in such conditions. It is relatively easy to train the permanent staff manning a building, and for that matter the artists concerned with the production, in the most safe way to exit from the area of work. It becomes much more difficult with the public because of the inability to train them in the direction of where to go safely when a fire breaks out. Thus, there is a need for clearly marked 'exits', correctly defined passageways for staff, artists and audience to evacuate a building. Although sprinkler systems are commonly used in the theatre due to the fact they can extinguish fires very effectively, they are somewhat of a hazard in the film and television industry as generally much more lighting will be involved together with a lot of technical equipment. There is obviously a need, if a fire breaks out, not to damage too much of the existing technical plant. To this end, smoke detectors and 'rate of temperature rise' detectors have been used in more recent years to warn the local staff of problems and these can also be coupled through via the telephone network to the local fire department.

With any planned development of any premises, either existing or proposed, it is most important to involve the local fire authority at an early stage so that they are consulted on what should take place within the building. Having discussed the general entertainment area itself, such as the stage or studio, there is also a requirement that all the adjacent areas have to be safe as well, such as dressing rooms, control rooms, dimmer rooms, etc. A good example of applied safety is that of a dimmer room which may have a door opening into the active area itself, will require another access door, generally at the opposite end of the room so that operators can evacuate away from areas of potential hazard. In film and television studios, there is a need to have defined fire lanes within the studio active area, so that people can exit safely from an area of great potential danger. Most modern television studios are built with a marked fire lane, which has to remain clear of any obstructions, around the perimeter. They also have to be equipped with a certain number of exits according to size. In television and film studios, acoustic barriers are often formed by having twin doors through a small lobby from the corridors adjacent to studios to the studio area itself. It is obviously important that these allow a safe exit. The various codes of practice which have to be adhered to and which will probably be the main concern of the architect, are laid down in British Standards and by various Acts published by Parliament in the British Isles.

Grid loading

An area of great concern for safety is the mechanical structure formed above the acting area. This will usually weigh several tonnes and will have pieces of moving machinery sitting on the structure itself. Thus, other than the static load of the weight of the equipment, we have the dynamic loads when the motors and lifting gear are operated, lifting scenery and luminaires from the acting area. Devices rigged to the mechanical structure such as the luminaires, pantographs, technical fittings of any description and scenery equipment all pose areas of potential danger. Almost on a par with the mechanical problems are the electrical problems. Although it is not very likely that an electrical socket will suddenly work free and fall to the studio floor in normal operation, it is possible that any malfunction of the electrical system may cause a fire. It is also important from the operators point of view that the electrical system is installed to all known regulations so that the highest safety standards are maintained.

9.3 Green field sites and refurbishment of existing premises

The architect is given a brief which may be that of a 'green field' site, which means building new premises from scratch, or the refurbishment of existing premises. In the first case, that of new premises, the architect obviously starts with a blank piece of paper and can incorporate many new ideas and suggestions. If, however, it is the refurbishment of existing premises, the architect is constrained by what can done within the building, the limits caused by the physical structure of the building and the loads that would be acceptable to that structure, how much space there is for the development or how can extra space be created within the development. Unfortunately, for the poor architect, every interested technical person has an input which usually conflicts with the rest of the team. For example, it might be that the lighting consultant, to meet the needs of the client, must make the area as large as possible, together with extremely high lighting and thus electrical loads, which will cause problems for the air conditioning and electrical engineers. With all these changes to the structure and shape, the poor acoustics specialist starts to worry about all the extra work that this is going to entail. The structural engineer, at this point, probably has eyes firmly fixed on the ceiling thinking of all the calculations to be made so that the architect will be convinced that the building won't fall down.

Having said this, of course, most project teams work extremely harmoniously and usually generate a good team spirit. It is more than obvious at this stage that a great deal of compromise will have to be reached on the installation itself. Thus, where do we start?

Design considerations

In an existing installation, the size of the studio or for that matter, stage area, will be fixed, and very seldom will it be changed. It might be that new mechanical devices are incorporated in the new installation or the electrical installation is changed, but generally the size and height of the area is fixed. This is probably a good thing from the architect's point of view because it places quite logical constraints on what can happen within the area chosen for development. It may be that the existing lighting grid structure remains unchanged, the only alterations being changing the luminaires supplied to the premises. If this is the case, the constraints already laid down by the lifting capacity of the equipment installed will dictate the type of luminaires purchased. If however, some of the facilities are to be changed so that greater lifting capacity can be used, this will have a knock on effect on the structural engineers' calculations, due to the devices imposing greater loads on the structure. It is quite conceivable that although the weight of the equipment doesn't increase, the power required for the equipment is higher, thus the electrical engineer will have to update the power system and the ventilation engineer will probably have a potential problem with the existing air conditioning plant. The room used to house the dimmers, if such a room exists, which was probably quite adequate, possibly now becomes inadequate by an increase in the number of dimmers required. All of this presupposes that the lighting consultant can actually do what he wants. Unfortunately, in any modern system, we also have to handle scenery. Therefore this places constraints on the disposition of lighting bars in a system and it also dictates the spacing between lighting bars or trackways. The size of the luminaires involved will also dictate spacing in the grid.

A modern controversy that reigns quite a lot these days, is where do we put control rooms? In the theatre, control rooms with a window having a clear view of the stage are obviously desired for those staff operating sound systems and the lighting control console. In television there is not an overwhelming need to see in the studio as the pictures from the cameras will tell the operating staff what is happening. There is however, a need for rapid access for the LD and people concerned with the production from the control rooms to the studio and to this end, many studios built today have control rooms at floor level. In the theatre, and for that matter film or television, a walkover grid is highly desirable for the ease of suspending items of equipment from the grid itself.

One of the major problems of walkover grids is the building is required to be higher, or in a fixed building, the proposed grid is forced to be lower. In an existing building, the walls may not be capable of taking additional loads and any new equipment installed would require either building alterations to the walls themselves so that the loads become spread or that structures are used that use the floor area as support. If we are building from scratch on a green field site, most of the problems can be taken care of, hopefully with the ingenuity of the architect and the structural engineer. The main requirement in a green field site would be that of the acting area and its associated facilities. There is always a need for large theatre stages, but common-sense has to prevail and generally the architect, having been briefed by the client as to what the requirements are, has to work within the budget to meet the planned objectives.

Film studios

If we were building from scratch in the film industry, which at this point in time is extremely doubtful, generally we would be building studios with very large acting areas, e.g. around 1500 to 3000 m². In the film industry, the feeling generally is that a small production can fit into a large studio area but not the other way around. This might appear to be the case for the TV industry as well, but because the studios have defined purposes, such as small news areas, small presentation areas, medium sized news and current affairs studios or large multi-purpose production studios, there are finite limits to areas required. Most of these are established by custom and practice within the industry itself. Another aspect of film studios is that they are not, generally, permanently equipped with lighting equipment but are usually provided with a fairly basic lighting grid and power supply system.

TV studios

Television studios are generally integrated into production centres, which may vary from fairly small to very large, such as the BBC Television Centre in London. By integrating a series of box like structures into a building, the design of the building is greatly influenced. In television there is a need for many adjacent areas to a studio such as make up and wardrobe areas, dimmer room, production, lighting, vision and sound control rooms. The disposition of all these areas has a bearing on access ways and vantage points to the studio. In the theatre there is not the need for so many technical rooms as the production is controlled from the stage area. Most of the support areas have to be close to the stage so that artists are provided with good access to dressing rooms and quick change areas. A requirement of theatre productions is to have complex mechanical stage lifting arrangements, possibly integrated with orchestral facilities. All of these will have to be considered by the architect so as to integrate the whole system to a meaningful production area and the following sections give the various parameters that have to be observed so that the various requirements of the building are met.

9.4 Building construction and how it can be influenced

Fly tower

In the theatre the height of the grid which will be used for both scenery and lighting, will be dictated by the height of the fly tower. Fly towers are used to take scenery from the stage to a safe parking space above the stage area. The height of the fly tower is generally dictated by the audience's sight line from the front seats of the auditorium; thus when the scenery is suspended it should be out of

Figure 9.1 Audience sight lines

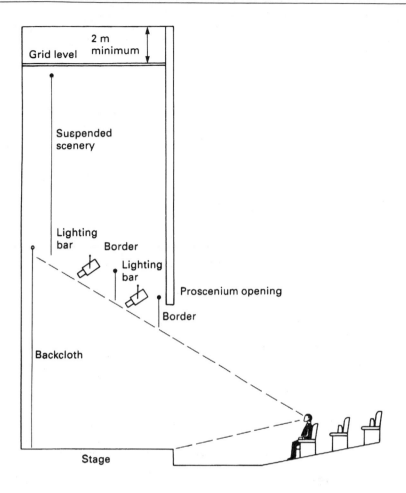

sight and not obstructive to the audience viewing. As a general guide the height of the grid is between two and a half and three times the height of the proscenium opening.

Theatre bars

A practical spacing for the counterweighted barrels used in theatres is around 200–250 mm. This is generally dictated by the requirements for flying cloths and scenery. As counterweight bars may be used for both scenery or for lighting, it should be noted that there are practical limitations to the distance between the suspension lines used on the bars themselves. For lightly loaded bars it might be possible to get away with a span of four metres between suspension points but with heavier loaded bars, several lines have to be attached to each bar and these would be at around three metre intervals. Unfortunately, although several suspension lines may be used, if heavy point loads are applied to a bar this will cause distortion, and it is preferable to use bars formed as trusses in these circumstances. Several forms of power assistance have been used on counterweight bars in the theatre but in general bars are manually operated. Due to the beam spread of the lights usually used above the stage, it is

Figure 9.2 Positioning stage
luminaires

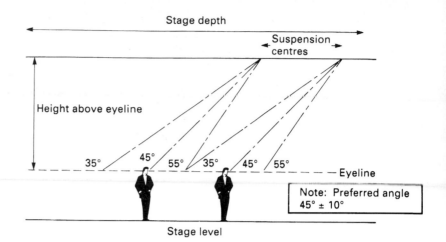

possible by using a drawing showing the side elevation, to calculate the coverage of the lights on the stage itself (Figure 9.2). This will then dictate the position and rows of units required to effectively light the whole stage area. If this is the case, it might be that some of the bars could be motor driven and these would be extremely useful for the lighting units themselves.

In addition to the lights above the stage, the front of house lights also have to be considered and the best solution for this type of lighting is to use lighting bridges across the auditorium which hopefully will be concealed but sometimes can be in view of the audience without being too distracting, due to their height above the paying customers. Wall slots for lighting positions will have to be provided in the sides of the auditorium but generally in existing theatres it is often necessary to rig some vertical scaffolding bars to suspend the lighting units. These luminaires at the sides of the stage can be fairly low in height and thus provide nice low frontal key lights from the sides of the stage.

In all the cases discussed, we must have access to the lighting units, so that they can be focused, pointed in the right direction, have their colour filters changed and at times be maintained. It is generally impossible to provide access to reach the bar units above the stage area. Thus most of the lighting will be adjusted either with bars at low level or with the aid of mobile platforms so that the electricians can adjust the units in situ. This is a case where pole operation will probably be justified on the grounds of speed of adjustments during rehearsals. As the front of house luminaires are rigged from a lighting bridge over the auditorium it will be easy for the electricians to reach these units. Luminaires at the side of the auditorium pointing towards the stage also require access and in new installations, this is usually possible to achieve by having one or two access platforms at reasonable heights. In existing premises, where the equivalent of temporary scaffolding has to be rigged, it is probably a climbing job for the electricians to do most of the adjustments.

Grid clearance

Where access is required, such as in the grid, and from any of the lighting bridges, sufficient head room has to be allowed so that space is given for safe operation from the electrician's point of view. In general, a head clearance height of 2.5 m tends to be reasonably sufficient.

To sum up then, in the theatre the lighting is usually an adjunct in the design to the scenery system itself. The requirements for power, dimmers and luminaires is somewhat similar to all other systems. In general, highly specialized architects work on theatre design and have many years of experience in this field. Thus, they are aware of many of the pitfalls of modern stage design.

Cyc height

If we turn now to the construction of film and television studios, the decisions are somewhat dictated by the needs of the set designer and not by the needs of the audience as in the theatre. Generally, in the case of the film industry, 'big is beautiful'. Large scale studios often have wide vista shots taking place, which dictate the height of any cycloramas used. A studio 32 m long will require cycs at least 9.5m high and probably higher. If we allow a clearance above the cyc sight line so that luminaires do not intrude, we additionally need at least a 1.5 m clearance from the top of the cycs to the grid. If, for instance, boats are used in the studio, then even more clearance is required above the cyc line and this would imply an extra 2.5 m, thus allowing operators to work at this level without hitting their heads on the grid structure.

Access

Film studios are not traditionally equipped with walkover grids, but they do require access at high level, even if its only walkways to allow access for rigging and de-rigging of the block and tackle units to suspend lines for scenery and luminaires. There is obviously also a need to reach the electrical distribution system at this level where luminaires are being used or power feeds have been dropped from the grid down to lights which may be suspended on block and tackle or some other lifting device.

Boats

Attempts have been made in the past to provide some form of mechanized system similar to those used in the television industry. The most famous of these was the installation of a monopole system in two studios at Pinewood in England. The BBC also experimented with the use of motorized barrels at its facility at the old Ealing film studios in London. For most of the time however, the film industry is content to continue lighting in the same way that has been practised lighting for many years. Thus the prime requirements of the film studio are suspensions trackways at fairly frequent intervals down a studio so that lifting equipment or 'boats' may be attached where and when desired. Due to the sheer physical size and subsequent weight of the luminaires used in the film industry over many years, the grid structures have had to be reasonably robust to take the weights of the equipment. However, it should be borne in mind that saturated lighting with its well distributed weight load, is not used in the film industry. One of their main requirements is high point loadings caused by several large high intensity luminaires or a 'boat' with luminaires attached, in one small area of the grid structure.

Power systems

With the construction, if desired, of a new film studio, it might be that we would have to integrate its use for either film or video shooting. Much of the economy of the film industry these days is based upon the shooting of pop videos and commercials for television. Film studios are fairly simple in their nature being rather large 'box-like' structures immune to outside noise if designed as sound stages, and constructed in such a way that almost any production can be fitted in them with the provision of high cycloramas. The actual lighting arrangements are extremely basic. The film industry occasionally uses dimmer units for some control on productions. The one big advance that has helped in the film studio is the introduction of discharge lighting taking away the need for the large carbon arcs. These units, with their highly efficient output require much less power from the electrical system. Talking about power in systems, reminds us that some film stages may still have dc voltage feeders, although in most cases these are being converted to ac systems. Generally there is no need to provide permanent dimmer rooms adjacent to film studios, although if new studios did evolve for dual purpose film/vision systems, then a provision should be made so that fairly large dimmer installations could be added at a later date in the studio's life. The general requirement in film studios is for large power distribution cabinets, placed at regular intervals around the studio from which can be taken all the temporary feeds to the lighting units themselves. Whereas in TV studios highly sophisticated air conditioning systems are used, the film industry is still fairly basic in its requirements. Due to the nature of filming, which may be a rehearsal period and then a 'take' with long extended intervals between, it is easy to allow the premises to cool over periods of time. It must be said, however, that in modern television studios the use of rehearse/record techniques using a few sets at a time diminishes the requirement for the large air conditioning systems at present employed.

Refurbishing existing studios

Due to the need to contain costs within the television industry, it is strongly suspected that other than refurbishing existing studios, very few new studios will now be constructed, in either Europe or America. What may be required is the conversion of some premises for studio use and this is highlighted by the case of the Greenwood Theatre in London, converted from a theatre for use as a multi-purpose television studio in 1979 by the BBC. It is interesting to examine this installation to see some of the problems that arise during the conversion process.

GREENWOOD THEATRE

The Greenwood Theatre, when acquired for use by the BBC was some four years old, therefore all its facilities were very modern and

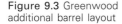

Figure 9.3 Greenwood additional barrel layout

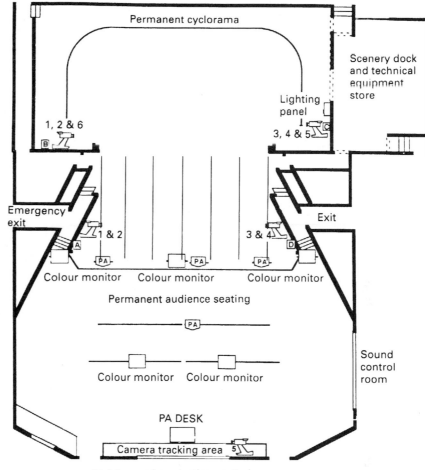

the basic structure was very good. The stage area was reasonably generous and it had a section of the stage capable of being raised and lowered on jacks, thus allowing part of the stage to be converted for use as an orchestral pit. To maximize its use for television the stage was extended by removing some of the audience seating. This stage extension was built from wood and had to be capable of taking loads up to 488 kg/m² (100 lbs/ft²). Thus it was possible for cameras and sets to be on the audience side of the proscenium, which transgressed the normal fire curtain arrangements.

Other than the stage area to the rear of the proscenium opening, there was now a requirement to light 'television style' over the extension to the stage and also above the audience itself. The requirement over the stage extension was met by providing seven additional bars, each 7m long and spaced at approximately 1.7m intervals; the bars were arranged for coverage from front to back of the theatre and not across the area. Four bars were installed above the audience, each approximately 6m long to give frontal coverage to the stage and these were installed across the auditorium. The weight of the new bars didn't pose any problems with the structure itself being a very modern installation.

Two major problems emerged from the conversion of the Greenwood Theatre for television use and these were concerned with the provision of heavier television luminaires, using the existing counterweight bars, above the stage area as opposed to the normal fairly lightweight luminaires of less power used by the theatre industry. As the theatre was going to be used for three standard productions per week it was relatively easy to come up with standard lighting plots to cover these and thus choose the luminaires necessary for illumination. The final choice was to use 2.5/5kW Fresnel luminaires of fairly lightweight construction, together with standard 2.5/5kW soft lights. To make life easier on a day to day basis, and owing to the fact that the installation was possibly only for a period of two years, it was decided to wire the supply to all the bars in flexible cables, with free socket outlets at the end of each power feed. The majority of wiring was to provide 5kW circuits although a few 10kW circuits were used.

Bar loading

So that the lighting rig could be serviced relatively easily by electricians from tall step ladders on the stage itself, all the cables were fed from the fly gallery across to the bars on loops of cable so that they could be raised and lowered without having to disconnect any of the wiring, similar in principle to the 'tripe' cabling used in theatres. The wiring being taken along the bars and dropped off at regular intervals to suit the disposition of the luminaires. The problem arose when calculations revealed that the weight of the cables attached to the bars, plus the weight of the TV luminaires, would exceed the existing fly bar Safe Working Load. To reduce the load per bar, it was decided to operate pairs of bars for the lighting system so that one bar had all the luminaires fitted and its adjacent bar carried the cables, thus the load was fairly well spread. To avoid any errors in operation, the two bars were tethered together by wire bonds. The counterweight buckets were also incapable of taking any more standard cast iron weights to enable these lighting bars to be balanced easily, therefore special lead weights were manufactured and introduced onto the buckets to enable balance to be achieved.

The theatre had 30 fly bars installed and of these eight were used for luminaires and cables. Three twin barrels were used for the main lighting over the stage. Additionally, two single barrels less densely loaded, were used at the rear of the stage for back lights and effects. One bar was used for the house tabs and 11 other bars were used for either drapes or scenery to be used on the three productions in the theatre.

Heat loads

Having surmounted the loading problems on the bars, it appeared that there might be a problem with the heat generated by the new luminaires over the stage area and going into the fly tower, where a sprinkler system was installed. Experiments took place over many hours with maximum lighting load (we might add with the sprinkler system drained down!) to ascertain whether the sprinkler heads would rupture and thus cause a problem in practice. Luckily the experiments proved that the existing sprinkler system was capable of handling the

200 kW of lighting over the stage area. The original theatre dimmers were installed at the side of the theatre with electrical feeds going to the stage area, but due to the need for heavier cables and the consequent cost, it was felt that the television system should have its dimmers nearer the grid so that the cables had a shorter route and consequently 120 dimmers were installed on the fly gallery on the opposite side to the counterweight system. These dimmers, in low density racks of 20 to reduce floor weight loading, unfortunately caused problems as the fans forcing air through the dimmers created acoustic noise which was picked up by the microphones on stage. As the dimmers were contained in racks with a lot of space, it was felt that the solid state devices in them could run at slightly higher temperatures than normal. Thus, the fuses for the fan units were removed and over several days experiments took place to ascertain the temperature of the dimmers. Luckily, they performed satisfactorily with no problems and worked satisfactorily over several years. This may be a case for lower density dimmer racks on some occasions. Please note!

The Greenwood Theatre was converted for a forecast period of two years' temporary use to ease the BBC's studio usage at that time, and although not now owned by the BBC, the premises are still in use today.

Let us now turn our attention to the design of lighting systems for television studios and how those designs will influence the building construction. Large television studios generally use a complex grid which in itself poses installation problems but prior to that is the need to ascertain the height of the grid and clearance above for services and personnel. There have been cases over the years where the management and accountants were convinced by the arguments put forward by architects saying that for each 300 mm of additional height in a studio enormous additional costs were incurred. Thus certain studios were limited in height, only to find the programme makers were forever complaining about the limitations imposed in these studios. As a starting point it is extremely important to get the height of the studio correct and the following system gives the method of calculation. It is relatively easy to decide upon the acting area that is required and consequently the floor dimensions. However, an important parameter that can only be ascertained by examination of the camera viewing angles is that of the cyc height and its subsequent effect on wide shots in a studio.

CYCLORAMA DESIGN

In small studios, more than likely, the cyclorama track and hence the cloth hanging from it will be relatively close to some of the walls, the only space required behind is for the odd low level lighting outlet box with space to plug in sources without impeding on the cyc cloth itself. In larger studios it is normal to have a walkway behind the cycs where space is not so critical from the point of view of the cable outlet boxes. When designing lighting for a cyclorama, the question is often asked, is top or bottom cyc lighting the best? The answer is, neither; it depends what type of result is required. One of the main essentials is to have good coving arrangements at the base of the cyc to get a blend between the horizontal and vertical so that there appears to be one continuous surface from the camera's viewpoint.

Top cyc lighting

Top cyc lighting, which is plotted at 3.1 m away from the cyc at 2.5m intervals, will give very good results from a height of 10 m down to floor level. However, bearing in mind that the light is striking the cyc cloth at a very acute angle, and striking the floor almost straight on, gives differentials between the base of the cyc and the floor which are very difficult to overcome. The great advantage of top cyc lighting is that no floor space is required, and indeed, in small news and current affairs studios, almost essential to prevent problems with space in the studio.

Bottom cyc lighting

Bottom cyc lighting, which is generally used 1 m away from the base of the cyc, with each individual source of light at 1.2 m intervals, can give a very even horizontal wash on the cyc but gives a very bright horizon effect at the base of the cyc and fades off rather rapidly in the vertical. If the units are taken out into the studio by the same amount as top units, i.e. about 3 m then we could generally expect a much more even result but as is obvious, this is not practical and it may be that the bright horizon effect is quite desirable. However, it is essential with ground row units that they are hidden in some way unless the units themselves are not too unattractive to appear in shot. Two methods of hiding ground row units are used, one of which is to have a short cove around the studio on the inside surface between the cyc units and the acting area. The other is to place the ground row units in a well which runs parallel to the base of the cyc, which can be very effective in long shot, but unfortunately when cameras are used off centre, can pose a problem inasmuch that the well itself may become noticeable.

Cyclorama heights

Camera viewing aspect ratio = 4:3. Assume a 36° lens angle is used this gives a vertical angle of 27° (Figure 9.4).

Note: By knowing the aspect ratio and horizontal angle of view, the vertical angle can always be derived.

Assume a lens height of 1.8 m above floor level. Cyclorama height = (L × tan 13.5°) + 1.8 m (where L is the length of the studio). Cyclorama heights (in metres) for studios with varying maximum lengths (in metres) are shown in Table 9.1.

Figure 9.4 Cyclorama heights

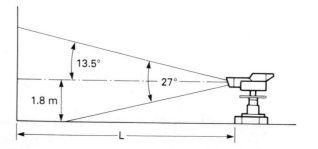

Table 9.1

Studio length	Cyclorama height	Studio length	Cyclorama height
6	3.2	20	6.6
8	3.7	22	7.1
10	4.2	24	7.6
12	4.7	26	8.0
14	5.2	28	8.5
16	5.6	30	9.0
18	6.1	32	9.5

As an example to see how the studio height has been influenced by the choice of the cyclorama height the following example is given:

Studio dimensions	= 30 m × 24 m
Cyclorama height for 30 m	= 9 m
Height allowance above the top of the cyc for luminaires and pantographs from the suspension system	= 2 m
Therefore the grid height	= 11 m
Allowance above the grid for maintenance	= 2.5 m
Allowance for air conditioning and services above the grid maintenance area	= 2.5 m
Total studio height	= 11 + 2.5 + 2.5 = 16 m

The example quoted is for a conventional studio with a barrel grid. The figures still hold for monopole grids, but if no access is required above the grid, or ventilation is provided such that access is not impeded, then the total height could be reduced. In the smaller studios little or no access is required at high level, the only space requirements generally are for the air conditioning equipment and electrical services.

9.5 Structural loads

MONOPOLE INSTALLATIONS

Monopole grids consist of continuous longitudinal trackways at very regular intervals usually engineered from steel, because they will wear so much better than lighter weight materials such as aluminium. At right angles to the main trackways, again at regular intervals, are the changeover tracks to enable monopoles to be wheeled from one track to another.

The method of construction of a monopole grid is to have a series of oblong platforms, made from steel with aluminium decking infill, individually suspended from the under side of the primary steels which will generally be used to support the roof of the studio. The long sides of the platforms form the main trackways and the short sides are the cross over tracks. The slots provided in the grid for the monopoles are conventionally 63.5 mm (2.5 inches) wide.

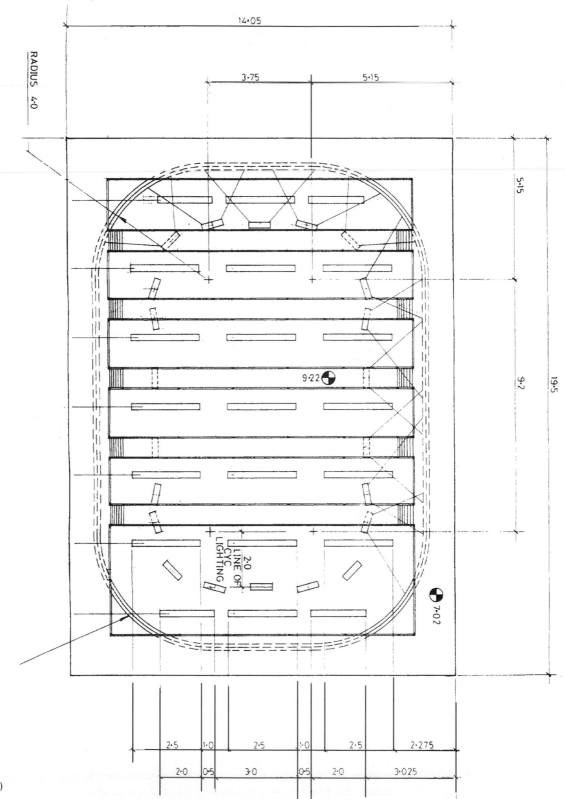

(a)

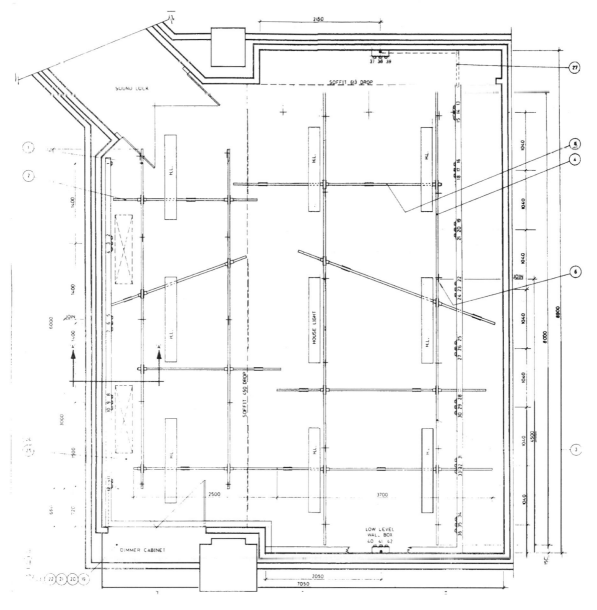

(b)

Figure 9.5 Typical studio layouts: (a) motorized barrels; (b) roller barrels; (c) fixed barrel grid

Mechanical loads

In the monopole system the mechanical loads on the structure can move around the grid; in comparison, a barrel grid, because of the design of the system, spreads the structural load fairly evenly. If we take as an example a monopole capable of lifting 60 kg, it will have a self weight of approximately the same amount, thus its total overall weight will be 120 kg. Therefore the point loading on the grid is 120 kg every time one of these units is used. The next problem arises

(c)

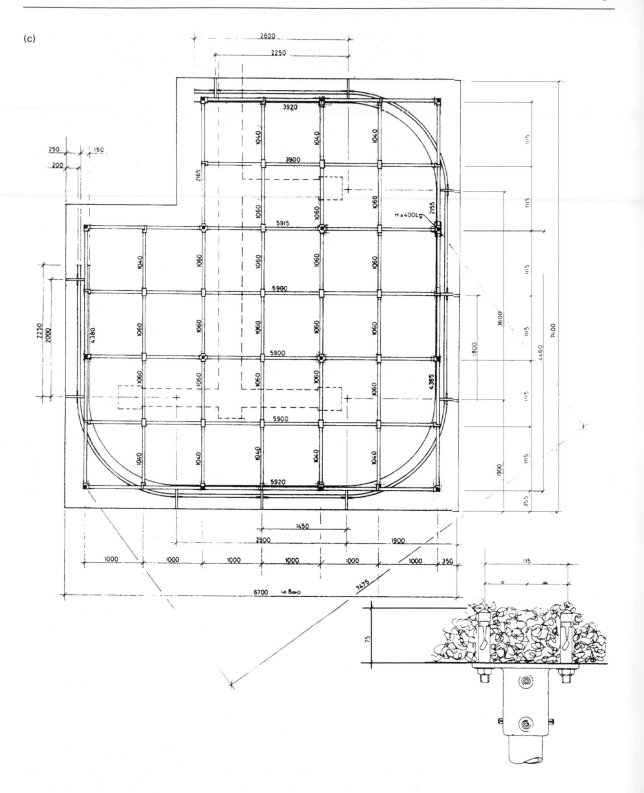

when considering how many units per linear run could we use and for television is it quite possible that a high density of monopoles have to be provided and allowance has to be made for the units to work almost next to each other, although it is doubtful that more than about 20 would be used in any one cluster. For the structural engineer concerned, the problem is that these large lumps of metal can move around the structure and can appear almost anywhere. Therefore a monopole grid has to be extremely strong and thus tends to be quite heavy. All this creates loading problems for the structural engineer and the architect to incorporate in their design. To give some idea of possible loadings in a studio it may be that 120 motorized monopoles are used in a studio of some 600 m². This represents a load, just for positioning the lights, of 14.4 tonnes. Sometimes there is a need to cluster the light sources; as an example, 16 lights formed into a square would occupy approximately 4 × 4 m and present a load of 1.92 tonnes to that area, which of course is a high point loading.

Another problem arises inasmuch that if we started all the units up at the same time, the dynamic load on that portion of the grid would be quite considerable and we certainly don't want it springing and oscillating every time we move equipment. Therefore, it has to be reasonably rigid, and this requirement also dictates the needs for fairly massive grid structures. In addition to the basic grid, there will be a need for loading platforms adjacent to the grid for rigging monopoles into the trackways. Possibly suspended just below grid level around the studio, are walkways, used for access to power feeds and specially rigged peripheral luminaires. Approximately 1 m from the edge of the studio a permanent cyc track will be provided. Trap doors have to be provided for lifting equipment into the grid area: either built into the grid itself or provided at the side of the studio. Due to the highly flexible nature of monopole grids they only require a certain basic amount of luminaires because these can be moved around to suit the production. Figures for luminaire requirements are given in the next section.

BARREL INSTALLATIONS

Counterweight barrel systems

Many American studios are equipped with counterweight barrel systems where the length of the bar may be around 4–5 m long. Studios are generally equipped with a reasonable density of this type of barrel. The nice thing about counterweight bars from the structural point of view is that the load on the grid is usually the basic safe working load of the bar itself and most of the weight is contained within the counterweight system, usually mounted on the studio walls. Some barrel studios have been constructed with bar units in the studio area with the support wires taken via divertor pulleys to the edge of the studio where the motor units are mounted on the walls. In most modern barrel studios where the scenery handling facilities are integrated into the grid structure the motor winding units for the scenery lifting system are generally mounted on the side walls of the studio. Most of the problems for the structural engineer with grid designs, usually arise with the heavy motorized barrel units which may be of the standard type with motors

Figure 9.6 Winch unit mounted in grid

mounted at grid level or self climbing units with integral motors. Even if the system uses self-climbing units, the total weight presented to the grid structure at any point is approximately the same.

Grid construction

Most barrel studios are usually constructed with the bar units approximately 1.5 m apart with an end to end spacing of approximately 1 m. Thus, having been given the studio area which doesn't include the fire lane, it is relatively easy to work out how many bar units will be employed. To take account of cyclorama tracks which are radiused at the corners of the studio, short bar units may be employed in the four corners of the studio.

In a monopole grid, because the slots provided at grid level are very similar to those in the theatre, it is relatively easy to drop spot lines for holding scenery up or suspending scenery pieces. In barrel studios, it is important that provision is made for the use of scenery and many modern studios have specially installed scenery winching systems, which run in between the main bars themselves. It is fairly obvious that the easiest installation for scene winches is in the same orientation as the bars. Going crosswise across the bar system could pose considerable problems. Motorized barrel winch units when they are of the standard type, are usually supported lengthways along twin structural members.

In a studio of some considerable span, these members have to be supported at frequent intervals to take account of the load. Thus several upright members between the grid and the primary steels have to be used so consequently it is not totally unobstructed. This point has to be borne in mind when designing walkover grids so that access is reasonable. A typical barrel winch unit will weigh approximately 150 kg, with a lifting capacity of almost the same amount, so the total load on the grid from any one winch unit may be around 300 kg. The encouraging thing from the point of view of the structural engineer and architect is the fact these loads are fixed in position in the grid. The weights given here assume the use of bar units approximately 2.5 to 3.0 m long. If we use shorter units the relative weights are somewhat similar from the point of view of the structural person, e.g. a shorter bar unit may have only half the lifting capacity of a long unit and its motor unit, mounted at the grid, may be only around 75% of a big unit but we will use twice as many bars in the studio. Thus the total load on the grid is approximately the same.

Most studios fitted with barrel systems operate with a high density of lighting. It may be at the BBC where multi-purpose luminaires are rigged permanently to the barrels, or like some of the studios in New York where many 2 kW and 1 kW luminaires are rigged per barrel, just for the ease of the general operation.

It is more than likely, in many of the studios that use motorized devices, for some restriction to be placed on the amount of units used at any one time, to stop dynamic loading problems on the grid.

Small studio pantograph systems

Smaller studios such as those using motorized or spring pantographs will have long trackways where, rather like the monopole studio, the loads can be grouped in areas. The weight of equipment in these studios is significantly less than motorized barrel and monopole systems. However, due to the nature of operations in studios of this type, their load is fairly well spread throughout the structure and of course, can be contained by loading notices which prohibit too much clustering within the studio area (Figure 9.7).

Perhaps only about 40 luminaires may be used together with 40 suspension points and of course this does not present the problems that exist in a large studio. Small roller barrel grids can also present a moving load to the main structure, although by not using motorized units, the weight on the structure is considerably less. In the

Figure 9.7 Mechanical loading notice

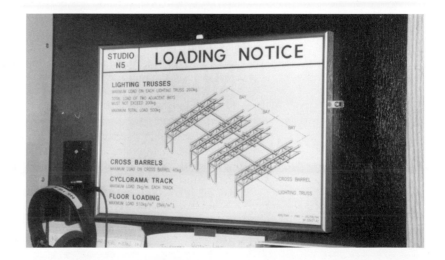

larger studios such as those used with monopoles and motorized barrels which may have their motor units mounted at grid level, or be the self-climbing type, special metal structures have to be arranged usually by the structural engineer in consultation with the architect, so that the rather heavy lighting grid system can be installed safely. This may require the use of special large beams being incorporated into the structure at high level. It must also be remembered that other than a lighting grid, air conditioning requirements exist and there will be a lot of additional weight from the power wiring system, etc. In smaller studios it may be that grid attachments can be made to, for example, a concrete roof going over the studio which can be made sufficiently strong by the astute use of reinforcing rod. The saving grace in a smaller studio is that the spans are not so great.

System installation problems

So far we have discussed the installation of grid systems and their subsequent structural loading, on the assumption that we are in a new building and can influence the design. What happens if we need to put a lighting system in existing premises? First of all it is important to come up with the lighting scheme itself, which can then be presented with all its facts and figures to the architect and structural engineer concerned. They will obviously be able either to accept the scheme as it stands for the new design, or it may be that they are able to modify the building in some way to accept the new design. Therefore it's back to the poor old lighting consultant to come up with an idea to be contained within the parameters set by the architect and structural engineer. It's quite possible that the idea could be acceptable but with some change to the structure itself, such as spreading the loadings between the walls and the roof, not just using the roof itself.

Structural loading problems

It may be that the roof structure cannot accept any load other than the one existing, therefore all the new installation would have to be supported from the side walls or from a structure built up from the floor level. The first of these requires that the walls are strong enough, and the second that the floor is also strong enough. Any of these solutions may be acceptable and it might even be a combination of any of them or all three. It must be remembered when discussing the structural arrangements with the architect and structural engineer, that these figures have to allow for all the lights, all the rigging system, all the power system and any ancillaries that may be added at any time.

In addition to the structural loads presented by the lighting system in the studio, the structural engineer will also be concerned with the size of plant installed in areas adjacent to the studio. Generally, the weight of the switchgear will be spread out in a fairly uniform fashion. The input power cables to the switchgear and the cables from the switchgear to the dimmer racks will also be fairly well distributed throughout the area. Most of the problem will be concerned with the weight of the dimmer racks where in a large installation the structural engineer may be confronted with a room with up to 20 or 30 dimmer racks. The biggest concern at the present time is the use of high density dimmer racks containing anything up to 108 dimmers. Whereas a small rack containing 30 dimmers may be around 200 kg, a large high density rack may weigh anything up to 1000 kg. Dimensions of dimmer racks vary quite considerably, and as an example, a lightweight rack of 200 kg from one manufacturer has base dimensions of 905 × 510 mm whereas another, which is a high density rack weighing 900 kg with base dimensions of 850 × 600 mm. The latter rack obviously gives floor loading problems, being a large weight over a small area. It would seem at first sight that the best solution to any of the loading problems in dimmer rooms is to keep the weights of the racks low and use more racks so that the loadings are well spread. However, the size of the room dictates how many racks may be used and the economics of the situation is that more racks generally put up the cost. In a new building, the structural engineer would obviously cater for the high floor loading at the planning stage; in existing buildings however, special precautions will have to be taken, or it may be that additional building work is required.

In practice, over many years of experience, it is very seldom that we have found buildings to be so bad that they would preclude some form of solution being adopted albeit possibly far removed from the original concept.

9.6   Television studio requirements

Lighting calculations (power)

The influence on the structure caused by the lighting grid has nothing to do with the amount of luminaires to be provided. Grids are there to hang lights, almost anywhere, using whatever quantities of luminaires that may be available. The basic requirement in any television studio is for a certain amount of light to satisfy the technical requirements of the cameras. This quantity of light will be determined by the average reflectivity of scenery together with the exposure time of the camera coupled with the aperture of the lens in use. Based upon incandescent sources with an efficacy of around 26 lumens per watt we can measure the amount of power required for the acting area to be adequately lit and this is given in watts per square metre. At the present time, a figure of around 300 watts of lighting per square metre for the basic lighting is considered adequate for the majority of general purpose requirements in television. Many television studios today will use prompters mounted on the cameras; these reduce the reflected light to a camera to about 75%; in other words, the incident light level has to be raised by 25% to compensate (Fig. 9.8).

This is usually accomplished by utilizing higher powered light sources or raising the dimmer output levels. It may be that the dimmer settings are quite high e.g. '8' or '9', and it is impossible to achieve the correct incident light level. This may necessitate, for example, having to choose 2 kW instead of 1 kW luminaires, as very few intermediate low powered sources are available. In larger luminaires, this can be overcome by using twin filament lamps or moving from 2kW to 3kW lamps.

Figure 9.8 Autocue

Although the figure of 300 W/m² is satisfactory for most basic purposes, it should be borne in mind that additional requirements, such as cyc and effects lighting, will impose an additional burden. A colour mixing system used on cycloramas will probably require loads of anything up to 2000 W per metre of linear run, thus a 40 m cyclorama cloth might require anything up to 80 kW being provided for adequate effects purposes. Although the cyc lighting power figure seems over generous it must be noted that when using highly saturated filter colours with transmissions as low as 5% the light output needs to be high to create the maximum effect and it is therefore suggested that a slightly higher estimating figure of around 450 W/m² is used on any studio above about 250 m². An important fact in the choice of luminaires is the size of the studio. Studios up to about 150 m² will generally work quite happily with a 2kW as the highest power luminaire required. However, above this size of studio, the majority of luminaires will probably settle at 2 kW, 3 kW or 1.25/2.5/5 kW. These powers of course, are related to working distances involved between the lights and the various subjects.

Whatever estimating figure we use for the power requirements for a studio, be it 300 or 450 W per square metre, it is obviously relatively easy to work out the power requirement by taking the active area in square metres and multiplying it by the appropriate wattage figure. In the case of monopole studios, and the smaller pantograph type studios, it is more than likely that the power requirements of the supply system will more or less match the available total wattage of the luminaires used. However, in the case of saturated lighting grids, the total power of the luminaires installed will probably exceed the power available by a factor of anything up to three times. As an example of this, a BBC studio of 800 m² will be supplied with approximately 450 kW of power. The 100 bars installed will each have two 5 kW luminaires rigged on them, thus the load presented by the luminaires to the system is 1 MW. In practice this is not a problem as only selected numbers of lights are used and therefore it is a basic requirement that the LD must have current meters and/or an alarm system indicating the maximum electrical load. The figures that follow have been worked out from typical studio usage over many years and represent reasonable requirements of any studio. It is obviously easy to start equipping a studio by covering the basic lighting requirements and in the fullness of time purchase more equipment to suit the installation. As an approximate guide, the 'luminaire power' required is divided into two thirds hard sources and one third soft sources.

50 m²
Minimum power required: 24 kW
6 × 2 kW Fresnel spots
12 × 1 kW Fresnel spots
8 × 625 W soft lights
4 × 1 kW profile spots
4 × 1 kW Parcans
4 × floor stands
Cyc:
12 × 625 W single compartment top units (1.2 m from cyc)

100 m²
Minimum power required: 45 kW
16 × 2 kW Fresnel spots
10 × 1 kW Fresnel spots
10 × 1.25 kW soft lights
6 × 1 kW profile spots
6 × 1 kW Parcans
6 × floor stands
Cyc:
16 × 625 W single compartment top units (1.2 m from cyc)

150 m²
Minimum power required: 70 kW
24 × 2 kW Fresnel spots
10 × 1 kW Fresnel spots
or
28 × 1.25/2.5 kW Fresnel spots

6 × 1 kW Fresnel spots
and
10 × 1.25/2.5 kW soft lights
6 × 1 kW profile spots
10 × 1 kW Parcans
8 × Floor stands
Cyc:
30 × 625 W single top units
(1.2 m from cyc)
and/or
30 × 625 W 4-compartment groundrow units

250 m²
Minimum power required: 100 kW
10 × 3 kW Fresnel spots
30 × 2 kW Fresnel spots
or
30 × 1.25/2.5/3.75 kW Fresnel spots
10 × 1 kW Fresnel spots
and
16 × 1.25/2.5 kW soft lights
6 × 1 kW profile spots
15 × 1 kW Parcans
10 × Floor stands
Cyc:
20 × 1.25 kW twin top units
(3 m from cyc)
and/or
40 × 625 W 4-compartment ground row units

400 m²
Minimum power required: 180 kW
3 × 10 kW Fresnel spots
and
20 × 3 kW Fresnel spots
40 × 2 kW Fresnel spots
or
60 × 1.25/2.5/3.75 kW Fresnel spots

and
12 × 1 kW Fresnel spots
24 × 1.25/2.5 kW soft lights
 8 × 1 kW profile spots
20 × 1 kW Parcans
12 floor stands
Cyc:
16 × 1.25 kW 4-compartment
top units (3 m from cyc)
and/or
40 × 625 W 4-compartment
groundrow units

750 m²
Minimum power required: 350 kW
6 × 10 kW Fresnel spots
and
35 × 3 kW Fresnel spots
70 × 2 kW Fresnel spots
or
105 × 1.25/2.5/3.75 kW Fresnel
spots
and
20 × 1 kW Fresnel spots
40 × 1.25/2.5 kW soft lights
12 × 1 kW profile spots
40 × 1 kW Parcans
16 floor stands
Cyc:
30 × 1.25 kW 4-compartment
top units (3 m from cyc)
and/or
70 × 625 W 4-compartment
groundrow units

9.7   The smaller studio

The smaller studio (those from 20 m² to 80 m²) usually provide for 'fixed head' presentation.

They are quite often conversions of existing premises with little or no air conditioning. The floors are usually strong, but the walls or ceiling may require some modification to allow a simple grid to be installed and this is generally because of the imposed weight of the grid and luminaires. If the main grid can be suspended from the ceiling all that is needed at the sides of the studio are cyc rail supports. Or it may be that the cyc system is integrated into the main grid structure. On occasions, however, the ceiling will not be strong enough to support the weight of the grid and it will be necessary to either fix to the walls or have a floor standing structure to support the grid. Quite often height is a problem and deep primary support beams, for the grid, across the studio will make matters worse. The use of a lightweight truss can be advantageous if a floor standing structure has to be installed (see Fig. 9.9).

The most basic grid is a fixed matrix of steel barrels, although if weight is a problem aluminium can be used at a cost premium. The matrix should provide a spacing no greater than 1 metre and preferably 600 mm. However, the less the spacing the more the weight load and cost! A good alternative is to use roller barrels which allow for better positioning of luminaires and can cut down the amount of metal in the grid structure. Usually a twin cyc rail is quite sufficient and the cyc cloths will usually be lit from above to conserve the limited floor space. There will be a need for Chroma Key backings which can be provided by a cloth or by a fluorescent back lit panel. Access behind the cyc cloth will be fairly restricted, but there will be a need for some power sockets at studio floor level for floor-stand mounted luminaires and effects lights.

The choice of lighting is made from the following criteria:

Figure 9.9 Grid trusses

1. **Tungsten:** for the best control of both optical performance and lighting level – controlled by a dimmer.
2. **Fluorescent:** limited optical performance with some energy saving – lighting level controlled by a dimmer.
3. **Discharge:** very efficient with good optical control but only capable of being dimmed down to 50% output.

The choice of luminaires can be either open face with high efficiency, or Fresnels with better optical performance. The dimmers will be 2.5 or 3 kW, controlled by a very basic lighting console. The amount of facilities will depend upon the complexity of programmes, which in a small studio are very limited. The main requirement of the lighting console will be very rapid access to any channel as it is more than likely that rehearsals will be very brief affairs.

Studio specification

The following details give the specification of an actual European studio to be used for talks and current affairs programmes. The studio has several small fixed set ups, hence the quantity of luminaires supplied. Only a few of the luminaires will be used at any one time.

Studio size:	88 m^2 (6.85 m × 12.9 m)
Light level:	Set at 700 lux with dimmers @ '7'
Power required (300 W/m^2):	26.4 kW: 120 A @ 220 V
	40 A/3 ph @ 380 V
Maximum load	
(for 48 × 2.5 kW dimmers):	545 A (182 A/3 ph)
Dimmer rack circuit protection:	By fuse
Dimmer circuit protection:	By mcb
Heat load (typical):	18 kW

STUDIO GRID AND LUMINAIRES

The grid consists of two parallel trackways supporting 16 rolling barrel units (eight in each trackway). Each rolling barrel would be fitted with two roller trolleys with female socket for luminaire suspension. Therefore all the luminaires can traverse the barrel as well as the barrel being positioned anywhere in its associated trackway.

As the height of the studio is not generous, it is proposed to fit the grid immediately below the ceiling support beams, to gain maximum luminaire height. Centrally positioned above each trackway is an electrical distribution system, on which would be mounted 20 twin 2.5 kW 16A CEE17 sockets, with each pair of sockets fed from **one** 2.5 kW dimmer. As two trackways are provided with associated electrical distribution, this gives a total of forty 2.5 kW dimmer feeds at high level. The remaining eight dimmers would feed wallboxes at floor level, each fitted with four twin 2.5 kW 16 A CEE17 sockets with each pair of sockets fed from **one** 2.5 kW dimmer.

The roller barrels give a total of 32 suspension points. As it is estimated that around forty luminaires may be required at high level, additional 'C' clamps are also provided to suspend luminaires either directly from the moving barrels or, from the primary grid which supports the main lighting grid. Some luminaires will be used on the studio floor. The studio is supplied with 57 luminaires, all capable of being hung from the lighting grid. Each of these will be fitted with a safety bond.

Two cyclorama tracks are provided so that two cyclorama cloths can be used simultaneously, thus avoiding rigging and de-rigging, which inevitably soils the cloth. The outer of these tracks is positioned 200 mm from the studio wall (thus allowing for sockets and luminaire cables behind the cloth). One long white cyclorama cloth is allowed for, together with a narrower Chroma Key blue cloth. The height of the cloths is only 3 metres due to the restrictions placed on the height of the cyc track by the studio ceiling height and the main grid structure.

All Fresnel spotlights and soft lights are provided with pole operation to enable quick adjustment from the studio floor without the need to use step ladders. A generous supply of cyc units is proposed to give the set designers maximum flexibility with regard to simple sets and colour wash on backings. The control system would be complete with VDU, a soft patch and memory system together with a reasonable electronic effects software drive package.

9.8   Air conditioning requirements

If we install 100 kW of lighting in any area, we have to expect that, ultimately, all of this will appear as waste heat and most of this will rise vertically. From the point of view of air conditioning, two effects take place. The first is that the luminaires will radiate infrared energy in the direction of the artists. This radiation is in direct proportion to the efficiency of the luminaires themselves, thus a luminaire with a claimed efficiency of 26% will have approximately 26% radiant energy in the light beam; the remainder will be contained within the luminaire and subsequently re-radiated from the luminaire body or as exhaust

LIGHTING EQUIPMENT SCHEDULE

Roller barrel grid mounted below ceiling support beams and consisting of sixteen 2.65 m long barrels suspended from twin trackways
Twin cyclorama track (30 metres) with 4 curves at 1500 mm radius, inclusive of end stops, roller bobbins and suspension
White canvas cyc cloth 24 m × 3 m, chain weighted
Chroma Key blue cloth 12 m × 3 m, chain weighted

Luminaires

17	1 kW Fresnel spotlights, pole operated
10	500 W Fresnel spotlights, pole operated
8	1 kW/2 kW Softlites inc. eggcrate, pole operated
22	Multi-purpose cyc units (used either on the studio floor or suspended from the grid)

Lamps

17	CP40
10	CP82
38	1000W linear lamps for soft and cyc lights

(Note: No allowance has been made for spares)

Plugs *(for luminaires)*
57   CEE 17, 16 A wired plugs

Roller barrel trolleys for barrel system

'C' clamps for hanging luminaires on secondary grid

Safety bonds All luminaires will be supplied with bonds

Spigot adapters 28 mm–16 mm (6 off)

Studio power distribution
Comprises 48 twin 16 A sockets on 48 2.5 kW dimmer circuits
Control system
One 48-way control board complete with VDU, soft patch and memory system
Dimmers
48 2.5 kW digital dimmers in rack complete with digital interface to control system

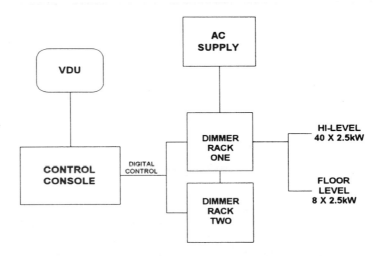

from the ventilation system on the luminaire itself. Generally older premises are never provided with adequate air conditioning systems and in fact, in older theatres, it always seems 'that you have to sweat to earn your money'! However, in new premises or where premises are capable of being successfully converted, it is possible to have adequate air conditioning installed. There are thus two important areas from the point of view of the air conditioning technician: first of all, the conditions that create a comfortable atmosphere at the acting level and secondly, the conditions for people working either in the flies or at grid level itself, and it is at grid level where the maximum heat will eventually settle, assuming nothing is done to prevent it.

Estimating heat loads

Heat loads are rather like the domestic electrical load and are somewhat subject to diversity of use. It is very seldom that *all* the installed lighting in any system will be used at the same time, and over a period of some years it has been established, certainly in television and the theatre, that an average load of 66% of the maximum installed kilowatts will be used over a period of time. So, for a studio using 400 kW of lighting power, we need to worry about 264 kW worth, thus easing the burden on the air conditioning technician. Theatre practices haven't changed very much over the years so the situation from the air conditioning point of view is fairly well established. In film studios, although large amounts of power are used on film sets, they are usually used for reasonably short periods of time with breaks between, which allows the temperature, although perhaps having reached high levels, to be dissipated fairly quickly by the use of large fans in the roof or walls. Television has changed greatly in recent years and the technique of rehearse/shoot, generally means that only perhaps one or two sets of the possible 10 to 13 sets in a large studio are in use at any one time, thus the load on the air conditioning system is considerably less and it may be in the future that the estimating figure of 66% has to be looked at once again and possibly reduced.

It's all very well having air conditioning that works effectively and keeps the ambient temperature to reasonable limits, to the relief of everybody concerned; however air conditioning can only be achieved by moving a large volume of air down small ducting or an equal volume of air down a large ducting system. The latter will create, in general, much less noise, and in fact for television use, we have to be extremely careful with the generation of noise from the air conditioning system. An interesting coincidence occurs inasmuch that by moving large volumes of air we don't create some of the air movement that causes problems in practice, such as a cyc cloth being moved by the sheer volume of air flowing around a studio. Other than the needs of the studio, air conditioning will be required in the dimmer room, as there is a reasonable amount of waste heat generated.

Zone control

This is particularly important if the dimmer room doubles as a maintenance room for the electricians to use. In a large studio it may be that the air conditioning engineer concerned will be able to have a zonal control system so that when only one quarter of the studio is used only that quarter is air conditioned to any reasonable degree. The requirement for a large volume of air to be moved down large ducting, obviously implies a large space being occupied by the air conditioning system at grid level. Thus, it is extremely important, when planning a studio, to integrate the air conditioning system and the lighting grid system together, so that a clash of interest does not occur and certainly access to the lighting equipment is not prevented. Others affected by the requirements of air conditioning are sound, vision and electrical technicians who also require the use of certain portions of the grid for some of their systems. Some air conditioning systems, when moving the volumes of air suggested in this section, require large rooms in which to put plant, and these rooms can almost approach the size of some of the studios they service. Further problems associated with air conditioning are that chilled water is required and if compressor units are used, it is important they do not create any undue noise in the studio. It also happens that introduction of air conditioning breaches the walls around the area which consequently cause problems to the acoustic specialist; this latter problem will be discussed in Section 9.10.

9.9   Power requirements

We are sometimes asked about the problems of interference with the use of discharge lighting in a studio as opposed to tungsten lighting with dimmers. Solid state flicker free discharge ballasts, although capable of generating high levels of interference, are usually engineered in such a way that interference is minimized. At the present time the EMC regulations would ensure that all solid state ballasts conform to a low degree of interference capability in the same way that dimmers have to be treated.

Irrespective of whether we use 1kW, 2kW, 3kW, 5kW or 10kW luminaires, or whatever type of dimmers drive them, power has to flow from one area to another in the theatre or the studio, and this involves large numbers of cables which have to be routed from one area to another with absolute safety. The system that supplies the power has to be carefully worked out and this is conditioned by whether or not it is a new installation or the refurbishment of an old installation. Various parameters concern us when we move power from one location to another and most important of these would be cable size. What affects the cable size? All cables have a small resistance and the larger the cable the less they impede the flow of current. Therefore if we use cables which are high in resistance to the flow of current we will waste some power in the cables themselves and this can cause problems from two points of view, one of which is the cables' heat, which is dangerous, and, secondly, we lose valuable power in the cables and do not deliver it to the lamps, thus we get a volts' drop and the lamps do not work at their maximum efficiency. How do we get around this problem?

Volt drop problems

The best method is to use generous sized cables and keep the distance from the dimmers to the luminaires as short as possible,

Figure 9.10 Grid-mounted dimmer

bearing in mind possible acoustic noise problems. Unlike the film and TV industries, the theatre luminaires tend to be used with reasonably short flexible leads attached so that most of the volts drop is in the fixed wiring. The loss of volts in theatre installations is not a serious problem from the productions' point of view, the change of colour temperature of the lamps will generally not be noticeable. The heating of the cables by not being large enough in current carrying capacity is, however, very serious. With new installations the present legislation in this country prevents cables being used which are quite simply not up to the job. However, in old installations, it is more than likely, if refurbished, they will have to have a completely new electrical system.

Plugs and sockets

Most of the lighting circuits at 240 V in theatres are 2.5 kW (10 A), although sometimes 5 kWs are used and occasionally 10 kWs may be employed. It is preferable that all dimmers are grouped together in a purpose built room where the noise can be contained and ventilation controlled fairly easily. Circuits should be run as phase/neutral pairs usually with a common earth provided either by large cables to groups of sockets or by the trunking used to distribute the power system. Unswitched sockets should be used and at the present time in the United Kingdom theatre industry, 15A plugs and sockets are common. It is much better that modern plugs and sockets to BS 4343 are used in 16A, 32A and 63A ratings, and these should be installed as a matter of course in a new installation and wherever possible used as replacements in existing installations. Parallel sockets are provided for convenience on the radial circuits used with the responsibility for the electrical loading of the system being placed on the operators.

Most dimmers in use today will be the thyristor type, and we have already discussed the interference that these units can generate. Because there is usually good separation between the power wiring and the microphone cables, particularly with the use of radio micro-

Figure 9.11 Wall-mounted electrical distribution

phones, high specification dimmers with low interference, such as used in TV, are not usually required in stage installations. In addition to the thyristor dimming circuits, independent or 'non-dimmable' circuits are also required. These are used for electrical loads such as the motors on effects lighting units, fan units and discharge lights including follow spots. It is relatively easy to provide such circuits from contactor switched power although most dimmer manufacturers offer 'non-dim' circuits through their dimmer racks, by either bypassing the action of the thyristors or having thyristor dimmers that, in full conduction, stay relatively stable when this type of load is applied. Other than the permanently supplied lighting power for the units contained within the premises, there is a need for additional power supplies when temporary lighting and sound equipment is provided by touring companies. From the point of view of cost, it is important that the dimmer room is as near as possible to the socket outlets used for the lighting system, thus cutting down the amount of cables required between the dimmers and the lights themselves.

The requirements of the film studio for luminaires and dimmers are less demanding than those for a theatre installation and the majority of cables used will be flexible feeders and not part of the fixed installation. The biggest difference will be the provision of much larger power supplies. Whereas, for years, the film industry generated their own dc voltage, they now rely on the incoming ac mains supply.

The requirements of TV in most respects is very similar to the theatre with large numbers of dimmers used and a multiplicity of light sources. The type of luminaires used will vary much more and thus their power needs will be different. The dimmers provided will be of the highest specification to prevent interference in practice. The majority of the wiring will be fixed, although the length of cable runs will mean keeping a close eye on the voltage drop.

Light levels

In general, we are looking at half the light level of old, which was set at 1600 lux and is now 800 lux, which roughly equates to 500 lux from keylights; 300 lux from the fill to give a reasonable contrast ratio. Therefore the estimating figure should be 300 W/m². This reduction in light level does not reduce the number of luminaires required, only the size and power. In studios which are equipped with dual source luminaires, there is no effect on the luminaires, the only requirement is that lower powered lamps are fitted.

Floor lights

With a more energy conscious society and owing to the need of lower power in installations and heat loads, it is worthwhile considering either fluorescent lighting – although this gives reasonable light levels, it is somewhat uninteresting light, and is not good for modelling – or, it is possible to use discharge lighting such as the MSR, HMI, etc., to give high light levels and less heat in an installation.

Discharge lights

One problem with using discharge sources is that they are only capable of being dimmed from a maximum down to 50% light output, and this somewhat limits the control available to the lighting designer. Although they may be designated 'hot restrike' lamps, they only come on at full power if they have been off for a short period of time. When struck from cold, they still require a warm up period to achieve maximum light output, which may be a minute or more. It is possible, of course, to fit some type of mechanical dimming to discharge sources and the drawback to this is the noise that may be generated. It is not possible to do lighting changes as such due to the fact that we can never go below 50% light output on the dimming curve. Therefore, discharge lighting is only suitable for studios where the lighting set up is fixed, i.e. no lighting changes take place. To integrate discharge and tungsten lighting requires one or other being filtered to the correct colour temperature. Another problem that exists in this type of installation, is that all the devices require ballasts and a choice has to be made between standard and flicker free, and it is only the flicker free that allow the 50% dimming to take place; therefore the costs are much higher than would be with standard ballast units. Furthermore, when using flicker free ballasts, some care has to be taken in the installation so that the levels of electromagnetic interference are kept to a minimum. Generally the housekeeping concerned should be the same as when using dimmer systems, i.e. that the wiring feeding the fluorescents, etc., should be kept reasonably well separated from all the sound and vision circuits.

9.10   Acoustic requirements

The Greeks and the Romans together with the builders of cathedrals and concert halls of the past had little or no knowledge of the decibel. A mixture of luck on one hand and the fact that all buildings appear to be structurally designed for at least three times the strength needed, seems to play a part in the acoustics of old buildings. Apparently, with the high technology of today's construction methods, there is a greater need for acoustic architects than ever before, but why is this so?

It's no good having a wonderful building where we are unable to hear the artists perform or for that matter resolve the sound spectrum fairly accurately within a broadcast studio. It is somewhat distracting when sitting in an auditorium to hear a jet aircraft go overhead. This is one area where the architects of old didn't have problems, they weren't confronted with jet engined aircraft or for that matter the motor vehicle going by on the roads outside. The buildings of old didn't seem to require much air conditioning as such, as due to their massive construction they appear to be inherently cool in the hot weather and not too cold in the coldest of weather. They were constructed more like a storage heater rather than a slim line radiator. It's pretty obvious if we don't get the construction right and the building does not meet the requirements for good acoustics then all is lost.

What has lighting got that influences the acoustics to any degree? In the theatre, probably not a lot, the only problems arise usually with the noise generated by dimmer units which may be loud enough to take people's attention away from the performance, secondly the installation of lots of pieces of metal at high level over a stage area introduces many reflecting surfaces. The fly tower, if we're not careful, reacts just a little bit like a large organ pipe. The architect when designing in theatres and similar premises still has to worry about the natural acoustics without much consideration to sound reinforcement or the use of radio microphones, etc. Because we need walkways over the front of the theatre to position some of the front of house lighting, we breach the ceiling in the theatre with slots for our front of house lighting, which may give problems to the acoustic architect and be something of a compromise between decor and the needs of audibility. The air conditioning in the theatre will not be of the levels required for the film and television studio and thus it may be relatively easy to keep the noise from the air movement to a low level. What would be important however, is that the noise of the ventilation plant should be kept separate from the structure so to reduce noise through the building.

Dimmer room noise

In the film and television studios where large power feeders are used, there may be a requirement to ensure that noise does not come from any of the electrical plant into the studio area. In film studios, generally, this shouldn't cause too much of a problem as dimmers are not the norm in this situation. They will probably have more problems with the use of discharge light sources on the sets themselves and the ballast units used with them. In television however, there is a problem with the use of many dimmers which are usually positioned very close to the studio, and one of the problems we have is that we make holes in the walls by taking the trunking from one area through to the studio and hence allow some form of vibration to go through the structures. Even if we inhibit vibration by using rubber mounts, or even discontinuous pieces of trunking, it may be that the noise comes from around the hole made in the studio wall and this does cause a real problem in studios. It's very convenient to have a door from the studio through to the dimmer room, but in most cases these have to be carefully selected acoustic doors, and usually double ones, to prevent noise coming from the dimmer room to the studio.

Studios are usually formed as rather large box-like structures with a metal grid, some 3 m below the actual roof. TV studios are generally designed to have a fairly 'dead' sound and any reverberation required is added artificially, thus the acoustic specialist has to provide some form of acoustic boxes on the ceilings above the grid where space is at a premium. There is little or nothing which can be done below the grid owing to the nature of productions and the usage of the system. The acoustic specialist will also want to cover the walls in acoustic cladding of some description, but unfortunately is bedevilled by lots of trunking and large control consoles at fairly regular intervals around the walls of the studios. This would either be for the lighting system or the sound and vision system. However good the acoustic specialist is, matters are not always controlled by his skills. The biggest problem in studios can be the noise generated by the lights. If the choice of luminaires leads to creaking bodywork on heating up and cooling down of a luminaire, this is absolutely disastrous. Lamp sing can penetrate the quietest of conversations. So whether we like it or not, the lighting systems have a major impact on the acoustics and sound quality of any building used for entertainment.

10
Lighting for sports, special events and locations

Introduction

Event and location lighting falls into two main types. The first is sports lighting, which is usually permanently installed or in some cases, temporarily rigged on towers or truss systems especially for the event. Sports lighting, generally using specially designed luminaires, is a broad wash of fairly even illumination to convey the action to the viewer, either live at the event or possibly by television. The second is, by specially designed lighting systems using suspended truss, scaffold towers or truss systems on ground support legs, for the lighting of concerts, fashion shows, car launches and even party political conferences. The lighting will use several types of luminaire and will not have some of the technical constraints of sports lighting. Some large rigs are used for several weeks and could be dismantled and re-assembled almost on a daily basis, therefore they have to be extremely well built and robust enough to stand lots of punishment.

Buildings, of course, are also floodlit but as this book is about entertainment lighting it is felt that this technique should be left to the practitioners of general floodlighting as they do not have the same constraints, such as the colour of the light source and uniformity, that are discussed in this section. The colour of the light sources selected for additional sports lighting have to blend with any existing lighting but most importantly must be capable of giving good colour rendition. A prime requirement of lighting for sports is that the sources are as efficient as possible due to the reasonably high light levels required. It would seem on the surface that the 'pop' world do not have to worry about colour rendition and efficiency of light sources, however, the use of Parcans with their very high output means that other sources also have to have a high output so that an artistic blend is achieved. An area where efficiency is of paramount importance is in automated luminaires because of the need to prevent heat and the subsequent problems it may give with internal colour filters, gobos and other mechanisms.

Floodlighting and its principles haven't changed a lot over the years, the only new approach has been to use much higher quality light sources. However, in all other areas there has been a tremendous influx of light sources of various types and although years ago outside lighting, or any event lighting, used specialized luminaires, all branches of the trade now use each other's luminaires to gain maximum effect. It is therefore possible to see a pop rig containing large Fresnel luminaires, and of course, many of the automated luminaires used in pop rigs and other events are fitted with discharge lamps. Many of today's TV lighting designers will use tungsten Parcans and automated luminaires from the world of pop. When we started our careers in the lighting industry, it was quite common, particularly on sports events floodlit for television, to see several huge carbon arcs positioned on top of scaffolding towers, nowadays we would get a similar result by using 4 kW or 6 kW discharge PAR sources.

In a studio, or for that matter, on a stage, the lighting sources and system are usually permanently in position for the operators to manipulate according to the lighting plot issued by the lighting director. On film stages, lights tend to be introduced almost in the same way that location lighting is used in the film industry, i.e. the type of lights used are not normally present in the studio but only placed there according to the demands of the director of photography. However, when lighting on location for film, television, special events and concerts, the luminaires, generators, and luminaire rigging systems all have to be specially supplied. At some events, there will also be a requirement to set up a television studio, together with designated interview areas on televized events, e.g. talking to ice skaters at the side of a rink.

Due to the obvious safety requirements on any temporary installation, such as huge pop rigs, with very big mechanical structures and electrical supply systems, it is essential that good inter-communication systems are installed for the use of all personnel so that danger is avoided and problems quickly averted.

As an example of a practical safety hazard, the Parcan, which is one of the most widely used luminaires in the lighting industry, can be electrically unsafe when being focused by electricians or riggers, because it is necessary to rotate the lampholder to position the beam in the correct aspect and this, of course, means getting very close to live terminals. The electrical current might not kill the person involved but the reaction to the shock might cause the person to fall off the truss and this might be fatal. To circumvent this problem Rolight Theatertechniek, a company based in the Netherlands, have introduced a shrouded receptacle, called the 'Parsafe' which completely covers the terminals of the lampholder, thus allowing manipulation of the lamp without the danger of coming into contact with the live wiring (see Figures 10.1 and 10.2).

10.1   Floodlighting

Floodlighting is required for both outdoor and inside venues, such as football grounds, athletics tracks, tennis courts, cycling tracks, and large indoor arenas, such as basketball, ice hockey and multi-purpose

Figure 10.1 Parsafe (courtesy
Rolight Theatertechnick)

Figure 10.2 Parsafe socket
(courtesy Rolight Theatertechnick)

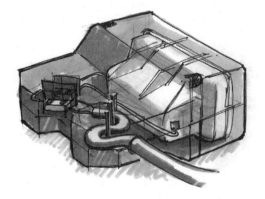

arenas where the floor area is converted for a variety of sporting
events. In a large venue the spectators may be a long way away from
the action, and to be able to see small detail and pick out the
athletes' actions, a higher level of illuminance will be needed than
that dictated by the needs of the participants.

Floodlighting basics

Floodlighting in years gone by, certainly on sports stadia and
football grounds, tended to be from a tower at each corner of the
arena/pitch, and usually 25 metres and above in height. This system
when used with many fixtures at the top of each mast provided good
illumination of the whole area. This system was based on the fact
that increasing the mounting height reduced the number of towers
required. Although generally the four tower system will give pretty
good horizontal illumination over the playing area, the vertical
illumination near the towers falls away quite dramatically, due to
the steep incidence of light close to the towers. Various tower
arrangements can be used varying from one in each corner to a
number on either side of the playing area. There is a need, of
course, to light all around a running area, motor racing, greyhound

Figure 10.3 (a) Floodlights
(courtesy Sheffield Utd FC and
MUSCO Lighting)

Figure 10.3 (b) Stand-mounted
floodlights (courtesy Sheffield Utd
FC and MUSCO Lighting)

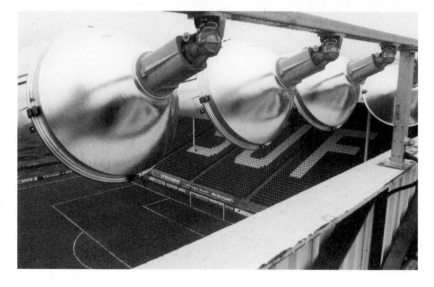

racing or horse racing tracks. In these cases there obviously has to
be many smaller floodlighting poles used to cover the whole perimeter of the track. With large athletics stadia and football grounds,
there has been a move away from the traditional 'tower in each
corner' approach and in many modern installations, much of the
lighting is provided along the front of the grandstands, and although
this can give satisfactory results across the pitch it is somewhat
lacking at the ends of the playing area. If we have a series of
luminaires, spaced reasonably close together, say all along the front
edge of a grandstand, the effect on the field of play is rather like
that of a very wide soft light. The lighting tends to be somewhat
featureless and although visually acceptable, is less able to produce
a sense of depth, as far as a TV camera is concerned, than point
lighting from four floodlight towers.

Lighting levels

Most modern large indoor arenas will have floodlights fitted which provide lighting levels quite adequate for modern television and usually are designed to do just this. Because the lighting levels for TV coverage are quite high, some venues will have a three stage floodlighting system which provides for normal level of play, expert level of play and for television coverage. Most floodlights have discharge lamps fitted because of their greater efficiency and in the past did not always have high colour rendition properties. However, most systems installed today will follow the guidelines set by the Sports Council in the UK and the CIE in Europe.

FLOODLIGHTING REQUIREMENTS FOR SPORTS

(Extract from Sports Council Guidance Notes for Floodlighting)

Horizontal values **at ground level**

Sport	Class III Lux	Ra	Class II Lux	Ra	Class I Lux	Ra
Association football	75	20	200	60	500	60
Athletics	100	20	200	60	500	60
Basketball	75	20	200	60	500	60
Cycle racing	100	20	300	60	500	60
Hockey	300	20	350	60	500	60
Lawn tennis *(court only)*	300	20	300	60	500	60
(Total playing area)	250	20	250	60	400	60
Rugby (league/union)	75	20	200	60	500	60

Lux: Illuminance level. **Ra**: Colour rendering

Class III   Low level competition such as local or small club events. This generally does not involve spectators, but may include general training and recreational participation.

Class II   Medium level competition such as regional, county or local club events. This will often entail medium size spectator capacities and viewing distances, and may involve high level training.

Class I   Top level competition such as national and international events. This will often include large spectator capacities with long potential viewing distances, and top level training.

Setting up

Floodlights consist of groups of luminaires aimed at the playing area with over-lapping beams to achieve a smooth result. In the past most of the floodlights were set by a team working to a drawn plan issued by the lighting designer after some laborious calculations, with luminaires having aiming sights. Today, it is more than likely that all the lighting calculations will have been done on a computer which then produces data which allows the luminaire settings to be pre-configured at the manufacturing plant. Once on site all that is necessary is to erect the masts at their designated positions, fit the luminaires and align them to the pre-set marks.

Design constraints

When designing lighting systems for a studio, the walls and the ceiling are all definite boundaries that contain the lighting system, whereas floodlighting can be placed almost anywhere within the vicinity of the area to be lit. The lighting may be positioned on the front of grandstands or on towers within the stadium close to the playing area. Alternatively, much taller towers can be well outside the spectator area at greater distances from the playing area. In general, floodlighting for sports usually falls into a fairly regular pattern, due to the layout of the playing area or pitch. By mounting the floodlights on high masts, it is possible to cover a fairly wide area with a very small number of masts; however, there is a relationship between the height of the masts and the distance from the base of the mast to the playing area. The steeper the light becomes, the better the horizontal illumination, but the vertical illumination diminishes. This is caused by the cosine effect.

Example: Area 60 × 100 m

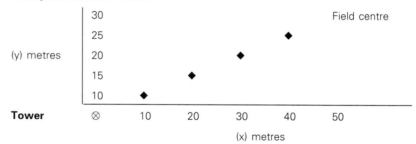

The following figures give typical distances from the tower floodlights to positions on the field (given by the 'x' and 'y' co-ordinates).

Table 10.1 Tower height of 20 metres

(x) (metres)	(y) (metres)	Throw (metres)	Cos ∅ (vert)
10	10	24.50	0.577
20	15	32.00	0.781
30	20	41.23	0.874
40	25	51.23	0.921
50	30	61.64	0.946

Table 10.2 Tower height of 35 metres

(x) (metres)	(y) (metres)	Throw (metres)	Cos ∅ (vert)
10	10	37.75	0.375
20	15	43.01	0.580
30	20	50.25	0.718
40	25	58.74	0.803
50	30	68.00	0.857

As can be seen from the above figures the distance of throw is much longer than would appear at first glance. The cosine figures are given to show the dramatic fall off in vertical illumination when close to the floodlight towers. The problem is less with shorter towers and/or greater distances.

Figure 10.4 Cosine effect

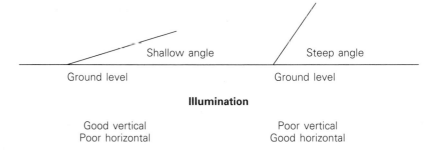

Shallow angle　　　　　　　Steep angle

Ground level　　　　　　　　Ground level

Illumination

Good vertical　　　　　　　Poor vertical
Poor horizontal　　　　　　Good horizontal

Aim point

It is usual to design the floodlighting system so that the centre of the beam is directed to a point roughly two thirds of the way across the area to be covered. The relationship between the mounting height (H) and the depth of the area (D) is extremely important (see Figure 10.5a and b).

Floodlights are made with various light output characteristics and are chosen for the particular installation concerned. Where the depth is greater than the height, by a factor of three or more, it is necessary to provide supplementary floodlights, usually with wide angle distributions, to fill in the area close to the base of the floodlight towers. Generally, floodlights aimed at a long range will have narrower beams than those aimed at short range.

Towers or columns

If using towers or columns, there is usually not too much restriction on the height, however the horizontal position of the towers or columns will be critical within the area to be lit. The spacing between the individual columns is most important because if they are too widely spaced we may end up with unacceptable uniformity of illumination over the playing area. Obviously, there are financial considerations when it comes down to how many columns should be around an area and there must be a finite number which equates between good floodlighting and the cost of the installation. One important point that may be overlooked is that each floodlight tower will require several kilowatts of power supply, and additionally has to be provided with some housing for the ballasts associated with discharge sources. The floodlighting will have to be controlled from some central source so that it can be switched on, either in stages or all at once.

It is possible to use either columns or towers. Columns can be made in steel, aluminium or concrete and are usually used for heights up to 30 metres. Towers, which are usually a lattice construction in steel,

Figure 10.5 (a) Floodlight aiming angles; (b) cosine effect

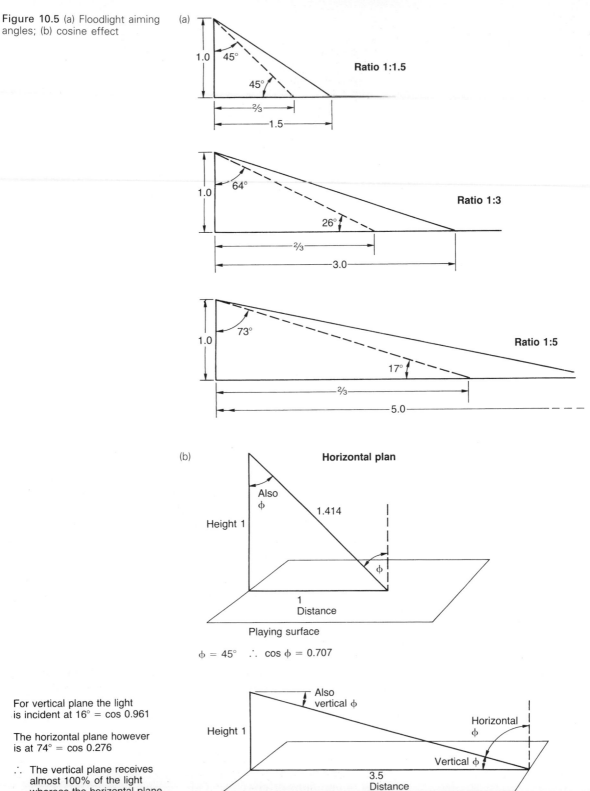

(a)

Ratio 1:1.5

Ratio 1:3

Ratio 1:5

(b)

Horizontal plan

Also φ

1.414

Height 1

Distance

Playing surface

φ = 45°   ∴   cos φ = 0.707

For vertical plane the light is incident at 16° = cos 0.961

The horizontal plane however is at 74° = cos 0.276

∴ The vertical plane receives almost 100% of the light whereas the horizontal plane receives about 78%

Also vertical φ

Horizontal φ

Height 1

Vertical φ

3.5
Distance

Playing surface

Figure 10.6 Light Structure
System™: typical service platform
detail (courtesy MUSCO Lighting)

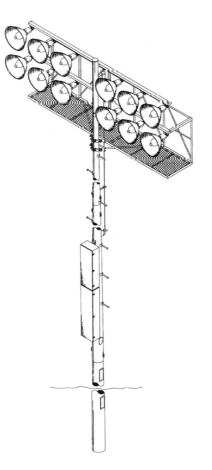

can be an economic alternative to the use of a column. Although a
lattice tower isn't as aesthetic as a single column, it can carry a large
number of floodlights safely and its construction enables platforms to
be installed at high level with ladders for access usually contained
within the structure. Any column or tower has to be able to withstand
high wind forces and it is fairly obvious that the greater the thickness
of the tower or column and the larger the area of floodlights that it
carries has an influence on how much wind the structure will be able
to withstand.

Power supplies

As already stated floodlights are usually discharge sources and come
in a variety of lamp power outputs. Simple installations will generally be fed from single phase supplies, i.e. a small tennis court, etc.
However, for large areas, three phase supplies are essential for two
reasons:

1. It is easier to balance the electrical load.
2. The flicker problems that are associated with discharge sources
   can be minimized by providing a degree of overlap of the light
   outputs.

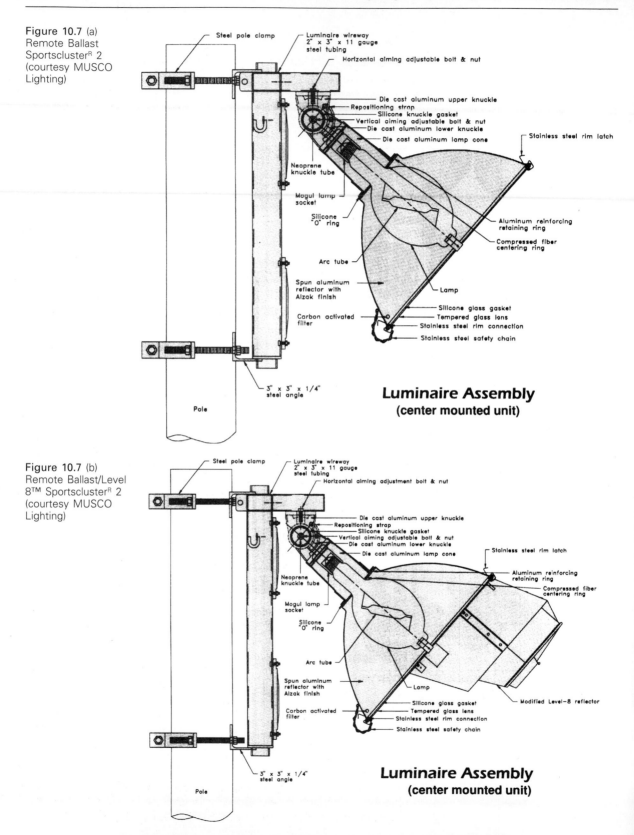

Figure 10.7 (a) Remote Ballast Sportscluster[R] 2 (courtesy MUSCO Lighting)

Figure 10.7 (b) Remote Ballast/Level 8™ Sportscluster[R] 2 (courtesy MUSCO Lighting)

Luminaire Assembly
(center mounted unit)

Luminaire Assembly
(center mounted unit)

Glare

Floodlighting must supply adequate illumination levels with a reasonably uniform light distribution and provide relatively glare free lighting to both the sporting participants and the spectators. Why do we need to guard against glare. First of all it may interfere with the event competitors and secondly it causes a great deal of annoyance to the spectators.

Glare is noticeable on the periphery of the visual field of view and increases significantly as the light output from the luminaires moves towards the centre of the observers' field of view. Discomfort glare can be caused by very bright lights against dark backgrounds. Within a floodlight area glare can be reduced by increasing the height of the floodlights or by providing louvres to prevent direct light entering the field of view and also by attempting to ensure that the background is not too dark; but this is obviously difficult to achieve on outside locations as there is no control over the dark night sky. Increasing the height of the floodlights can present problems with the vertical illumination as it will change the angle of incidence and hence affect the 'cosine law'.

10.2   Sports lighting for film and television

CIE guidelines

Beyond the needs of the spectators, there is a need for the lighting levels to satisfy film and television cameras and this is particularly true today when much sport is televised. In Europe the CIE have laid down guidelines for sports stadia lighting. These days, with many cameras used on sporting events, particularly small portable cameras that go anywhere in the playing area, any individual camera must have sufficient light levels for its requirements wherever it may be.

Colour rendering index

The Sports Council recommend that the colour rendering index (Ra) for sports at the highest level should be at least 60. However, it is generally accepted that the colour rendering index for film and television coverage at the highest level of competition should be at least 65 and this is the recommended figure given by the CIE (Commission Internationale d'Eclairage).

Measurement techniques

The CIE also state that vertical illuminance should be used to assess the lighting for good quality film and television pictures. Vertical illuminance is used because all objects of interest are generally vertical to the playing area. The positions at which the vertical illumination measurements should be made depends on:

1.   If the cameras are positioned along one side of the playing area then the incident illumination on the plane only facing the cameras has to meet the required light level (Figure 10.8).

Figure 10.8 Single plane incident
light readings

2. Where the cameras are positioned anywhere around the playing area, it is essential for the illumination in all four vertical planes to meet the required levels (Figure 10.9).

In isolation, each camera trained on a particular area may be able to correctly expose for a picture but the overall effect of the lighting has to be reasonably consistent to allow for those cameras which follow the action, for example all around a running track, and a figure of around 0.4 minimum to maximum vertical illumination is usually acceptable.

Illumination factors

As the illuminated horizontal area can form a large part of the field of view of a camera it is essential that a good balance is maintained between the vertical and horizontal lighting levels and a figure of between 0.5 and 2.0 is considered satisfactory. This figure is obtained from the ratio of the average horizontal illumination to the average vertical illumination, E_h av : E_v av.

The factors that decide the level of vertical illuminance required are based upon the following CIE guidelines.

1. Speed of action
The arm movements of a freestyle swimmer might be considered fast, but the progress through water is relatively slow. Similarly, rifle shooting and darts involve fast moving projectiles but the camera will concentrate on the marksman and the target, which are static. In most track events, movements along the track may be relatively fast, but the camera follows the action along predetermined courses and there is

Figure 10.9 360° incident light
readings

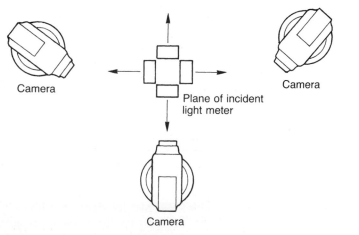

rarely sudden movement to be observed. Thus athletics will usually be classed as slow, and dog, horse and motor racing as of medium speed.

In some sports, although the players may move no faster than a sprinter, the direction of place changes frequently and rapidly. Where the object of play is small and travels at high speed, e.g. the puck in ice hockey, or there is action involving split second judgements, these all involve high speeds of movement.

2. Shooting distance and lens angle

Apparent speed for those watching the sport on television is dependent on whether the camera is using a wide angle or telephoto lens. This means that where the camera locations are a considerable distance from the action, the use of telephoto shots will be more likely.

3. Classes of sport

Sports can be divided into three groups, A, B and C, characterized mainly by the speed of the action occurring during camera shots.

- **Group A:** Archery, athletics, billiards, curling, darts, diving, horse jumping, shooting, snooker, swimming.
- **Group B:** Badminton, baseball, basketball, bob-sleigh luge, football, gymnastics, handball, hockey (indoor/outdoor), ice skating, judo, karate, lawn tennis (indoor/outdoor), racing (motorcycle, motor, cycle, dog and horse), roller skating, ski jumping, ski racing, softball, speed skating, volleyball, wrestling.
- **Group C:** Boxing, cricket, fencing, ice hockey, lacrosse, tennis, squash, table tennis.

Each of these groups is then subdivided into three according to the maximum shooting distance. Each value of vertical illuminance given applies to a particular class of sport and a specified maximum shooting distance.

The figures given in Table 10.3 reflect the illumination levels required for sport, they do not give any guidance as to glare and in practice most of the sports governing bodies have their own recommendations as to the way they prefer their individual sport to be lit. A good example would be fencing, where due to the nature of the sport, any small interference with the participants' eyeline from the lighting can cause problems. It is therefore preferable that the lighting is arranged parallel to either side of the fencing mat and sufficiently high to be out of the participants' eyeline. Another good example of a possible glare problem is for tennis players when they throw the ball up to serve. If towers are erected at the corners of the court there will be every chance that the player may look into

Table 10.3 Recommended illuminance levels (lux)

Maximum shooting distance	25m	75m	150m
Sports group A	500	700	1000
Sports group B	700	1000	1400
Sports group C	1000	1400	–

the luminaires and careful glare prevention techniques such as louvres have to be employed to reduce problems. It is generally much better to position the floodlight towers slightly to the side of the court to enable a better control of glare.

Additional lighting

Having said that the majority of modern stadia will have floodlighting based upon the requirements of television coverage, there are occasions when additional lighting may be required. A good example of this was in the main athletics stadium for the Olympic Games in Barcelona where the existing floodlighting consisted of two rows of luminaires in the upper part of the main stand balanced across the main area by five towers, each carrying a large array of the same type of fixture, supplemented at each end by two short towers with a small number of similar fixtures. The light level in the vertical plane on the main arena varied from a maximum of just over 2000 lux to a minimum of 355 lux, which was outside the recommended standards and was also considered unacceptable for film and television coverage. The lower readings were usually registered at the ends near the short towers, on the bends of the track. The minimum requirement for the arena was 1400 lux in the vertical plane. Bearing in mind that over 80 cameras were used in the stadium; it was essential that anywhere within the competitive area was lit correctly from almost every direction.

The finishing straight which was immediately under the canopy of the main stand and, although adequate for most purposes, was required to be lit to a minimum of 2000 lux for the film and high definition cameras deployed along that side of the stadium. The solution on the finishing straight was to provide 16 4kW discharge Fresnels along the rear of the stand and projected over the heads of the spectators so that the finishing straight reached a level of 2000 lux. Additionally, four extra 33-metre high towers were placed, two either end close to the small original towers so that the ends of the stadium could be raised to the necessary light level. This additional lighting was provided by 24 12kW discharge Fresnel luminaires, although if done now, would be using 6kW PAR discharge sources with their greater efficiency. Incidentally, the additional lighting power load was nearly as much as the installed floodlighting.

10.3   Events and locations

With specially installed temporary sports lighting there are guidelines for either the participants' benefit or for the filming and televising of sporting events, which will have a limiting effect on the choice of luminaires and the type of rig to be used. The suspension system will be very straightforward and is there just to get the lights in the right position. The main points are that, generally, the rig should not be too obvious and that the lighting will be fairly even.

The other type of lighting required which has to be more artistic and generally more uneven by design, can be for:

(a) a pop concert - either inside or outside,
(b) special videos shot on location,

Table 10.4 Luminaire functions

Parcan and profile spots	Limited colour effects available	Limited gobo patterns	Static positions	Large number required for effects lighting
Automated luminaire	Wide range of colour available in each luminaire	Multi and variable gobo patterns available in each luminaire	Motorized 'pan and tilt' of luminaire or mirror system to give dynamic effect	Very few required for effects lighting

(c) televised events, which may be a major outside broadcast such as the Last Night of the Proms,

(d) fashion shows, car launches, etc.

In all of the above lighting is paramount in importance and the tools for lighting all of these types of event are wide and various. Lighting for pop, fashion and other special events requires an approach which allows the rig to incorporate all of the theatrical effects from the lighting designer's special luminaires but at the same time allows speed of construction and servicing. In many cases the rig becomes an important part of the performance. The lighting is there for effect and does not necessarily have to conform to any set of technical standards or rules, although it still requires to be artistically balanced and is mainly biased to theatre lighting. In the past the Parcan was useful because it was cheap and enabled lighting directors to have many light sources with different colours and from a variety of directions for effect; nowadays the automated luminaire is being used more and more with its versatility as well as its ability to be programmed, thus replacing many luminaires in a lighting rig.

Table 10.4 compares the functions and use of luminaires. In addition, the individual luminaires are also required to move from a set position to ensure that the desired incident angle of lighting to the subject is correct, and this is usually accomplished by motorized trolleys moving around sections of the grid system. On occasions sections of truss may also be required to move to provide changes to its geometric shape.

Lighting types

The lighting can be anything from a small fluorescent source up to 20kW tungsten sources and 18kW discharge sources. TV and film will use tungsten and discharge lighting for location and events, with discharge predominating due to its greater efficiency, thus providing a cooler environment for the competitors or artistes. This type of lighting will be balanced by the use of dimmable ballasts, scrims and gels, and can remain on for periods of time without dynamic lighting changes. Concert and stage lighting, on the other hand, relies upon lighting changes which may be subtle and slow or fast and dynamic. The luminaires will be profile spots, Parcans and automated lighting units. The profiles and Parcans will use tungsten lamps fed from conventional dimmers and the majority of the automated luminaires will be fitted with discharge sources which are controlled by mechanical dimming systems, such as an iris placed in the optical path.

Providing facilities

Before we progress into arranging the facilities for any show in any location, there are several questions that need to be answered and these are:

1. Location of site?
2. Has the site been used before, and if so, are there records showing rigging arrangements, electrical supply, access routes, communication facilities and points of contact?
3. How much time is there to rig and de-rig the event?
4. Access to and from site?
5. There will obviously be a need for a truss system to be erected to support the luminaires, sound systems, etc. Additionally there could be a requirement for scaffolding arrangements which may be for proscenium arches or tall platforms for follow spots, etc.
6. Where is the technical equipment to be situated, i.e. lighting, sound and on occasions, vision?
7. Is there a requirement for a control position? If so, where is it in relation to the other equipment?
8. Does the location have a sufficiently large power supply or does it require power generation equipment?
9. If generators are required, where can they be positioned, bearing in mind they are very heavy and fairly noisy devices?
10. How do we get power from the generators to a fairly central position where it can be distributed throughout the venue or location without large volt drops on the long cable runs?
11. Does the location have sufficient air conditioning or does it require additional air conditioning according to the type of event? This is particularly important with sporting events and may affect the choice of luminaires.

Tower lights

Many small outside locations used for film and television probably only require the use of a few luminaires and the majority of these will be used on stands. Where more complex arrangements are required for this type of location, it is possible to hire trucks complete with generator and a working platform capable of going up to great heights, to enable lights to be positioned very high above a scene. These can vary from a single Fresnel discharge source on a jib arm similar to the Elstree Light and Power truck (Figure 10.10) through to more powerful sources such as the tower trucks made by Musco Lighting of America capable of raising an array of 15 6kW discharge sources to around 35 metres.

Because each 6kW luminaire is an open-faced fitting, its light output is more than twice that of a 12kW Fresnel discharge luminaire. The trucks, which are fitted with soundproofed generators, weigh around 33 tonnes; the boom extension is fitted behind the drivers' cab and towards the front of the generator. This obviously gives a very stable base for the heights required, with an extremely low centre of gravity. The lights can be controlled from a small hand-held remote control unit or by an operator with levers at the base of the boom arm; and each light can be panned through

Figure 10.10 Moonbeam crane and generator. Courtesy of Elstree Light and Power

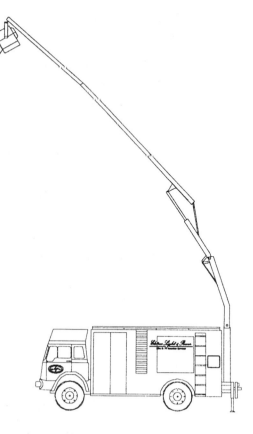

359°, tilted through 220°, flooded and spotted. Additionally, the boom arm is capable of rotating 180° on its base.

10.4   Electrical distribution

During 1975 following complaints from electricians that discharge lighting was a possible cause of high UV levels, a meeting was convened at the BBC Outside Broadcast base in London to examine the safety of discharge sources. All of the major manufacturers and suppliers of lighting attended, together with senior representatives of the Health and Safety Executive. During the course of this meeting, the electrical inspector concerned noticed a strange plug and socket (for him) and asked one of the BBC representatives what the device was. The reply was that the connector was a 'half inch' Kleigel which was introduced in Hollywood and had been used in the British film industry, subsequently being used in the TV industry in the UK. The inspector asked what voltage would be used with this connector and was told it would be 240V, at which point he said that due to the construction of the device, it was condemned! To say the least, this caused slight consternation amongst the assembled gathering as the whole industry had based many of their distribution systems around the half and one inch Kleigel connectors.

The introduction of BS 5550

The outcome of this seemingly innocuous statement from the Health and Safety inspector caused a complete rethink in the industry of the supply arrangements used for all outside broadcasts and film locations and to that end BS 5550 was introduced as a code of practice for the distribution of ac electrical supplies. The code of practice was finally introduced in 1981 (six years on) and has been in use ever since. Recently, it has been restructured to cover all aspects of temporary ac electrical supplies for entertainment lighting and other relevant fields. BS 5550 lays down the requirements for the types of cable, connector and distribution units so that the selection of mcbs and fusing arrangements are to required standards. The standard is produced so that guidance is given on common matters of interest to manufacturing companies, equipment hire suppliers, the various electrical installation contractors that may be employed and electricity supply companies. The electricity used may come from the public supply or other suppliers or from portable generators. The distribution systems themselves can be for lighting, general house lighting and power supplied for cameras, audio equipment, various types of broadcast equipment and associated services such as wardrobe, make up, scenery, etc. By bringing in an appropriate standard, it ensures that all manufacturers of equipment used in the entertainment industry meet minimum safety standards. Much of the code of practice is based upon the BS 7671 (the IEE Regulations now published as a British Standard) but with emphasis on the need for portability, robustness and suitability for use in a variety of weather conditions.

Oh, by the way, the problems with UV radiation were referred to the National Physical Laboratory to ascertain the 'danger' levels and any hazards in practice.

Power system design

When designing a power system for a special event, various requirements will have to be taken into account. These are:

1. What are the show or production requirements?
2. What are the site conditions?
3. The design of a safe and suitable electrical system, which will have to take account of the fact that some electronic control systems may have large neutral currents, e.g. some manufacturers' flicker free ballasts, etc.
4. Ensure that any installation meets the requirements of the local authorities such as the fire brigade, etc.

In areas where lightning is a high risk, it is essential that precautions are taken to prevent any unnecessary hazards.

Connectors

The various connectors used must be approved to either a British Standard or an international standard to suit its actual use. The main requirement with connectors would be that they should only be used in association with a correct pin connections and relevant colour codes, etc. Due to the fact there is now a tremendous overlap between the theatre, television, film and pop lighting world, it may be the various connectors are used in areas where they have not been used before and it is essential that the connectors are carefully chosen for the purpose in hand. The main power distribution cables generally use large single pole connectors due to the high currents involved and it is essential to identify each of these connectors clearly to show whether it is a phase, neutral or earth conductor. It is fairly obvious that any misplugging can cause a huge fault, or a very dangerous situation. Several modern distribution systems do have sensing circuits to prevent any misplugging. Several distribution units in use today have all the necessary intake switchgear and sub-distribution fuses or mcbs contained within one unit, which makes the whole process so much safer by reducing the amount of inter-connections on site (Figure 10.11).

Multi-core connectors and cables

Generally, multi-core connectors and cables are used for circuits up to 125A. Above this point single core connections are generally used. An important factor with the cable rating is that they may be taken to areas where the temperatures are extremely high and due to the installations, will probably be bunched or grouped in close proximity which can cause problems, and this is a factor which must be taken into account by the designer concerned. All items used on the temporary installation should have been tested for electrical safety prior to being delivered to site; they should be marked that the test was satisfactory. It is essential when in the areas where the public are, that the cables are routed carefully, possibly up and over gangways so that there is no danger of anyone tripping over cables.

A problem with temporary cables is that they may have to go through various doorways, etc., and it is essential that they would not break any fire regulations by breaching openings in the building which should be closed during a performance or normal working conditions. The power will be either from the public supply or from a generator and the distribution system will feed dimmers and other subsidiary equipment, which may be located in many places within the temporary installation. It is essential that all feeds to all these items of equipment are adequately fused or have the correct mcbs fitted to ensure protection for the cables and equipment. One of the problems with temporary installations is the variety of weather that may be encountered. For instance, outside events in very humid or wet conditions would no doubt require special precautions to be taken to prevent any safety hazards and the use of RCDs is encouraged. Most modern distribution units are fitted with RCDs and to prevent nuisance tripping they are also fitted with a by-pass system accessed by the use of a key (Figure 10.12).

It is essential that when the temporary installation is complete it is fully checked to ensure, as far as possible, that all connections and equipment are installed correctly prior to the application of power to the system.

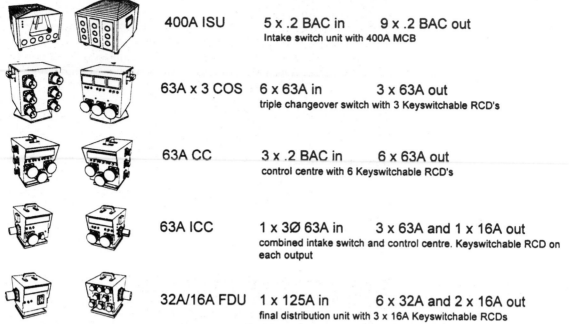

400A ISU   5 x .2 BAC in   9 x .2 BAC out
Intake switch unit with 400A MCB

63A x 3 COS   6 x 63A in   3 x 63A out
triple changeover switch with 3 Keyswitchable RCD's

63A CC   3 x .2 BAC in   6 x 63A out
control centre with 6 Keyswitchable RCD's

63A ICC   1 x 3Ø 63A in   3 x 63A and 1 x 16A out
combined intake switch and control centre. Keyswitchable RCD on each output

32A/16A FDU   1 x 125A in   6 x 32A and 2 x 16A out
final distribution unit with 3 x 16A Keyswitchable RCDs

(a)

Figure 10.11 (a) Power distribution (courtesy Elstree Light and Power)

Figure 10.11 (b) High density dimmer rack (courtesy Elstree Light and Power)

(b)

Figure 10.11 (c) Dimmer rack load meters and MCBs (courtesy Elstree Light and Power)

Figure 10.11 (d) Distribution unit (front and rear view) (courtesy Elstree Light and Power)

Multi-way connector systems

Multi-way connector systems together with multicore cables are used to supply from dimmer racks to points on a truss where fanout cables are used for six dimmer circuits, each comprising a live, neutral and an earth connection. Many of the companies in the supply of systems for the entertainment industry do not necessarily conform to a standard multi-connector pin connection and the new standard is welcomed so that some standardization will be possible.

The public

With permanent installations, purpose built switch rooms and areas which are used for electrical supplies, can be built in such a way that they are not capable of being entered by members of the public. On

Figure 10.12 Distribution unit
(courtesy Elstree Light and Power)

outside broadcasts, locations or special events where temporary lighting is used, it is essential that the public are kept away from any source of electrical danger which might come from the distribution units or cable system.

Most supply systems encountered are 'star' connected three phase systems, but it is possible on some locations, to encounter 'delta' connected systems and the best method to overcome any difficulties with the connected equipment is to employ 'star' output transformers which are fed from the 'delta' supply.

If the power requirement for additional lighting in any venue or premises is not too great, it is possible that there will be sufficient capacity on the house supplies to allow the extra luminaires to be used. However, in the majority of cases there is no slack capacity and the generator will have to be employed. Whatever the system of obtaining a power supply, the fact is that it needs to be adequately fused, the cables need to be of sufficient size and they need to be run in such a manner that they do not cause danger to members of the public and/or artists.

Cable systems and power loads

In the past, usually three-core cables were fed to each luminaire, generally from some switchgear or dimmers. The pop industry found this was too time consuming when they were on the road with the large rigs employed and resorted to multi-core cable systems feeding banks of luminaires. However, there is a finite limit to the size of cables used, due to the weight and flexibility. If they are heavy, it is important that the actual runs of cable, when coiled, would be within the handling capability say, a rigger or sparks on trussing, etc. An important point to bear in mind is where are dimmers, if used, being placed in relation to the luminaires themselves. Obviously long cable runs should be

60 kW

Vehicle
Bedford TL.

Gross weight:	12.5 T
Unladen weight:	8.9 T
Length:	7620mm (25ft)
Width:	2590mm (8ft 6in)
Height:	2819mm (9ft 3in)

Generator
TV Silenced generator with Sync Lock control

Output:	60Kw single phase
	on 3 x 125A, 1 x 63A CEE17, or Busbars
Output:	24Kw three phase
	on Busbars

Figure 10.13 (a) TV silenced generator. Courtesy of Elstree Light and Power

500KVA Twin Generator Set

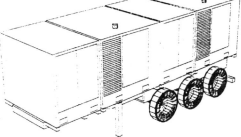

Gross weight:	
Width:	2438mm (8ft)
Length:	7823mm (25ft 8in)
Height:	3309mm (11ft)
Fuel Capacity:	6,200 litres (60 hours running time at full load)
Equipment Cap.:	8.5 cubic metres / 3000Kg

Two sets can be configured as two separate power systems, or linked to provide either a 500 kVA supply or a 250 kVA supply with 100% redundancy for failsafe operation.

Figure 10.13 (b) Silent Flight 250 generator system. Courtesy of Elstree Light and Power

avoided if possible and additionally, the power loads shouldn't be too far away from the generator due to the need to have large cables coming through any premises. Over the years, several dubious practices have been used with regard to cable systems and the connectors used. With the application of BS 5550, together with the Electricity at Work Act and other various directives with regard to electrical safety, the industry is having to get its act together and try to make them safer than before. Distribution can be broken down into three areas:

1. The main intake, where large cables are taken from a generator into subsidiary switchgear, probably of around 400 A per phase, and then distributed from these units protected by mcbs
2. To smaller units placed strategically in the premises and probably protected at around 125 A.
3. Finally these circuits would feed the dimmer racks with individual outputs anywhere between 2 and 10 kW.

Neutral currents and power factor

Special arrangements have to be made to feed the ballast units associated with discharge sources. As well as the power feeds, there will also be a need for the control cables used with automated lighting systems, dimming shutters and hoist motors all placed in the temporary grid system. With tungsten lighting on dimmers, a power factor very close to unity will be achieved most of the time. However if using discharge lighting without power factor correction, it is possible to find that there are large neutral currents flowing and this can cause problems with the distribution system. With choke ballasts the power factor will be that dictated by the inductive load. With flicker free ballasts, it is generally a capacitive out of balance, either of these causing the same problem in the neutral. Normally, with a three-phase supply if the load is balanced uniformly across the three phases, there would be no need for a neutral return. However, with out-of-phase currents, there is a need for a neutral and the neutral is then in relation to the currents which are out of phase. So, it's no good providing a small neutral in relation to the large phase conductors, it is essential that the neutral conductor and the phase conductors are all the same.

Heat problems

Special arrangements may have to be made for any areas where heat may build to excessive levels, and the following is a case of where the best laid plans of mice and men can go astray due to the needs of the competitors in the sporting event.

The Olympic badminton venue at Marbella on the sea front at Barcelona contained three courts and the roof in this building did not allow for very much weight to be added. It was therefore decided that four trusses, each 10 metres long, would carry 90 2 kW 'Blondes', with 30 Blondes used on each court. Blondes were selected because of their high light output and low weight. If discharge sources had been chosen, there was the additional problem of using quite heavy ballasts, and for convenience these would have to be in the actual rig. The building was fitted with quite a reasonable air conditioning system which was needed due to the fact the building construction was metal framed with glass infill - rather like a large greenhouse. All the multi-core feeder cable ran through the existing roof space and down to the trusses. Obviously all the heat was near the roof, but with the air conditioning working there was little or no problem. When the competitors started to practise, long silk ribbons were lowered from the roof to ascertain the amount of breeze in the building, which was claimed would affect the movement of shuttlecocks. Having established that the silk ribbons were blowing sufficiently that there could be a disturbance to the play, the competitors and the organizing committee of the event requested that the air conditioning be switched off. This caused the competitors to have to play in temperatures often exceeding 40°C. The problem now arose that the roof space became increasingly hot and the ambient temperature in which the cables were working was excessive in the extreme. The local authorities, concerned with the running of the building, became concerned that the cables themselves were running hot, and although under the maximum limit imposed by the British cable makers, it was felt, on the grounds of diplomacy, that it would be best to change all the cables. As events were taking place all day long, it meant that the actual riggers and electricians concerned could only work from about

10 o'clock at night to the next morning to accomplish the changeover of all the cables. Normally, this would be quite easy but the roof space consisted of a series of deep latticed beams supporting a fairly flimsy roof, and there were no proper access ways at roof level, which meant that the work was relatively dangerous and it was necessary for the crew to go up a wire ladder into the roof itself, as no access route had ever been provided. With the changeover completed, the cables ran cooler, the authorities were happy and the contestants still sweated it out!

10.5 Generators

Generators and diesel engines

Generators come in various sizes, from the small Honda sets giving a few kilowatts to the large 100 kVA generators. All modern generators are driven by and are provided with large fuel tanks so that the generator can run for many hours without being replenished. One of the problems with diesels is that if they runs out of fuel, it would be necessary to bleed the fuel lines to allow the diesel to run again. On occasions, when it is necessary to run generators for long periods of time without switching off, it may be necessary to make special arrangements to introduce fuel from an external fuel tank system. The generators are normally three-phase and the phases must be fairly well balanced to ensure that the diesel runs smoothly; the diesels used for the entertainment industry need to be silent running. It is essential that the frequency of supply is kept stable, and this is usually done by fitting electronic governor systems. Normally, the rear of the generator contains a distribution panel which is fitted with voltmeters, ammeters and the various switches required to run the diesel itself. The normal procedure is to wire to the generator from the local distribution units, check all the electrical system is OK and safe and then run the generator. When the generator is running the main switches are applied and electricity is supplied to the system.

Power factor

Although a generator may be rated at say, 1000 kVA, if this is not feeding units which have a good power factor, it can be that the output is considerably reduced and in the past with using discharge sources with standard ballasts, a 1000kVA generator may be only worth 700 kVA with all the luminaires connected.

10.6 Trussing and support systems

Weight loads

Truss used for suspension systems comes in different sizes and lengths with a variety of joining pieces to enable intricate arrangements to be built (Figure 10.14). The physical size would be determined by the weight loads such as cables and luminaires imposed on the truss. The larger the load, the larger the cross section of the truss. The length of section will be decided by the maximum deflection under a load that can be applied safely without any defamation of the truss. The size and length of truss may be decided by the ability to suspend only from a few points rather than regular intervals, e.g. a fairly long truss only suspended at its ends will obviously have a limit of deflection due to the lack of a central suspension point.

Chain hoist motors

The first requirement of truss is that it should be lightweight but capable of taking quite high point loads on the structure with a pretty reasonable overall safe working load. The sections have to be small enough to be manhandled and transported; they also have to be capable of being assembled quickly and safely. Trusses come in various sizes; and various lengths. Having established the pattern of truss required, it is now essential to lift it to the height required in the venue by using inverted chain hoist motors, with capacities anywhere between 1/8 to 3 tonnes, the most favoured of these being 1 tonne. Obviously with just one straight section of truss, it may be possible to hoist it into place with two motors, but the first requirement of hoisting is the fact that the motors must run synchronously together so that it is easy for the operator on the control unit at floor level to ascertain the correct height and enable the unit to be positioned accurately. If three motors are used on a straight section of truss, it is essential that all three take the load simultaneously and no one motor ends up taking the majority of the load. As the rigs become more complex it may be that several motors have to be used simultaneously to lift a pre-arranged pattern of truss to a set position above the performing area.

Any chain hoist motor unit will probably be capable of up to 40 m of lift, be protected for overload and have upper and lower limit switches fitted to ensure safety when working with these units. They may be used on either single- or three-phase supply, the majority being three-phase.

Parcans and pre-wired groups

The vast majority of the lights used on truss are Parcans, and these are usually in pre-wired groups on short bars, easily attached to the truss itself, and capable of being plugged to the multicore electrical feeder system very rapidly (Figures 10.17 and 10.18). However, there is a need to identify all the feeder cables so that the console operators concerned will know which dimmers control which lights. In addition to the Parcan, there is generally a multiplicity of automated luminaires to provide dynamic lighting effects on the set and there also may be a requirement for laser projection. Sound reinforcement loudspeakers may also be required to be rigged on the truss.

In addition to the chain motors which take the truss to high level, once in position, it is essential that extra bonding is provided so that the system is absolutely safe. In addition to bonding the truss by a secondary means of support, it is essential that all luminaires attached to the truss are also safety bonded to avoid any accidents, either to the performers, audience or technicians involved.

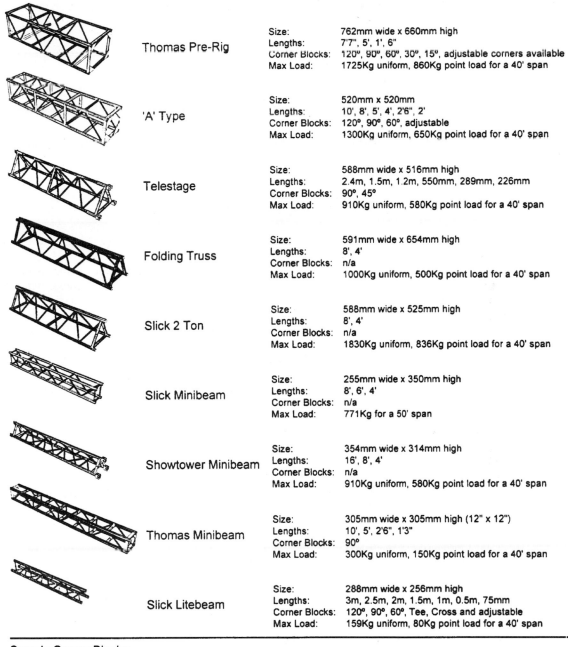

Thomas Pre-Rig

Size: 762mm wide x 660mm high
Lengths: 7'7", 5', 1', 6"
Corner Blocks: 120º, 90º, 60º, 30º, 15º, adjustable corners available
Max Load: 1725Kg uniform, 860Kg point load for a 40' span

'A' Type

Size: 520mm x 520mm
Lengths: 10', 8', 5', 4', 2'6", 2'
Corner Blocks: 120º, 90º, 60º, adjustable
Max Load: 1300Kg uniform, 650Kg point load for a 40' span

Telestage

Size: 588mm wide x 516mm high
Lengths: 2.4m, 1.5m, 1.2m, 550mm, 289mm, 226mm
Corner Blocks: 90º, 45º
Max Load: 910Kg uniform, 580Kg point load for a 40' span

Folding Truss

Size: 591mm wide x 654mm high
Lengths: 8', 4'
Corner Blocks: n/a
Max Load: 1000Kg uniform, 500Kg point load for a 40' span

Slick 2 Ton

Size: 588mm wide x 525mm high
Lengths: 8', 4'
Corner Blocks: n/a
Max Load: 1830Kg uniform, 836Kg point load for a 40' span

Slick Minibeam

Size: 255mm wide x 350mm high
Lengths: 8', 6', 4'
Corner Blocks: n/a
Max Load: 771Kg for a 50' span

Showtower Minibeam

Size: 354mm wide x 314mm high
Lengths: 16', 8', 4'
Corner Blocks: n/a
Max Load: 910Kg uniform, 580Kg point load for a 40' span

Thomas Minibeam

Size: 305mm wide x 305mm high (12" x 12")
Lengths: 10', 5', 2'6", 1'3"
Corner Blocks: 90º
Max Load: 300Kg uniform, 150Kg point load for a 40' span

Slick Litebeam

Size: 288mm wide x 256mm high
Lengths: 3m, 2.5m, 2m, 1.5m, 1m, 0.5m, 75mm
Corner Blocks: 120º, 90º, 60º, Tee, Cross and adjustable
Max Load: 159Kg uniform, 80Kg point load for a 40' span

Sample Corner Blocks

120º 2 way   90º 4 way   60º 3 way   30º 2 way   15º 2 way

Figure 10.14 Trusses. Courtesy of
Universal Rigging Services

Figure 10.15 Ground support
towers. Courtesy of Universal
Rigging Services

Self Climbing Ground Support System

Description
The ground support system comprises of a small footprint base
with levelling jacks, 12" square tower sections that are bolted
together to the desired height with a hinged section at the base.
A sleeve block fits round the tower and holds an electric chain
hoist. The chain is passed up to the top of the tower over a roller
beam and back down to the sleeve block to allow the hoist to pull
the sleeve block up.
Four towers are normally used in a square, connected together by
truss sections bolted to the sleeve blocks. If fewer towers are
used, outriggers are available for added stability. Note that 32A
three phase power is required for the motors.

Specifications
Max Load:	1 Ton per leg
Max Height:	11.5m
Tower Sections:	12" square mini beam, 10', 5', 2'6", 1'3"
Sleeve Blocks:	Available for Pre-Rig, Telestage and 'A' Type truss

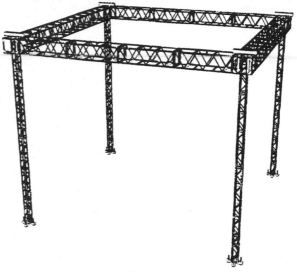

System using 4 towers and Thomas Pre-Rig truss to give a 35' box.

Showtower Ground Support Mast

Description
The Showtower system uses free standing towers with a suspended load. This allows a variety of loads to be lifted such as
speaker clusters or angled truss.

The towers are self-erecting by means of a motor in the base unit
that is also used to raise the load. Outriggers are fitted to the
base section to ensure stability. Note that 32A three phase power
is required for the motors.

Specifications
Max Load:	1 Ton per tower
Max Height:	11m
Tower Sections:	16', 8', 4'

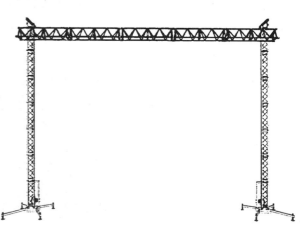

System using 2 towers and Telestage truss to give a 40' arch.

Figure 10.16 Truss sections
(courtesy Universal Rigging
Services)

Figure 10.17 Parcan groups
(courtesy Elstree Light and
Power)

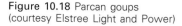

Figure 10.18 Parcan goups
(courtesy Elstree Light and Power)

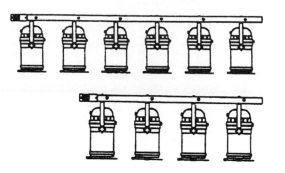

Lighting at sports events is quite often the application of reasonable illumination in a studied way onto an area. The skill generally is positioning trussing and lights so that they do not interfere with the competitors' eyelines and they also give a reasonable result on the playing area without affecting the spectators' eyelines.

Problems in practice

The following example emphasizes the flexibility of trussing when used for the lighting support system. The venue for the fencing at the 1992 Olympics consisted of an old exhibition hall spanned by large steel trusses supporting the roof, all of which were quite capable of carrying any mechanical loads imposed by the trussing, the cables and the luminaires. The original plan was that all the fencing mats ran parallel to the length of the hall, thus there was a centre court, with just one mat and either side were three pairs of mats making 13 mats in all. In the run up to the Games, with only a short time left, the organizers decided that, mainly for television coverage, the two sets of mats either side of the centre court would have to be placed at 45° to the hall, thus ruining the carefully arranged lighting system that had already been installed. Due to the fact that all the areas at ground level were now complete, it was virtually impossible to lower everything to the floor, de-rig, move it and re-rig; and the solution was to actually move things whilst in the air – a feat accomplished in a remarkably short time, considering that there were eight large trusses, a considerable length of multi-core feeder cable and 64 luminaires to re-rig. Of course, needless to say, all the pre-arranged cable routes had to be scrapped and a new system introduced. During the rigging process in this hall, an accident occurred which showed just how careful you have to be with temporary audience seating and handrails. One of the riggers, who incidentally was a mountain climbing expert, leant back on a handrail approximately three metres above the concrete floor; unfortunately the rail had not been fixed properly and he fell off the back of the staging onto his spine. Luckily, being a trained climber, he relaxed his body sufficiently so he didn't sustain a major injury to the spine, only a cracked vertebrae. The lessons learnt from working on events such as this are always be prepared for the unexpected, never take anything for granted and always be on your guard for seemingly simple requests that eventually may turn out to take hours of effort.

11
Automated lighting systems

Introduction

The dictionary defines automation as 'a high degree of mechanization in manufacture, the handling of material between processes being automatic, and the whole automatically controlled'. A technical dictionary defines automation as 'industrial closed loop control system in which manual operation of controls is replaced by servo operation'. In the entertainment industry, we have come to use the word 'automation' incorrectly, to describe several different types of system which are, in the main, generally motorized and responsive to some degree, *with human intervention*. The whole point about an automatic process is that it occurs *without* human intervention, and with many robotic machines in use today a learning process takes place and after that process the machine works without a human operator. On car assembly lines, with this type of machine, the operator goes through the motions of, say, a paint spraying process on a car body. The machine follows every movement of the human being and then replicates these when returned to the automatic mode. If we use the definition as laid down, the only automatic system we have in use today is the memory playback on lighting control consoles. In addition to this, we also have motorized luminaire control systems that are memorized and then replayed. However, it is doubtful if we will ever get to the stage where the lighting system responds 'automatically' without human intervention. Although this section of the book discusses automated lighting systems, it really should be entitled 'Mechanized systems with some form of memory control and their application to lighting'.

Remote controlled luminaires were introduced on a large scale for the disco scene closely followed by the pop groups on tour, for roadshows and live concerts. The idea of moving the light beams by either a mirror or moving the luminaire was a progression from purely placing colour and patterns in them. Eventually, television and film borrowed the techniques to create, in their own media, a simulation of a live pop show. Having experienced the joy of moving a luminaire with fingertip control, without getting anywhere near the luminaire itself, the television industry promoted the idea to manufacturers to develop all-singing, all-dancing studio luminaires.

The technical designers soon discovered that the pop/theatre and television requirements were poles apart. The pop and theatre industry required extremely fast movement for effect with as many colour changes as possible, using multi-layer dichroic filters, all combined in a lightweight portable unit that could be rigged on overhead trusses. Theatre and television systems do not always require the same degree of speed and number of colour changes, but do require accurate positioning. This is highlighted in the case of a motorized spot luminaire, with hard edged focus. With a projected distance of say, 10 metres, the beam must stop within a repeatable accuracy of at least 10 centimetres.

In the case of Fresnel or PC luminaires, focusing from flood to spot does not require a great accuracy of setting; the same is true for hard edge to soft edge focus on a profile spot. In televison and film, a motorized Fresnel with a set of barndoors requires movement of the four barndoor flaps together with clockwise/anticlockwise rotation. A colour changing system is an essential requirement, with a suggested minimum of 20 colours, which may be provided by a colour scroller or built in filtration. In a profile projector, two lenses have to be moved to change the spot size and a set of shutters with some degree of rotation are required to shape the beam with optical adjustments to produce the beam distribution required.

The acoustic noise associated with movement and accuracy of alignment can be overcome by either reducing the speed of movement, or by using very high grade drive systems. The motorized luminaires in theatre and television are not always intended to stimulate emotional effects; the aim is to produce fast turn round times in a television studio and in the theatre, with the demands of 'rep', to allow different luminaire settings without having to get to those difficult luminaires tucked away in the 'gods'.

Ask any lighting director for a desirable list of requirements for a motorized luminaire and they will certainly cite all of the above controls, plus many personal foibles. They would also like to control the luminaires by standing in the middle of the acting area, pointing a magic wand at the appropriate luminaire and creating any number of effects. Added to these requirements is a memory system that would record every movement, the time of that movement and the position of the end result.

In the pop world, the greatest need would seem to be for moving beams of light to heighten the effect of the performers on stage, thus the luminaires concerned could be from a Parcan through to the high intensity movable Xenon sources used rather like searchlights. All of these of course, have to be controlled in some way and the degree of accuracy of their requirements depends upon the effects desired. The world of the theatre however, will probably use motorized luminaires with remote control systems, quite often tied into the lighting control system of the theatre concerned, to achieve a lower rate of luminaire usage. In other words, where before two or three lights were used to create an effect, mainly on the grounds that colours had to be changed, one luminaire with its integral control of beam and colour may replace three luminaires. All these changes have to meet two criteria:

1. They have to be extremely quiet to avoid being a nuisance to the audience enjoying the theatre show.
2. They must have rapid response to their positional or colour changes so that the effect is virtually instantaneous from the audience viewpoint.

The trouble is, speed and quietness are not too easy bedfellows.

We come to the requirements of the TV and film industry. Any luminaires used in these industries would invariably have to be supplied to go with rigging systems and the whole has to be integrated very carefully. In TV one luminaire without lateral movement will not be able to take the place of three other luminaires. One of the problems in TV and film is that we've always got an obtrusive object called a boom microphone that hovers around creating rather nasty shadows if the lighting is not correctly positioned; therefore the position of the luminaire is extremely critical. There would appear to be two forms of control desirable when using automated lighting, one of which is the ability of an LD to implement the intended plot from a home computer. The second form of control would be that when the rehearsals and takes or transmissions are involved, the LD has full control of the luminaires from a control room adjacent to the stage or studio. In television the control of the lights is relatively easy because the LD will have camera preview monitors to see the effect of any adjustments made. However in the film industry, this might not be the case although some systems do use combined video/film techniques. The biggest snag in the TV and film industry is the fact that the units would probably be too noisy for the quiet conditions demanded by the realization team in any studio.

11.1 Automated luminaires

Modern fittings such as those produced by Vari-lite, Inc., High End Systems and other moving light companies are capable of rapid lighting changes, but in much theatre work such as drama, rapid movement is not needed. As Francis Reid has said, 'one of the most important aspects of lighting is the angle at which the light beam hits the artists' and although one light may be capable of several modes, by moving the beam around the stage we would get several incident light angles. From the point of view of changing the effect of an individual luminaire, its light output and colour, there are many useful features in the modern generation of automated luminaires.

One area where a big advantage is seen is for colour mixing. With automated luminaires, the multiplicity of colour available for one luminaire may obviate the use of two or three for effect. There is obviously a distinct advantage in being able to programme sets of luminaires if used in a repertory situation with show following show fairly quickly.

There would also be a tremendous advantage when touring, when if the lights were rigged in the same manner over any stage area, it would be simply a matter of coupling them to the necessary computer control and they would all be set to the correct scene setting.

If we look at any trade magazine, or manufacturers catalogue at this moment in time, we will find that the amount of automated luminaires on offer is quite exceptional and it would therefore be impossible to cover for all these devices, so we have attempted to concentrate on two major manufacturers, just to emphasize how automated luminaires have developed in a few short years since 1981.

What functions need to be automated on any luminaire? First of all we will examine what types of luminaire should be automated for their particular application and the functions used for that application.

Mirrors

A high proportion of lighting used in discotheques is a motorized form of illumination. Due to the need to create mood and atmosphere in fairly dark conditions, the intensity of source illumination is not too high. There is also a need to shape the light beam in many ways and to introduce a multiplicity of colour effects. In the luminaires provided by manufacturers for the disco and pop industry, much of the movement is created by the use of mirrors moving at high velocity to divert the light beam in various directions. Mirrors are used because they are extremely lightweight devices in comparison to the luminaire itself and to move luminaires at high velocity to achieve the rapidly moving effects desired by the pop industry, requires quite sophisticated drive systems. For the television, film and theatre industry, the movements required from automated luminaires is usually slower. It is necessary to move higher intensity sources in the film and television industry and generally the luminaires are larger.

Pan and tilt

The basic functions required for any type of automated luminaire are as outlined below. With motorized 'pan and tilt' mechanisms, we can remotely direct the luminaire to the position required. On the surface this seems relatively straightforward to achieve but there are several snags that have to be watched for and these are:

(a) What is the speed of motion required?
(b) How is the speed controlled?
(c) Is it variable and does it have a finite maximum to avoid any structural damage to any component parts of the luminaire?

If the speed is too slow it will be annoying to the viewer, and if too fast difficult to control. How far do we take the directional movement? It would obviously be quite ludicrous to have a device that allowed the 'tilt' mode to keep travelling in the same direction and thus rotate within its yoke. This would cause rather a lot of damage to any power feeding cables or control cables for that matter. By the same token the 'pan' has to be restricted in some way with a feedback system that tells the control that it has reached a finite distance of travel. It is suggested that for 'pan' the motion must be restricted to just over 360° to cover for all situations. Is the device

Figure 11.1 Motorized TV
luminaires

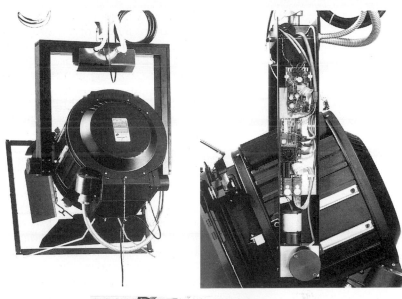

equipped with a system that allows control of 'pan and tilt' simultaneously and does the device have sufficient intelligence to work out
its final destination from two co-ordinates being provided? Perhaps
most important of all is how accurately does the device position itself
and how noisy is it in operation?

Accuracy

As an example, let us take the case of an effects luminaire with a beam
width of 30° with a throw of 10 m: the beam diameter would be
5.36 m. On the assumption that an error of 50 mm at the edge of the
beam would not produce too disturbing a result, we discover that this
would be caused by the beam being misaligned by 0.29°. In the world

of digital electronics where the binary system is used, we find that 2 raised to the power of 10 gives 1024. As this would be a convenient number to use within our digital electronic control system, if we divide 360° (the maximum rotation within one full circle) by 1024 we discover it produces 0.35° and in fact most of the systems in use today work to an accuracy of roughly this amount; usually, in most manufacturers' literature, called 'one third of a degree'. This error, applied to our original beam at 10m throw, produces an error of 61 mm, which is just over 1% of the width of the beam. Obviously as the beam width becomes narrower, the proportion of error in relation to the projected beam is greater. With wide beam luminaires, the result would not be so noticeable. The accuracy of the electronics involved is still, however, greatly influenced by the mechanical coupling of the systems themselves and if much slack exists in either the 'pan' or 'tilt' mechanism accuracies such as those discussed will not be attained. The practical limitations of 'pan and tilt' would appear to be a fraction over 360° in 'pan' and 270° for the 'tilt' operation.

Velocity

One point to be observed when going through the 'tilt' angles is that it would be quite possible to exceed the lamp manufacturers' stated operating angles when using tungsten halogen lamps, although possibly quite satisfactory for discharge sources. Because a fixed speed of movement would be a disadvantage it is preferable that it is a smoothly controlled variable, governed by the control electronics. One manufacturer publishes figures of a minimum velocity of 0.5° per second, and a maximum velocity of 120° per second, which translated into more meaningful terms means rotations varying from 3 seconds in duration to 12 minutes. The 'pan and tilt' drive motors and decoding mechanisms are generally contained within the yoke fitted to the luminaire.

Clutches

Mechanical slipping clutches should be fitted to the 'pan and tilt' system so that in the event of hitting an obstruction the unit will not drive against a motor. This avoids the possibility of either damaging scenery, the luminaire body or burning out the motors.

Optical adjustment

Having adjusted the 'pan and tilt' so that the luminaire is pointing in the right direction, or the direction of reflection from the mirrors, what type of beam do we require? There are two ways of varying the beam angle of a luminaire, one of which is to adjust the lamp in relation to the optics to give varying outputs. This would be the case with Fresnel lens type luminaires. If we are focusing projector type luminaires such as the profile spot, it is desirable to have adjustment of the optics or if fitted, zoom optics, thus being able to give a continuously variable beam angle over the operating range of the optics. Another desirable feature on a luminaire is that we should be able to have a soft or hard edge to the light beam as would be desirable with profile projectors used in the theatre and pop world.

Figure 11.2 (a) Semaphore colour
changer. (b) Scroll colour changer

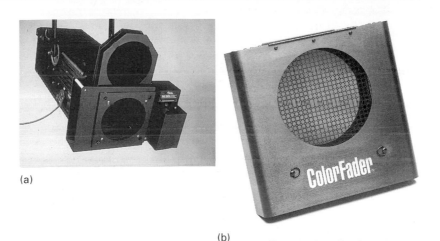

(a)

(b)

Luminaire focus

Obviously it is difficult to put a time or speed to the adjustment of
the focus or any of the optics as this would probably be observed,
and adjusted accordingly by the operators concerned. With all types
of luminaire in use, patterns or 'gobos' will be desired and these
should obviously be inbuilt to the device so that they are instantly
available upon selection.

Colour

Many of today's effects luminaires are often fitted with discharge
lamps. If this is the case and they have to be integrated with other
units, it should be borne in mind that their colour output will probably be around 5600K and to match with other sources within sets or
on the stage, they may have to be colour corrected to 3200K. Even
allowing for the colour of the source, we would wish to change the
basic colour of the light output for effects purposes in any of the
venues where these devices may be used. There are two ways by
which this can be accomplished, one of which is to put electro-
mechanically driven colour changing units on the front of the
luminaires (see Fig. 11.2) or have integral colour changing usually
accomplished by a 'dichroic' system. Electromechanical colour
changers are invariably noisy whereas the use of integral dichroics
may be less obtrusive from the point of view of acoustics. A dichroic
colour changer has to be able to feature a wide range of colours.
Colour changes should occur fairly rapidly so that it would appear
to the viewer that a snap change between two independent light
sources had occurred, not a slow mix of colour on one source which
would probably not give the effects desired by the operators. It may
be of course, that slow changes are required and that the system
should allow for colour mixing within its programme.

Light output

If we are using tungsten luminaires obviously these can be dimmed
by electronic dimmers in the normal way. However, if we are using

discharge sources, even if they were of the 'instant restrike' type, they always have to go through a period of colour and intensity change upon any degree of warming up after being activated. Generally discharge sources require a separate mains supply and do not work satisfactorily from dimming circuits, therefore the most satisfactory method is to use a mechanical dimming shutter to control the light output. This possibly would take the form of an iris which works in a similar manner to that of a still camera. Although the iris would give good control of the light beam, we would have to allow for complete blackout for effect and the time from maximum 'open' to maximum 'close' has to be carefully controlled. Two variations of operation occur, one of which is the appearance of the luminaire having been switched off, or it might be programmable over a long period of time to give the effect of a very slow fade, as used in the theatre world. Being a mechanical device, it once again is a source of acoustic noise.

Real time systems

Although many attempts had been made to introduce automated lighting, the first true all embracing lighting system made its debut at a concert by Genesis in 1981 held in a bull ring in Barcelona. This show marked the first time that a truly automated lighting system, in which all the major functions are under the real time control of a remote console, was put to practical use. This system managed and combined all the important features i.e. high speed reliable mechanisms and control of pan, tilt, beam size, intensity and colour. It did so with dichroic filter colour changing, a compact arc source and a well designed control console. This system was the Vari*lite Series 100™ and was a new product of Vari-lite Inc which was founded in 1981 by a group from ShowCo Inc from Dallas together with members of the British music group Genesis. Prior to the Series 100™ system, touring musicians usually used coloured lighting in their performances but the colour was created through the use of gels and the lighting design was generally limited by the number of luminaires and gels that could be successfully hung in the support system. The key for the development of the Series 100™ and all subsequent lighting systems is the use of dichroic filters to create a wide spectrum of colours together with the use of high efficiency metal halide discharge lamps. The use of dichroics was essential as gels would invariably bleach and possibly disintegrate with some light sources. The use of discharge sources enabled much higher light outputs with lower radiation levels in the beam; thus the filtering materials had a much longer life.

Luminaire types

Ultimately, the Vari*lite Series 200™ system was launched in 1986 and featured both spot and wash luminaires, by taking full advantage of the development in computer technology. Each Series 200™ luminaire was equipped with its own computer which allows for two-way communication between the console and each luminaire's microprocessor. This overcomes any delay in response of the system and provides a much greater processing capacity to allow expansion of the system. Today Vari-lite Inc produces a Series 300™ automated lighting system uses a VL6 spot luminaire with MSR discharge lamps; the VL5 wash luminaire using tungsten halogen lamps and cold mirrors to reduce heat in the light beam; the Mini-Artisan 2 control console allows up to 1000 cues for up 1000 luminaires. The console is normally linked to a Mackintosh computer, which when using proprietary programs devised by Vari-lite Inc allow a high degree of fast and easy programming.

In the VL6 spot luminaire, there are now two independently controlled gobo/filter wheels each with 12 positions, thus allowing several configuration of 22 gobos or colours. It is possible for two gobos to be in the beam simultaneously and thus, by moving the focus from one gobo to the other, a dissolve or 'morph' effect can be achieved.

Whereas the Vari-lite uses pan and tilt on the luminaire with a motorized yoke system, to achieve movement of the light beam, the Cyberlite from High End Systems of the USA uses moving mirror light beam. The Cyberlite uses a 1200W MSR lamp to give a very high output from especially designed ellipsoidal reflector. The colour mixing system uses an array of dichroic filters; it is also fitted with an 8-position colour wheel, containing seven fairly highly saturated dichroic colours plus an open white. The unit has four variable speed indexed rotating gobos with selectable forward or reverse rotation. All the effects are fully programmable to any position. The luminaire is also fitted with an 8-position index gobo system with three fixed and four replaceable gobos. Various gobo effects are possible by combining the rotating and stationery gobos. It is also possible to get high resolution glass gobos to achieve very high quality image projection. The Cyberlite uses a built in computer system and allows for the programming of items such as selectable diffusion, variable frost, full optical dimming, fade to black, colour and gobo selection, zoom, focus and variable iris. The units are used with a lighting console, using DMX 512 control protocol and is used with a 486 microprocessor based PC, which in turn interfaces with the Cyberlite fixtures. The system runs with Microsoft Windows on a desktop PC and use window-driven displays for editing and programme storage.

An interesting development from Whybron of America is the AUTO-PILOT system. The system is designed to send signals through a system of luminaires so that the luminaires will track the performer as they move around on the stage. The AUTO-PILOT system consists of a DMX compatible system controller, four belt packs and eight ceiling receivers. The system controller is connected between the lighting console and the automated lights. The controller receives DMX 512 data from the lighting console and passes along all the lighting parameters except the pan and tilt information to the luminaires. A performer wears a belt pack powered by a 9V battery which sends signals to the receivers overhead. The system controller then uses this data to generate and insert the necessary pan and tilt information into the DMX data stream. As the artists move around, so is the pan and tilt information updated and thus the lights respond, following the performers' every move. The system can accommodate up to four performers, using the same eight-receiver array; the system is capable of controlling up to 24 lights simultaneously and it can be adjusted to suit performers of different heights.

Figure 11.3 Motorized barndoors

Barndoor systems

If we are using automated lighting for television or film, the larger luminaires used will always have barndoor systems fitted. Although some barndoors come with either four flaps, each with adjustable width of flap, or for that matter, eight independent flaps, we will examine the effect of mechanization on a four-door system. Because barndoors are made with two small and two large flaps, the orientation of the doors allows oblong shapes at various rotational angles to be projected onto the sets. We must be able to regulate this rotation and it can be seen immediately that we will have to have some method by which the rotation is carefully governed so that we do not exceed a reasonable operating range and run into problems with control cable feeds, etc. Thus the rotation of the barndoor flaps is similar to that of the 'pan' system which allows for just over 360° of rotation. Each of the individual barndoor flaps has to be capable to being adjusted from fully open to fully closed and one of the problems with this would be that if two flaps are allowed to operate simultaneously, and they have to intermesh, there must be some safeguard so that they intermesh safely and do not cause mechanical jamming. This obviously requires a great deal of feedback from the angle of flap movement to the control system to compare the angle of each flap to ensure correct intermeshing. How far do we take the control of the barndoor system? Should we be able to rotate and adjust all four flaps at the same time? If so this probably poses bigger problems for the control system.

One of the biggest problems with having small motors attached to the flaps of barndoors, is that the barndoor system regulates the light beam, which unfortunately is one of the hottest parts of the luminaire, thus all the devices used on the doors have to be either carefully insulated or be in such a position that they are not affected too much by the light beam and hence heat. Having said that, the same would be true of any motors that are close to the body of a high powered light source in use, due to the radiant heat from the luminaire body.

In a manner similar to that of the 'pan and tilt' the repeatability of barndoor positioning must be obviously high. If for instance, a set of barndoors were used to project an oblong shape on a doorway within a film or TV set, the accuracy of that type of positioning needs to be extremely high.

11.2   System control

System control

We have talked at great length about the luminaires but somehow all the functions have to be controlled from a console of some description. It's more than likely that the console we have will bear a great similarity to a lighting control system and in many cases, the two are integrated as one unit. With more functions requiring control, the system has to be more complex, which brings us to the point of how do the control signals go from the console to the functional parts on the luminaires? Well, we turn to our friend the 'digit' which rapidly goes down pieces of wire from the control area to the luminaires themselves. If the control system used means that a luminaire has to wait until another luminaire has finished all its functional movements, then this is much slower than a system which allows two or more luminaires to be adjusted simultaneously. The limiting point in the speed of operation is that, as more functions are required, each luminaire needs more control signals. These take a finite time to be accepted and made operable. If a large number of adjustments are having to be made at the same time, the system itself may become slow and cumbersome. Thus, the effects are observable and not acceptable as far as the LD is concerned.

Control signals

Having decided that we need to get signals from point A to point B to control the luminaires, how are these distributed in the premises? It's impractical to take an individual feed to each luminaire, therefore a superior way is to provide a digital control 'bus' with provision made for take off points for the luminaires involved. This then means that each luminaire plugged into the 'bus' has to have a code number which is recognized by the control system itself. If any luminaire is changed within the lighting rig due to possible failure or a requirement change, a definite code has to be sent, on substitution, so that the system recognizes the type of luminaire in use and its position in the system.

One of the reasons for using motorized systems is the requirement to reduce operating costs, and as can be imagined the cost of automated lighting systems is fairly high. The cost of any system will be dictated by the complexity of the luminaires concerned: if simple functions such as 'pan and tilt' only are desired to be automated then this is obviously much cheaper than a TV studio full of multi-purpose luminaires where many functions would have to be controlled. It may be that our need for using motorized luminaires is the fact that it makes life so much easier when the amount of luminaires in a lighting rig is reduced; this would be particularly so on large scale musicals mounted in major theatres.

11.3 TV studio installations

Before looking at modern systems, it is worthwhile going back to examine the events and reasons for the mechanization of the lighting system. At the turn of the century, film makers had studios that were able to rotate on trackways, so that they took advantage of the sun's direction this being the main source of illumination. With some of the earlier studios, although labour was relatively cheap during this period, operational needs sometimes required some form of mechanization, the earliest example in film studios being that of long poles to adjust the lighting. Owing to the nature of luminaires being used it was more than likely to adjust the 'on/off' function. As the film industry developed they tended to rig luminaires from grid structures by means of block and tackle arrangements, either with single light sources or using 'boats'. In the theatre, quite complicated and involved hoist systems were being used. It was unfortunate however, that the film industry didn't take account of some of these earlier experiments with mechanized lifting and suspension systems and has operated a very labour intensive lighting system which has remained unchanged – even today. The film industry's motto seems to be 'why use one person when two will suffice'.

Television in its earlier days adopted the techniques of the film studios and in the ensuing years rapidly learnt that productivity was extremely low, using this means of rigging. This either meant that the producers had to reduce the rehearsal time to meet programme deadlines, or it necessitated the building of many more studios to meet the needs of the programme makers. To make cost effective television requires high utilization of studio premises with a rapid turnround of programmes. In the days of monochrome television, the first attempts to increase productivity were by the introduction of mechanized lifting systems, together with simple pole operated luminaires. This was followed by experiments with dual purpose luminaires where a soft and hard light were combined in one unit. In the late 1960s, the introduction of colour to British television caused a dramatic rethink of many systems. The BBC, for example, commenced the use of dual source luminaires, with pole operation, which enabled switching between the soft source colour system and the hard source. The power output could be varied between 2.5 and 5 kW and it was easy to adjust the spot/flood mechanism together with the pan and tilt controls. The purpose of the introduction of this unit was to enable the same rigging time as previously used for black and white television. In other areas, the needs of the studio required that the control of intensity of lights was also improved, thus lessening the necessity for 'light reducing' scrims to be placed in the older type of luminaires. Over a very short period of time, television moved away from the old resistance dimmer units, as used in film studios and theatres, to thyristor dimming units so that instantaneous control of all luminaires in the studio was achieved. The original control systems, inherited from the theatre industry, were

Figure 11.4 Manual shift controlled dimmers

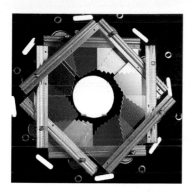

Plate 4 CYM colour mixing

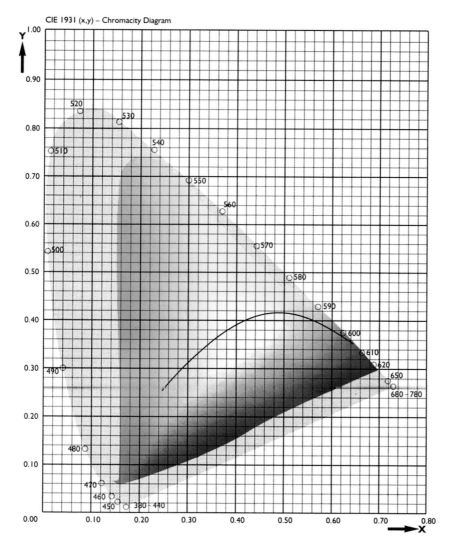

Plate 5 VL5 Wash luminaire

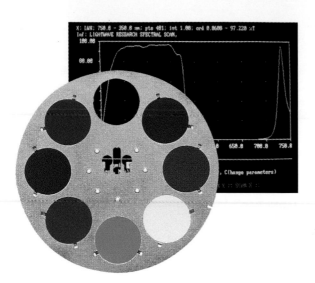

Plate 6 Fixed colour wheel base

Plate 7 Electronics ballast

Plate 8 Interior of electronic ballast ∧

Plate 9 Pearl console ∨

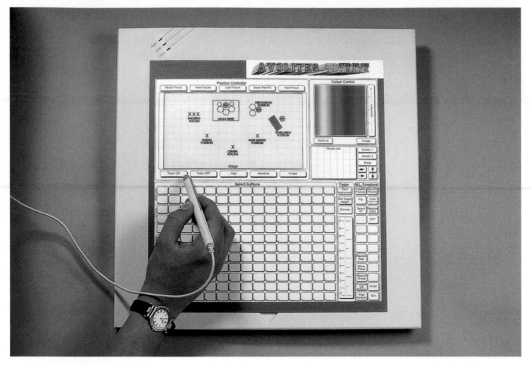

Plate 10 Graphics tablet

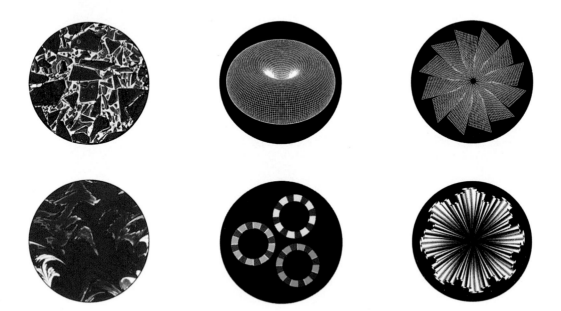

Plate 11 A selection of gobos. Courtesy High End Systems Inc

replaced by systems using digital electronics, with relatively unlimited capability. Earlier attempts in America with computerized lighting control were not brought into general service use there as rapidly as those introduced in Europe. Television required that the methods of rigging traditionally used by the film industry had to be mechanized. This was done mainly by two methods:

1. The use of single point suspension units, such as the monopole or pantograph enabled accurate rigging of light sources. Even from an early stage of development, mechanical control, such as portable electrical or air driven tools were used to reduce the amount of staff required to operate the monopole systems.
2. By using lighting winch units, which generally consisted of barrels approximately 2.5 m long being raised by motors mounted at grid level.

Theatres also introduced motorized barrel units to ease rigging problems with lighting systems in the theatre. It should appreciated that it was very much easier to introduce up to date mechanized systems into new television studios than to convert old theatres to new systems. Generally, with old premises the mere weight of new equipment might impose loads on the structure that were unacceptable to the architects concerned.

In recent years, units such as self-climbing barrel winches have been introduced to enable fairly simple structures to be adapted to motorized units. Control of suspension systems was usually by switches controlling analogue circuits which often require several kilometres of multi-core cable to be installed whereas some systems being installed today use digital information to control the suspension system.

Applying controlled mechanization to the luminaires is not new and attempts were made in Europe during the 1970s to achieve some crude form of control. The units themselves were fairly cumbersome, utilizing standard drive systems, such as small ac or dc motors.

AUTOMATED LIGHTING SYSTEMS

Small studios

What type of studio is suitable for an automated lighting system? If we start at the lower end of the scale with small interview situations, there is probably no need to automate any small studio that has only two or three handed interview situations. The lighting could be left for the majority of the time and even when changes are desired, these would be small and relatively insignificant. Studios of this type often run with few or no electrical staff involved and in fact the lighting may be adjusted by any of the vision operators concerned. Moving up a notch, we get to a small studio of approximately 150 m² which would be the type used for small regional programmes and local news input. In this type of studio the programmes are usually based around an anchor man/woman sitting at one position with two or three set-ups to cover for much of the news intake of the day and local current affairs programmes. They have, on occasions in the past, been used for small dramas and for small audience participation shows – all of which lead to variations in the lighting rig itself. Owing to the repertory nature and repeatability of the lighting over quite long periods, possibly over a programme period of 13/26/52 weeks, there is a definite need for a repeatable rigging system, and an automated lighting control system in a studio such as this is highly desirable. The idea is that the LD could, in fact, have the studio rigged with about eight basic but different set-ups to cover most of the situations likely to be encountered day by day. Having received the information as to the programme content on a day to day basis, it would then be very easy for the LD to dial up 'Set 1', 'Set 2', etc. until the combination of desired sets for the programme content of the day. If the luminaires are generally fixed in their application, such as a 'key' light, these will invariably be Fresnel spotlights, together with a requirement for softlights as fillers. However, to allow the LD a greater degree of flexibility, the use of multi-purposes is to be encouraged so that any luminaire can perform any function, within reason. Subsequently, there will probably be a reduction in the overall rig. This type of installation lends itself to the use of the motorized pantograph working within a reasonable range of lateral flexibility and height, together with a multi-purpose luminaire. This system, as already noted, allows space for luminaires to move alongside each other so accuracy of rigging is reasonable. It might be that the control system is clever enough to know if one luminaire is not within striking distance of another luminaire, it can move to a new position thus allowing accurate rigging. It may be an operational requirement that all luminaires are parked at one end of any trackway and the system should be intelligent enough to allow this operation to take place without any problems.

Large studios

What happens when we go to a mainline studio, say of about 500 m^2, where we would expect to cover any production such as drama, dance, music, light entertainment, audience participation, comedy shows, etc. If we take drama, it is quite possible that we will not necessarily be confined to single storey sets, but we may have multiple storey sets which causes problems because of their height. There could be scaffold arrangements built in studios of this type, which might be for high cameras, for example. It might be that we need special follow spot positions rigged which again involves scaffolding towers and special positions within the studio. There will be a need to light the cyc cloths to a higher degree of evenness than would be required in a smaller studio and this would therefore require special cyc lights to be rigged at high level. There will also be a need in the largest studio for scenery to be suspended from the grid itself; this necessitates the use of spot winching systems, lines and supplementary barrels or drapes to be positioned; all of which conspire against the movement of luminaires along the grid system, thus traversing becomes extremely difficult. The problem can be eased in a monopole studio by restricting the lateral movement of the units themselves. If we're considering a barrel rigged studio, such as the BBC's, then the problem is not so acute because the basic barrel system allows spaces for the scenery suspension system. It is only where supplementary barrels have to be placed, possibly at right angles to normal, that there could be problems.

The major drawback to automation in studios of this size is the fact that the programmes are not repertory by nature and are usually 'one offs'. A series of six situation comedy programmes will be different in their content on a weekly basis. It's no good pretending that although we have a 'stock set' every week, such as a police station in a series of programmes, that lighting within that set will stay the same, because it will vary according to the action within that area. Therefore 'normal' lighting does not exist. This highlights the main problem when trying to apply automated systems to large studios. The lighting is extremely varied, there are difficulties in moving the lights themselves and this also requires that on every individual programme the LD would have to re-programme all the lights in the studio, or most of the lights, on that production, even on the repetitive week to week series that may be shot in the studios. If the system could be made as sophisticated as possible, the LD would have the pleasure of sitting at home with a computer, working out the lighting plot and then sending it down the modem to the studio centre to have it rigged automatically. The problem comes - when does it get rigged? We are certain the scenery department will be most indignant while they are rigging to find that lights keep moving around. Do the scenery department have to say to the lighting engineer's computer 'We've finished, you can carry on now'?

Large studio productions rely for speed and efficiency upon scene and electrical crews largely integrating their work output so that time is reduced in the rig and pre-light session. If we have to have a situation where the lighting has to be allowed to reset itself, rejig itself to new positions, is this done before the sets are placed in position? Because this is not the normal way of doing things. At the present time, sets are rigged and the lights are dropped in to suit the action on the sets. What happens if the scenic designer has made a change or for that matter the sets have been placed off their marks in the studio. This actually happened to one of the authors, working on a very famous police programme in the 1960s, where the whole studio had to be relit from scratch, due to a design mix up prior to the first day of rehearsals. Would the lighting engineer's computer know this? And when the luminaires position themselves, would they be able to ascertain this? Not without extremely good intelligence which would require enormous computer capacity with a very sophisticated feedback system from the luminaires.

Costs and savings

It would seem therefore that there is a case for automation in the smaller to medium sized studio but its application to large production studios is probably a remote dream and will probably never be realized. Even if equipment of the intelligence required to solve many of the problems existed, could we actually afford all this equipment? Would our capital costs be recovered by the savings on the operating costs? Possibly with some of the clever young accountants of today this might be the case; but we believe in actual practice this is unlikely. With regard to the larger studio, what is desired is a better degree of control of the luminaires to help the LD. Remote control of the functions on a key light would allow the LD to adjust the effect while sitting in the correct viewing position. This applies equally to all forms of entertainment lighting.

A TV studio using a hundred motorized luminaires would have its installation costs quadrupled. The difference in costs from using normal luminaires would have to be paid back over a reasonable period of time to keep the accountants happy. The labour saved may produce a reduction in operating costs, but we may be confronted with a higher maintenance cost. Based on the experience of lighting control systems, which these days are extremely robust, it is more than likely that the system will give few problems over a ten year period. If the new luminaires are more complex than the luminaires they have replaced, they will obviously have to be taken out for longer periods of time for maintenance.

The standard luminaires used in the TV and film industry, although they have generally high power outputs, give very little trouble if relatively basic maintenance is performed annually. In the case of automated luminaires, this maintenance will have to be much more stringent. In discussing maintenance, we have to bear in mind that this is generally only required because of breakdowns. What actually happens if a fully automated luminaire breaks down? If it was replacing three luminaires, the loss would be most noticeable.

Finally, and most important of all, what happens when the systems malfunction and every cue is uncontrollable?

11.4   Grid system functions

Control of lighting breaks down into three distinct areas:

(a) control of the intensity of luminaires and their on/off function in some combination;
(b) the elevation and positioning of the luminaires by motorized lifting systems;
(c) control of the directional properties of luminaires and further functions for effect such as iris, shutters and barndoors together with the control of the colour output.

Grid system

First of all, what is the basic function we require if we apply mechanization to a grid system? It would be nice to be able to control the hanging of any luminaire in three planes, i.e. its attitude across and along the acting area, coupled with the height of the luminaire over the acting area. The control of height is very straightforward. When using motorized pantographs and motorized monopoles, control of direction in either the x or y co-ordinates of the studio is extremely easy as the unit will invariably only have to motor backwards and forwards along a fixed trackway consisting of either barrel or RSJ, or a 'C' section channel system. Movement in the other plane would be more difficult to accomplish although not impossible. When rigging a monopole, and its associated luminaire, the only problem that exists for the operators is to have a nominated position for the luminaire to be hung in the studio and also sufficient space to hang it in the position required.

Motorized barrel systems

Motorized barrel systems require a slightly different technique inasmuch as there is no individual control of any single luminaire except when using short barrels, other than by use of supplementary spring pantographs on the barrel unit. The height of a motorized barrel unit is generally dictated by the LD's requirements. The luminaire on its associated trolley is then moved along the bar to a point as near as possible to the nominated position in the studio rig. As has already been stated, this is something of a compromise in practice. Where a horizontal bar some 2.5 m long is raised and lowered in a studio, its position in relation to the scenery is extremely important and in fact, it might be impossible to put the bar at the desired position due to the height of intervening scenery.

Motorized pantographs

Motorized pantographs pose similar positioning problems to the motorized monopole with one big distinction. Where necessary, monopoles can be removed from their associated trackways and either lifted out to another trackway or by using crossover point systems between trackways, be diverted to adjacent trackways. The motorized pantograph system is generally permanently installed to the trackways and is not normally rigged or derigged in practice.

If we motorize the elevation of monopoles, barrel winches or pantographs, the safety cut-out systems employed on them should guarantee not too many mis-haps in operational use. The slack wire cut-out operates very rapidly on these devices when meeting an obstruction on their downward travel: however, when individual units are not fully loaded, the overload system may not trip, even when starting to pick up inadvertently a relatively large piece of scenery. This highlights one of the major problems with total mechanization of winching systems in that dangers are always inherent with scenery flats and other obstructions in the acting area, which really do require human supervision to ensure no malfunction of the system.

It is obviously relatively easy to add a motor to allow a unit to traverse along its trackway, but what happens to the luminaire at the base of the lifting device? Does it know that a scenery flat is in the way or that a luminaire in the trackway is in the position which we've nominated for the new luminaire? At what speed will our nominated luminaire approach the fixed luminaires within the rig? If we are using barrel systems and to avoid problems, it might be that only one motorized traversing unit has to be fitted to each barrel. However, to cover the studio area adequately, we would have to provide a large number of short barrels all over the studio. If we extend this principle of restricting the movement of the traversing system, would it not be sensible to restrict the movement of the monopoles in their trackways and the motorized pantographs in theirs, so that they are only allowed to travel in 'safe space'? It is strongly suspected that this would be extremely undesirable operationally.

Let's look a little closer at the individual systems themselves and the problems they may pose and primarily look at the barrel system.

Barrel systems

Barrels which may be 2.4 m long or a shorter one at 1.2 m long are installed to give as much coverage as possible within the studio. The length of the bars dictates the actual operational flexibility of the system. The more short bars are obviously preferable to fewer long bars. The BBC, for instance, use systems where two luminaire are permanently rigged to 2.4m bars and one luminaire is permanently rigged to a 1.2m bar, but there is always the provision to add extra lights to any of the bars in use for special requirements within a production. How would we get over the problem of the peak demand of studios where we do not necessarily always require the largest number of luminaires to be permanently rigged?

This brings us to the point as to how do we set about rigging a studio with motorized luminaires which are attached to barrel units. Although the barrel unit only has the problem of finding its nominated height as dictated by the LD, the luminaires, if motorized, would have to pan and tilt to meet the requirements of the LD. Two problems exist with motor driven pan and tilt with luminaires on barrel systems used in this way. One, is to avoid a luminaire on panning around crashing into its neighbour; and secondly, if the starting torque is high, it is more than likely this would impart motion to the barrel unit itself which would probably react by swinging like a pendulum for some time during the rigging period. The problem comes when adjustments are made to the lights in the rehearsal period, where motion is totally undesirable and would be extremely annoying from the point of view of the LD and even more so from the programme director's viewpoint.

Stability

Barrel units always have a tendency for some motion generally caused by their position near the floor which involves relatively long wire rope drops from the grid level. This statement holds true for standard winches with motors at grid level or for self climbing winches with integral motors. Other problems exist with installing mechanized luminaires on barrel rigs. Firstly there is the cost of installing fully automated luminaires on the bars themselves and secondly, what functions are required and how are these units actually controlled? The existing barrel systems usually have a reasonably generous safe working load but it is marginal when additional temporary equipment is rigged. The additional loads presented by the motorized units may prohibit some types of temporary equipment being used.

Motorized pantograph systems

The BBC have installed studios, varying from 140 m² to 220 m², with motorized pantograph systems. The reasons for their introduction are twofold, one of which is that they are much safer than the traditional spring pantographs used in small studios and secondly, if they are motorized for elevation and track position, they can be controlled from a remote point by one person, relatively easily. The basic premise of the original system installed was that if each motorized pantograph unit was fitted with a multi-purpose luminaire, a man with a pole in one hand and a remote control unit in the other, could rig and adjust the lighting in the studio with consummate ease. This system, although mechanized, has no inherent positional memory provided and thus cannot be claimed to be an automated lighting system. Additionally, the luminaires chosen for use have no motorized functions and are standard multi-purpose units.

Unit spacing

The pantograph trackways are spaced at intervals so that the luminaires can pass each other when moving along their associated trackways, generally, with the barndoors open. It is possible to obtain greater flexibility to have the trackways spaced at smaller intervals but the barndoors may have to be closed when units pass each other. It is also possible to lower the luminaire to the floor so that its supporting pantograph, which is smaller in cross section, can pass between adjacent luminaires. Grids in this type of studio are approximately 6 m above floor level, thus extra long pantograph units are not necessarily required. The pantograph only needs to reach 1 m above floor level so that luminaires can be rigged and derigged with ease. The signals coming from the control system could be in many forms, but in the BBC were chosen to be ac mains signals, so that the amount of control gear built within any pantograph unit was kept to a minimum, thus reducing the possibility of operational failure. The electrical signals required for any unit is the 'up/down' function and the 'traverse' function. In the event of control system failure, it was felt necessary to provide a pole operated control switch on the pantograph unit that could, by injecting mains signals, replace the incoming control signals and allow for local control of up/down and traverse motion. To avoid damage to adjacent units, buffers were fitted to the trolley units at the top of the pantograph rather in the style of an elongated version of buffers as fitted to railway locomotives. It is important that the traversing speed is not too high, so that the units themselves do not swing when in a lowered condition. To this end, all the pantographs have to be fitted with pivoting mechanisms at high level to avoid damage.

Breakdowns

If either of the motor units fail, this is a severe operational problem in practice and to that end, the unit should be relatively easy to move off the trackway if the need arises. They would be rather unwieldy for the operational personnel to manhandle without safety problems being encountered, so this operation will probably require the use of a small local winch unit to raise and lower the old and new pantograph units into position. In practice, however, this type of unit has proved to be extremely reliable.

As the units are fitted with one luminaire, only one 5kW supply cable and socket for lighting power is needed at the base of each pantograph unit. The controlling ac mains feeds together with the lighting power, are fed to the motor unit at high level by a catenary cable system rather like those used with overhead electrical cranes.

At the moment it sounds as though we're discussing one unit in the track, which of course in practice is not the case, and more than likely six motorized pantograph units will be used in each trackway. If we assume three units would be fed by catenary cables from each side of the studio, then some degree of flexibility has to be inbuilt to the cabling system. It has to be noted that to reduce the amount of trackways for the cable systems, bunches of cable are suspended from either one or two trackways. These trackways are adjacent to their respective pantographs and carry one set of triple cables from one side of the studio and another triple set from the other. The flexibility requires that all the units have to be able to be positioned anywhere along the trackway, the only limitation being the space taken up by adjacent units. To achieve this means that the cables themselves have to be sufficiently long to allow any unit to reach its maximum towards the other side of the studio, allowing for parked luminaires, and that the cable between each unit also has to be long enough (say 8 m) to allow precise positioning of the luminaire.

Control

The operator in charge of the rigging is provided with a small hand-held controller. This controller, although it could be connected by flexible cable back to a wall termination point, is much better for use if it is not constrained by a length of cable. The hand-held unit could be infrared, rather like the controller for TV/video systems, but generally is radio controlled, the reason for this being that some problems have occurred in practice when using infrared systems and their reception, usually occasioned by flats and cloths and other devices being in the way in the studio area. The intensity of lighting itself however, has proved little or no problem for IR systems in the studios and experiments did take place where receptor units were exposed to the light of a fully spotted 5 kW luminaire and still were able to distinguish the infrared signals being received.

The small hand held controller is used to select the luminaire required in the studio and its associated pantograph and controls the luminaires 'on/off' function. It also enables the control of the 'up/down' and 'traversing' motion of the pantograph unit while the channel is selected. It is possible that, having selected the channel to be 'on' or 'off', to leave it in either state so that all the lights on any one area can be controlled easily. Initially, it was felt desirable to control the mechanical functions of only one unit at a time, thus avoiding any dangerous situations, such as a unit being moved inadvertently out of the operator's eyeline. It would be possible, however, to control more units if it is assumed that the operator has a clear view of all units selected.

Radio control

If radio control is used in an area, it is essential that the control unit is not operated outside of that area as the signals will be received by the base station and this would mean that the units in the studio would be controlled by somebody having no idea of what was happening. In practice this is overcome by ensuring that only trained operators use the system and they have strict instructions that **under no circumstances is the controller to be used outside the studio.** To prevent malpractice, the operators have to input an access code to the system.

Upon completion of the rigging period, the studio control system is switched off and the normal lighting control console takes over control of the luminaires themselves. The actual rig is now in position and, unless small adjustments are required, is left unattended.

The biggest advantage of the motorized pantograph unit is the fact that springs are not required, thus the unit itself is not load dependent. Any luminaire from the smallest to the largest allowed on the unit may be rigged and derigged in absolute safety.

Motorized monopole systems

We now come to studios which are utilizing motorized monopole units for mechanization. One of the problems with monopoles, as has been noted elsewhere in this book, is the problem that to move them around requires personnel working at grid level, possibly above artists and other personnel during rehearsals. In recent times, with the advent of stricter safety legislation, this practice has had to be tightened up considerably and quite often people are moved away from the area in which monopoles are being rigged and derigged, for safety reasons. It would be difficult to move the monopoles in their x and y axes without very complicated mechanical arrangements being made and it is preferable that they only traverse along sections of trackway. It would be desirable to limit that movement to certain sections of trackway, due to the need to avoid one unit hitting another or the possibility of fouling other pieces of studio equipment. If we limit the traversing of units to a specific distance, what distance should be involved? Probably, as a guide, it could be similar to that of the barrels on barrel winches, and therefore approximately 1.5 m. Monopole studios are usually constructed with trackways that are very close to each other to enable luminaires to be positioned almost anywhere. If we have a system where traversing is allowed even over short distances, we have to make allowances for luminaires to pass each other for overlap purposes and this would dictate the spacing of the trackways and invariably make them wider spaced. By doing this, we have negated one of the great advantages of monopole rigs, the fact that luminaires can be positioned anywhere. If we follow this argument to its logical conclusion, it would seem more acceptable to rig monopoles incapable of traverse in a standard monopole grid and only use 'up and down' motors on the units themselves. Having done this, we have taken away another advantage of motorized monopole systems, the fact that rigging still has to take place to a considerable degree, requiring a reasonable number of electrical staff.

If we make the systems more efficient, it is the reduction of staff that is important from the point of view of cost saving. Rigging is the situation where the most staff are required, but any studio, once rigged, requires very few electricians to do the fine 'trim' that is

Figure 11.5 Icarus system

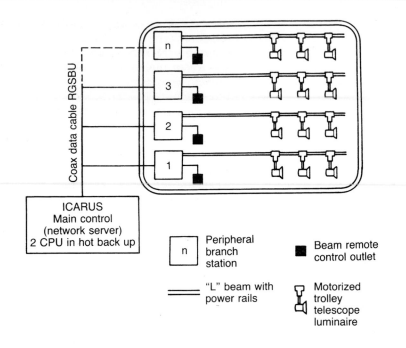

ICARUS
Main control
(network server)
2 CPU in hot back up

	n	Peripheral branch station

Beam remote control outlet

"L" beam with power rails

Motorized trolley telescope luminaire

desired by the LDs. If we automate a monopole rigged studio, what type of luminaires should be used? A motorized version of a multi-purpose luminaire seems to be the most logical choice.

The ICARUS system is the first one introduced into general studio use that offers control of the luminaires and also suspension equipment. The controls are as follows:

1. horizontal movement on the trackway;
2. vertical movement of the suspension;
3. luminaire pan, tilt and focus; barndoor rotation and barndoor positioning.

The system can control motorized monopoles and motorized pantographs with fully motorized luminaires, or standard self climbing and conventional winches with fully motorized luminaires.

The capacity of the ICARUS system using winches together with sets of luminaires is for control of up to 336 hoists, each one equipped with three motorized luminaires giving a total of 1008 luminaires. There is no system limitation to the grouping arrangements, but the dynamic loads on the supporting grid system caused by the simultaneous movement of a large number of units have to be borne in mind.

The control console uses the standard PC using Windows programmes with appropriate graphics of the various modes selected and these positioning luminaires, singly or in groups. The system also allows for live and preset settings. The various preset functions of the luminaires and winches or support systems can be memorized by simply giving it a file name and recording in the PC. The system also allows for handheld remote control units for setting up in the studio.

The trolley is driven by one motor drivewheel with a torque limiter which provides a degree of protection if the unit hits an object and comes to a stop. Feedback to the control system warns the operator and the software stops the motor after a few seconds. Information is input into the control system on installation which imposes a minimum distance between two or more moving trolleys, which is maintained even when they are moving. This is obviously necessary to prevent luminaires clashing.

Trolley movement is controlled by optical incremental encoders which give an accuracy of ±8 mm on 10 m of travel. The motors are equipped with soft start and soft stop functions to avoid any jerky movements. Telescopes are also equipped with optical incremental encoders for height information with an accuracy of ±8 mm on a 10 m extension.

The following table gives the conductors within the electrical track system. This works by sliding contacts on copper conductors similar to those used with overhead cranes, and the following figures are for 18 metres of track. Each conductor rail is rated for 80 amps.

Table 11.1

| Motor side of trolley | | | Opposite face | | |
Rail	Function	Circuit	Rail	Function	Circuit
1	Dimmer phase	Channel 3 (blue phase)	11	Dimmer phase	Channel 4 (red phase)
2	Dimmer phase	Channel 2 (yellow phase)	12	Dimmer phase	Channel 5 (yellow phase)
3	Dimmer phase	Channel 1 (red phase)	13	Dimmer phase	Channel 6 (blue phase)
4	Dimmer neutral	Channels 7 and 8	14	Dimmer phase	Channel 7 (red phase)
5	Dimmer neutral	Channels 4, 5 and 6	15	Dimmer phase	Channel 8 (yellow phase)
6	Protective conductor	Earth	16	Dimmer neutral	Channels 1, 2 and 3
7	Protocol bus	RS422	17	Motor phase	Blue phase
8	Protocol bus	RS422	18	Motor phase	Yellow phase
9	Protocol bus	RS422	19	Motor phase	Red phase
10	Protocol bus	RS422	20	Motor neutral	Neutral (three motors)

12
Electrical distribution

Introduction

Historical

In the past and indeed up to recently, film studios often generated their own power. This was in the form of a dc voltage, usually at 120 V, and mainly used because of the need to supply carbon arc sources used in the film industry. The basis of the 120V was the importation from America of the lighting technology used in film studios. As the public supply authorities did not in general, supply dc voltage, it was necessary for the film studio to install large diesel driven generators. Associated with the 120V systems used was the need to have much larger copper feeder cables than would be normal in Great Britain, due to the current being used. With the advent of much more sophisticated d.c. power supplies, particularly of a size such as the film industry would demand, it was easier to supply systems with ac voltage and transform and rectify it to the 120 V needed.

AC power supplies

Nearly all entertainment premises these days use ac power supplies provided by the local electricity authority. In the smaller installation one three phase transformer will usually be fed from an 11kV high voltage main. In the larger installations, it is quite possible that a high voltage ring main will be used with several sub stations to transform from 11 kV to 415 V within the building and positioned adjacent to the areas of maximum demand. A big problem for supply authorities these days is the fact that the supply system itself contains a high proportion of harmonics and this has been created by the use of discharge lighting systems such as fluorescents and in many cases the use of solid state semi-conductor equipment such as computer power supplies. Unfortunately in large entertainment premises using lighting systems, we do have a high proportion of fluorescent lighting in the offices, we may have a high proportion of discharge lighting on the sets and we certainly have many dimmer racks full of solid state equipment generating harmonics. In theory, in a balanced three-phase system all the current will flow in the phase conductors and not in the neutral. Unfortunately in the situations quoted, it is possible to have as much current in the neutral as contained in the phases themselves.

Back-up generators

So far we have discussed the supply of power for use in an entertainment situation from the public supply system, but of course it is possible to have a back-up generator used within the premises to prevent any problems if the public power supply fails. If back-up power systems are used only for technical equipment then the loads may not be too great and small diesel generators are a good proposition. When applied to the lighting systems where considerable amounts of power are required, it is not always economically viable to install standby power equipment. Most television companies install a small generator, sufficiently large to keep a small amount of crucial equipment operating and capable of being used for transmission; with sufficient power spare to enable say, captions and one announcer to be lit.

In very large installations, it is more than likely that two incoming supplies from the local 11kV distribution system are provided to the premises and obviously there has to be an arrangement made to have changeover facilities in the event of failure. It is extremely advantageous in a large building to use a ring main for the high voltage supplies so that in the event of any damage or faults on any equipment, an alternative supply route can be utilized. In premises such as a large television studio complex, there is a need to keep the studios working as much as possible, therefore when maintenance is required, it is important that the local transformer can be bypassed and the area supplied from another area so that essential maintenance is carried out. Routine maintenance will obviously have to be carried out on all the switchgear on a regular basis.

Substations

Within any installation, the siting of the main transformers and switchgear either connected with high voltage or low voltage systems has to be carefully considered and the installation carefully planned. In the smaller installation, only one low voltage substation will probably be provided, additionally one switch room will be installed close to the incoming supply and within this room will be a factory built assembly from specialist manufacturers which will incorporate the circuit breakers, fuses, mcbs and metering systems. A very important point in the selection of the electrical power systems is the fact that the electrical designer concerned should ensure that most equipment is fairly standard, therefore any problems can be quickly overcome and the spares holding is reasonable in size.

Switchgear

Usually the lighting power is controlled by a special switch on the lighting console, probably remotely engaging a large contactor in the

Figure 12.1 Main
switchgear/dimmer room

Figure 12.1 Main
switchgear/dimmer room

switch room. Although it would be nice to think that this contactor would be operated as a 'no load' device, thus ensuring that the contacts within the switchgear are not burnt by opening under large electrical loads and thus causing arcing, there is no guarantee that this will not happen. In practice therefore the switchgear has to interrupt large currents.

In general in the entertainment industry, it's not a good idea to install systems that would automatically shut off the supply in the event of an overload. In the theatre, this would spoil the audience's enjoyment of the production and in television where large audiences may be watching a live programme, an auto switch down of the system would be annoying in the extreme. Systems are therefore generally designed to have warnings displayed for overloads so that the operating staff can take avoiding action. The installed capacity of luminaires can quite often exceed that of the power allowed for any installation, therefore generally the discipline of the operators is required to ensure there is no overload of the system.

For ease of operation and to ensure the minimum disruption in the event of any faults, generally with lighting installations, it is wise to have several small pieces of switchgear feeding dimmer racks, thus ensuring no one item of equipment on failing would take the whole system out of action. One good thing about most modern dimming equipment is that it is generally well protected by fuses or mcbs and therefore faults are contained within individual parts of the system and not reflected back into the main system.

In the theatre and generally in film studios and television studios, lighting creates the greatest single demand for electricity. With demands ranging from hundreds of kilowatts to possibly even thousands of kilowatts, lighting generally has to be considered almost separately from the rest of the installation. The loads it can impose on a three phase system can have quite severe effects on the rest of that system.

quality transformers on one hand and modern self-stabilizing dimming systems on the other.

Isolation

If we take the distribution in a large dimmer room the main incoming power from the adjacent transformer will be fed through armoured cables to the switchgear and then via a busbar system through the switchgear. The switchgear provides for an isolator per dimmer rack. This is for (a) safe isolation for maintenance and (b) to isolate parts of the equipment in the event of a major fault. It is important to have individual isolators for the equipment and not a common isolator to more than one piece of equipment which could cause a problem during the normal operation of the premises; and of course it is not very useful when you have to shut down the entire system just to maintain one dimmer. All of the lighting power will usually be under the control of a contactor on the input to the switchboard, so that lighting power can be remotely switched from the lighting control room. This contactor will have to be quite large: it will also have to be rated for live working conditions. There is no guarantee that no load conditions will exist at the time the contactor operates.

It is usual to feed from the isolators on the switchgear to the dimmer racks with armoured multi-core cable and as this has a definite bending radius, it is often advantageous to use parallel multi-core cables of a slightly smaller physical size so that they may be manipulated easily within the dimmer room. Generally dimmer racks are fed via the top of the units which makes access fairly easy although on some occasions we are likely to find the air conditioning installation technicians trying to impose their trunking in the most awkward places. Other than armoured cables, the use of trunking to enclose PVC power feeder cables can be advantageous, due to the fact that PVC cables are much easier to manipulate then their armoured counterparts. We have already noted in Chapter 8 that it is extremely important to provide sufficient space for the termination of the mains input cables. The rack s incoming cables may range from 16 mm^2 cables on smaller installations up to 400 mm^2 cables or the equivalent on very large dimmer racks.

12.2 Power and balance for three phases

Phasing

In the past, due to the British regulations pertaining at the time which treated single- and three-phase working voltages differently, it was very difficult to feed the lighting system effectively from three phase supplies, owing to the need for defined limits of separation between socket outlets on different phases. In practice, this often meant that all floor sockets were on the same phase as the technical equipment. In trunking arrangements with socket outlets fitted and especially on barrels, it was difficult to prevent clusters of equipment appearing on the same phase causing large imbalances over the three phases. The main reason was that studios had to have the individual barrel outlets on the same phase; thus one third of the barrels would be connected to the red phase, one third to yellow and the remainder blue . Generally, the barrels were interspersed as sets of three for phase distribution. Thus barrel 1 would be red; barrel 2 blue, barrel 3 yellow and so on. Sometimes to get around loading problems in an installation, yellow and red phases would be used for lighting and blue for the remainder of the installation. Due to a change of IEE specification, which defines *any voltage up to that of 1000V ac between conductors, or 600V ac between conductors and earth, as low voltage*, we are now covered for both 230 V and 415 V in one voltage range and the requirement for separation has lapsed. We can now quite happily design the lighting distribution to be spread over three phases for the ease of balancing the power system. Although it s possible to design the studio to work on three phases, and for that matter to arrange some form of uniform distribution throughout the grid system and lighting sockets generally, we have no guarantee that the luminaires will be plugged in a balanced way or that the use of the lights controlled by the lighting console will not, by coincidence, only use those on one phase only, by some chance of fate.

Patching and balance

When the lighting director is producing the lighting plot for the electricians to use in the studio to plug the luminaires into the electrical supply system, the phase of the various lighting power socket outlets in the area concerned must be considered so hopefully he can ensure a reasonable balance over three phases may be ensured. If systems are using any form of patch it may be that the LD indicates the lighting positions that are required and allows the electricians to plug these into appropriate sockets. With a soft patch system in use it may be that the LD upon being given the dimmer numbers, can programme the console to suit the channel numbers in use. The main point that the LD will have to watch is the maximum capacity of each phase.

How is the lighting apportioned over the three phases so that one phase is not highly loaded in comparison to the others? It may be that the maximum current allowed on a phase dictates the amount of luminaires that the LD may use at any one time. Thus it is not always a simple matter for the LD to ask for various combinations of lighting equipment without having some regard for the supply concerned. For example, if the maximum current allowed is 200 A per phase, it will not be possible to allocate more than ten 5 kW luminaires to that phase. If there were some guarantee that diversity was applied, e.g., all the dimmers were never to be higher than say 8 then more luminaires could be allocated per phase due to the lower individual current consumption.

These days where many installations do not have permanent lighting directors but most are brought in on contract, it s more than likely that any LD doesn t have an intimate knowledge of the premises concerned. It is extremely important therefore, that any technical literature that may be given to any guest lighting director in any premises, is extremely accurate and reflects faithfully the lighting electrical system together with details of the lighting console installation and any quirks within the installation with regard to the general power supplies. In practice, it s no good calling for six 10kW luminaires to be used when the system does not even have any 10kW dimmers, or for that matter sockets, supplied.

12.3 Distribution systems

Volt drop

Probably the best place to start in our distribution system is to look at an individual circuit and see the initial effects of lighting power in a practical way and then how it affects the rest of the system. The current carrying capacity of a 4 mm^2 PVC cable is 30 A and a 240 V 5 kW circuit will draw 20.83 A, therefore superficially it would appear that this cable would be sufficient for our purposes; but unfortunately that s not the end of the story. It is important in any installation that the volts dropped by the currents flowing down the cables do not exceed certain limits. The concern with voltage drop is that items of equipment might cease to operate correctly and therefore constitute some form of danger. In the latest British regulations, the maximum stipulated voltage drop is 4% of the nominal voltage, which is 9.6 V with a 240 V supply.

Obviously with the majority of lighting equipment, we are not so much concerned with the volt drop to the luminaire as the tungsten lamps will operate on any voltage from zero to their maximum. Our problem, in practice, if we lose too many volts down the cable is that the lamps will commence to burn at a lower colour temperature than that desired even at maximum applied volts, and although not critical in a theatres, this might prove to be a problem with aligning cameras. Voltage drop on a domestic installation will not be very high as the length of cables involved are relatively short. However, let s take a practical example in an installation using a 240 V 5 kW dimmer, feeding a socket in the acting area and the cable from the dimmer to the socket is 80 metres long.

PVC single-core cable (in trunking)		Voltage drop for 80 m
4 mm^2	11 mV per amp per metre of run	18.3 V
6 mm^2	7.3 mV per amp per metre of run	12.2 V
10 mm^2	4.4 mV per amp per metre of run	7.3 V

It will be readily appreciated that the first two voltage drops exceed the limit as laid down by the present regulations, and only the 10 mm^2 cable would be acceptable

A further problem now arises. Most luminaires are fed via flexible cables and if we assume this to be a 4 mm^2 three-cored flexible cable, then even a short lead, 5 m long, will give us 1.3 V of voltage drop on a 5 kW luminaire. This has to be added to the 10 mm^2 figure.

An even bigger problem occurs when the 80 metres of 10 mm2 cable is terminated at grid level, instead of going directly to a socket in the acting area. This is usually to allow the inter-connection of a 4 mm^2 flexible cable from the termination point, via a flip flop cable system, down to a socket on a suspension bar. If this cable was

15 m long, we would get a further voltage drop of 4 V. If we run all
the figures together, which might be quite possible in a TV studio
installation, we therefore have, using 10mm² cable, a loss of 7.3 V.
We have a further loss of 4 V on the feeder from the grid system to
the bar outlet socket and the luminaire lead will also have a loss
amounting to 1.3 V, so our total loss is 12.6 V, which is above the
desired IEE technical parameters.

However, in the studio, this might not give a problem with the
intensity of light, but we do have to bear in mind that if this was a
240 V system, we would have a colour temperature change of 5K per
volt. When calculated this gives 12.6 × 5K = 63K. It is not unknown
in practice, unfortunately, that lamps are delivered from manufacturers with low operating colour temperatures and these may be
around 3100K for a nominal 3200K lamp. So instead of our system
now producing a start point of 3200K, it may be we are closer to
3000K, and of course we intended lining the TV cameras up around
this point. If we reduce the dimmer to 7 which would be our normal
starting point for technical line up, we would have a colour temperature output from the lamp of about 2850K, which is really at the
lower acceptable limit of the video camera and thus does not allow
for any further dimming of the light sources if we are to maintain
the camera s colour integrity.

Thus it is extremely important that cables between the areas and
on the equipment themselves are as generous as possible to avoid
voltage drop. It is, of course, possible to have the input transformers feeding the switchgear and dimmer racks adjusted so that they
deliver high volts on input, say 250 V, to offset some of the voltage
drop in a system, but this is a practice which should not be encouraged. By starting with high volts, which would be presented to the
dimming system, and by suddenly getting a voltage surge, it might
be that we rapidly exceed safe limits on the dimmers and this would
be quite disastrous.

In most installations in the entertainment industry these days,
electrical services will be generally conveyed by trunking or cable
trays. Due to the amount of cables used in installations, which may
be pairs of single conductors or multi-core cables, the trunking and
tray systems installed will have to be prefabricated from steel, due
to its strength and rigidity. Cables fed by either system at high level
in the premises will unfortunately be in the area of the highest
temperatures. It may be that the use of cable trays is more advantageous with the cables being exposed to the air, particularly if not
bunched, and probably not having the same electrical requirements
of those that are totally enclosed.

EM interference problems

However, due to the need to keep the EM interference as low as
possible, it is preferable to keep all cables from dimming systems in
trunking rather than on trays and this is particularly important when
the dimmers are feeding low level sockets within the premises where
they may be in close proximity to sound circuits. As a guide, if
separations of approximately 300 mm or greater are used between
the lighting power cables, and any other installed cables, there generally will not be a problem. Another major advantage of metal trunk-

ing systems is that they can provide an extremely good earth continuity throughout the installation and in addition afford a high degree of mechanical protection to the cables. In the theatre, the trunking systems will be provided generally to the periphery of the stage area so that power feeds can be taken across to the lighting bars on flexible cables. In film studios, as already noted, most of the distribution will be at floor level. In television studios however, nearly all the distribution is at high level and this means that the system has to be carefully integrated with the layout of any monopole system, bar system, motorized pantograph system or even a fairly simple lighting system such as fixed barrels. If we require clearance above a grid for access, it is important that trunking is not put in the most awkward places, thus creating possible hazards to the operational staff working in the area. As can be seen from Figure 12.2, most systems will use trunking at high level, dropping it down to outlet points on a fairly regular basis and usually this will be a central box feeding four winch units at the same time. In the case of monopoles, quite complex socket arrangements are provided.

One problem with using dimmer systems is that the harmonic content of the waveforms is extremely high when they are in 90° conduction, and if we are not careful, we will have high circulating currents in the neutral and earth conductors.

Practical problems

Two basic rules are extremely important.

All circuits wired from the dimmer room to the acting area should be wired as live/neutral pairs of conductors in the same conductor size. The use of several small independent phase conductors with a large common neutral is to be deprecated, because this in itself can cause a problem. For example, in one large broadcasting studio that was converted from saturable reactors to thyristor dimmers using common neutral systems, the circulating harmonics caused severe eddy currents in the trunking in the studio and created conditions where it was extremely difficult to hold a conversation against the noise, other than the fact the trunking was getting rather hot. It s worth noting that it cost quite a lot of money to correct this design error.

Equally important and at times capable of causing more problems, is the correct earthing of the system.

Earth loops

It is essential that the earthing system does not form a ring conductor within the system but all earths should be radial conductors, and if possible, taken to a nominated star point. To avoid problems on most installations these days, it is usual practice to adopt a clean earth policy where the technical equipment is on a separate earth system to the dimming system — if this is at all possible. Any circulating earth currents can cause a greater problem with the sound and vision equipment than the electromagnetic interference radiated by the cables from the dimmers.

In addition to the power cables for the individual circuits from dimmer racks, there is a need for the control system inputs from the control room to all dimmer racks and these will be conveyed in either separate trunking or by small flexible cables fed within the racks themselves. On the whole the control cable is relatively immune from interference problems. The main precaution to take with analogue signal cables is to ensure that the cables are well screened internally. With digital inputs becoming more normal these days, control system interference is virtually non existent, as any random signals can be prevented from causing problems by checking all the data for error signals.

Other than the power wiring in the studio, there will be a need for additional trunking which provides for the control cables to and from the various control consoles within the studio and these would be as follows:

1.   local electricians panel
2.   lighting hoist control panel
3.   scenery winch control panel.

These may be placed anywhere at studio floor level for the ease of the local operators, but in general they will tend to be grouped, particularly those for the electricians panel and the lighting hoist panel.

12.4   Distribution problems

The following example actually occurred in a small television studio, where the windows overlooked a waterfront which was used as backing to the camera shots.

The air conditioning was not functioning as effectively as it should have been, the movement of air in the studio was not enough and the ceiling area was accumulating a pocket of very hot air. This was mainly caused by the use of several 5kW tungsten sources, fitted with IL blue correction filters to counterbalance the daylight, rather than using IL orange on the windows to correct to 3200K or using discharge sources of a quarter the power for the same light level. There were also some 2kW circuits in use for effects lighting.

The studio had originally been wired with flexible cables from the dimmer room, mounted on cable trays. However, it was felt that the cables could be tidier and the tray was replaced by PVC cables in trunking. It was then discovered that the trunking and cables were running at around 80¡C.

In normal circumstances, the cables installed from the dimmer room to the studio may possibly have sufficed, if all the circuits were not selected simultaneously, thus avoiding a grouping problem. However, due to the need to light the studio to a high level, all the luminaires had to be used and thus no diversity took place.

Taking into account the ambient temperature, together with the grouping factor of the cables in the trunking, it was essential to increase the cable size for the 5kW circuits, which also had the advantage of reducing the voltage drop to the studio where even 5 volts lost represents around 5% light loss in the studio.

There were two solutions to the cable heating problem, assuming no other changes.

(a) Leave the existing trunking and cable for 2kW circuits only and remove the 5kW feed cables. Install new 100×100 mm trunking for the 5kW circuits with the cable size increased to a minimum of 10 mm².
(b) Remove all the existing trunking and cable and rewire in rubber flexible (85¡C) cable on perforated trays. No more than a double layer with a minimum of 6 mm² for the 5kW circuits and 4 mm² for the 2kW circuits. **Note:** The use of tray allows a smaller cable size for the 5kW circuits.

The second course of action (b) was adopted as the solution to the problem. As can be appreciated, this merely reverted the situation to square one .

12.5 Plugs, sockets and distribution

Most of the sockets used in the theatre are supplied by 2.5kW dimmers although there are requirements for some 5kW circuits and on occasions 10kW circuits are used. In the theatre, parallel sockets can be advantageous on the dimmer outputs to enable pairs of light sources to be coupled together. This is obviously very convenient for two cross lights on the artists. Many theatres, even today, still use the traditional 15A plugs and sockets. There is however, a slow change taking place over to BS 4343 (CEE 17), 16A, 32A and 63A plugs and sockets.

With a limited number of dimmers, it is possible to have a power patch system so that the sockets to be powered in the active lit area can be connected to dimmers as appropriate to the area concerned. This is often done in smaller installations where perhaps 24 dimmers

Figure 12.3 Lighting power
sockets

are provided feeding 48 sockets. A good thing about patch systems
is the fact that, usually, the power from the dimmer to the socket is
on a 'one to one' basis with very little chance of circuit overloads
occurring. If however, the dimmer units are provided with parallel
sockets on the front panels for convenience, there is the danger of
overloads when the operators are not careful.

Due to the flexible nature of monopole grids, it is necessary to
provide a reasonable number of dimmers which cater for the
maximum size of production in the studio but because of the need
to keep continually repositioning monopoles and to prevent long
flexible leads, several parallel sockets at high level are required.

Figure 12.4 Cyclorama lighting
distribution

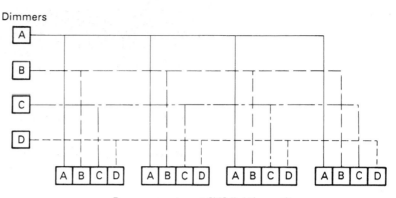

Four-compartment CYC lighting units

Either we have a very clever switching system to prevent any of the individual circuits being overloaded or we rely upon the operators making the right decision when plugging up the various luminaire feeder cables.

In pantograph systems, when permanent catenary systems are employed feeding the individual luminaires on the base of the pantographs it is very rare to find circuit overloads. This is because the system is strictly 'one to one'.

Motorized barrel systems will employ a variety of sockets mounted adjacent to the suspension barrel for the luminaires. In general, the circuits will be 5 kW and the minimum number usually supplied per 2.5 metre bar, for example, will be three circuits. It is possible that one of these circuits or more, may be installed with parallel sockets across the dimmer circuit so that two small luminaires can be

Figure 12.5 Permanently installed
cyclorama distribution

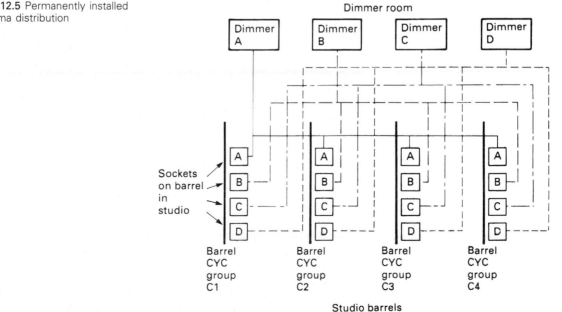

Studio barrels

patched to one dimmer from the bar itself. In addition to the normal outlets for the Fresnels and soft lights used, there will be a requirement for either additional standard sockets or for special sockets for cyclorama lighting units.

The distribution system will also feed floor outlets but the circuits are generally connected directly to the dimmer units. On occasions, it may be advantageous to switch between floor lighting power sockets and high level lighting power sockets, but if this is switched in the correct manner the power can only be in one place at any one time, therefore a circuit overload is avoided.

In a television studio, other than the need for the power sockets for the normal lighting on any of the types of suspension used, there is a need for additional sockets to be used for effects lighting, cyc lighting and discharge lighting which may require connection to a three-phase system, and this is usually provided by special sockets in selected locations to suit the installation.

One area where special sockets are required is for the lighting of cyclorama cloths. Ground row cyclorama units invariably are supplied with 625 W lamps per compartment. If we use 4-compartment ground row units for 4-colour mixing, we can feed a string of eight of the same colour compartments from one dimmer, e.g. 8×625 W = 5 kW. Special cables are supplied by manufacturers to allow the linking of several ground row units (see Fig. 12.6a). These may be integral to the unit itself or supplied as separate pre-formed cables in eight, four and single connector configurations. The cyc end of these cables are usually fitted with nine-pin connectors to mate with the cyc units; the other end is split into four standard studio plugs for circuits A, B, C and D.

Cyclorama lighting units when employed at the top of cycs invariably use 1250W lamps and we could therefore light four of the same compartments from one dimmer, i.e. 4×1250 W = 5 kW. Top cyc units can be supplied by manufacturers with input cables to suit the installation power sockets. They can vary from a single cable and plug attached to each compartment to a nine-pin male connector, used for the four circuits, going to special sockets provided in the grid system (see Fig. 12.6d).

As an example, let s take the case of overhead cyc lighting with four units used, each with four compartments fed from four 5kW dimmers. Dimmer A feeds the first colour, dimmer B the second colour, dimmer C the third colour and finally dimmer D the fourth colour. In the case of ground row units, obviously the four dimmers are still required but we now can feed eight sets of four-compartment units rather than the four used at high level. For convenience, we can install sockets in groups of four representing A, B, C, D for use by either cyclorama system. It may be that the barrel system at high level also has a permanent cyclorama lighting installation which would utilize groups of 9-pin A, B, C, D sockets where the sockets would be paralleled in groups of four, where each group, i.e. $4 \times$ A, is fed from one dimmer output; $4 \times$ B from another dimmer, etc. (see Fig. 12.6b). As an alternative, the nine-pin cyc sockets can be fed by four flexible cables, the ends of which are fitted with standard plugs, allowing them to be patched to any standard studio socket (Figure 12.6c).

In addition to this type of socket used in the studio, there will be a need for distribution, in some studios, of 10 kW sockets when

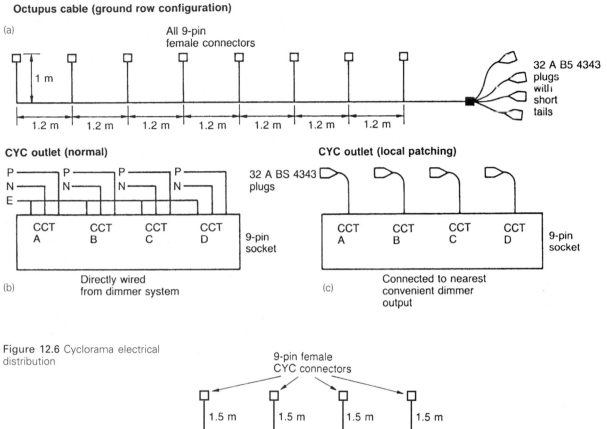

Octupus cable (ground row configuration)

(a)

All 9-pin female connectors

32 A B5 4343 plugs with short tails

CYC outlet (normal)

Directly wired from dimmer system

(b)

CYC outlet (local patching)

32 A BS 4343 plugs

Connected to nearest convenient dimmer output

(c)

Figure 12.6 Cyclorama electrical distribution

9-pin female CYC connectors

9-pin male CYC connector

Octupus cable (top CYC configuration)

(d)

higher powered luminaires may be required. When the 10 kW socket is not being used, it is preferential to supply two 5 kW sockets in parallel, switched from and adjoining the 10 kW socket and all fed from the same 10 kW dimmer, thus upon selection, one 10 kW socket could be used or two parallel 5 kW sockets. These 5 kW sockets would have to be subfused on the adjacent panel next to the selection switch.

12.6   Fuses and circuit breakers

There are two functions required from the protective devices we use, one of which is that they will protect for normal overload conditions, such as lamps failing or incorrectly plugged luminaires creating too much current on a circuit. In addition, the devices have to be adequately rated so that they safely stand fault currents caused by short circuits.

The wiring going from the switchgear to the dimmer racks has to be protected by either fuses or some form of circuit breaker. Before we go any further it would perhaps be wise to look at the magnitude of currents that flow from the main switchgear to the dimmer racks. In a fairly straightforward simple installation using packs of 6 × 2.5 kW dimmers, each pack, which would probably be connected to 240 V single phase, would consume 62.5 A on full load. At the other end of the scale, using a high density dimmer rack containing 192 5 kW dimmers, spread over three phases, we would have 1333 A per phase on full load. With smaller systems it is probably just as easy to protect the input to the dimmer racks by fuses. However, with higher current systems, it is more than likely that the electrical installation engineer will install circuit breakers of sufficient rating to meet the demands of the dimmer racks. As far as the output of the individual dimmers themselves goes these can be protected by either mcbs or fuses.

At this point it would be worthwhile looking at fault currents. What do we mean by fault current?

Fault current

If we are stupid enough to place a piece of wire across a 240 V supply and switch on, the wire disappears rather quickly. By using a simple bit of Ohm s law it will soon be realized that the current is governed by the resistance of the piece of wire and if the piece of wire does not have much resistance the current can become quite large. For example, if a piece of wire with a resistance of 0.01 ‰is placed across a 240 V supply, the current flowing through the piece of wire would be 24 000 A. It is reasonably obvious that with a current flow of this magnitude, unless we are using an enormously thick piece of wire, the wire would actually vapourize and thus fuse. In practice we wouldn t just be concerned with a piece of wire across the 240 V supply, because in addition to the resistance of the wire will be the resistance of all the cables feeding to the initial point where the wire is inserted in the circuit. Thus, the nearer we are to the point of supply the greater will be the fault current. On the input to the main switchgear from the substation and its transformer we can get very high fault currents indeed. If, however, the fault occurs at the end of a 100-metre cable run, the fault current will be relatively low. Although in practice it would be rare to have a short circuit at the output of a dimmer for example, the rules and regulations regarding protection state that we have to protect for a short circuit at this point. Thus the prospective fault current has to be verified for this point. Why should we be worried about a short circuit in the wiring system? We are concerned with avoiding short circuits in our lighting feeders because of the danger due to the magnetic and thermal effects it can produce in the conductors and on busbar systems. We must therefore place protective devices in the conductors which must operate sufficiently quickly and in absolute safety to prevent this kind of danger. If we are going to use a fuse, we can meet the fault current requirement by selecting fuses with a high rupturing capacity, for example BS 88 in the United Kingdom allows for a rupturing capacity of 80 kA. Another method of protecting circuits is by using an air circuit breaker (acb) or a moulded case circuit breaker (mccb). These will also have to be rated to meet the prospective fault current.

Thus the switchgear feeding the dimmer racks will be provided with, say, fuses to handle 400A running current and if a normal overload occurs will rupture relatively quickly. In addition, they will have to fuse immediately a with a fault current of around 20 000 A. Acbs and mccbs are often specified for high current applications of about 400 A and greater on switchgear. Fuses are generally used below this point.

MCB rating

Many mcbs that are used for circuits with much lower current capacity have fault current ratings of somewhere between 6000 and 9000 A, particularly in the type that we would select for dimmers. It is more than likely that the potential fault current of the circuits involved will exceed these values. It would seem at this point that an mcb could not be used to protect our outgoing circuits. However, in practice this is not the case, because we are allowed to use a device which is not quite adequate if we back it up with a fuse which adequately protects the complete circuit. Thus, if the prospective fault current was 8000 A and the breaking capacity of the mcb we had selected was 6000 A, we would have to back up the mcb with a fuse with a breaking capacity in excess of 8000 A so that the circuit was fully protected.

Most of the devices to protect the installation will have to be carefully selected. We have to bear in mind that there will be more than one device protecting the circuits so the protection devices have to be carefully integrated with each other so that discrimination is achieved. For example, it s no good having the mccb feeding the dimmer rack failing when only one outgoing dimmer circuit has a fault.

12.7   Meters

It s fairly obvious that the fault conditions can be calculated and appropriate measures be incorporated in the switchgear, dimmer racks and any ancillary equipment feeding a stage or studio area. Overload conditions are catered for by the selection of devices that disconnect the supply when a certain current level is reached.

From an operational point of view it is important that we monitor the parameters of the supply so that we do not create overloads on the main power intake. It may be that if you are on a special tariff, going over the top costs real money. By putting voltmeters across the phases it will be possible to see the state of the voltage within the premises, although in general these are something of a luxury because even if the volts are wrong you can do little or nothing about it. One of the problems with supplying voltmeters is where do you actually take the reading. If it s taken at the switchgear, it s quite possible that the voltage will be reasonable; if we took it at a studio socket it s more than likely it would be several volts lower and due to the varying lengths of run in a studio, it would be highly impractical to adopt a policy of looking at socket voltage outputs. Therefore

Figure 12.7 Power meters

the best voltage guide is probably the one provided by the switchgear but, due to the various volt drops within the studio, this can be rather misleading in practice.

Remote metering

What can be done however, is to ensure that the capacity of the system is not exceeded by trying to draw too much current. If ammeters are supplied which monitor the current of the total system, and individually monitor supply to various parts of the system, then we can ensure an overload does not take place. On any lighting system it is preferable that an ammeter is placed in the incoming supply to the dimmer rack installation so that the total current can be monitored. This can then be displayed on remote metering systems in control rooms and in the dimmer room and at stage or studio floor level. The ammeters are also necessary for the operators to see the current in each phase so that the lighting load can be balanced across all three phases to avoid heavy neutral currents and the financial penalties imposed by supply companies for out of balance loads. Modern metering systems use low volt signals to convey the information from special transducers built into the equipment. The metering systems should be placed for the operators benefit; it is essential that the operators can read clearly what is indicated. It is very frustrating to have a meter with a red segment indicating the overload area, when you actually can t see the needle and where it s pointing. Thus, generally, if meters are supplied, they will require little lights to illuminate the panels. Of course, self-illuminating meters could be used and in recent years some use of gas discharge bar graphs have been used where rising columns of bars indicate the voltage and current levels reached. On the whole, analogue meters are preferable, although there s much to be said for a digital display where the current level is clearly displayed in figures and not open to the operators interpretation.

Trip systems

It s not a good idea to have a trip system which on sensing an overload would shut down that phase to avoid any further problems because from an operational point of view this would be highly undesirable. Warning systems have been incorporated into metering systems in the past which, for instance, give some indication of either approaching the danger point or the actual overload condition per phase, but unfortunately the buzzers themselves can become a nuisance in practice and they have never been brought into general use.

It is essential to ensure there is no leakage of any currents down to earth, they should always come back up the correct paths. To ensure this, it is preferable that the earth leakage currents are monitored at the input to each dimmer rack and this can be achieved by having a current transformer mounted at the input of any rack where the input cables are taken through and then terminated. This ensures that the current flowing into the rack should equal the current flowing back up the return conductors and thus cancel out. Any imbalance would indicate a current flowing elsewhere and hence a fault condition. Earth leakage can be monitored in each rack and then, if a fault occurs a local indicator is activated. All the individual rack EL warning systems can be fed to a central unit which in turn sends a master warning signal to all interested parties. Isolating the problem is simply achieved by going to the dimmer room and seeing which individual rack has the fault.

12.8   Distribution on the set

In addition to the suspended production lighting, there will be a need for luminaires mounted on floor stands around the sets, together with small luminaires on special clamps attached to the top of scenery flats for local lighting in the sets. There will also be a requirement to have practical lights. These will be similar to those found in any normal house or business premises and consist of table lamps, fluorescent fittings, wall mounted units and pendant fittings hanging from a ceiling. The use of these fittings is to give a realistic effect to the scene. However, the general lighting effect will not be provided by the practical lamps but by the main lighting being used cleverly by the LD to supplement the effect of say, a 100 W bulb.

Cables and fuses

We have to be careful with this 100 W practical lamp, because it will no doubt be fed by a relatively small electrical flex so that it looks right as far as the viewer is concerned, but unfortunately in practice the circuit may not have the correct back-up protection if anything goes wrong. It has already been noted in the section on dimming that it is very important to select the correct fuse for the circuit involved. If we take the standard studio or stage set up, the 240 V dimmers will be fused at about 10 or 20 A, or possibly even more on some occasions. The problem that occurs when the practical is plugged into a lighting power outlet is that the cable size has reduced considerably with the use of flex for the practical and we must insert a subsidiary fuse at this point where the cable sizes change. If the practical is supplied from a wall outlet and the flex has to progress several metres across the acting area this also constitutes a source of danger. Our best bet is to ensure that we get as near to the practical as possible with well rated cable and then introduce an additional fuse at this point so that only a short piece of flex is used. The best method is to use special extension leads, but whereas the normal lead will just have a socket at the end of it, the special leads for practicals will have fuses fitted adjacent to the final socket.

Obviously for convenience when two practicals have to be used together in a room, the extension cables should be supplied with parallel sockets, each one of these fitted with a small local fuse. Thus, the 20 A fuse used with a 240 V 5 kW dimmer, will protect the cable all the way down to the sub-distribution outlet. This can then be sub-fused at 5 A to supply the final piece of flex and the subsequent 100 W lamp.

Other than practical lamps, it is quite possible that some of the lights used on the scenery flats are also low wattage sources. These luminaires may be supplied from within the premises or are hired pieces of equipment, but in most cases they will be supplied with small mains leads fitted. Once again, we have to ensure that they are only plugged into a circuit that is correctly protected by a subsidiary fuse rather than directly plugged into the main lighting circuits.

With set dressing lights, which are often supplied from overhead sockets, it may be more convenient to have an adaptor unit with a plug that goes into a bar outlet, is sub-fused at that point and provides a smaller connector on its output. As an example, a 32 A BS 4343 plug may be used to go into the 32 A socket on the bar but the outlet from the adaptor unit would be a 16 A BS 4343 socket supplied via a fuse fitted in the adaptor.

Having said that we need to protect the circuits by the choice of the correct fuses, we must also ensure any cables feeding either set or practical lights are routed in such a manner that they are protected from mechanical damage at all times. This will require special covers over cables at floor level together with a careful choice of route through the scenery labyrinth.

Isolating transformers

On occasions, there may be a need to use an isolating transformer to give a higher degree of protection to some of the circuits appearing at floor level. Generally these will be those circuits used for musical instruments and of course, these will not be dimmed circuits. However, it is important to ensure that at any time any load such as a transformer, or motor, when plugged into the system, is going to work correctly with the dimmers installed in that system. Some items of equipment that may be provided from hired-in items may not be of the same voltage as the supply system in the premises and it would be somewhat disastrous to put a 120 V hired-in device across the output of a 240 V dimmer.

The main lessons to be learnt are to:

(a) check every point of detail at any time with regard to the disposition of small pieces of lighting equipment within sets;
(b) check particularly on their ability to handle current and that they are suitable for the system voltage.

Finally, it s no good having protected a 100 W lamp with a small fuse to have the cable draped across a corner of the set in such a way that the first person going that way trips over and breaks a leg!

13

Working lights and emergency systems

Introduction

In any area used for entertainment, there will be a requirement for four types of lighting:

1. Lighting for performance.
2. Lighting for working practices when the performance lights are not in use.
3. Houselights; provided for the benefit of audiences.
4. In the event of failure of the performance lighting, the working lights or the house lighting, an emergency lighting system has to be provided.

Houselights and working lights tend to describe lighting systems that may be achieving a somewhat similar result. In theatres, we would describe houselights as those used to illuminate the auditorium for the benefit of the audience. Working lights are used in the more technically orientated areas of the installation. In television and film studios, houselights describe the fittings provided in a studio for general illumination and they are also the working lights.

Working lights

When not using the performance lighting, we need to be able to see to work on rigging sets and to make changes to the production lighting within a building. In the so called 'good old days' this seemed to be answered, if one views any Hollywood movie, with a 60 W lamp stuck in a stand in the centre of a stage. Unfortunately, in this day and age, that's not good enough, because with the advent of measures to increase safety within working premises used for entertainment, light levels have to be sufficiently high so that hazards to staff and artists are avoided. There are no hard and fast rules for light levels for working lights and it is generally left for the users to decide what is best for their installation. Guidance for light levels in various areas is given by the IES Code For Interior Lighting in the UK.

13.1   Types of sources

Before we discuss where to put working lights in any premises, perhaps it would be a good idea to review the light sources available, their advantages and disadvantages. For many years, tungsten lamps have been used for house lighting and working lights and there really is not much of a problem when using this type of source. By choosing the correct lamp it is possible to get a reasonable light level commensurate with a reasonably long life. It is helpful if lamps don't have to be changed too frequently, because they are invariably in slightly inaccessible positions. The main snag with tungsten lamps is that their efficiency is low and they produce quite large amounts of waste heat. In big theatres, film and TV studio installations, a considerable amount of power can be used for the house and working lights and in fact, in some studios, this might be as high as 30 or 40 kW.

It would seem advantageous, therefore, to go to other sources of light and the first of these would be the fluorescent lamp. Fluorescent lamps, which are more efficient, generate much less waste heat, which is advantageous from both the electrical and air conditioning viewpoints. One of the problems however, is that unless used close to the working area, fluorescent lamps provide broad sources of illumination and are not as convenient as focused downlights which may be required when the working area has a high grid. It would seem fairly obvious that we might be able to employ high bay lighting, such as in factories, using mercury discharge lights. The advantage of this type of lighting is that it is more efficient with much less wastage of power. But mercury discharge lights have one major drawback – they take time to reach full light output; and if they fail whilst they are burning – and thus are hot – they take a long time to cool down. This means a long wait before the lamps can be restruck.

Discharge lighting in the studio

During the 1970s, the BBC experimented with the use of discharge lighting in a studio at the Television Centre in London. The installation made use of reasonable quality mercury discharge lamps in parabolic reflectors aimed down to the studio floor area. To get around the problem of the warm up time of a discharge lamp, a tungsten lamp was positioned adjacent to each of the discharge sources. Upon initial 'switch-on' the tungsten light was activated as well as the discharge lamp; after about ten minutes, the tungsten lamp was extinguished because by this time the discharge lamps had reached their stable working condition. In normal use, if the supply to the discharge sources was interrupted, either by the operators switching 'off' the working lights, or by failure of the incoming mains, the tungsten lamps were re-activated and the control circuits waited for the discharge lights to cool down for a set period of time before re-applying their ignition pulses. This required a reasonable amount of intelligence to be built into the control system for the studio, particularly as the working lights were split into four quadrants and each was treated independently.

Several facts emerged from this experimental installation, one of which was the lamps used did not maintain a good colour over their operational life and therefore some distortion was caused in the colour rendering of materials and drawings in use, being particularly troublesome to the lighting and scene crews involved. There was also a reasonably high degree of flicker present from the discharge sources. The periods of changeover from tungsten to discharge were annoying in practice and the operators much preferred the tungsten light, although it had a slightly lower light intensity. Finally, but not least, the installation of the system incurred high capital costs and although it was felt that these would be recovered in a reasonable period of time, this was not the case in practice.

A major problem that has emerged in recent times in the application of discharge lamps for working lights is the need to have an emergency switch to switch off the production lighting in the event of any electrical hazard occurring in the working area. When the main production lighting is removed, the working lights need to be activated immediately, and discharge sources take too long to come up to full light output.

Having looked at the light output of sources used for working lights, what about the colour? We find tungsten lights will invariably give good colour rendition and cause very few problems in practice. If we choose to use fluorescent tubes for lighting the working area we have to be careful in the choice of tube so that the colour rendition is of a high order. Modern discharge sources can now be obtained with very good colour rendition and greater stability throughout their working life but for the reasons stated are not being adopted for general use in entertainment working lights.

The light levels in Table 13.1 are given as guidance for installations.

Table 13.1

Theatre auditorium (houselights)	100 lux
Theatre stage area (working lights)	100–300 lux
Film studios (working/houselights)	200–400 lux
TV studios (working/houselights)	300–400 lux

13.2   Integrating the system

Having decided upon the type of light source that we will use for a working light, where will we provide it? In the theatre, the main areas will be in the wings, above the grid, on the fly galleries and a general illumination on the stage itself. In all these areas a reasonably high illumination is required so that the operators can see clearly what they are doing, thus avoiding any accidents when handling scenery, luminaires and counterweight sets. Other than the working lights in any area, there is also a need to have some level of lighting backstage during the performance. This is to enable the

Figure 13.1 House lights – unwanted shadows

stage operatives to react to cues and thus perform lighting and scene changes. It's fairly obvious that this shouldn't disrupt the performance lighting on the stage itself and thus interfere with the effect intended by the LD. This background lighting must be of a sufficiently high standard so that it too avoids any safety problems.

All of this activity is occasioned by the 'live' performance. In television and film this is not the case! Having set up the scene, movement is then restricted to keep background noise to a minimum while the scene is recorded on either film or via television cameras. Thus, the need in television and film studios is for working lights over the whole area to enable sets to be erected, dressed and lit and then ultimately used for production shooting when the working lights will be switched off. In film and television, if there is a need for some special working lights within a production area, due, for example, to quick change dressing room facilities being required, localized lighting is usually provided.

Types of sources

In the larger television and film studios fluorescent lights are not generally used, tungsten sources being preferred and these are usually in the form of long life 1000 W linear lamps mounted in floodlight fittings pointing downwards or in the general direction of the acting area. This enables a reasonably high illumination level in the main area. In smaller studios, it is quite possible to use fluorescent fittings to provide an adequate light level on the studio floor. However, it may require several twin units to produce the light level required as it is more difficult to provide focused beams with fluorescent lamps as a source. One of the problems of mounting any form of working light in a grid system is the fact that there are so many objects hanging from the grid, obscuring the working light. In a large studio, we get the crazy situation when all the winches are raised towards the grid level, we have unobstructed lighting of the studio floor, but when we lower the winches to their operational height, which would be the main requirement when rigging and setting, the working lights are obscured.

When illuminating the acting area it's bad enough trying to position a small floodlight fitting about 300 mm square within a grid system, but when trying to install fluorescent fittings up to 2 m in length, it's almost impossible. Small lighting units can be installed between the ends of barrel winch units and not interfere with the main production lighting layout. Fluorescent fittings, however, can only be positioned between rows of production lighting units and this, of course, in practice means valuable space is occupied.

Other than the fittings below the grid level which illuminate the main area, there is also a requirement to illuminate above the grid for operators working at that level, although these lights will only be used occasionally and not permanently switched on.

In large studios there is a provision for some emergency lighting that is left alight all the time, usually fed from a central battery power supply. This has to be carefully integrated with the rest of the system, although the light level provided is low in comparison to the main house lighting and therefore generally does not affect the production lighting.

We've now got lights all over the place! How do we switch them on and off, because it's pretty obvious that switching them all off at the same time may be inconvenient and possibly dangerous. Most studios have the lights switched in four quadrants, thus it is possible to have a quarter of the working lights on, with three quarters off and this switching arrangement can be in any combination for convenience. One big problem with a high light level from the working lights in a studio is the fact they are also a major source of illumination and can project quite obtrusive, unwanted shadows (see Fig. 13.1). So although the lighting can be removed in certain segments, it is usually necessary to switch off most of the working lights during a production so that any undesired effects are avoided.

Emergency 'off' switch

It is necessary to have an emergency 'off' button which operates the main lighting power. This is provided to remove the power from the active area in the event of fire or any electrical hazard. The application of this switch, which removes the main lighting, could plunge the area into darkness and so that this does not happen, an interlock system has to be provided so that when the production lighting is switched 'off', the working lights are immediately switched 'on', thus avoiding any danger. The emergency 'off' buttons operate on a latching system and therefore are not allowed to be reset until an authorized person investigates the problem and clears the situation for normal operation again.

Whatever type of lights we choose for our working lights, there will be a need to maintain them. This might be simply changing a lamp when it fails or cleaning the fittings on a regular basis to ensure maximum light output. This requirement means we have to carefully consider where we put the fittings and how they are accessed in normal use. Obviously in a small studio, using tungsten or fluorescent fittings, or, for that matter, a theatre using fluorescent lighting for some of its peripheral illumination around fly galleries, probably a pair of steps or a reasonably short ladder may be used by operators to gain access. In premises where high grids are installed, there will be a need to provide access to the working lights, generally from the grid system itself to avoid the use of high portable towers. On occasions there will be a need to lower the fittings to the floor and this requires lifting devices to be installed for every lighting unit.

Dimmers

Tungsten working lights and houselight systems usually have thyristor dimmers to control them. Some modern studio installations have sophisticated control systems in an attempt to save power. The method of control is to have a period when the lights are fully on which is usually worked out from normal rigging practices and this amounts to say, four hours. At this point the lights will slowly fade down to half brightness, thus saving some energy. If the operators are still working and require the higher light level, the action of touching the 'on' button of the system, re-activates the circuits to maximum and a further four hour cycle commences.

Safety precautions

On all types of working lights where there is a lamp involved we obviously have to take safety precautions. It is rather unnerving to have a lamp explode above members of staff or the public. Having only a mesh in front of any of these working luminaires is insufficient, and it is essential that no material escapes from one of these fittings when it is above people. In the case of tungsten or discharge fittings, it is possible to have safety glasses fitted which are toughened and in addition to the safety glass to also have a mesh to prevent pieces of the safety glass falling to the floor level. With fluorescent fittings, specially designed units can be obtained that are generally safe in most aspects. It goes without saying that all these fittings have to be fireproof!

We have already mentioned that around the edge of a stage area there will have to be working lights left on to enable staff to perform some of the functions during a live performance. In television particularly, there is a need for items of equipment to be illuminated around the edge of the studio for normal use, but which must not be too obtrusive when using the studio for recordings or transmissions.

Many television studios are often fitted with cyclorama cloths that at times can encompass two thirds of the periphery of a studio and this can pose a problem inasmuch that direct access towards an exit doorway is not possible, and an alternative route has to be available. There are strict rules concerning how much of a studio can be encompassed by pieces of cloth or sets and there must be definite access ways provided for safety. A problem that often occurs in television studios is that the exit lights have to be left on and if a cyclorama cloth is hung across the face of the exit light the camera will see the outline of the 'exit' sign through the cloth, thus the exit sign has to be obscured in some way. The safest method, by far, in these circumstances is to hang some form of material in front of the sign but this must be hung as near to the cyc cloth as possible, so that the normal sight line to the 'exit' from the fire lane at the rear of the cyc, is maintained.

Additionally, around the edge of the studio there will be consoles for local control of the winches, pantographs, monopoles, together with controls for switching lights on and off. All of these need illumination for the operators to see what they are doing, and this is generally accomplished by having fluorescent downlighters mounted above the panels which can be obscured from the view of the camera. Unfortunately at times the outline of the panels can be seen through cyc cloths and therefore local switching arrangements have to be provided so that the fluorescent units can be switched off if the camera is looking in that direction. A fire lane will invariably be provided all the way round the edge of the studio and to ensure that illumination is sufficient for rapid access in the case of an emergency, fluorescent lights are provided at frequent intervals, attached to the studio walls. These also require baffles so that the cameras cannot see this illumination.

In a theatre, there will be permanent arrangements for an audience, this being part of the normal operation. However, in film and television studios, audiences are not the 'norm'. When they are there, it is essential that the safety arrangements made are as good as those in theatres. Special arrangements have to be made to indicate clearly the exit routes; although in most modern studios the audience seating is generally integrated into the building, so there are definite access routes. If, however, the audience seating is placed in the area on an 'ad hoc' basis, then special arrangements have to be made. This is particularly important with regard to the lighting. In the event of an emergency it is essential that the audience is safely conveyed away from the technical area being used for the production, which is the high risk area. Thus special temporary lighting arrangements have to be made to light the exit routes, particularly around the audience rostra.

13.3 Lighting in control areas and dressing rooms

Lighting console

Although not usually of direct concern to a technical consultant planning lighting systems the requirements for control rooms and dressing rooms should be borne in mind. In the control room used by the LD, there will be a need for downlighters onto the desk adjacent to the lighting console so that the prepared lighting plot for the production in question may be interpreted. It may be that colour coded symbols have been used to indicate cyc lighting colours, for instance. Therefore, in addition to a reasonable light level, there is also a requirement to have faithful colour rendition. In television, the lighting director is intimately involved with the technical picture quality from the cameras and therefore has to use high grade monitors in good viewing conditions, which implies almost dark surroundings. The only areas of light will be those on the control desk. Desk lighting these days is usually achieved by having fluorescent fittings to give a general background illumination along the working edge of the desk, with small tungsten spotlights to pick out areas of special interest. Both the fluorescent and tungsten lighting have to be provided with dimmers so that a balanced working light level is achieved.

Dressing rooms

Traditionally, dressing rooms are lit by banks of tungsten lamps around a make-up mirror. In recent times, however, fluorescent lighting has been used in an attempt to give a more even illumination which is kinder on the performers' eyes and also helps to save energy. The most important aspect is that the fluorescent tubes chosen must be a very good quality from the point of view of colour rendition.

This latter fact also applies to the fluorescent tubes used over control desks.

13.4 Emergency systems

Emergency lighting can take two forms:

1. 'Standby lighting'
This is needed so that essential work may be allowed to continue (this would obviously be more applicable to a hospital operating theatre). In general in the entertainment industry, standby lighting is not normally installed. It may be provided on occasions in those areas concerned with television master transmission suites which have generators backing the public electrical supply systems, feeding the technical plant, so that a minimum 'on air' presence is maintained.

2. Escape lighting
This is required in areas occupied by staff, artists and audiences so that a rapid but controlled exit can be made from an entertainment area in the event of fire. It is the most important form of emergency lighting as its main requirement is to ultimately save lives.

The essential requirement for emergency lighting is that it will operate reliably from an independent source other than the mains supply. The light level required by British legislation for safety lighting is remarkably low and in fact for most areas a level of 1 lux is considered sufficient. However, the light level is really up to the installers and operators of the premises to review, and if necessary, increase upon this base level. Other important purposes of emergency lighting are:

1. It must clearly define the exits and all the emergency exits.
2. All escape routes must be clearly indicated and adequately lit so that people can see their way to exits.
3. It is essential that the lighting along escape routes is relatively even and does not have wide variations in light level.

4. It is absolutely essential that, having got out of the building, all the people evacuated don't blunder into pitch blackness, therefore outside illumination must be provided.

One of the most onerous requirements of emergency lighting is the fact that it has to reach the desired light level within five seconds of failure of the main lighting system. It is possible that the response time of the emergency system can be increased up to 15 seconds with the permission of the local authority, providing people in the building concerned are very familiar with their surroundings. However, in most cases it is preferable if the five seconds is maintained. Due to the five second limitation, it would obviously be impossible to use discharge sources for emergency lighting, and in fact the only types of lamps preferred for emergency lighting are from the tungsten and fluorescent families.

It is also extremely difficult to use a generator for the emergency lighting system due to the fact that they, also, need a finite time to run up and in most cases will probably exceed the five second limit. The main source of supply for emergency lighting is a battery system, this can be either a central system where the emergency power is distributed to the areas concerned, or self-contained systems where each individual luminaire used comes complete with its own battery. In the past many large installations used large banks of batteries contained within a battery room in the premises to provide dc voltage to the emergency lighting systems. In essence, the battery system works rather like the battery in a car: in normal use, any drain on the battery systems by maintained exit signs or maintained house lights would be catered for by a charging plant in the same manner that the alternator on a car keeps a battery topped up. With failure of the mains, the batteries are always in a state to provide an emergency power source for a reasonable period of time. Battery powered emergency lighting is usually designed to be activated for a period of up to three hours, according to the size of the premises and with due regard to all the problems of escape from the building.

Batteries

Battery backed luminaires used for emergency systems are usually reliant upon the normal mains input to provide a trickle charge so that the batteries are maintained in a working condition at all times. Luminaires for emergency systems come in three types:

1. The first of these is where a lamp is 'off' until any emergency arises, in which case the lamp will be powered from the internal battery pack. Normally the mains feeding the unit will trickle charge the battery pack.
2. The second type of unit is where the lamp is always in use and under normal circumstances powered from the mains, but in an emergency situation will use the internal battery supply. Once again, the incoming mains trickle charges the battery.
3. It is possible to combine the two types of operation in a third sort of luminaire for emergency systems, and this luminaire contains two lamps; one which is used normally, powered from

the mains, and a second lamp for use only in emergency conditions, powered from the internal battery pack. In the event of mains failure the second lamp will switch on. As before, the unit relies upon a trickle charge from the normal mains to keep the batteries in good condition.

Performance checks

A problem that arises with emergency lighting luminaires is that if the lamp in the fitting is used all the time it is in a constant process of ageing, hence some notice must be taken of its life cycle so that lamps are changed to avoid failure in emergency conditions. Units that employ lamps which are only switched on in emergency conditions need to have these lamps checked at fairly frequent intervals to ensure no possible malfunction when used. It is also extremely important that all units installed in the premises are switched onto the emergency state at fairly frequent intervals to ensure that the batteries are working correctly.

In the entertainment industry the members of staff working on the premises will be aware of the escape routes, exits and emergency exits. Unfortunately, many members of the public may come into the premises and will be totally unfamiliar with the layout of the building. This requires that the operators of any premises have to ensure that all exits, be they permanent or temporary, are clearly marked. As well as the need to have clear exit signs and lighting for the emergency routes, there is a need for additional lighting where hazards may exist along a route, such as stairways and any other type of obstruction. Obviously these must be clearly lit so that no additional problems are caused by people tripping over obstacles. It goes without saying that, **if in doubt, install more emergency lighting**.

14
Safety

14.1   Luminaires and EN 60598-2-17

Historic

After World War II, the European countries continued to follow their own electrical and mechanical standards without regard to their neighbours or the adverse effect that this created on their export trade. Germany and Britain were the dominant standard makers and adopted the attitude that the other countries should fall in line with one of them. The thought of getting together and thrashing out a common set of safety standards was not only unheard of, but would have been tantamount to heresy. However, in 1979, common sense prevailed and the International Electrotechnical Commission (IEC) published the first edition of a safety standard for luminaires that had been agreed by 23 participating countries. This standard was called 'Luminaires: General Requirements and Tests Publication 598/1'.

In 1984 a proposed standard for luminaires used in the entertainment business was circulated to all participating countries to try to reach a common agreement in the industry. After six years of debate by all the 23 countries, it is a wonder that the proposed standard was ever adopted.

One of the authors of this book sat on the United Kingdom Committee and cogitated with the rest of the team – however, modesty prevents us saying which one. Suffice it to say that our proud committee member sallied forth full of hope and encouragement to introduce a luminaire design to the whole of Europe with one set of European safety standards incorporated into it. The journey took our intrepid designer to many of the participating countries and, just to check on acceptance by the various national authorities he stopped by at the appropriate safety standards office in each country and to say 'hello' and to gloat over our new found commonality and to get agreement that we were working to the same set of rules. The result of his labours is best demonstrated in Norway, by the inspector of NEMKO.

Question: Do you accept IEC/598/2/17 in Norway?
Answer: Yes, of course we are one of the participating countries.

The inspector then picked up a huge mound of books from his desk, placed them on top of IEC/598/2/17 and said, 'However, we still require you to conform to the NEMKO standards as well'. And so it was in each country visited.

Back in the UK a colleague put this into perspective by saying, 'You wouldn't expect British Standards or the Institute of Electrical Engineers to give up their regulations, would you?' So there we were with all the different standards that we had before and a brand new one in addition.

Fortunately the situation was resolved several years later when the European Norms (ENs) modified and accepted the IEC 598/2/17 and issued them as EN 60598-2-17. British Standards then adopted this legislation and issued it as BS 4533 in 1990.

The following suggestions and remarks regarding safety considerations in the design and operation of luminaires should be taken as a guide to help you through EN 60598-2-17 which is now harmonized across Europe (EEC and EFTA) and Canada accepts it as an alternative to CSA standards. However the USA will only accept UL 1573 which is considerably different to the European standards.

The main basis of the following is EN 60598-2-17 with an overlay of good practice accumulated by the authors over many years of experience. However, it is up to the individual to determine their own interpretation of the standards because the authors cannot accept responsibility for their accuracy. It is also assumed that the reader already has a sound knowledge of good electrical practice.

Glass fragments from luminaires

The luminaire should be designed in such a way that in the event of a lamp exploding, fragments of glass or quartz 3 mm in size should not escape directly in line, from a lamp, through a ventilator or other aperture. If the ventilation system is designed with a labyrinth or fitted with a mesh to prevent pieces of glass or quartz 3 mm in size coming out from a directly exploding lamp in such a way that the glass is caught within the labyrinth or by the mesh, this is accepted within the standard.

Safety glass/mesh

Open faced luminaires require either a safety glass with a minimum thickness of 3 mm or a safety mesh that will not permit pieces of glass or quartz 3 mm in size to pass through it. Luminaires that have a single lens require a safety mesh in front of the lens of such a size as to prevent pieces of glass 25 mm passing through it. However, luminaires with more than one lens do not require a mesh, but it is our opinion that it is good practice to fit one. Luminaires that have a safety glass require a safety mesh in front of it, of such a size as to prevent pieces of glass 12 mm passing through it. The glass and mesh must be captive in the luminaire. In the event of a safety glass or lens cracking, its mounting must retain the broken pieces in position. The mechanical heat test for the safety glass is carried out by placing the luminaire in the horizontal position and burning it until it reaches a stable temperature, then water at a temperature of 15°C is sprinkled onto it by hand. The unit is allowed to cool and reheated and the test is repeated three times; the glass can crack, but it must be retained in its position in the housing. Tests for halogen lamp shields require that they withstand an exploding lamp and to ensure that any hot fragments that do escape do not ignite a gauze placed under the luminaire.

The yoke

The mechanical connection between the yoke and the luminaire must be locked against loosening. This is to prevent the pivots working loose, during operational use, by tilting the housing. Forms of locking may consist of either fitting a locknut or drilling and pinning the pivot shaft.

The yoke must have earth continuity to the housing if there is a risk of a single electrical fault. Since there is normally no wiring in the yoke there is no necessity for a separate earth bond on the yoke.

The mechanical safety of the yoke requires a 10:1 safety factor on each leg of the yoke so that if one side of the yoke is disconnected from the housing the remaining leg provides a 10:1 safety factor.

The test procedure is to hang the luminaire from its spigot and apply a test load to the luminaire. Since the safety factor is to 10:1, a weight of *nine times* the total weight of the luminaire (including all accessories) is added to the housing, making a total of *ten times* the original weight. The yoke may deform under test, but it must not break. At the time of going to print, discussions are taking place to determine if the safety factor could be reduced to 6:1, but this is a matter for the future.

The male spigot

The size and type of spigot to be used can be determined as follows. Luminaires weighing up to 7.5 kg may use a 16mm diameter spigot and it can be made of either steel or aluminium. Over 7.5 kg, a 28.6mm spigot is required and it must be manufactured from steel (aluminium is not permitted). A hybrid spigot has been developed (see Fig. 14.1) which dimensionally suits the German DIN specification together with the British and US standards. This has not been accepted by the Standards Committee but is suggested here as the only reasonable solution to a universal spigot. In 1995, this design was submitted to British Standards for consideration and we await the outcome.

Safety anchor point and bond

A dedicated anchor point must be provided on the housing (unless it is intended for floor mounting or to be used as a hand held luminaire) whereby the safety bond can be passed over the primary means of suspension, through the yoke and terminated at the anchor point. In this way the housing will be arrested even if the yoke breaks. The test procedure is as follows. The unit will have all its accessories attached and lifted 300 mm and allowed to free fall until it is arrested

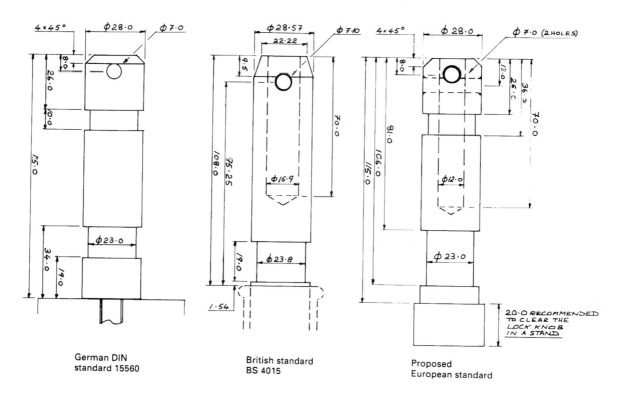

German DIN
standard 15560

British standard
BS 4015

Proposed
European standard

Figure 14.1 Spigots

by the safety bond. This procedure is repeated 30 times. During the test it is not permitted for any part of the luminaire or its accessories to become detached although they may become deformed.

Barndoors and colour frames

A German DIN specification exists for the size of receptacles for colour frames and barndoors. This is to ensure a good mechanical fit of component parts together with ease of interchangeability with other manufacturers items of equipment. Although this is not a formal requirement it represents a very desirable feature.

If possible, luminaires should be designed to cater for the sizes quoted in these standards. The major manufacturers in Europe have already adopted these sizes.

Nominal size of colour frames – German DIN standard No. 15-560 part 38

The following dimensions (in millimetres) can be the diameter of a round colour frame or the size of a square frame: 120, 150, 160, 180, 210, 240, 270, 360, 390, 450, 480 and 540.

The top latch which is normally provided for retaining the colour frame and barndoors must be self-applying so that it does not rely on the operator to close it. In this way, the operator is obliged to hold the retaining clip out of the way whilst the barndoor or colour frame is withdrawn. On letting go of the catch, it returns to its locked position.

Cables

PVC or other plastic cables should not be used on luminaires. This is because the cable will deform with the heat if it touches the side of the housing. The mains input cable must have a sleeve of insulation where it is clamped at the cable entry.

Any cable passing through a hole in sheet metal must be protected by a secondary sleeving to avoid mechanical damage to its insulation.

Electrical components and cables

All electrical components such as switches, cables, terminal blocks, lampholders, etc., must be manufactured to the appropriate standards for the individual items concerned. Otherwise the luminaires could fail acceptance tests due to the use of unsatisfactory component parts.

Earthing

The termination point of the incoming earth should be in view when the mains input terminals are exposed to enable an inspector to see that the earth is connected. The international earth symbol must be used adjacent to the incoming earth terminal. This must be punched into the metal or stuck onto it, so that it cannot be removed. The earth symbol must be a minimum of 5 mm high. Earthing washers are to be used to cut through the paint and ensure a good earth. The earthing screw is to be a minimum of 4 mm diameter with a machine cut thread, self-tapping screws are not acceptable. The screw size will increase with electrical current requirements but cannot be reduced for mechanical strength reasons. The screw must be plated steel or manufactured from brass or copper.

All metal parts that can be touched on the outside of the luminaire, that could come into contact with a live part under a single fault condition, must be earthed. The lamp carriage must have a direct earth continuity wire, a scraping earth conducted along tracks is usually insufficient. Under no circumstances can push-on terminals be used for earth connections to luminaires that draw more than 3 A from the mains supply.

Terminal blocks

The terminal block should be designed so that it would allow one strand of wire to turn back from its connection by 8 mm and *not touch* adjacent terminals or metalwork in the luminaire. If the terminal block employed does not automatically perform this function, an insulating material must be placed under the block or used as a barrier between terminals so that isolation is achieved.

Warning labels required on the housing

The following recommended warnings are so numerous that it would require a larger housing just to display them on small luminaires. However, they are being quoted verbatim from the standards.

- **Before opening disconnect all poles from the electrical supply.** (The minimum height for the lettering is to be not less than 2 mm and 5 mm for graphical symbols)
- **The top of the unit must be indicated to prevent it being mounted upside down.** (A broad arrow symbol may be used with the addition of the word 'TOP' or 'OBEN' in German. The minimum height of the arrow symbol is 5 mm).
- **Replace any cracked protective shield**
- **To be serviced by qualified personnel**
- **State the distance from the lens to a flammable surface.** (When the temperature in the centre of the beam is $\leq 90^{\circ}$C with an ambient temperature of 25°C. Use the international symbol.)
- **The burning angle must be stated x° above horizontal, y° below horizontal**
- **Observe the lamp manufacturer's recommendations**
- **Maximum voltage with an ac or dc symbol**
- **The maximum current**
- **The maximum wattage.** (State if there is more than one lamp used, e.g. 4×1250 W.)
- **The frequency of the supply** (which may be in the instruction leaflet)
- **The maximum case temperature in degrees Celsius.** (This is defined as the hottest part of the housing that could be touched from the outside, also the maximum ambient temperature (Ta) if it is not 25°C.)
- **The weight, complete with lamp and all accessories**
- **The manufacturer's name and type number.** The label must have permanent print and must be attached to the luminaire with rivets or stuck so that it cannot be removed.)

Safety instruction sheet

This must be provided with every luminaire when it is sold. The sheet must describe all the hazards involved with lamps and luminaires.
     The following should also be noted:

- **Ambient temperature:** All luminaires should be designed to work in a maximum ambient temperature of 45°C (good practice but not a standard).
- **Fuses:** The value of an integral fuse must be stated adjacent to the fuseholder, so that it is apparent to the operator when changing a fuse what value it should be.
- **Luminaire data sheet:** *This must be enclosed with each luminaire and include the following*:
  - The same information that appears on the warning labels.
  - The fixing instructions of how the unit should be mounted or suspended.
  - A description and location of the safety bond anchor point and how to correctly attach the safety bond.

  In addition, a description and reference numbers for the following items:
  - Safety glass
  - Wire guard

- Lens
- Safety bond
- A list of all lamps that can be used in the luminaire with details of their voltage, wattage, life, colour temperature and any other parameters that are relevant.
- A list of all accessories
- Recommended stands
- Spares. **Note:** It is not a standard requirement to provide spares information, because the sheet will be particular to each unit. It is however, a good opportunity for the manufacturer to identify the spares at this time.

Discharge sources

Additional requirements include:

- **Luminaires:** These require the same standards as the tungsten halogen units, plus the following:
  - *UV protection:* Where a luminaire is not fitted with a glass lens it is recommended that a safety glass is provided to absorb the UV radiation from the lamp. The glass should have a minimum thickness of 3 mm to provide adequate mechanical strength. However, with higher wattage luminaires, an increased thickness of glass will be required to give added strength.
  - *UV radiation:* It is prudent for a manufacturer to have an independent test certificate from a test house such as the National Physical Laboratory to determine that luminaires do not exceed any dangerous UV radiation levels or to conduct the UV tests themselves and 'self certify' to the appropriate standards.
- **Warning on housing:** For UV protection, the safety glass must remain in position and be replaced if it is cracked, broken or has deep scratches.
- **Door opening:** The lens door may be screwed closed, in which case it would not require a safety switch. In the event that the door can be opened without a tool, then a double pole mains isolation switch can be used (good practice but not a standard) which must be activated by the glass of the lens so that the unit will not work if the lens is removed or the door is open. The activator must be designed so that it cannot be operated by hand, i.e. enclosed in a tube with a push rod to prevent the operator holding the switch closed and operating the unit. Some manufacturers use a trip relay that does not re-activate until it is manually reset. The same safety requirements apply to open fronted discharge luminaires that are fitted with a safety glass.
- The following warning is required: **'Do not open for 'x' seconds after switching off'. Note:** This is due to the hot lamps having high internal pressures and seeks to avoid explosions caused by cold air blowing on the lamp. This instruction is only required on luminaires declared by the manufacturer 'a danger when hot', particularly xenon lamps.

Operating and safety instructions: lamps and luminaires

Manufacturers are required to provide the following information for the safe operation of luminaires and their associated lamps in the entertainment industry.

It is in the interests of every person purchasing or operating luminaires to read the following *typical* instructions, because the manufacturer is making you aware of the possible safety problems. This will prevent you being in the unenviable position, after an accident, of the manufacturer saying 'I told you so!'

1. Luminaires should be marked with the maximum operating current. Observe the following colour code (Europe):
   Brown wire: live
   Blue wire: neutral
   Green/yellow wire: earth
2. When connecting the luminaire to the mains supply, ensure that it is effectively earthed, that the mains supply is at the rated voltage and that the correct polarity is observed.
3. Each circuit must be protected by rapid acting, high rupturing capacity fuse or miniature circuit breaker of suitable voltage and current rating.
4. Lamp replacement must only be carried out after the luminaire has been disconnected from the electricity supply. Allow sufficient time for the lamp to cool before removing it from the equipment. (Cooling could take as long as five minutes.)
5. Only use lamps of the recommended type and observe the maximum wattage limitation marked on the luminaire. Observe the lamp manufacturer's recommendations relating to lamp type.
6. Insertion of the lamp into the lampholder by holding the envelope may cause mechanical breakage of the lamp and/or seal. For safety, install by holding the lamp cap or protective sleeve and use eye protection where appropriate.
7. Do not handle the quartz envelope with bare hands. Oil or grease from the skin may contaminate the surface of the envelope and in operation reduce performance and cause premature failure. If the quartz is accidentally handled, clean it before operation with a cloth moistened with alcohol or methylated spirit.
8. In certain circumstances, items made from quartz or glass may shatter. Prevent water droplets splashing onto a hot lamp as they may cause the envelope to break.
9. A suitable safety mesh or glass must be fitted to protect persons and property in the event of a lamp shattering – this is most important when lamps are used in open fronted luminaires. If the safety glass or lens should become damaged with deep scratches or chipped edges, they must be replaced.
10. The lamp shall be changed if it has become damaged or thermally deformed.
11. At the end of life, lamps should be broken in a suitable robust container or wrapped to retain quartz fragments. The gas filling has a slight toxic content and large quantities of lamps should only be broken in a well ventilated area.

12. Direct exposure to discharge and high intensity tungsten halogen lamps can cause ultraviolet irritation to the skin and eyes. The use of glass or other UV filters is advised if the lamp is used in close proximity or for a prolonged period. When reflector fittings are used to concentrate the light in open fronted luminaires, the safe exposure period will be reduced. Appropriate screening of people and surroundings must be provided.

13. The luminaire must be mounted on a firm support or stand and positioned at a safe distance from any flammable material, e.g. curtains, background paper or scenery.

14. A high amount of radiant heat is produced and high surface temperatures are developed. Avoid operation in close proximity to human skin, as burns could result.

15. Avoid improper operation of the lamp, e.g. over voltage, or at burning angles not designed for the lamp type.

16. Luminaires must not be operated in explosive or flammable atmospheres or other hazardous areas.

17. All luminaires that are suspended must be fitted with a secondary independent means of support, e.g. a chain or bond. Removable accessories must be retained to prevent them falling if they become dislodged.

18. A dedicated anchor point should be provided on the housing so that the safety bond can be passed around a firm support through the yoke and terminated at the anchor point on the housing.

19. The top of the unit has been indicated to prevent it being mounted upside down.

20. Special care must be taken with portable luminaires and handheld lamps. When demounting the luminaires, allow them to completely cool before standing them on a flammable surface or placing them in a carrying case.

21. For replacement parts, refer to the manufacturers parts list for the recommended type of safety glass, wire guard, safety suspension bond and any relevant accessories.

22. Service and repairs must only be carried out by a qualified person.

14.2 The Supply of Machinery (Safety) Regulations 1992 (1992 No. 3073) together with Amendment 1994 (1994 No. 2063)

For any person engaged in the entertainment industry who is involved with either motorized luminaires, grid systems or pop rigs, these regulations have to be fully understood as they are not just recommendations but Statutory Instruments where failure to comply could lead to imprisonment and/or a heavy fine.

It is obviously impossible in this publication to cover the documents completely but the following is given as a brief guide. It is strongly recommended that the full regulations are obtained and studied in full.

Definition of 'responsible person'

(a) the manufacturer of the machinery
(b) the manufacturer's authorized representative in the Community
(c) the person who first supplies the relevant machinery in the Community

Definition of machinery

(a) an assembly of linked parts or components, at least one of which moves, including, without prejudice to the generality of the foregoing, the appropriate actuators, control and power circuits, joined together for a specific application, in particular for the processing, treatment, moving or packaging of a material;
(b) an assembly of machines, that is to say, an assembly of items of machinery as referred to in (a) above which, in order to achieve the same end, are arranged and controlled so that they function as an integral whole notwithstanding that the items of machinery may themselves be relevant machinery and accordingly severally required to comply with these Regulations; or
(c) interchangeable equipment modifying the function of a machine which is supplied for the purpose of being assembled with an item of machinery as referred to in (a) above or with a series of different items of machinery or with a tractor by the operator himself save for any such equipment which is a spare part or tool.

There are exclusions regarding certain types of machinery and the Regulations should be consulted with regard to these.

GENERAL REQUIREMENTS

No person shall supply relevant machinery or safety component unless the requirements of regulation 12 below are complied with in relation thereto.

Where a person –
(a) being the manufacturer of relevant machinery or relevant safety component, himself put that relevant machinery or safety component into service in the course of a business; or
(b) having imported relevant machinery or safety component from a country or territory outside the Community, himself puts that relevant machinery or safety component into service in the course of a business.

Requirements for the supply of machinery

12 The requirements of this regulation are that:
(a) the relevant machinery satisfies the relevant essential health and safety requirements;
(b) the appropriate conformity assessment procedure in respect of the relevant machinery has been carried out;
(c) the responsible person, at his election, has issued either –
 i)   an EC declaration of conformity, or
 ii) a declaration of incorporation

(d) the CE mark has been properly affixed by the responsible person;
(e) the relevant machinery is in fact safe.

Machinery manufactured for European standards

The responsible person must:
(a) draw up and forward to an approved body a technical file;
(b) submit the technical file for verification that the standards have been correctly applied; and request that a certificate of adequacy is issued; or
(c) submit the technical file together with an example of the relevant machinery for EC type examination

*The '**Technical File**' must include the following:*
(a) A overall drawing of the machinery and control circuits
(b) Fully detailed drawings together with calculations, test results and any other data that may be required to check the conformity of the machinery with the health and safety requirements
(c) A description of methods adopted to eliminate hazards presented by the machinery
(d) A copy of the instructions for the machinery
(e) For series manufacture, the internal measures that will be implemented to ensure that all the items of machinery are in conformity with the provisions of the Machinery Directive

CE MARKING

For the purposes of these Regulations, the CE marking shall not be regarded as properly affixed to relevant machinery unless:

(a) that machinery –
   i)   satisfies the relevant health and safety requirements; and
   ii) is safe; and
(b) the responsible person who affixes the CE marking to the relevant machinery –
   i)   has carried out the appropriate conformity assessment procedure and issued an EC declaration of conformity in respect thereof;
   ii) affixes the said marking in a distinct, visible, legible and indelible manner; and
   iii) in the case of relevant machinery which is the subject of Community Directives other than the Machinery Directive, which also provide for the affixing of the CE marking, has complied with the requirements of those other Directives in respect of that machinery:
(c) No markings which
   i)   are likely to deceive any person as regards the meaning and form of the CE marking; or
   ii) reduce the visibility of legibility of the CE marking shall be fixed to relevant machinery.

MODIFICATIONS

Where the responsible person complies with one of the conformity assessment procedures he must inform the approved body of any

modifications, even of a minor nature which he or, where the respon-
sible person is not the manufacturer, the manufacturer has made or
plans to make to the relevent machinery to which the technical file
relates.

14.3   BS 7671 (The IEE Regulations) in practice

In any installation that a lighting consultant is concerned with, the
electrical engineer appointed will in the main ensure that the current
regulations are adopted and enforced to ensure that the system is
built to any required standards. There are however, some aspects of
the regulations which have to be borne in mind by the lighting
consultant as well. The first of these is the selection of the equipment that meets the requirements of the permanently installed lighting system such as the dimmer racks. It is obviously no good having
a piece of equipment that has a reasonable metal shell around it but
leaving it possible to poke your finger through a ventilation louvre
enabling you to touch a live terminal or a busbar.

There are several aspects to the safety of equipment such as this.
Some of these items may seem very obvious but it's very useful to
ensure that equipment meets some of the basic parameters. Any
item of equipment selected must meet the requirements of the
voltages present in the installation, together with the normal current
consumption and additionally has to perform satisfactorily and not
create any danger by the abnormal current flow during fault conditions.

Dimmer racks

In the case of dimmer systems, it's obvious that we have to be aware
of the voltage and frequency of the mains used. Dimmer racks are
defined as 'factory built assemblies' and the rules for these must be
complied with. There are various degrees of protection required in
a dimmer rack and without going into all the details, the first of these
that we are concerned with is a degree of protection to IP2X. This
means that the rack is protected against the entry of solid objects
greater than **12 mm** across and this is defined as a 'finger' or a similar
object not exceeding 80 mm in length. This can be checked by using
a 'standard test finger'. This degree of protection is required on all
vertical surfaces of a dimmer rack. On the horizontal top surface
however, an even greater protection is required and this is IP4X,
where the top surface must be protected against the entry of solid
objects greater than **1 mm**. The definition refers to wire or strips of
metal in thickness greater than 1 mm and solid objects exceeding
1 mm in diameter. This requirement is to protect against the
dropping of small screwdrivers through slots on the top of a rack or
strands of copper wire being used for the installation penetrating the
slots, thus 'shorting out' equipment within the rack, possibly causing
an electrical explosion.

The IEE regulations state that 'where an opening larger than that
permitted for IP2X or IPXXB is necessary to allow the replacement
of parts' two requirements will apply:

suitable precautions shall be taken to prevent persons from touching a live part unintentionally

and

it shall be established as far as practicable, that a person will be aware that a live part can be touched through the opening and should not be touched.

Plug-in dimmers

It is this particular requirement that makes the use of 'plug in' dimmers particularly onerous. When a 'plug in' dimmer is removed from a rack, quite a large space is left and terminals at the rear of the dimmer are exposed. Most dimmer racks these days have dimmers that are totally enclosed with terminals that are either very difficult to reach from the front surface of a dimmer rack or meet an IP2X requirement.

Dimmer rack security

One of the most important regulations that concerns us with dimmer racks, is the one that states:

where it is necessary to remove a barrier or open an enclosure, or to remove a part of an enclosure, one or more of the following requirements shall be satisfied:

(i)   the removal or opening shall be possible only by use of a key or tool.
(ii)   the removal or opening shall be possible only after disconnection of the supply to the live part against which the barrier or enclosure affords protection, restoration of the supply being possible only after replacement or reclosure of the barrier or enclosure.
(iii)   an intermediate barrier shall be provided to prevent contact with a live part, such a barrier affording a degree of protection of at least IP2X or IPXXB and removable only by the use of a tool.

Item (i) is generally met on dimmer racks by a front door being fitted which is usually locked with a key, and by the fact that any rear access requires screwdrivers or special tools to remove screws or nuts. Item (ii) is met by an automatic disconnection of a supply, probably realized by having a microswitch operating a contactor for example, but this is not usually used in our installation systems although a microswitch on the lens door of a discharge luminaire is somewhat similar in operation. An example of an intermediate barrier such as quoted in (iii), would be a Perspex cover such as that provided to enclose the terminals on a transformer or across terminals at the input of the rack.

Each of the pieces of equipment that we wish to install will have to have a label or other suitable means of identification to indicate what the purpose of each item is. There will be wiring going to and from any apparatus installed and this must ensure that colour codes for identification of cables meet the requirements of the country where the system is to be used. It is essential that correct colour codes are maintained so there are no misunderstandings as to their purpose.

Cables and connections

In a lighting system we have to make many electrical connections and there are strict rules with regard to these. The most obvious one is the fact that the terminals should be large enough to make a good connection with the type of cable in use. Thus the means of connection has to take into account the following:

(i)   the material of the conductor and its insulation
(ii)   the number and shape of the wires forming the conductor
(iii)   the cross sectional area of the conductor
(iv)   the number of conductors to be connected together
(v)   the temperature attained by the terminals in normal service such that the effectiveness of the insulation of the conductors connected to them is not impaired
(vi)   where a soldered connection is used the design shall take account of creep, mechanical stress and temperature rise under fault current conditions
(vii)   the provision of adequate locking arrangements in situations subject to vibration or thermal cycling.

Items (i), (ii), (iii) and (iv) cover the size of terminals including the provision of two or more parallel connections; Item (v) covers for high temperature switches where deterioration of the insulation will cause problems in practice; Item (vi) prevents the melting and breaking of soldered connections which could lead to wires floating about in cabinets; Item (vii) seeks to prevent terminals coming loose either by the extremes of being cold and hot or by vibration which again could lead to wires floating about.

When using armoured cables for the input circuits to dimmer racks, there are strict rules regarding the type of cable used. One of the most important is that single core cables armoured with steel wire or tape should not be used, thus preventing any eddy currents being induced in the armour system. At the input to the dimmer rack, which is usually constructed from steel, an arrangement has to be made so that the individual conductors are not surrounded by a ferrous material thus preventing eddy (induced) currents. It's fairly obvious that any system using electrical conductors should provide a method of self-cancellation to prevent harmful electromagnetic fields.

Conductors of ac circuits installed in ferromagnetic enclosures shall be arranged so that the conductors of all phases and the neutral conductor (if any) and the appropriate protective conductor of each circuit are contained in the same enclosure.

Every cable has to have adequate strength and be installed so that it can withstand any electromechanical forces caused by high fault currents or any other current that may occur in service. The same principle is applied to any busbar systems within dimmer racks.

As well as having regard for the regulations when we take the cables from the dimmer room to the production area (and this has already been discussed), another point to be borne in mind is that any outlets either at the bottom of bars, along bars, attached to monopoles or pantographs, are all governed by regulations to ensure electrical safety is maintained.

An important element of the installation is the ambient temperatures that the racks and wiring can be subjected to, and there are rules regarding the limits and these have to be kept. The type of fusing, or protection afforded by mcbs, has to be carefully integrated with the size of cables and the loads that they are handling, although in practice the use of say a 20A fuse on a 240V 5kW dimmer circuit will more than adequately protect the wiring installed which will invariably be generous in size to prevent voltage drop.

Another important element covered by regulations that we would be most concerned with is the mechanical strength of the equipment. We have to be aware of areas of high humidity, which although not usually a problem in the United Kingdom, can be a problem with equipment in other countries. Much of the equipment used for entertainment will be subject to vibration, and this is another area which is governed by modern regulations.

Phase balance

If we could ensure a balanced distribution through our three-phase network, we wouldn't have to worry too much about the neutral conductor and it could be of a reasonable size in relation to the phase conductors. However, in many of our installations, we will have out-of-balance three-phase systems, therefore the neutral conductor must always have a cross sectional area appropriate to the expected value of the neutral current. In general this means the neutral conductor and the three-phase conductors are of similar size.

Fire precautions

We are obviously concerned with the spread of fire within the systems we install, and another regulation states:

where a wiring system passes through elements of building construction, such as floors, walls, roofs, ceilings, partitions or cavity barriers, the openings remaining after passage of the wiring system shall be sealed according to the degree of fire resistance required of the element concerned (if any).

In addition:

where a wiring system such as conduit, cable ducting, cable trunking, busbar or busbar trunking penetrates elements of building construction having specified fire resistance it shall be internally sealed so as to maintain the degree of fire resistance of the respective element as well as being externally sealed to maintain the required fire resistance.

The two regulations quoted cover for the instances when we go from one area to another and thus create holes in the structure. The first covers for unenclosed wiring systems where it may be just cables going from one area to another. The second regulation quoted covers for the fact that we might have trunking going through a wall and the trunking itself is sealed to the wall surround but unfortunately the internal part of the trunking allows fire to move from one area to another and this, of course, would be just as dangerous.

Additionally the regulation that covers all of the above states:

each sealing arrangement used in accordance with the regulations shall comply with the following requirements:

(i)   It should be compatible with the material of the wiring system with which it is in contact.

(ii)   It shall permit thermal movement of the wiring system without reduction of the sealing quality.

(iii)   It shall be removable without damage to existing cable where space permits future extension to be made.

(iv)   It shall resist relevant external influences to the same degree as the wiring system with which it is used.

and that

Each sealing arrangement shall be visually inspected at an appropriate time during erection to verify that it conforms to the manufacturers' erection instructions and the details shall be recorded.

Regulation (i) above seeks to prevent harmful chemical reactions between the wiring system itself and any materials used for fireproofing; regulation (ii) is fairly obvious in that it would be no good having fireproofing that with gradual movement allowed gaps to appear. Unfortunately fire doesn't need too much of a gap to go from one area to another; regulation (iii) covers for the situation where it would be quite easy to spray, for instance, around cables with some foam which would be fire retardant but unfortunately, if you then needed to do anything with the cables, it would be physically impossible because they'd all be glued together. Regulation (iv) prevents the use of materials which would be less robust than the cables themselves.

Thus we have to be careful with the methods used for fire prevention because by covering for this eventuality it may make life difficult when expansion of a system is required.

During an installation temporary sealing arrangements have to be provided as appropriate and when any work is done, any sealing that has been disturbed has to be re-instated as soon as possible.

Signal cables

In lighting systems we have the normal mains supply cable going to the luminaires, in addition we will have low voltage multi-core cables or smaller digital signal cables provided for the control systems. This type of situation is covered by the regulations which state that we are not allowed to mix cables with various voltages present unless the insulation of all of the cables used is insulated for the highest voltage present in any of the cables, or alternative methods are adopted:

(i)   Each conductor in a multicore cable is insulated for the highest voltage present in the cable, or is enclosed within an earthed metallic screen of a current carrying capacity equivalent to that of the largest conductor enclosed within the screen,

or

(ii)   the cables are insulated for their respective system voltage and installed in a separate compartment of a cable ducting or cable trunking system, or have an earthed metallic covering.

It is obviously extremely dangerous to pick up a conductor where we expect to find safe low voltage and in fact find mains, and the above regulations seek to prevent this happening.

The two methods are either to have good insulation of the systems so voltages can't travel from one cable to another, or conductors that are surrounded by an earthed shield where any harmful voltage will be conveyed safely away.

In practice, we generally run the mains feeds around the building separately from the control feeds, the only time where they may come into close proximity is perhaps on monopoles, pantographs or motorized barrel units where technical cables for the sound and vision system are installed in addition to the lighting circuits.

Plugs and sockets

In places of entertainment and for those concerned with the production of entertainment we have a multiplicity of plugs and sockets used. These may be the normal 13A supplies for domestic use, special sockets concerned with lighting outlets and there will invariably be provision for three phase supplies for portable machinery. We have to be extremely careful that we don't intermix any of these socket outlets or plugs so that people are not placed in danger or machines receive voltages for which they are not designed. The main requirement for plugs and socket outlets is as follows:

(i)   *It shall not be possible for any pin of a plug to make contact with any live contact of its associated socket outlet while any other pin of the plug is completely exposed.*

(ii)   *It shall not be possible for any pin of a plug to make contact with any live contact of any socket outlet within the same installation other than the type of socket outlet for which the plug is designed.*

(iii)   *Every plug and socket outlet shall be of the non reversible type with provision for the connection of a protective conductor.*

Emergency systems

Finally but certainly not least, is the provision of devices for emergency switching. The regulations requires that a means of interrupting the supply for the purpose of emergency switching shall be capable of cutting off the full load current of the relevant part of the installation.

means for emergency switching shall consist of:

(i)   *A single switching device directly cutting off the incoming supply, or*

(ii)   *A combination of several items of equipment operated by a single action and resulting in the removal of the hazard by cutting off the appropriate supply; emergency stopping may include the retention of supply for electric braking facilities.*

The regulations go on to state:

where practical a device for emergency switching shall be manually operated directly interrupting the main circuit. A device such as a circuit breaker or a contactor operated by remote control shall open on de-energization of the coil, or another technique of suitable reliability shall be employed.

The operating means (such as handle or push button) for a device for emergency switching shall be clearly identifiable and preferably coloured **'red'**. *It shall be installed in a readily accessible position where the hazard might occur and where appropriate, further devices shall be provided where additional emergency switching may be needed.*

The operating means of a device for emergency switching shall be of the latching type or capable of being restrained in the 'OFF' or 'STOP' position. The release of the emergency switching device shall not re-energize the equipment concerned.

Although it is possible, in a further qualified part of the regulations, to allow an automatic reset under specified conditions, we in the entertainment industry are mainly concerned with the fact that nearly all of the operatives involved with a production could de-energize the system by operating the emergency switching. The re-energizing of the equipment has to be carried out by approved personnel, such as engineers or electricians concerned, to ensure that the hazard that caused the 'emergency' has been dealt with correctly.

14.4   Electricity at Work Regulations in practice

The Health and Safety Executive issued the Electricity at Work Regulations 1989 and they came into force on 1 April 1990. The Regulations are mandatory, and are enforceable by law. The intention of the Regulations is to require precautions to be taken against the risk of death or personal injury from electricity in the place of work. Whilst the Regulations cover all electrical supplies and equipment, we will restrict our coverage to portable items that can be plugged into the mains via a plug and socket. These are obviously the most vulnerable to damage and are by their description the most likely items to be handled.

The Regulations cover every portable item to be found on the premises from luminaires to kettles, from typewriters to electric drills, in fact every item fitted with a plug must be included. The wiring of the premises and permanently connected machinery and apparatus are also included, but are not being considered by us at this time. The question is how to comply with the Regulations. The first step is to obtain a copy of 'Electricity at Work Regulations, 1989' and 'Statutory Instruments No. 635'. There are also two very useful Guidance Notes PM 32 'The Safe Use of Portable Electrical Apparatus' and GS 37 'Flexible Leads, Plugs and Sockets'. All are issued by the Health and Safety Executive, Her Majesty's Stationery Office or from the safety officer for your area. The following notes are our interpretation of some of the requirements and should not be taken as a statement of the Regulations.

The statement that all portable electrical equipment must be as far as possible electrically safe is the starting point and it really means **all and every item** found on the premises and does not take into account who owns it. It can be a personal radio or a rented item, it still comes under the umbrella of the Regulations. When the area safety officer calls to inspect your premises, he will ask to see the duty holder. This is any responsible person that has been nominated to keep a register of every item of electrical equipment; he will ask the duty holder for the register and expect to find certain information in it. Identify the item, the date that it was tested, the result of the test, which can only be pass or fail, action taken and the date of the next test. The period between tests can only be established by the duty holder and the operator and will depend on how often the appliance is used and the history of damage that can be sustained by the environment in which it is used. Examples could be: an electric drill being used all day, every day on a production line, in which case three-monthly tests could be deemed appropriate; equipment in frequent use and subject to transit damage could be tested every six months, and so on. Until a history is built up in the register no definite period can be established.

Most portable items in entertainment that are not out on rental or travelling shows, and are normally used in the same premises, could be considered to have light duty and might be considered for an annual test. Portable electrical equipment can be divided into three groups:

- **Class I:** Requiring an earth connection to any metal part that could become live in a fault condition.
- **Class II:** A totally insulated electrical device where no part can become live in the event of a fault condition. This type of equipment does not require an earth wire.
- **Class III:** Low voltage equipment that has special regulations.

A typical test for Class I equipment could be a visual inspection of the cable, the plug top, the cord grip at the plug and the cord grip at the appliance and an inpsection inside the plug top to determine that it is correctly wired. Any damage to these items would fail the test and the equipment would not be allowed to continue to the electrical test. The reported accidents show that 80% of electrical accidents could have been avoided by a visual inspection. If the equipment passes the visual test it will be tested electrically for earth continuity from the plug top to the frame of the appliance and the earth resistance will be recorded and must be within the Regulations' requirements. The insulation is tested from the plug top through the earth and live conductors and must have the required resistance. Finally, a run test is conducted to determine that the equipment conforms to the Regulations in its working state. Other tests are available on some products; a high voltage test might be carried out, normally 1500 V for Class I equipment and 3000 V for Class II, but these are made at the discretion of the electrical engineer conducting the tests.

14.5 Safety checklists and inspections

Much of the equipment used in the entertainment industry is well built and a superficial examination usually would lead one to expect the equipment would work safely for long periods of time with little or nothing going wrong. However, life is not as easy as that and modern legislation requires that moving equipment such as monopoles, winches, pantographs and devices used to suspend equipment over stage areas, studio areas and particularly above audiences is regularly inspected to see no danger is present. Many items concerned with mechanical safety can be verified by visual inspection, but this is not necessarily the case with electrical equipment when the fault may lie in a piece of copper somewhere. All items of electrical equipment also have to undergo routine checks to ensure that they are not posing any hazard.

To ensure that the necessary inspections are carried out correctly, all items of equipment must be coded and numbered and a register of equipment and tests kept on the premises. When items of equipment are purchased, they must have a CE mark (including year of construction), name and address of manufacturer, designation of series or type, an identification number of the particular piece of equipment. All equipment must be accompanied by clear operating and maintenance instructions.

Routine testing (which covers many of the points of the EEC Machinery Directive) of lifting equipment has to provide checks against the following items:

1. Undue wear of any part.
2. The wire ropes used for lifting must be inspected to ensure they haven't been damaged in any way and that no strands are broken.
3. The points where wire ropes are made off to provide permanent anchor points to other parts of the structure are to be inspected to ensure they are not loose or damaged.
4. All parts of the motor assembly are firmly in place and not loose in any way.
5. All pulleys or scroll drums are to be examined for undue signs of wear which would indicate possible problems with the winding of the wire ropes.
6. All diverter pulleys are to be examined for signs of wear and the fact that they are free to rotate.
7. A visual inspection of the top and bottom limit system in addition to visual inspection of overload and slack wire system.
8. To apply load tests to ensure that the slack wire and overload system works correctly. In addition to traverse the unit from top to bottom to see that limit switches are operating correctly.
9. Ensure that all warning labels are present and all indicators are fully functional.
10. Ensure that the equipment is capable of being controlled from all nominated control positions, e.g. studio floor level or on the local controls at grid level.
11. All covers and guards are correctly positioned and fastened securely.

Electrical safety is covered, in the main, in the United Kingdom, by the Electricity at Work Regulations which would cover for items of equipment that are portable and in addition the latest edition of the IEE regulations pertaining to the installation of the electrical system in the building. As well as the regular checks for electrical safety under the Electricity at Work Regulations, it is also wise to check for the mechanical safety of any luminaire or other type of light source used in the entertainment industry. Most premises will, on a fairly regular basis, do some maintenance to ensure the equipment works correctly, and this obviously makes life much easier from the point of view of the electricians concerned with lighting equipment. At the time these checks for maintenance are made, it is very easy to go over some of the mechanical items to ensure that they are not damaged in any way. Testing the pan and tilt mechanism for movement and slackness might reveal problems in this area. A visual examination of a yoke for instance, would not necessarily indicate problems with the devices used to lock the yoke to the body of the luminaire. A fairly careful examination of the bodywork of any luminaire would reveal any loose parts that may be suspect and therefore in danger of falling off.

To give an example of a problem that can occur and in fact did, many years ago and had tremendous implications for safety in the studio, a luminaire mounted above two actors suddenly discharged molten aluminium down to the studio floor. The amount was quite considerable and would have caused a severe burn had it hit one of the actors. An investigation was carried out and revealed that a small internal aluminium cover in the luminaire had come loose, possibly through vibration by being raised and lowered in the studio on a bar unit. This small aluminium cover had fallen across the primary reflector of a 1250W linear lamp. Instead of melting the offending piece of aluminium that had become dislodged, the lamp chose to melt the reflector around it. The molten aluminium fell through the bottom louvres used for air flow in the unit concerned and dropped to the studio floor. One horrifying aspect of this case was that during the tests to reproduce the fault, it was found that with the dimmer held at about '7' and thus applying about 200 V to a 240V 1250W linear lamp, no problem occurred and, in fact, this might have been the case for a long period of time. However, as soon as the lamp was raised to full output the fault was reproduced. Thus, it was rather like playing Russian roulette with molten aluminium.

Therefore a suggested checklist for luminaires is as follows:

1. Is the yoke functioning correctly and are the pan and tilt controls, if fitted, working satisfactorily?
2. Do all locking knobs fitted correctly tighten the moving part so it can be held in the position as set?
3. Examine the spud fitted to see that it hasn't become loose from the yoke assembly.
4. Check internally for any loose parts, particularly with regard to reflectors and lamp holder assemblies.
5. Check internal wiring for any signs of wear.
6. Check all switches fitted to see that mechanically they function correctly. Although they may appear to be satisfactory from an electrical standpoint, it might be that they are not mechanically perfect. This generally avoids any arcing problems within switches, caused by springs or levers being slack.
7. Check to see that all accessories attached to the luminaire are not loose, i.e. barndoors, colour frames, etc.
8. Check all louvres which allow air flow through the luminaire for signs of damage and ensure they are working correctly to make certain that the luminaire does not get over hot. This can usually be ascertained by signs of burning on the bodywork.
9. Check to see that barndoors function correctly and are sufficiently tight to do the job needed.
10. If a base or feet are provided to stand a luminaire on, ensure they haven't become damaged in any way.
11. Luminaire leads and plugs should be tested *at least* once a year but it's quite useful to inspect them on a more frequent basis to see that no arcing is occurring on any of the pins, which would also indicate deterioration in any of the permanent sockets fitted in the system.
12. A useful point is to listen out whilst in operation for any nasty frying noises, which would indicate lamp contacts arcing and thus a lampholder which would need replacing.

Although all the foregoing seems a bit of a chore and probably most people generally say, 'it's not my responsibility', if most of the tests listed above are carried out, it ensures a safe working environment in which it is easier to work because all the equipment is functioning correctly.

15
Maintaining and hiring lighting equipment

15.1 Standardization for maintenance and spares

Maintenance can be in house or in the case of hired equipment, the hirer does the maintenance. What follows applies to anyone concerned with maintenance. One of the problems with a variety of equipment used, is the fact that to maintain it requires different procedures for each type of equipment. This generally poses a problem for the maintenance engineer and, secondly it can lead to items being overlooked by the staff being unfamiliar with all the equipment concerned.

Although a 1kW profile spot luminaire may appear to be very similar between two manufacturers, there are many points of detail that will vary in its construction, and it's quite possible, for example, that parts used are sourced from different manufacturers. It might be that different lampbases are used on very similar pieces of equipment and this will cause a problem when trying to repair them. This leads us on to spares holding.

It's very well worth repeating at this point that it's essential to keep the amount of spares held on premises as low as possible, because it is plant that just gathers dust and usually accomplishes no useful purpose, other than tying up sums of money that could be well spent elsewhere. If we are lucky, it may be that the solid state devices used by three or four dimmer manufacturers are common to any of their pieces of equipment. For example, it may be that the output thyristors on a 5kW dimmer need to be 40A devices, say, and these could be sourced, provided they meet the technical specification, from several manufacturers. This enables prices to be kept low. A good example of standardization is with motorized winches. In an installation containing, say, 100 units, it would be nice to think that only one motor unit had to be kept in stores in case of failure. It would also be preferable that any limit switches in use on the units were the same type of microswitch. Although sometimes necessary, it's not desirable to have several types of switch on any unit because it only puts up the spares holding within the premises. In the negotiation process with a company when tendering for work, a point that has to be discussed is how many items need to be kept as spares for the particular pieces of equipment. Items of equipment such as monopoles, winch systems and mechanical items require very few spares to be held as most components will be relatively lightly used. Similarly lighting consoles and dimmers have very low failure rates. It would be nice if the same could be said for the luminaires, but unfortunately they are subject to heat, to mechanical movement, to being rigged and de rigged and thus suffer more damage in use.

One of the problems with standardisation of products is that any company concerned may hesitate before going in another direction for the supply of equipment. Hopefully, in practice, this is not the case because it would inhibit any development work by the various manufacturers servicing the entertainment industry. However, the point remains that some standardization is beneficial to the customer and can also be beneficial to the manufacturer. One of the best examples of standardization is where luminaires for discharge and tungsten lighting, can use the same luminaire body, yoke and pole operation controls, the only items varying being the reflector, lens combination and the lampholders.

15.2   Maintenance rooms and test equipment

In Europe we have a wonderful legacy of splendid theatres handed down to us over the ages; some have beautiful architecture, some have splendid auditoria but they all have one thing in common – a dividing line drawn at the proscenium arch separating the paying audience from the theatre's working area. The average theatre goer would not believe the cramped conditions and in some cases the squalor that exists in the world beyond the proscenium arch. To find any space for a maintenance area is difficult and the electrician often resorts to a bench in a dark corner somewhere. The luxury of a purpose designed maintenance room in a modern theatre can only be upstaged by the maintenance areas provided in the modern television studios. So if we are given an opportunity to plan our own maintenance area in film, television or theatre, what should we look for?

The first requirement is an area large enough to store the spare lights and equipment plus enough room to stack the equipment requiring repair, leaving room to test luminaires and have enough racking for spares and consumables such as lamps and filters. Obviously we would require a good electrical supply terminated into a purpose built distribution board which will provide all the types of socket outlets required together with a three-phase outlet; a large bench, with an equally large vice, covered in a thick linoleum that is also a good insulator. A large lock up cupboard stocked with taps and dies and nuts and bolts of all sizes, complete with all of the normal tools including an electric drill, soldering irons large and small and an adequate supply of various plugs, sockets and cables. Test equipment should also include a good quality multi-meter, a incident light meter and a tri stimulus colour meter to perform light tests.

To comply with the Electricity at Work Regulations 1989, each piece of electrical equipment must be entered into a register and periodically tested. Purpose built electrical test instruments are available offering all the test facilities required and are a good investment for everyday use and to use for the periodic tests. To be given these conditions and a good lock on the door, is no more than the electrical staff deserve to enable them to keep a well ordered house in good working condition.

15.3 Luminaire maintenance

A common misunderstanding of maintenance is that the electrician walks round with a duster and flicks dust from lights and repairs the ones that do not work. Nothing could be further from the truth. Electrical maintenance is a legal requirement, laid down in the Electricity at Work Regulations, 1989.

Over and above the electrical safety tests, there are three main problem areas to be considered when carrying out luminaire maintenance: heat, mechanical damage and the ingress of dirt. It is inevitable that luminaires are going to attract the dust and dirt that is in the air by virtue of the fact that the instrument is designed to have a cold air intake to cool the lamp and electrical equipment, which also sucks in the associated grime. As it does so, it deposits the dirt on the lens, reflector and any other surface which is subject to change of temperature. Therefore, periodic cleaning is required to maintain the efficiency of the luminaire. Most reflectors are made from brightly polished anodized aluminium. These are surface reflectors and should only be cleaned by wiping them with a damp cloth and liquid soap. A conventional wipe down with a wet rag afterwards to remove the soap will suffice and dry with a lint free rag. The same method can be used to clean the lenses, however, in the case of the tungsten halogen lamps which do have a large deposit of grime on them, these should be wiped clean with alcohol and then polished with a clean lint free rag. Fingermarks must be avoided on tungsten halogen lamps to prevent the fingerprints becoming etched into the envelope when they are hot, causing hot spots which can collect extra heat and form a blister on the envelope.

Regular examination of the internal cables, which are flexed when the unit is focused, are needed to determine if the insulation has been damaged. Switches and lampholders are targets for excessive heat. One indication of a lampholder overheating is to remove the lamp and inspect the pins. If they show signs of 'arcing' then the lampholder must be replaced, because if a new lamp is inserted into a lampholder that already has arcing on the contacts, it will transmit the same problem to the new lamp. The safety bond must be visually inspected for damaged or frayed strands. Any bond or chain must be replaced if it has arrested one fall of the luminaire so any distortion in its shape should alert you to this problem. Barndoors and colour frames are retained by safety catches which must be in good working order. If cables are to be replaced they must be of the recommended temperature range; do not be tempted to use just any old cable. Lenses must be examined for chips or cracks, the most obvious place is around the edge of the lens which when continuously heated and cooled progresses the chip into a crack and the lens will ultimately fracture. Change any damaged lenses. Look for dents in the housing that could cause problems to the electrical internal switches and wiring. The yoke must be examined to determine that it is mechanically sound.

Suspension system maintenance

Trusses, counterweight bars, motorized barrels, telescopes and pantographs are basically the same device: a means of supporting luminaires from above with variable height. They may employ electrical drives, with various sensing switches together with cable support systems or alternatively, spring balanced. We can therefore generalize about support systems and state that a secondary means of support should be provided. This usually takes the form of a wire cable (safety bond), as a means of arresting the device if the primary means of support is broken. Therefore the first step in mechanical maintenance must be to inspect these areas which provide the ultimate safety.

Well designed winches allow inspection of the cable termination on the winding drum and at the bottom end of the cables. Look for loose or frayed ends, examine the whole length of the cable as it is wound in and out for any loose threads. If any such signs are seen, the cables must be changed. Each lifting apparatus has a safe working load stated on it; a periodic inspection must include the application of a test load to determine that the unit is safe. Many insurance companies require such tests annually. Most designs employ a top and bottom limit, the unit should be run through the whole range to determine that both limits are working and also the overload and underload limits. These are normally provided to switch the device off in the event of it picking up an additional load such as piece of scenery or a safeguard against the operator placing too many luminaires on the barrel. The underload switch is required if the luminaire is lowered onto the top of a set where cable would be spewed out until the luminaire toppled off the set and presents a real hazard. This test can easily be simulated by lowering the luminaire onto a rostrum where it should cut out immediately it touches the floor.

In the case of traversing monopoles and pantographs, they are normally fitted with end stop switches for traverse, which must be operated and the electrical cables should be examined for damage, particularly in the case of pantographs where cables are laced up the side of the links and can easily be caught between them. In general gearboxes should not require maintenance, unless they have been stripped down for repair. Care should be taken on the type of grease or oil used, some types of gearbox rely on a heavy lubricant to help them to become self sustaining to avoid the luminaire running away under a no volt condition. Any lubricants used must be at the recommendation of the manufacturer. A good guide to all lifting devices is that two turns should be left on the hoisting drum when the device is at the bottom limit. This will determine that the cables retain the load and not the end fixing. The cables used in lifting devices are special and normally of a flexible nature. Only use the manufacturer's replacements.

Pantographs should be inspected for mechanical damage of the links and the hinge pin retaining clips; these have been known to pop off and not affect the operation until the pin slides out. The springs used on pantographs normally have a 10 000 cycle working life; this doesn't meant they will fall to pieces in 10 000 cycles but an early warning of fatigue can be found by inspecting the edge of the springs, which show small cracks developing along the edges towards the end of life. At any sign of fractures, the springs should be replaced. Extreme caution must be taken in removing the springs from pantographs; with a pantograph on a bench, the spring should be pulled down by the ring provided and allowed up slowly until it touches its winding drum. In this state, the spring will be stationary and can be released. The assembly can be removed from the pantograph. Under no circumstances attempt to remove the spring from the drum; it is under considerable tension and can only be removed from the drum by the manufacturer. Barrel roller trolleys have stops screwed to them which engage under the barrel to prevent the trolley jumping off. On inspection ensure that the stops are present and undamaged. Where monopoles are concerned, sticking tubes are often caused by external damage. If this is the case, it is recommended that a complete set of tubes is replaced, in view of the fact that these are mated during manufacture for not only size tolerance, but the bow that occurs in their length. Any attempt to replace one particular tube could result in many hours of work and problems of fit and alignment that you were not aware of.

15.4   Holding spares and expendables

The seemingly simple task of holding spare parts and replacement items is anything but simple. The problems are mainly trying to identify the parts required and the quantities to hold in stock and monitoring the usage of expendable items.

Major items of equipment, such as winch systems, dimmers and luminaires will be changed with replacement of worn out plant programmes and these may vary in length of time from a seven to twenty year cycle. However, on a day to day basis, we have operating costs that are concerned with the maintenance of plant and the use of lamps, filters and certain types of accessories.

With a new installation it is a good policy to ask the manufacturer for a 'spares list' identifying all of the likely parts that will be required to keep the product in good repair. This request in itself causes some manufacturers to research their own products to determine the likely spares requirement for the future, whereas other manufacturers produce pictorial spares sheets, with photographs of the parts for easy identification. This practice also helps the user to determine the particular model in the years to come after the product has undergone several modifications and upgrades, and also overcomes the language problem when trying to describe the parts that are required. If your make of equipment does not provide this luxury it is expedient to ask for a written parts list which will identify your model and the parts required at that point in time.

If you are fortunate enough to be at the planning meeting when the products that are to be ordered are chosen, then it will be expedient to include the spares at the same time and as a condition of the original purchase. That part is easy. The question is: how many spares should be held?

Manufacturers have often taken part in discussions with the user to determine a sensible spares holding. In the first place this can only be an educated estimate from past experience and a percentage applied to the purchase order. A typical spares list for a luminaire could be as follows, with a percentage applied for orders from 100–300 units.

Lenses	5%
Lampholders	6%
Switches	5%
Internal electrical harnesses	3%
Yokes	2%
Reflector	6%
Wire guard	2%
Barndoors	4%
Colour frames	10%
Housing	1%
Mains cable assembly	5%

This could be a good starting point but don't forget that paradoxically, the older the equipment gets, and therefore the more likely to require spares, the less likely they are to be available, because the manufacturer has moved on to other designs. However, most reputable manufacturers keep spares for seven years from the first model – so beware if you have purchased in the last year of manufacture.

Holding spares in an existing installation reduces the problem of how many to stock, because a good record of purchases over the years will give a good guide to the likely requirement. The main problem is availability, because many luminaires are kept working long after their useful life. If this is the case and the original equipment manufacturer cannot supply the spare parts, there are specialist companies that carry out repairs and make special parts for old products.

Expendable items are much easier to predict. With a good record of purchases, a working quantity can be arrived at. Some of the most expensive items are the lamps. In many organizations the advent of computer databases has enabled the recording of faults and replacement items a relatively easy chore, which enables an analysis to be made of problems encountered. Fortunately, there are several main stockists that hold the large range of lamps used in TV, film and theatre, so the spares holding can be reduced to a nominal amount to cover day to day needs and calling on the stock of the main stockists for unscheduled requirements. From records, a guide of lamp usage in theatre and TV studios is approximately 1.3 lamps per year per luminaire. This is assuming that the lamps are supplied from dimmers. In the theatre the lamps will be providing different light levels, but the average dimmer output level could be similar to that adopted in television, where it is common practice to line up the cameras with the dimmers set to level '7'. In both cases this has the effect of greatly extending the life of the lamp. However, in film lighting the lamps are normally run at full voltage, resulting in a much shorter life. Typically for a tungsten halogen lamp, rated at 3200K, this is likely to be from 200–400 hours. One way of easing the pain of the lamp costs in the first two years of a new installation is to order two lamps for each luminaire at the same time that the equipment is purchased. In this way it is paid for out of the capital investment and does not come out of the expendable budget. By the second year, sufficient experience will be gained to determine a fairly accurate expendable requirement.

Whereas lamp manufacturers supply figures of typical life in use, filter manufacturers don't. This is obviously extremely difficult to do, because the life of filters is dependent upon the light source being used. However, from the customers point of view, it's very useful to do some tests to ascertain which filter material has a good life. This can be done very simply by putting up similar colours on the same light source and seeing which one deteriorates the most.

Stocking colour filters can be a big problem, the variables being 100 different colours sold in sheets and rolls. Although there are several good stockists who can normally respond quickly to your needs, it is expedient to keep a working stock of filter to call on. To remove one of the variables, it is normally a good practice to stock colour filters in rolls, this makes racking simple, with a colour swatch and number attached to the end of the roll. Rolls are also more economical because different sizes can be cut with the minimum of waste. However, the second variable of 100 colours needs a lot more thought. If one applies the 20/80 principle which seems to work in most cases, then 80% of the filters used will be in 20% of the colours offered. This would appear to be a simple solution; just stock filters for the 20 most popular colours. After much discussion and heated exchanges with the LDs, you might arrive at a compromise short list but be prepared for a long and arduous debate.

Filters used for colour correction are, of course, out of this category and are stocked separately as the need dictates.

Some accessories disappear as if they were expendable items and require special attention, otherwise a constant state of annoyance will persist. Barndoors usually suffer from damage preventing them from rotating and the flaps suffer from that infuriating malady known in the trade as 'a droopy flap'. This is when the hinges have become so weak that they cannot support the weight of the flap. Replacements will save a lot of aggravation between the LDs and the electrical staff. Safety bonds have a habit of disappearing, whether an alternative use has been found for them that we have not yet discovered, or a private hoard is hidden somewhere in the building, we will most likely never find out, but one thing that is certain is that every luminaire must have one to meet the safety requirements, so good replacement stocks must be maintained. Colour frames suffer from the same problems but have the additional requirement in theatre to be 'gelled up' between shows, so a complete set of spares is required as well as replacements.

Control and dimming should not require a large spares stock; the modern systems are very reliable and offer electronic card replacements and dimmer modules which should suffice. However, do not forget that when a tungsten halogen lamp ends its life with an arc-over across the filament, that it draws a large current and normally blows the fuse, so it is necessary to keep a good stock of spare fuses. Finally be sure that you have made your case for expendable items by submitting your budget for next year in plenty of time. No one else in management is going to remind you to spend their money.

15.5 Monitoring equipment usage for replacement programmes

It is quite common for a lighting manufacturer to be asked for spares to repair a luminaire that is 30 years old, not for a sentimental enthusiast to restore the instrument as an antique, but by necessity to keep the luminaire working long past its useful life. It is normally not too difficult to get management to replace a control system after some years of service, because there is always a good case for having the latest development in 'thingummy bobs and wotsits' that the designers of lighting control systems are constantly adding to their products. The simple luminaire or lifting device stands very little chance of becoming more desirable because it is a new model so the attitude of some management is 'light still comes out of it' or 'it still lifts up and down, doesn't it?', mainly brought on by the sudden realization of a big capital investment. Whilst we can blame the management for not wanting to invest more money, what have we done over the preceding years to develop a replacement programme? In most establishments, the accountant will depreciate the capital equipment by 25% per year, in this way the book value will reduce to 23.72% of the original value in five years.

This method of amortization will never remove the item from the books, but will show the management that the equipment that will be scrapped when it is replaced has very little capital value so that it can be written off. It is therefore a good practice to keep records of your own in the maintenance department of purchases and the date and cost, and make this information part of your inventory. To support your argument for replacements, you should keep a record of breakdowns, cause and effect, and so build up a case for replacements because of the nuisance to the production. Other factors are the size, weight and performance of a piece of equipment compared with a modern equivalent. In this way additional items can be introduced into your capital replacement budget each year in the hope that some money will be made available. If this is not forthcoming, keep the running total and add to it each year, then if you eventually get a percentage of your requested capital investment allowance, it will at least be a percentage of a much higher figure. The last question that management cannot ignore is 'does it conform to **current** safety standards?'

15.6 Hired equipment

At some time or the other, most lighting engineers will require the services of a lighting rental company to supply the extra equipment for a particular occasion or to provide a total installation on a temporary basis. There are many good rental companies available, providing an excellent service to the industry. Rental companies tend to specialize in film, television or theatre, normally dictated by the specialized equipment required in each of the lighting disciplines. A film company normally registers a film as a business name and trades as a limited company for the duration of the film. This sometimes makes it advantageous for equipment and cameras to be hired from a rental company and are therefore costed directly to that film. If the equipment had been purchased, it would present a problem at the end of the film of what to do with the equipment. In theatre, most professional houses have a small complement of lighting and control equipment but do not provide the quantity or choice of equipment for a large production. This dictates that the production company rents the additional lighting control and dimming required. The advantages are that the desired type and make of equipment can be chosen with the cost paid weekly from the takings or at the worst the equipment can be returned in the event of a disaster.

In television the main requirement is for outside broadcast lighting, and on occasions, to supplement the normal studio lighting with special units used for effects lighting. In the case of the pop industry, specialist companies usually provide the rig and the lights.

While the rental system is most helpful and seems to fill a very real need it should not be entered into lightly, without reading the small print, usually found on the back of acceptance delivery notes and contracts issued at the time of ordering. Each rental company has its own conditions. The following are some of the more important ones found by the authors.

- The customer hiring the equipment must check and test it before it is used and satisfy himself as to its fitness for the purpose.
- Further the customer must have adequate insurance cover to protect the rental company from claims against it for its products or personnel employed by the rental company for legal actions, proceedings, costs, charges, expenses and indemnity of third parties.
- The equipment must only be operated by people with the appropriate qualifications.
- If the customer uses labour provided by the rental company, the customer is responsible for them whilst on site, including any damages done, expenses or consequential indirect loss.

Finally, many an expensive argument can be avoided by determining if the cost of the hired lighting equipment includes the lamps.

Appendix I:
Glossary of terms

Absorption filter A filter which transmits selected wavelengths. The absorbed energy is converted to heat which raises the temperature of the filter.

Acting area That portion of a stage used by the actors during a performance.

Additive colour mixing The superimposition of light beams, usually consisting of the primary colours, whereby the resultant light is the *addition* of the various wavelengths concerned. See **Subtractive colour mixing**.

Alternating current (ac) Electric current whose flow alternates in direction. The time of flow in one direction is a half period and the length of all half periods is the same. The normal waveform of ac is sinusoidal.

Ambient light General background light.

American National Standards Institute (ANSI) An independent association that establishes standards to promote consistency and interchangeability among manufacturers. This organization was formerly known as the United States of America Standards Institute (USASI or ASI) and previously as the American Standards Association (ASA).

Ampere-hour A measure of a battery capacity given by the current/time characteristic.

Arc light Usually a luminaire using a carbon arc discharge as the source of illumination. Also describes modern discharge sources such as MSR, HMI, CSI, etc.

Aspect ratio The ratio of the width to the height of any imaging system. Generally refers to the final picture on the television or film screen (e.g. HDTV is 16:9).

Automation The ability of a piece of equipment to go to predetermined operational points by means of a closed loop servo system without the need for human intervention. Often confused with 'power assisted systems'.

Baby 1kW Fresnel luminaire.

Backing Scenery used behind sets to limit the view of the audience or a camera through openings such as doorways or windows.

Backing lighting The illumination provided for scenery and backcloths.

Backlight A luminaire used to light the subject from the rear to help separation from backings and to increase the three-dimensional effect.

Ballast The electrical device, required for all discharge lamps, that limits current through the lamp. Additional functions may be incorporated in the basic unit such as starting circuits and dimming control.

Barndoor Movable flaps attached to a Fresnel or PC luminaire to shape the light beam.

Barrel (Colloq. Bar) A metal tube, generally 48mm diameter, for suspending luminaires or scenery. Usually manufactured from steel or aluminium.

Base light The basic intensity of 'soft' lighting required to satisfy the minimum viewing or technical requirements.

Batten (a) Horizontal pipe on which luminaires or scenery can be hung. (b) Compartmented multi-colour floodlight unit for theatrical lighting.

Battery belt A battery pack mounted on a belt that can be worn around the waist during location shooting.

Beam The unidirectional flow of total light output from a source, usually a luminaire.

Beam angle Those points on the light output curve which are 50% of maximum output. The included angle between these two points is the beam angle.

Beam light Lensless luminaire with a parabolic reflector to give a parallel light beam.

Best boy The assistant chief lighting technician or second electrician

Black wrap Thick aluminium foil painted with matt black to control spill light from luminaires

Black body A body which completely absorbs any heat or light radiation falling upon it.

Black body radiation Radiation that comes from an ideal blackbody. The distribution of energy is dependent only on the temperature of the blackbody and is governed by Planck's radiation law.

Blackout To switch all channels to 'off' on a lighting console. Also refers to switching off all illumination, except the exit lights.

Blackout switch A master on/off switch used for controlling the overall production lighting for either stage or studios.

Blind Refers to changes made on a lighting console which do not effect the 'live' console output (usually called blind plotting)

Blonde A 2kW open faced luminaire.

Board A name for a control desk (derived from 'switchboard').

Bounce lighting Directing light onto a large diffuse surface to produce a soft reflected light.

Brail To pull a lighting suspension or piece of scenery out of its normal hanging position by means of attached rope lines.

Bridge A narrow platform suspended over the acting area. Luminaires and projection devices mounted on the bridge are accessible during performance.

Brightness See **Luminance**.

Brightness ratio The ratio of maximum-to-minimum luminances occurring within a scene.

British Standards Institution (BSI) Produce technical specifications and other documents which are made generally available. The main aim of the Institute is to maintain standards, quality and safety in goods and products.

Broad A wide angle floodlight.

Brute A 225 ampere dc high intensity carbon spotlight with a 24 inch diameter Fresnel lens.

Bubble Slang term used to describe lamps of any type.

Build A gradual increase in light level or in the number of light sources used.

Bulb An old term describing the bulbous glass envelope of an electric lamp.

Bump To briefly flash lighting channels 'up' or 'down'.

'C' clamp See **Hook clamp**.

Cam-lok A type of single pole connector used for feeder cables.

Camera light A luminaire mounted on a camera for lighting along or near the optical axis, usually to provide catch lights for the subjects' eyes.

Candela Unit of luminous intensity.

Candlepower A term that was used for intensity but has been replaced by the candela.

Carbon arc A dc arc source in which the arc is produced in air between a pair of carbon electrodes. These electrodes burn away and must be advanced during operation.

Catwalk A metal or wooden walkway usually used in the film industry to provide access and additional suspension points for luminaires.

Channel The circuit from the lighting control console to its associated dimmer.

Channel number Reference number entered by a key pad, or used by dedicated faders.

Chase A series of programmed sequential steps activating channels from a lighting console.

Chaser lights A linear string of lamps wired and controlled so that the lights appear to be following in sequence.

Chroma In television, the information which gives the colour of the image as distinct from its luminance (brightness).

Chroma Key A television special effect which uses a monochromatic coloured background to allow electronic switching to another picture. Deep blue is commonly used for the background when the foreground involves people.

Chromaticity The colour of light, as defined by its chromaticity co-ordinates, generally using the CIE diagram.

Circuit The electrical path from a dimmer to the luminaire.

Circuit breaker An electrical switch positioned in the circuit that will automatically operate to break the flow of current under abnormal conditions.

Cold mirror A dichroic coated glass surface which reflects visible light but allows infrared energy to pass through the reflector so that the reflected light contains less heat.

Colour A sensation of light induced in the eye by electromagnetic waves of a certain frequency, the colour being determined by that frequency.

Colour compensation (CC) A colour meter reading indicating the amount of filter required. Usually used in the film industry.

Colour frame A frame used to support colour media at the front of the luminaire.

Colour media Any coloured transparent material that can be placed in front of a luminaire. These are often referred to as 'gels' (for gelatine). Glass and other plastic materials are also used.

Colour rendering index (Ra) The evaluation of the effect of a light source on a set of coloured test pieces representing portions of the visible spectrum. The higher the Index towards its maximum of '**100**' the better the colour reproduction. Sources in general require an Index greater than **90** to prevent noticeable colour distortion.

Colour temperature A method of specifying the colour of a source which emits light in a continuous spectrum. Expressed in Kelvin units, the range used in media lighting is from 2600K (white light with a high red content) to 6000K (white light with a high blue content). Note: Cannot be used with discharge sources, although sometimes used as a guide to approximation of colour. (See **Correlated colour temperature**).

Colour wheel A circular mechanism holding several different colours mounted in front of a luminaire which can be rotated by hand or by a motor drive.

Complementary colours A pair of colours in the additive colour mixing system which combine to make white light.

Condenser A lens or mirror used in an optical system to collect the light being radiated from a source, which is then directed onto the gate of the projection system.

Console Name for a control desk (derived from 'organ console').

Contactor An electrical switch used within an electrical system to control the on/off state of the supply. Usually operated by an electromagnetic coil.

Contrast range This is the ratio of the brightness between the lightest and darkest areas in a subject. In a video system, it is the range between the maximum signal which can be satisfactorily handled, without distortion and the acceptable electronic noise level of the system.

Correlated colour temperature (CCT) Many sources of light energy do not have the same characteristics as black body radiators, but sources which have a mainly white light output can be given a correlated colour temperature. This is defined as that temperature of the black body radiator which *most closely* matches that of the light source in question. It therefore gives a rough guide to the blueness or redness of the source.

Cosine law The equation which allows the calculation of illumination on a surface which is at an angle to the incident light.

Counterweight system Mechanical system for flying scenery in which the weight of the pieces of scenery is balanced by adjustable weights in a cradle running up and down in guides in a frame normally at the side of the stage. The system is also used for lighting bars.

Crank-up stand A heavy duty stand provided with gears and a cranked lever to raise and lower heavy luminaires.

Cross barrel Used between barrels to allow accurate positioning of luminaires.

Cross fade A gradual change in the lighting where one lighting set-up *completely* replaces another. Obviously, only one crossfade can occur at a time (see **Move fade**).

Crosslighting Illumination from two luminaires at approximately 180° to each other on opposite sides of the subject. They are generally hard sources.

CSI A discharge lamp which approximates to sunlight for colour balance (CCT 4000K).

Cue A signal, which may be written, verbal or by action, that causes motivation of artists or technical staff. Also refers to changes in the lighting set-up.

Cue number The reference number given to control system memories which contain the lighting set-up information.

Cyclorama A backing, mounted in the studio, to provide a continuous surface and an illusion of infinity.

Cyclorama (cyc) lights Luminaires with specially designed reflectors used either at the base or at the top of cycloramas to light in a smooth manner.

Daylight filter (a) A blue filter used to change the colour of a light source from tungsten at 3200K to approximately 5600K. (b) A blue filter used on a camera to allow daylight balanced film stock to be used with tungsten lighting.

Deuce A 2kW Fresnel.

Devitrification The process which causes a change from a 'glassy' state to a crystalline state.

Dichroic filter A filter which reflects chosen wavelengths and transmits the remainder. Usually for 3200K to 5600K (approximately).

Diffuser Sheets of frosted plastic or spun glass fibre used to soften the shadows produced by the light beam.

Dimmer An electronic device used to reduce current flow to a lamp and therefore allow its light intensity to be adjusted.

Dimmer curve A graph which shows the light output or voltage output of a dimmer against the channel control setting.

Dimmer room The area which has been allocated for the equipment racks which contain the dimmers and associated equipment.

Dipless crossfade When channels with the same level in different lighting set-ups do not vary in intensity during a crossfade.

Direct current (dc) Current that does not alternate in polarity.

Discharge sources Light produced by the passage of electricity, through a gas, across two electrodes enclosed in a quartz envelope, e.g. Xenon, CSI, HMI, MSR lamps (see **Arc**).

Distribution box An electrical box with circuit protection used to change cable and connector sizing and provide assorted outlets.

DMX Multiplex protocol for transmitting digital information from control consoles to dimmers and automated luminaires.

Double broad This is a twin lamp floodlight generally used on studio floors as a local filler.

Double purchase A suspension system used on counterweight bars which gears the movement of the counterweight bucket to half that of the bar itself (see **Single purchase**).

Douser (dowser) A small metal flag used in follow spots to cut off the light beam without having to switch off the electrical supply to the source.

Downlighter Usually refers to small ceiling mounted luminaires in control areas.

Downstage The stage or studio area which is nearest the audience.

Drop arm A device used to hang a luminaire lower than the normal suspension system permits.

Effects Sequence of lighting, usually pre-programmed to give a visual effect (chasers, etc.).

Effects projector A focusing luminaire used to project slides or shapes. The effects can also be motor driven.

Efficacy This is the efficiency of a light source in converting the electrical input power to light and is expressed in 'lumens per watt'.

Efficiency This is a measure of the *useful* light output in lumens against the total lumens generated by the light source.

Eggcrate A device consisting of small cross baffle plates to restrict the spread of the light beam on a soft light.

Ellipsoidal spotlight (profile projector) A luminaire which uses an ellipsoidal reflector and a reasonable quality optical system to project shapes and patterns with a hard edge.

Ethernet Data transmission system for computer networks; also used for inter-connection of lighting consoles, dimmers and VDUs in remote locations.

Extension bar This is used to extend lighting barrels for accurate positioning of luminaires.

Eye light A set of numbers used to express the aperture of a lens which represents its light transmission. It is worked out by dividing the focal length of the lens by the diameter of the opening in the lens diaphragm. It is also colloquially known as the 'stop'.

F-number A set of numbers used to express the aperture of a lens which represents its light transmission. It is worked out by dividing the focal length of the lens by the diameter of the opening in the lens diaphragm. It is also colloquially known as the 'stop'.

Fader A control device for indirectly setting the current output of a dimmer and thus varying the light intensity. Originally were levers, but are often 'wheels' in modern lighting control systems.

Fade time The time between the start and end of a lighting change.

Field angle Those points on the light output curve which are 10% of maximum output. The included angle between these two points is the field angle.

Filament The tungsten coil inside a lamp that glows when voltage is applied to it creating light.

Filler Light used to control shade areas. Usually a soft light but can be controlled hard light.

Film speed (a) A measure of the film's sensitivity to light expressed in numerical terms to given an 'exposure index' which is used in the ISO and ASA system on light meters. (b) The velocity of film passing through movie cameras or projectors and is measured in frames per second or in metres per minute.

Five K A colloquial term for a 5kW spotlight.

Fixture General term for a luminaire, light or lantern.

Flag A sheet of metal or card mounted a short distance in front of the luminaire to give a sharp cut off to the light beam

Flicker-free ballast A solid state ballast that provides square-waves of around 100 Hz to eliminate variations in the light output of discharge sources, thus avoiding problems with synchronization of film shutters and television field frequencies.

Flood By focusing a lamp close to a lens, the diameter of the light beam is enlarged and thus gives the widest field of illumination.

Floodlight A luminaire which has only a reflector to control the beam and has wide angle distribution. (See **Soft light** and **Cyclorama light**).

Fluorescence The ability of some materials to convert ultraviolet energy into visible light.

Fly To suspend scenery or equipment above a stage or studio floor by means of a suspension system which can be manually operated or driven by motorized units.

Fly gallery The gallery which extends around the side walls of the stage area approximately 10 m above the stage floor. It is used for operating the ropes which adjust the counterweight system and hence the height of the bars above the stage.

Fly tower The upper part of the stage area which is formed as a tower, usually with galleries, to suspend scenery out of sight of the audience.

Focal length The distance of the focal point from the lens is called the focal length of the lens.

Focal point The point where the incident parallel rays, which are bent by a lens, meet in focus.

Focus In optics, the adjustment to give a clearly defined image. Originally used in the lighting industry to indicate the process of 'spotting' or 'flooding' the light beam of a luminaire, but is now used to indicate the general setting of a luminaire on the stage or in a pop rig.

Follow spot A narrow angle, focusing hard edged spotlight used to follow moving artists.

Footcandle An old unit, now superseded by 'lux', used to describe illumination which was measured in 'lumens per square foot'.

Footlambert The old unit for luminance (brightness) which has been replaced by the 'nit'.

Footlights Lights mounted along the edge of a stage to provide uplighting.

FPS Frames per second

Frequency The number of cycles per second of ac, measured in hertz (Hz).

Fresnel lens A convex lens built with concentric steps to enable its thickness to be reduced.

Fresnel spotlight (Colloq. Fresnel) Luminaires fitted with Fresnel lenses of varying sizes, the width of the beam can be changed by varying the spacing between the lens and the lamp/reflector assembly.

Front of house lights (FOH) Luminaires usually mounted on barrels, and generally concealed, above the audience seats.

Frost Translucent gel or plastic used to diffuse light sources.

Fuse A protective device for electrical circuits; originally a piece of special wire but nowadays nearly always a metal link contained in a ceramic cartridge.

Gaffer Term used in the film industry to describe the chief technician.

Gaffer clamp See **Mafer clamp**.

Gamma A measure of the contrast in image reproduction. In television overall gamma relates to the receiver screen luminance and the brightness of the original scene.

Gate The optical centre of a profile projector where the shutters are positioned and an iris or 'gobo' can be inserted.

Gel See **Colour media**.

Generators A diesel powered unit used to generate power on location (also used in some film studios). They are sound baffled and provide either bus bars or other feeder connectors. Also called 'genny'.

GFI Ground fault interrupter.

Gobo A mask placed in the gate of a profile spot to shape the beam. It is a simple form of outline projection.

Grandmaster The device (wheel or fader) which has overall control of the output of a console.

Grey scale Chart showing gradations from white to black.

Grid See **Lighting grid**.

Ground row Compartmented lighting units usually arranged in linear fashion for lighting from the base of cyclorama.

Half scrim A semi-circular scrim used to attenuate part of the light beam (see **Scrim**).

Halogen cycle The cycle by which halogen in a lamp returns tungsten deposits back to the filament thereby preventing blackening of the inner lamp wall.

Hard glass halogen lamp A tungsten halogen lamp with an envelope of borosilicate glass.

Hard light A luminaire that produces well-defined shadows, normally a spotlight.

Heat filter A light filter which removes infrared from the beam to reduce heat from the source of illumination.

Hertz (Hz) The unit of frequency which is measured in cycles per second. Other units are kilohertz (kHz) and megahertz (MHz).

High key Describes a scene containing mainly light tones well illuminated without large areas of strong shadow.

Highest takes precedence (HTP) On a lighting control system, where the highest setting will win, when two or more pre-set levels are simultaneously selected for that channel, e.g. if '7' then '5' is selected for a particular channel, '7' will win (see also **Latest takes precedence**).

HMI (also CID and MSR) Discharge lamps which have a daylight colour balance (5600K).

Hoist (see **Winch**) Old term used to describe either manual or motorized lifting equipment.

Hook clamp A clamp used for suspending luminaires from lighting bars.

House electrician An electrician permanently employed by a theatre or concert hall to maintain and operate the electrical equipment in the premises.

House lights A lighting system permanently installed to either illuminate an audience area or provide worklights in studios.

Hue The quality by which one colour is distinguished from another as a result of their wavelengths. It does not take into account the brightness or intensity of the colour.

Illumination The luminous flux falling on unit area of a surface. The unit of illumination is the lux (1 lumen per square metre) and it is the measure of the quantity of *incident light.*

Impedance (z) A measure, in ohms, of the opposition to current flow in an ac circuit. Includes resistance and reactance.

Incandescence The emission of light by raising a material to a high temperature.

Incident light meter A light meter that reads the light falling onto the subject.

Independent Channels in a control system which only respond to one master and are 'independent' of the rest of the console.

Inductance Opposition to current changing in an ac circuit, which causes the current to lag behind the applied voltage. Inductance is created by turns of wire with or without an iron core.

Infrared (IR) Wavelengths below the visible wavelength of light, felt as heat.

Internal reflector An integral reflector formed on the inner rear surface of the envelope of a lamp and usually parabolic or elliptic in shape.

Inverse square law The equation which is used to calculate the illumination at a given distance from a source of light.

Iris A series of adjustable metal plates arranged to give a variable circular aperture. Used in lighting projectors to alter the size of the light beam.

Junior A 2 kW Fresnel.

Kelvin The SI unit of thermodynamic temperature. It uses the same size of degree as the Celsius scale (zero K = –273°C).

Key light The principal modelling light, usually a spotlight.

Kicker Generally a hard light source used to provide obvious highlights.

Kilowatt Electrical power term for 1000 watts.

LD Abbreviation for lighting designer or lighting director.

Lamp A glass or quartz envelope which contains filaments or electrodes. The term lamp is often used to describe a luminaire, which is to be avoided as it can cause confusion. (Colloq. terms include globe, bubble, source).

Lantern See **Luminaire**.

Latest takes precedence (LTP) On a lighting control system, where the last selected level for a particular channel will win, e.g. if '7' then '5' is selected for a particular channel, '5' will win (see also **Highest takes precedence**).

Leko A slang term used in America to describe ellipsoidal spotlights.

Life Usually refers to the manufacturer's rates for life in hours of a lamp at its normal voltage and is based on the average life of a number of lamps which have been tested.

Light centre length (LCL) The distance from the centre of the filament to a standard point at the base of the lamp.

Lighting batten A barrel assembly with integral power feeders for luminaires.

Lighting control console A unit which contains the controls for adjusting the channel levels and thus the dimmer outputs, 'group channel' control, memory control, playback system and special effects.

Lighting designer (director) The person who creates and implements the lighting design for a production.

Lighting grid In *television* a structure mounted at high level above the operational area, usually made from steel or aluminium or a combination of the two, for the purposes of suspending luminaires and ancillary lighting equipment. In *theatre*, it is the framework above the stage in a close gridiron formation to allow operators access for positioning lights and scenery.

Lighting plot The instructions and drawings of the various lighting set-ups for a production, used by the LD and electricians (sometimes simply known as the 'plot') .

Limbo Describes a state of lighting where the background details are suppressed. In television this is usually created by 'blackness' whereas the film industry tends to use a white background.

Linnebach projector A lighting unit, basically a box without a lens, which contains a small point source of illumination to project soft diffused images of cut-outs or glass slides.

Louvres Thin black metallic strips located on a luminaire to reduce spill light (see **Eggcrates**). When fitted in front of a luminaire may also be adjustable at various angles to provide dimming without colour change (see also **Shutters**).

Low key Describes a scene containing mostly dark tones with large areas of shadow and is often used to create a dramatic mood.

Lug A very heavy-duty connector for attaching feeder cables to bus bars.

Lumen The lumen is the unit of 'luminous flux' and is defined as the amount of light which falls on one square metre of a surface at a *constant* distance of one metre from a source of one candela.

Lumens per watt The light output in lumens produced by a source for each watt of electrical power supplied to the source.

Luminaire A general term for a complete lighting unit. It includes the housing, the reflector, lens and lamps. (Colloq. light, lantern, fixture, unit, instrument, fitting).

Luminance The measure of brightness of a surface, it is measured in 'nits'. The old unit was the 'foot lambert'.

Luminous intensity A measure of the energy from a light source emitted in a particular direction. It is measured in candelas.

Lux The unit of illuminance (illumination). It is the unit of measurement for the incident light arriving at a surface. The old measuring system used foot-candles. (One foot-candle equals 10.76 lux).

MacBeth A blue glass filter used on some open faced luminaires which converts tungsten sources to daylight.

Mafer clamp All purpose grip clamp which can utilize different mounting attachments.

Master/group master Usually refers to a lighting control system fader which over rides by electrical means a group of individual faders.

Maximum overall length (MOL) The overall physical length of a lamp including all electrical contacts.

Mcb Miniature circuit breaker

Mccb Moulded case circuit breaker

Memory The term used to denote electronically recorded information which contains the lighting set-ups.

Microphony The interference caused by the mechanical vibration of any electrode system. Particularly troublesome on the older type of camera pick up tube, such as the Image Orthicon and the Plumbicon tubes used in colour cameras.

MIDI (Musical Instrument Digital Interface) A communication protocol used to link control consoles for both lighting and automated luminaire systems.

Mirror ball A motor driven ball with its surface covered in small mirrors. When rotated, with spotlights shining to it, it produces moving points of light.

Modelling light The terms is used to describe any luminaire, generally a hard source, that reveals the depth, shade and texture of subjects.

Move fade A fade from one lighting set-up to another where *only those channels with a new intensity* change; the other channels remaining static. Several 'move' fades can occur at the same time (see **Crossfade**).

Nanometre (nm) A unit of metric measurement equal to one billionth of a metre, which is used to measure light wavelengths.

Neutral density filter A filter which attenuates the light passing through it without affecting the colour of that light.

Nit The unit of luminance, which is one candela per square metre of surface radiation. It is therefore the measure of the *brightness* of a surface.

Non-dim Describes the circuit which replaces the normal dimmer function, where the circuit is switched 'on' or 'off' *only,* either by a switch or relay system.

Nook light A small light-weight open-face luminaire using a double-ended lamp.

Objective lens See **Projection lens**.

Offstage Areas that are out of the eyeline of an audience.

On-stage In view of the audience.

Opaque Absorbance of electro-magnetic radiation at specific wavelengths, generally refers to the fact that light is not transmitted.

Open faced luminaire Describes luminaires with no lens system, such as the 'Redhead' and 'Blonde'.

Pcb Printed circuit board.

Pan Term describing the horizontal movement, about a point, of luminaires or equipment.

Pantograph A mechanical cross-armed device for varying the height of luminaires or other fittings. It is generally spring balanced but can be operated by a motor or manually driven gear system.

Parcan A simple luminaire, basically a metal tube, with a PAR lamp mounted in it. The type of lamp determines the beam spread.

Patching A term describing the connections made between channels on lighting consoles and dimming systems (when accomplished by software – known as 'soft patching').

Patch panel A system rather like an old telephone operators interconnection system (switchboard) to connect low voltage circuits or high voltage circuits (known as 'hard patching').

Pin matrix A method of coupling control channels into groups by the insertion of special pins into a 'x' and 'y' matrix, where the 'x' axis may represent channels and the 'y' represent groups.

Pipe clamp See **Hook clamp**.

Pixel A picture element. The smallest element of a CCD array. The definition is governed by the number of 'pixels per area'; the higher the amount the better the definition.

Plano-convex lens A lens which has one flat side and one convex side.

Plano-convex spotlight (PC spot) A luminaire that gives a reasonably even beam with a very sharp edge.

Playback That part of a lighting control system where the lighting memories and/or other lighting states are combined and controlled by output master faders or switches.

Polarity The orientation of the positive and negative wires of a dc circuit or the phase and neutral wires of ac circuits.

Pole cat Lighting support system consisting of sprung metal tubes capable of extension onto which luminaires can be mounted. Used between two surfaces, floor and ceiling or two walls.

Pole operation (Colloq. Pole op) The control of electrical and mechanical functions on luminaires and suspension equipment by means of a long metal pole.

Power assisted systems Luminaires and suspension equipment that are under the direct control of an operator, e.g. winch control motor systems.

Practical Describes a light, e.g. table lamp, that can be effectively switched on and off by an actor within a scene. In television, the light will usually be remotely switched from the lighting control console.

Pre-focus Denotes special lamp caps so that the filament lines up precisely to the optics of a luminaire.

Preset A group of faders on a manual desk which are connected to the dimmers and controlled by a 'master fader'. As there are usually two presets or more on manual lighting control systems it is possible for a lighting plot to be set up in one preset without affecting the active preset (this is known as blind plotting).

Primary colours The primary *additive* colours are red, green and blue. The primary *subtractive* colours are cyan, magenta and yellow.

Profile spot A luminaire used to project shapes or patterns.

Projection lens A lens specially designed to project slides or shapes onto a surface with considerable enlargement of the slide or original material.

Proscenium arch (opening) The surround to the stage area and through which the audience views the performance.

Pup A colloquial term for a 1 kW spotlight.

Quartz Crystalline silica which is glass like and used to make envelopes for lamps. It is generally transparent to ultraviolet radiation.

Record The action of recording a lighting set-up on a control system.

Reflectance (reflection factor) The ratio of the reflected light to the incident light falling on a surface, measured in lumens.

Remainder dim A lighting console instruction which maintains the levels of selected channels, while forcing all other active channels to zero.

Remote A method of controlling the lighting from a position away from the main control system.

Rig To set up scenery equipment and lighting.

Riggers control A remote portable handheld control unit for controlling either luminaires or winch systems.

Rigging Collective term for suspension equipment.

Risers The flat surfaces on the Fresnel lens rings that form the division between segments.

rms Abbreviation of root-mean-square. The rms value of the current is a measure of its effectiveness in producing the same heating effect in a resistance as a direct current. It therefore allows for various wave shapes and directly relates to the power in watts.

Safety bond (also safety chain) A short length of wire rope or chain formed into a loop around a suspension point, to act as a secondary means of suspension in the event of failure of the primary system.

Saturated rig A lighting installation where luminaires are installed in sufficient numbers to cover the total acting area without rigging and de-rigging.

Saturation A term used to describe the density of a colour between the pure colour concerned and white, i.e.: a deep red or pink.

Scissors arc A special carbon arc device used to create a lightning effect.

Scoop A simple elliptical shaped floodlight usually fitted with a large GLS lamp giving a soft light output.

SCR A silicon controlled rectifier. A solid state current switching device, used in dimmers for lighting systems. It comes from the *thyristor* family.

Scrim A fine mesh used in front of a luminaire to attenuate the light beam. They are made with various meshes to give different attenuation characteristics (see **Half-scrim**).

Secondary colours Those colours produced by mixing either additive primary colours or subtractive primary colours.

Senior A 5kW Fresnel.

Shock The nervous sensation imparted to a body by the passage of an electric current.

Short circuit Unwanted current flow of low impedance between conductors.

Shutter Metal flags of varying shapes used within a luminaire to block light. They are used to shape the light beam from effects spotlights and follow spots. In a motion picture camera, a butter-fly shaped device that spins in front of the film.

Shutters Venetian blind type metal slats mounted in front of a luminaire as a blackout device or dimmer.

Single purchase A suspension system for counterweight bars where no gearing is used. The distance of travel of the counterweight bucket will be the same as the barrel (see **Double purchase**).

Skycloth A scenery unit used to convey the impression of a open sky (see **Cyclorama**).

Skypan A very shallow scoop used in the film industry, which is rather like a metal dustbin lid with a bare lamp in the middle.

Snoot A conical metal tube fitted to the front of the luminaire to enable a reduction in beam size.

Soft light A luminaire designed to produce virtually shadowless light and is generally used to control contrast.

Spacelight A large cylinder consisting of a diffuser with an array of lamps inside to give soft ambient illumination.

Specular Describes a mirror like surface.

Spigot The male member attached to a yoke used for the suspension of the luminaire and also for insertion into a floor stand. Colloq. 'spud'.

Spill light Extraneous uncontrolled light from a luminaire.

Spot To focus a luminaire by moving the lamp/reflector away from the lens, giving a narrow beam.

Spotlight A luminaire with a focusing system to concentrate the light beam and thus giving greater operational control.

Stage left/right The performers' left and right as they face the audience.

Stand A telescopic floor mounted tripod device which provides a means of adjusting the height of luminaires above floor level. Can be manual lift, or by a geared wind-up system.

Studio area The total floor area contained within the walls of a studio which may not always be used as the acting area, due to fire lanes, etc.

Subtractive colour mixing The removal of light of various wavelengths, by filtering or reflection, e.g. a magenta filter *subtracts* the green from the light path, whereas the pigment of yellow paint reflects the red and green components of the incident light but absorbs (subtracts) the blue. (See **Additive colour mixing**).

Telescope A grid mounted device made from retractable sets of tubes that is used to suspend luminaires at varying heights in the studio. Older types of telescopes were driven by portable power tools, modern systems are generally equipped with integral electric motors.

Throw Generally describes the direction of light from a luminaire and also the effective distance between the luminaire and the area being lit.

Tilt Term describing the vertical movement, about a point, of luminaires or equipment.

Tower A temporary platform usually made from scaffolding, on which to mount luminaires.

Trombone American term for an adjustable drop arm (see also **Drop arm**).

Truss A framework, generally made from alloy bars together with cross bracing, to provide lightweight rigging structures.

Tungsten halogen Describes a family of lamps with either hard glass or quartz envelopes, *tungsten* filaments and *halogen* (usually iodine or bromine) fillings.

Turtle stand A very low stand with either three or four feet to position lights at ground level.

Two K A colloquial term for a 2 kW spotlight.

Ultraviolet (UV) The band of short wave radiation from 400 to 10 nm, although invisible to the eye the energy is extremely powerful and produces reddening of the skin (sunburn); it can also cause damage to the eye.

Underwriters' Laboratory (UL) An American independent test laboratory that ensures minimum safety standards of equipment.

Undo A memory system feature for cancelling the last instruction and returning the console to its previous set-up.

Variac An auto-transformer dimmer.

Voltage drop That loss of volts which occurs through energy wastage when a current passes through a cable or electronic device.

Wash General ambient light on the acting area.

Winch Term used to describe either manual or motorized lifting equipment.

Wind-up stand See **Crank-up stand**.

Wire rope Ropes formed from fine wires woven in complex patterns to give great strength.

Working lights See **Houselights**.

Yoke The suspension frame of a luminaire; possibly containing the drive mechanism for pan and tilt. Colloq. fork, stirrup, trunnion.

Zoom Used in profile spots and scenic projectors, consisting of the relative movement of two lenses in an optical system to change beam width and focus.

Appendix II:
World mains voltages

Country	Supply voltage	Supply frequency
Afghanistan	220	50
Algeria	127/220	50
Angola	220	50
Antigua and Barbuda	230	60
Argentina	220/225	50
Australia	240	50
Austria	220	50
Bahamas	120/240	60
Bahrain	230/110	50/60
Bangladesh	230	50
Barbados	115/200/230	50
Belgium	127/220	50
Benin	220	50
Bermuda	120/240	60
Bolivia	115/230	50
Bophutatswana	220	50
Brazil	127/220	60
Brunei	230	50
Bulgaria	220	50
Burma	230	50
Burundi	220	50
Cameroon	220	50
Canada	120/240	60
Canary Islands	127/220	50
Central African Rep.	220	50
Chile	220	50
China	220	50
Colombia	120/240	60
Congo	220	50
Costa Rica	120	60
Cuba	115/120	60

Country	Supply voltage	Supply frequency
Curacao and Aruba	127/220	50
Cyprus	240	50
Czechoslovakia	220	50
Denmark	220	50
Djibouti	220	50
Dominican Rep.	110	60
Ecuador	110/120/127	60
Egypt	220	50
El Salvador	120/240	60
Ethiopia	220	50
Finland	220	50
France	127/220	50
Gabon	230	50
Gambia	230	50
Germany	127/220	50
Ghana	250	50
Gibraltar	240	50
Greece	220	50
Grenada	230	50
Guadeloupe	220	50/60
Guatemala	120/240	60
Guinea Rep.	220	50
Haiti	115/220/230	60
Honduras	110	60
Hong Kong	200	50
Hungary	220	50
Iceland	220	50
India	230/250	50
Indonesia	127/220	50
Iran	220	50
Iraq	220	50
Ireland	220	50
Israel	230	50
Italy	127/220	50
Ivory Coast	220	50
Jamaica	110/220	50
Japan	100/200/210	50/60
Jordan	220	50
Kenya	240	50
Korea (N)	220	60
Korea (S)	100	60
Kuwait	240	50
Laos	220	50
Lebanon	110/220	50
Lesotho	220	50
Liberia	120/240	60 ·
Libya	17/230	50
Luxembourg	120/127/220	50
Macau	110/220	50
Madagascar	127/220	50
Madeira	220	50

Country	Supply voltage	Supply frequency
Malaysia	240	50
Mali	127/220	50
Malta	240	50
Mauretania	230	50
Mauritius	230	50
Mexico	120/127/220	60
Mongolia	127/220	50
Morocco	115/127/220	50
Mozambique	220	50
Nepal	220	50
Netherlands	220	50
New Zealand	230/240	50
Nicaragua	120/240	60
Niger	220	50
Nigeria	220/230	50
Norway	230	50
Oman	240	50
Pakistan	230	50
Panama	120/240	60
Papua New Guinea	240	50
Paraguay	220	50
Peru	225	60
Philippines	120/220/240	60
Poland	220	50
Portugal	220	50
Puerto Rico	120/240	60
Qatar	240	50
Reunion	220	50
Romania	220	50
Saudi Arabia	127/220	50
Senegal	127	50
Seychelles	230	50
Sierra Leone	230	50
Singapore	230	50
Somalia	110/220/230	50
South Africa	220/230/250	50
Spain	127/220	50
Sri Lanka	230	50
St Vincent	230	50
Sudan	240	50
Suriname	115/127	50/60
Swaziland	230	50
Sweden	220	50
Switzerland	220	50
Syria	115/220	50
Taiwan	110/220	60
Tanzania	230	50
Thailand	220	50
Togo	220	50
Trinidad and Tobago	115/230	60
Tunisia	220	50

Country	Supply voltage	Supply frequency
Turkey	220	50
Uganda	240	50
United Arab Emirates	220/240	50
United Kingdom	220/230/240	50
Uruguay	220	50
USA	120/208/240	60
Former USSR	127/220	50
Venezuela	120/208/240	60
Vietnam	120/220	60
Virgin Islands	110/220	60
Yemen Arab Rep.	220	50
Yemen Dem. Rep.	250	50
Former Yugoslavia	220	50
Zaire	220	50
Zambia	230	50
Zimbabwe	225	50

Appendix III:
Lamp tables

Incandescent lamps

In general, incandescent lamps for film, TV and theatre in Europe can be divided into three groups, having the codes of CP, P and T. The designations are given by the Lighting Industries Federation (LIF) and are broadly described as follows:

CP Originally stood for colour photography, because the first lamps were imported from the USA by the film industry. All CP lamps are 3200 K and are single ended, ranging in size from 300 W to 20 000 W.

P   This class of lamps are also 3200 K but they are linear, double ended types, ranging in size from 250 to 2000 W

T   Indicates lamps designed for theatre, because they are of the order 2900–3000 K with an appropriately longer life, ranging in size from 500–2000 W.

The American National Standards Institute (ANSI) have a different coding system, being three letters arranged in alphabetical order. The cross reference table gives the equivalent types in both systems and can be used not only as a substitute guide, but also to help the user to find alternative lamps of different wattage and voltage for his luminaire. To do this, identify the lamp base and the light centre length (LCL) and look for alternative lamps that have the same; but care must be taken not to exceed the maximum rated wattage of the luminaire as this will cause the lamp to overheat and shorten its life and can damage the housing and present a safety hazard. It is also extremely important that lamps designated as having 'pinch protection' should only be used in luminaires designed for them (see Pinch protected lamps, Section 2 of this appendix).

The tables have been collated from many different manufacturers' catalogues so it is not an easy task to select one catalogue and expect to find that it provides information on all types of lamps, but a good wholesaler should have the required information, if supplied with the code and the voltage required. When ordering lamps for Europe, be careful to specify 220 V or 240 V because if 220 V lamps are used at 240 V, the life will be reduced to only 30% of the manufacturer's stated life.

In the tables that follow the lamps light centre lengths are given in millimetres, life is given in hours and the colour temperature is in Kelvin degrees.

1. SINGLE ENDED TUNGSTEN HALOGEN INCANDESCENT LAMPS

	European code (LIF)	US code (ANSI)	Volts	Colour temp.	Life	LCL	Base
250 W	-	DYG	30	3400	15	36.0	GY 9.5
300 W	CP-81	FKW	120	3200	150	46.5	GY 9.5
	CP-81	FSL	220	3200	150	46.5	GY 9.5
	CP-81	FSK	240	3200	150	46.5	GY 9.5
	M-38	-	220/240	2900	2000	46.5	GY 9.5
500 W	T-25		220/240	3000	300	46.5	GY 9.5
	T-18	FRF	120	3050	400	46.5	GY 9.5
	T-18	GCV	220	3050	400	46.5	GY 9.5
	T-18	GCW	240	3050	400	46.5	GY 9.5
	CP-82	FRG	120	3200	150	46.5	GY 9.5
	CP-82	FRH	220	3200	150	46.5	GY 9.5
	CP-82	FRJ	240	3200	150	46.5	GY 9.5
	M-40	-	220/240	2900	2000	46.5	GY 9.5
	T-1	DNW	240	2900	200	55.5	P28s
	T-17	FKF	220/240	2950	750	55.5	P28s
	T-17	BTL	120	2950	750	55.5	P28s
	T-28	-	220/240	3000	300	55.5	P28s
	T-24	BTL	120	2950	750	55.5	P28s
	-	BTM	120	3200	150	55.5	P28s
	-	EHC	120	3200	300	60.5	G 9.5
	-	EHD	120	2900	2000	60.5	G 9.5
	-	EGN	120	3200	150	63.5	G 22
	-	EGE	120	2900	2000	88.9	P28s
575 W	HX600	FLK	115	3200	300	60.5	G 9.5
	HX601	-	115	3000	1500	60.5	G 9.5
600 W	-	DYS	120	3200	75	36.0	GY 9.5
	-	FMB	120	3050	2000	51.0	GY 9.5
	HX602	-	220/240	3100	300	60.5	GY 9.5
650 W	-	DYR	220/240	3200	50	36.0	GY 9.5
	-	DYS	120	3200	75	36.0	GY 9.5
		EKD	120	3400	25	36.0	GY 9.5
	T-26	FRE	120	3050	400	46.5	GY 9.5
	T-26	GCT	220	3050	400	46.5	GY 9.5
	T-26	GCS	240	3050	400	46.5	GY 9.5
	CP-89	FRK	120	3200	200	46.5	GY 9.5
	CP-89	FRL	220	3200	150	46.5	GY 9.5
	CP-89	FRM	240	3200	150	46.5	GY 9.5
	T-12/T21	-	220/240	3000	750	55.0	GX 9.5
	CP-23/CP-67	-	120	3200	100	55.0	GX 9.5

	European code (LIF)	US code (ANSI)	Volts	Colour temp.	Life	LCL	Base
650 W	CP-23/CP-67	FVD	220/240	3200	100	55.0	GX 9.5
	T-13	FKA	120	3000	750	55.5	P28s
	T-13	FKB	220/240	3000	750	55.5	P28s
	CP-51/CP-69	FKL	120	3200	100	55.5	P28s
	CP-51/CP-69	FKM	220/240	3200	100	55.5	P28s
	CP-49	-	220/240	3200	50	55.5	P28s
	-	FKR	220/240	3100	300	60.5	G 9.5
	-	FKV	120	3150	300	60.5	G 9.5
	CP-39/CP-68	FKG	120	3200	100	63.5	G22
	CP-39/CP-68	FKH	220/240	3200	100	63.5	G22
	-	DTA	120	3200	300	87.0	P40s
750 W	-	BTN	120	3000	750	55.5	P28s
	-	BTP	120	3200	200	55.5	P28s
	-	EHF	120	3200	300	60.5	G 9.5
	-	EHG	120	3000	2000	60.5	G 9.5
	-	EGR	120	3200	200	63.5	G22
	-	EGG	120	2900	2000	88.9	P28s
900 W	-	BVA	120	3200	75	44.5	GY 9.5
	-	DZJ	220/240	3200	75	44.5	GY 9.5
1000 W	CP-98	-	220/240	3200	125	46.0	GY 9.5
	T-11/T29	-	120	3050	750	55.0	GX 9.5
	T-11/T29	-	220/240	3050	750	55.0	GX 9.5
	T-19	FWP	220	3050	750	55.0	GX 9.5
	T-19	FWR	240	3050	750	55.0	GX 9.5
	CP-24	-	120	3200	200	55.0	GX 9.5
	CP-24	-	220/240	3200	200	55.0	GX 9.5
	CP-70	FVA	220	3200	200	55.0	GX 9.5
	CP-70	FVB	240	3200	200	55.0	GX 9.5
	T-14/T20	-	120	3050	750	55.5	P28s
	T-14/T20	FKD	220/240	3050	750	55.5	P28s
	CP-52	FKN	220/240	3200	200	55.5	P28s
	-	BTR	120	3200	250	55.5	P28s
	CP-77	FEL	120	3200	300	60.5	G 9.5
	CP-77	FEP	220/240	3200	300	60.5	G 9.5
	-	FCV	120	3200	300	60.5	G 9.5
	T-30	-	220/240	3000	750	63.5	G22
	CP-40/CP-71	FKJ	220/240	3200	200	63.5	G22
	-	EGT	120	3200	250	63.5	G22
	T-16	-	220/240	3050	750	87.0	P40s
	T-15/T23	FKE	220/240	3050	750	88.9	P28s
	-	EGJ	120	3200	500	88.9	P28s
	-	EWE	220/240	3200	250	88.9	P28s
	-	BVT	120	3050	500	100.0	P40s
	-	BVV	120	3200	250	100.0	P40s
	-	CYV	120	3200	250	127.0	G 38
	CP-106	-	220/240	3200	400	127	G38
	-	DSE	120	3200	500	N/A	E40s
1200 W	T-31	-	220/240	3050	400	63.5	G22
	CP-93	-	120	3200	200	63.5	G22
	CP-93	-	220/240	3200	200	63.5	G22
	T-29	-	120	3050	400	67.0	GX 9.5

	European code (LIF)	US code (ANSI)	Volts	Colour temp.	Life	LCL	Base
1200 W	T 29	FWS	220	3050	400	67.0	GX 9.5
	T-29	FWT	240	3050	400	67.0	GX 9.5
	CP-90	-	120	3200	200	67.0	GX 9.5
	CP-90	-	220/240	3200	200	67.0	GX 9.5
1500 W	-	DTA	120	3200	300	87.0	P40s
	-	CWZ	120	3200	300	100.0	P40s
	-	CXZ	120	3200	300	127.0	G 38
	-	DSF	120	3200	750	241.0	E40s
1900 W (2 filaments: 1250 W+650 W)							
	CP-105	-	220/240	3050	250	143.0	GX38q
2000 W	CP-43/CP-72	-	120	3200	400	70.0	GY 16
	CP-43/CP-72	FTM	220	3200	400	70.0	GY 16
	CP-43/CP-72	FTL	240	3200	400	70.0	GY 16
	CP-79	-	220/240	3200	350	70.0	GY 16
	CP-75	-	220/240	3200	400	75.0	G 22
	CP-53/CP-74	-	120	3200	400	87.0	P40s
	CP-53/CP-74	-	220/240	3200	400	87.0	P40s
	CP-28	-	220/240	3200	300	87.0	P40s
	CP-92	-	120	3200	400	90.0	G 22
	CP-92	-	220/240	3200	400	90.0	G 22
	-	BVW	120	3200	400	100.0	P40s
	CP-41/CP-73	FKK	220/240	3200	400	127.0	G 38
	-	CYX	120	3200	400	127.0	G 38
	CP-34	-	220/240	3200	300	127.0	G 38
	-	BWA	120	3200	500	127.0	G 38
	-	FWG	120	3200	500	128.0	E40s
	CP-59/CP-76	-	220/240	3200	300	133.0	E40s
	-	BWF	120	3200	400	133.0	E40s
	-	FWH	120	3200	500	171.0	E40s
2500 W	CP-91	-	120	3200	400	90.0	G22
	CP-91	-	220/240	3200	400	90.0	G22
	CP-94	-	220/240	3200	400	127.0	G 38
2500 W (2 filaments, each 1250 W)							
	CP-30	-	220/240	3200	300	143.0	GX 38q
3000 W	HX-48	-	120	3200	400	127.0	G38
	HX-48	-	220/240	3200	400	127.0	G38
3500 W	CP-107	-	220/240	3200	400	165.0	G38
3750 W (2 filaments: 2500 W + 1250 W)							
	CP-58	-	220/240	3200	300	143.0	GX 38q
5000 W (2 filaments, each 2500 W)							
	CP-32	-	220/240	3200	300	143.0	GX 38q
5000 W	CP-29/CP-85	-	220/240	3200	500	165.0	G 38
	CP-29/CP-85	DPY	120	3200	500	165.0	G 38
	CP-46	-	220/240	3200	400	165.0	G 38
	CP-46	ECN	120	3200	400	165.0	G 38

	European code (LIF)	US code (ANSI)	Volts	Colour temp.	Life	LCL	Base
10000 W	CP-80	-	220/240	3200	400	254.0	G 38
	CP-80	EBA	120	3200	400	254.0	G 38
	CP-83	-	220/240	3200	500	254.0	G 38
	CP-83	DTY	120	3200	500	254.0	G 38
20000 W	CP-27	-	220/240	3200	500	420	G 38
	CP-99	BCM	220/240	3200	350	354	G 38

2. SPECIAL 'PINCH PROTECTED' TUNGSTEN HALOGEN LAMPS

The lamp manufacturers state that 'pinch protected' lamps should only be used in dedicated 'pinch protected' luminaires and under no circumstances should they be used in existing standard luminaires. This is because 'pinch protected' lamps have either a shorter 'light centre length' than normal or a higher wattage for the same LCL to enable manufacturers to design smaller luminaires. If used in standard luminaires, over-heating of the lamp and/or housing could result, e.g. fitting a 'pinch protected' 2 kW lamp with a G 22 base into a standard 1kW Fresnel which has the same base and the same LCL. The pinch temperature of a standard tungsten halogen lamp is typically 400°C, whereas 'pinch protected' lamps can work at temperatures up to 500°C.

Wattage	Ref. no	Volts	Col. temp.	Life	LCL	Base
75	VL75BP	30	3200	75	36.5	GZ 9.5
150	VL175BP	30	3200	75	36.5	GZ 9.5
250	VL250	30	3200	75	36.5	GZ 9.5
400	VL400BP	120/230/240	3200	75	36.5	GZ 9.5
800	VL800BP	120/230/240	3200	75	36.5	GZ 9.5
1000	6995 IBP	120/230/240	3200	250	46.5	GY 9.5
2000	6994 MBP	120/230/240	3200	500	63.5	G 22
2500	86863 HBP	120/230/240	3200	500	179.0	Fa 4
5000	6963 MBP	120/230/240	3200	525	127.0	G 22
5000	6963 NBP	120/230/240	3200	525	127.0	G 38

3. DOUBLE ENDED TUNGSTEN HALOGEN INCANDESCENT LINEAR LAMPS

	European code (LIF)	US code (ANSI)	Volts	Colour temp.	LIFE	Length	End CAPS
250 W	P1/8	-	30	3400	12	78.0	R7s
300 W	-	EHM	120	2950	2000	78.0	R7s
400 W	-	EHR	120	2900	2000	78.0	R7s
420 W	-	FFM	120	3200	100	78.0	R7s

	European code (LIF)	US code (ANSI)	Volts	Colour temp.	LIFE	Length	CAP
500 W	P2/30	FDF	120	3200	400	118.0	R/s
	K1	-	220/240	2900	2000	118.0	R7s
	-	FCL	120	3000	2000	118.0	R7s
625 W	P2/10	-	220/240	3200	200	189.0	R7s
	P2/10	-	120	3200	200	189.0	R7s
	P2/15	-	220/240	3400	75	189.0	R7s
650 W	P2/6	FAD	120	3200	100	78.0	R7s
	-	DWY	120	3400	25	78.0	R7s
750 W	-	EJG	120	3200	400	78.0	R7s
800 W	P2/13	DXX	220/240	3200	75	78.0	R7s
	P2/11	EME	220/240	3200	150	118.0	R7s
1000 W	-	DXW	120	3200	150	93.0	R7s
	P2/35	-	220/240	3200	150	93.0	R7s
	P2/28	FCM	120	3200	300	118.0	R7s
	P2/28	-	220/240	3200	300	118.0	R7s
	P2/29	FHM	120	3200	300	118.0	R7s
	P2/20	-	220/240	3200	300	118.0	R7s
	K4	-	220/240	3000	2000	118.0	R7s
	-	FFT	120	3200	500	167.0	R7s
	P2/7	EKM	220/240	3200	200	189.0	R7s
1250 W	P2/12	-	220/240	3200	200	189.0	R7s
1500 W	-	FDB	120	3200	400	167.0	R7s
2000 W	P2/27	FEX	220/240	3200	300	143.0	R7s
	-	FEY	120	3200	300	143.0	R7s

4. PAR SEALED BEAM INCANDESCENT TUNGSTEN HALOGEN LAMPS

	Wattage	LIF	ANSI	Volts	Col. temp	Life	Beam angle (°)	Base
PAR 36	650	-	FCX	120	3200	100	40X30	Ferrule cap
	650	-	DWE	120	3200	100	40X30	Screw terminal
	650	-	FBO	120	3400	30	25X15	Screw terminal
	650	-	FBE	120	5000	35	25X15	Screw terminal
PAR 64	500	CP-86	-	220/240	3200	300	10X7	GX16d
	500	CP-87	-	220/240	3200	300	11X9	GX16d
	500	CP-88	-	220/240	3200	300	21X10	GX16d
	1000	-	FFN	120	3200	800	10X7	GX16d
	1000	CP-60	EXC	220/240	3200	300	12X6	GX16d
	1000	-	FFP	120	3200	800	13X10	GX16d
	1000	CP-61	EXD	220/240	3200	300	13X10	GX16d
	1000	-	FFR	120	3200	800	25X14	GX16d
	1000	CP-62	EXE	220/240	3200	300	25X14	GX16d
	1000	-	FFS	120	3200	800	70X70	GX16d
	1000	CP-95	EXG	220/240	3200	300	70X70	GX16d

Discharge lamps

Caution: When selecting an alternative discharge lamp consult the luminaire/ballast manufacturer or his representative for a suitable replacement. Lamps of the same rating may have different operating characteristics or may be 'hot restrike' (*instant restart*) which require higher ignition voltages.

1. DOUBLE ENDED LINEAR DISCHARGE LAMPS

Wattage	Code	Lamp volts	Correlated colour (K)	Life (hrs)	Maximum length (mm)	End CAPS
HMI (Osram) hot restrike						
200	HMI 200 W	80	6000	300	75	X515
575	HMI 575 W/GS	95	6000	750	135	SFc10
1200	HMI 1200 W/GS	100	6000	750	220	SFc15.5
2500	HMI 2500 W/GS	115	6000	500	355	SFa21
2500	HMI 2500 W/S	115	6000	500	210	SFa21
4000	HMI 4000 W	200	6000	500	405	SFa21
6000	HMI 4000 W	123	6000	500	450	S25.5
12000	HMI 12000 W	224	6000	500	450	S25.5
12000	HMI 12000 W/GS	160	6000	500	470	S30
18000	HMI 18000 W	225	6000	250	500	S30
HTI (Osram) hot restrike						
270	HTI 250 W/D	45	4600	250	93	MO-PIN-1mm
300	HTI 300 W/DE	100	6500	600	92	SFc10.4
400	HTI 400 W/D	55	4600	250	100	MO-PIN-1mm
600	HTI 600 W/D	95	5300	250	100	MO-PIN-1mm
MSI (Philips) hot restrike						
200	MSI 200 W	80	5600	300	75	X515
575	MSI 575 W	95	5600	750	145	SFc10.4
1200	MSI 1200 W	100	5600	750	220	SFc15.5.6
2500	MSI 2500 W	115	5600	500	355	SFa21.12
4000	MSI 4000 W	200	6000	500	405	SFa21.12
6000	MSI 6000 W	123	6000	350	450	S25 5x60
12000	MSI 12000 W	225	6000	250	470	S25 5x60

2. SINGLE ENDED DISCHARGE LAMPS

Wattage	Code	Lamp volts	Correlated colour (K)	Life (hrs)	Light centre length (mm)	Base
HMI (Osram) hot restrike						
125	HMI 123 W	80	6000	150	26.7	Special
200	HMI 200 W/SE	70	6000	200	39.0	GZY 9.5
270	HMI 250 W/SE	50	6000	250	35.0	FaX 1.5
400	HMI 400 W/SE	67	6000	650	60.0	GZZ 9.5
575	HMI 575 W/SE	95	6000	750	70.0	G22
1200	HMI 1200 W/SE	100	6000	750	107.0	G38
2500	HMI 2500 W/SE	115	6000	500	127.0	G38
4000	HMI 4000 W/SE	200	6000	500	142.0	G38

Wattage	Code	Lamp volts	Correlated colour (K)	Life (hrs)	Light centre length (mm)	Base
HTI (Osram) *not instant restart*						
150	HTI 150 W	90	6500	750	30	GY 9.5
HTI (Osram) hot restrike						
270	HTI 250 W/SE	45	4600	250	35	FaX 1.5
400	HTI 400 W/SE	55	4800	250	35	FaX 1.5
600	HTI 600 W/SE	95	5300	300	35	FaX 1.5
1200	HTI 1200 W/SE	100	6000	600	59	GY 22
2500	HTI 2500 W/SE	115	6000	600	85	G 22
HSR (Osram) *not instant restart*						
400	HSR 400 W	67	5600	650	62	GX 9.5
700	HSR 700 W	72	6000	1000	75	G22
MSR (Philips) *not hot restrike*						
200	MSR 200	70	5600	200	39	GY 9.5
400	MSR 400	70	5600	650	62	GX 9.5
575	MSR 575	95	5600	750	125	GX 9.5
700	MSR 700	72	5600	1000	75	G22 X42
1200	MSR 1200	100	5600	800	85	G22/30X53
MSR/SA (Philips) hot restrike						
220	MSR 200 SA	34	5400	500	36.5	GY 9.5
400	MSR 400 SA	54	5400	400	36.5	GY 9.5
MSR/HR (Philips) hot restrike						
125	MSR 125 HR	80	5600	200	39	GZX 9.5
200	MSR 200 HR	70	5600	200	39	GZX 9.5
400	MSR 400 HR	70	5600	650	60	GZZ 9.5
575	MSR 575 HR	95	5600	750	70	G22
1200	MSR 1200 HR	100	5600	800	107	G38
2500	MSR 2500 HR	115	5600	500	127	G38
4000	MSR 4000 HR	200	5600	500	142	G38
SN (Philips) *not instant restart*						
220	SN 250	75	5600	2000	55	GY 9.5
440	SN 500	75	5600	2000	70	GX 9.5
660	SN 660	65	5600	500	80	GY 16
880	SN 1000	75	5600	750	95	GY 16
MSD (Philips) *not instant restart*						
200	MDS 200	68	5600	750	55	GY 9.5
700	MDS 700	72	5900	2000	85	GY22
CSR (GE) *not instant restart*						
400	CSR 400/CS	67	5600	650	62	GX 9.5
700	CSR 700/CS	72	5600	1000	75	G22
1200	CSR 1200/CS	100	5600	750	85	G22

Wattage	Code	Lamp volts	Correlated colour (K)	Life (hrs)	Light centre length (mm)	Base
CSR (GE) hot restrike						
575	CSR 575/HR	95	6000	750	70	G22
1200	CSR 1200/HR	100	6000	750	107	G38
2500	CSR 2500/HR	115	6000	500	127	G38
4000	CSR 4000/HR	200	6000	500	142	G38
CSI (GE) *not instant restart*						
400	CSI 990201	100	4000	500	25.5	Special Pin
1000	CSI 990221	77	4000	500	63.5	G22
CID (GE) hot restrike						
200	CID 990211	70	5500	150	36.5	Special Pin
300	CID 990413	100	5500	350	36.5	Special Pin
575	CID 990415	95	5500	500	52.0	G22
1000	CID 990222	77	5500	500	63.5	G22
2500	CID 990431	100	5500	350	127.0	G38

3. PAR SEALED BEAM DISCHARGE LAMPS

Wattage	Code	Lamp volts	Correlated colour (K)	Life (hrs)	Par (1/8" units)	Base
HMI (Osram) hot restrike						
1200	HMI 1200 W PAR	100	6000	1000	64	G38
CSI (GE) *not instant restart*						
1000	CSI 991222	77	3800	3500	64	G38
CSI (GE) hot restrike						
1000	CSI 991422/HR	77	3800	3500	64	G38
CID (GE) *not instant restart*						
1000	CID 991225	77	5500	1500	64	G38
CID (GE) hot restrike						
1000	CID 991425/HR	77	5500	1000	64	G38
1200	CID 991435/HR	100	5500	1000	64	G38

Appendix IV:
Luminaire performances

Discharge sources

200 W

Distance (m)	Spot Intensity (lux)	Beam size (m)	Flood Intensity (lux)	Beam size (m)
4	5156	1.27	859	4.16
6	2291	1.90	381	6.24
8	1289	2.53	214	8.33

575 W

Distance (m)	Spot Intensity (lux)	Beam size (m)	Flood Intensity (lux)	Beam size (m)
4	12500	0.70	1250	4.00
6	5555	1.05	556	6.00
8	3125	1.40	313	8.00
10	2000	1.75	200	10.00

1.2 kW

Distance (m)	Spot Intensity (lux)	Beam size (m)	Flood Intensity (lux)	Beam size (m)
6	10278	1.16	1944	6.11
8	5781	1.54	1094	8.15
10	3700	1.93	700	10.20
12	2570	2.31	486	12.23
14	1888	2.70	357	14.27
16	1445	3.08	273	16.30

2.5 kW

Distance (m)	Spot Intensity (lux)	Beam size (m)	Flood Intensity (lux)	Beam size (m)
8	17187	1.19	1562	10.00
10	11000	1.49	1000	12.50
12	7638	1.78	694	15.00
14	5612	2.08	510	17.50
16	4297	2.38	390	20.00
18	3395	2.68	309	22.50
20	2750	2.97	250	25.00

4 kW

Distance (m)	Spot Intensity (lux)	Beam size (m)	Flood Intensity (lux)	Beam size (m)
10	30000	1.57	2000	9.97
14	15306	2.20	1020	14.00
18	9260	2.83	617	18.00
22	6198	3.46	413	21.94
26	4438	4.09	296	25.93
30	3333	4.72	222	29.91

6 kW

Distance (m)	Spot Intensity (lux)	Beam size (m)	Flood Intensity (lux)	Beam size (m)
14	24439	1.84	1531	12.47
18	14784	2.36	926	16.03
22	9897	2.88	620	19.60
26	7086	3.41	444	23.15
30	5322	3.93	333	26.71
34	4144	4.46	260	30.28

12 kW

Distance (m)	Spot Intensity (lux)	Beam size (m)	Flood Intensity (lux)	Beam size (m)
18	30864	1.82	1543	18.74
22	20661	2.23	1033	22.90
26	14793	2.63	740	27.07
30	11111	3.04	556	31.23
34	8650	3.44	433	35.40
38	6925	3.85	346	39.56
42	5669	4.26	283	43.73

18 kW

Distance (m)	Spot Intensity (lux)	Beam size (m)	Flood Intensity (lux)	Beam size (m)
20	24500	2.97	1625	21.27
24	17013	3.57	1128	25.50
28	12500	4.16	829	29.77
32	9570	4.76	635	34.02
36	7561	5.35	501	38.28
40	6125	5.95	406	42.54
44	5061	6.54	336	46.79

1.2 kW PAR

Distance (m)	Intensity (lux) Spot	Narrow flood	Flood	Super wide flood
10	25000	7250	2000	1100
15	11111	3222	889	489
20	6250	1812	500	275
25	4000	1160	320	176
30	2777	806	222	122

2.5 kW PAR

Distance (m)	Intensity (lux) Spot	Narrow flood	Flood	Super wide flood
10	33750	13700	4500	2000
15	15000	6088	2000	888
20	8438	3425	1125	500
25	5400	2192	720	320
30	3750	1522	500	222

4 kW PAR

Distance (m)	Intensity (lux) Spot	Narrow flood	Flood	Super wide flood
10	45000	16200	6000	2500
15	20000	7200	2667	1111
20	11250	4050	1500	625
25	7200	2592	960	400
30	5000	1800	667	278

6 kW PAR

Distance (m)	Intensity (lux) Spot	Narrow flood	Flood	Super wide flood
10	71750	35700	12200	6800
15	31889	15867	5422	3022
20	17937	8925	3050	1700
25	11480	5712	1952	1088
30	7972	3967	1356	756

Tungsten sources

800 W Redhead

Distance (m)	Spot Intensity (lux)	Beam size (m)	Flood Intensity (lux)	Beam size (m)
4	2500	3.07	406	7.46
6	1111	4.60	180	11.19
8	625	6.15	102	14.90

2 kW Blonde

Distance (m)	Spot Intensity (lux)	Beam size (m)	Flood Intensity (lux)	Beam size (m)
4	13500	1.63	1575	5.60
6	6000	2.44	700	8.40
8	3375	3.26	394	11.20
10	2160	4.07	252	14.00
12	1500	4.88	175	16.80

1 kW PAR

Distance (m)	Intensity (lux) Narrow spot	Spot	Flood
6	8889	7500	3472
8	5000	4218	1953
10	3200	2700	1250
12	2222	1875	868
14	1632	1378	638
16	1250	1055	488

1 kW Fresnel

Distance (m)	Spot Intensity (lux)	Beam size (m)	Flood Intensity (lux)	Beam size (m)
4	4609	0.77	675	4.8
6	2048	1.16	300	7.2
8	1152	1.54	169	9.61

2 kW Fresnel

Distance (m)	Spot Intensity (lux)	Beam size (m)	Flood Intensity (lux)	Beam size (m)
4	11562	0.70	1462	4.53
6	5139	1.05	650	6.79
8	2891	1.40	366	9.05
10	1850	1.75	234	11.32
12	1284	2.10	163	13.58

5 kW Fresnel

Distance (m)	Spot Intensity (lux)	Beam size (m)	Flood Intensity (lux)	Beam size (m)
6	13889	1.31	2083	6.79
8	7812	1.75	1172	9.05
10	5000	2.20	750	11.32
12	3472	2.63	521	13.58
14	2551	3.07	383	15.80

10 kW Fresnel

Distance (m)	Spot Intensity (lux)	Beam size (m)	Flood Intensity (lux)	Beam size (m)
8	19531	1.40	2656	7.30
10	12500	1.75	1700	9.10
12	8680	2.10	1181	10.90
14	6378	2.45	867	12.80
16	4883	2.80	664	14.60
18	3858	3.15	524	16.40
20	3125	3.50	425	18.20

1.25 kW Softlite

Distance (m)	Intensity (lux) (minus eggcrate)	Intensity (lux) (with eggcrate)
2	2700	2250
3	1200	1000
4	675	562

2.5 kW Softlite

Distance (m)	Intensity (lux) (minus eggcrate)	Intensity (lux) (with eggcrate)
4	1562	1234
6	694	548
8	391	309

5 kW Softlite

Distance (m)	Intensity (lux) (minus eggcrate)	Intensity (lux) (with eggcrate)
6	1215	972
8	684	546
10	438	350

650 W profile projector 25° Fixed

Distance (m)	Intensity (lux)	Beam size (m)
6	972	2.66
8	547	3.55
10	350	4.43
12	243	5.32

1 kW profile projector 30° Fixed

Distance (m)	Intensity (lux)	Beam size (m)
6	2419	3.20
8	1360	4.29
10	871	5.36
12	605	6.43

1 kW profile projector 15°/28°

Distance (m)	Narrow Intensity (lux)	Beam size (m)	Wide Intensity (lux)	Beam size (m)
6	5638	1.58	1620	2.99
8	3171	2.10	911	3.99
10	2030	2.63	583	4.99
12	1409	3.16	405	5.98
14	1035	3.69	298	6.98

1200 W profile projector 11°/26°

Distance (m)	Narrow Intensity (lux)	Beam size (m)	Wide Intensity (lux)	Beam size (m)
6	7083	1.15	3611	2.77
8	3984	1.54	2031	3.70
10	2550	1.92	1300	4.62
12	1771	2.31	903	5.54
14	1301	2.70	663	6.46

2 kW profile projector 12°/22°

	Narrow		Wide	
Distance (m)	Intensity (lux)	Beam size (m)	Intensity (lux)	Beam size (m)
10	4288	2.10	1856	3.90
12	2978	2.52	1289	4.66
14	2188	2.94	947	5.44
16	1675	3.36	725	6.22
18	1323	3.78	573	7.00
20	1072	4.20	464	7.78

2 kW tungsten follow spot 9°/15°

	Narrow		Wide	
Distance (m)	Intensity (lux)	Beam size (m)	Intensity (lux)	Beam size (m)
12	3955	1.89	1733	3.16
14	2906	2.20	1273	3.68
16	2225	2.52	975	4.21
18	1758	2.83	770	4.74
20	1424	3.15	624	5.27

1 kW discharge follow spot 9°/15°

	Narrow		Wide	
Distance (m)	Intensity (lux)	Beam size (m)	Intensity (lux)	Beam size (m)
20	4284	3.00	2556	5.34
22	3540	3.31	2112	5.87
24	2975	3.61	1775	6.40
26	2535	3.91	1512	6.94
28	2186	4.21	1304	7.47
30	1904	4.51	1136	8.00

2.5 kW discharge long throw follow spot 4.3°/7.5°

	Narrow		Wide	
Distance (m)	Intensity (lux)	Beam size (m)	Intensity (lux)	Beam size (m)
20	8250	1.50	3750	2.62
24	5729	1.80	2604	3.15
28	4209	2.10	1913	3.67
32	3222	2.40	1464	4.19
36	2546	2.70	1157	4.72
40	2062	3.00	937	5.24
44	1705	3.30	774	5.77
48	1432	3.60	651	6.29

Appendix V:
Formulae and conversion tables

Most scientific measurements are made using the International System of Units (Systeme International d'Unites) or SI for short.

The three basic units are the **metre**, **kilogram** and the **second**. From these are derived the whole range of units which cover the world of physics. For the ease of our readers we have picked out only those units which are applicable to the subject matter in this book.

Measurement of length

Basic unit: **metre** (m)
Other units:
    centimetre (cm)   = one hundreth of a metre (10^{-2} m)
    millimetre (mm) = one thousandth of a metre (10^{-3} m)
    nanometre (nm) = one thousandth millionth of a metre (10^{-9} m)

Measurement of area

Basic unit: **square metre** (m^2)
Other units:
    square centimetre= one ten thousandth of a square metre
                                   (10^{-4} m^2)

Measurement of mass

Basic unit: **kilogram** (kg)
Other units:
    gram (g)   = one thousandth of a kilogram (10^{-3} kg)
    tonne (t)   = one thousand kilograms (10^{3} kg)

Measurement of electric current

Basic unit: **ampere** (A)
Other units:
    milliampere   = one thousandth of an ampere (10^{-3} A)

Measurement of thermodynamic temperature

Basic unit: **kelvin** (K)
Note: The kelvin scale uses the same interval of degrees as the Celsius scale. 'Absolute zero' on the kelvin scale is **minus** 273 degrees Celsius.
     Thus: $K = (°C)+273$.

Measurement of light

	Physical units	Luminous units
Total light output	Radiant flux (watts)	Luminous flux (lumens)
Light emitted in a specific direction	Radiant intensity (watts per steradian)	Luminous intensity (**candelas**)
Light emitted from a unit area in a specific direction	Radiance (watts/cm² per steradian)	Luminance (candelas/cm²)
Light striking a unit area	Irradiance (watts/cm²)	Illuminance (lumens/m² = **lux**)

Law of illumination

Inverse square law $E = I/d^2$

where   E = Illuminance in lux
        I = Luminous intensity in candelas
        d = Distance of source to surface being illuminated

Cosine law $E = \dfrac{I}{d^2} Cos.A$

where A = The angle to the normal of the incident light.

Note: This is a modification to the inverse square law to take account of the angle of incidence.

Electrical formulae

Ohm's law states that the current (I) flowing in a circuit is directly proportional to the applied voltage (V) and inversely proportional to the resistance (R), thus:

$$I = \frac{V}{R} \quad V = IR \quad and \quad R = \frac{V}{I}$$

Power (P) in the circuit is given by the product of voltage (V) and current (I). The unit of power is the watt (W), thus:

$$P = V \times I \text{ watts}$$

alternatively as $V = IR$ therefore $P = I^2R$ watts

as $I = \dfrac{V}{R}$ therefore $P = \dfrac{V^2}{R}$ watts

The above formulae are those used for direct current (dc) circuits.

For alternating current (ac) circuits, the formulae only hold true when the circuit is purely resistive. That is, the voltage and current are in phase with each other. If the circuit contains inductance or capacitance the voltage and current will be out of phase to some degree.

To allow for this discrepancy we have to modify the formulae as follows:

In an ac circuit circuit the ratio of applied voltage (V) divided by current (I) is called the impedance (Z):

$$Z = \frac{V}{I}$$

The power is given by: P = VI cos φ watts where φ is the phase difference between the current and supply voltage. Cos φ is called the power factor (PF).

The power factor is also given by:

$$\frac{\text{power in watts}}{\text{rms volts} \times \text{rms amperes}}$$

For most practical measurements:

$$PF = \frac{\text{kilowatts}}{\text{kilovoltamperes}}$$

Figure AV.1 Single-phase sine wave

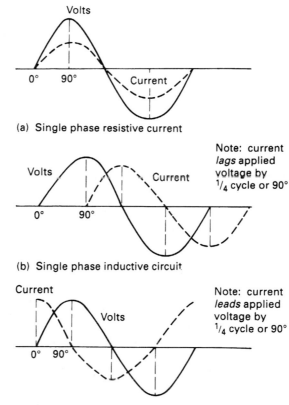

(a) Single phase resistive current

Note: current *lags* applied voltage by $^1/_4$ cycle or 90°

(b) Single phase inductive circuit

Note: current *leads* applied voltage by $^1/_4$ cycle or 90°

(c) Single phase capacitive circuit

Electrical energy

This is the measurement of power used over a period of time.

Thus: Watts $\times$ seconds $=$ watt-seconds or 'joules' (J)
             1 kWh $=$ 1000 $\times$ 3600 watt-seconds
                                                 $=$ 3 600 000 J

For practical purposes the units most used are:

   kilowatts $\times$ hours $=$ kilowatt-hours (kWh)

Generally called a unit of electricity

Figure AV.2 (a) Star connection
and neutral point. (b) Three-phase
sine wave

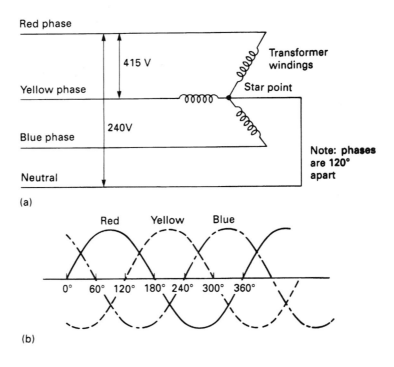

Conversion factors

Imperial to metric

Metric to imperial

Length

Imperial to metric			Metric to imperial		
Inches × 25.4	=	millimetres	Millimetres × 0.03937	–	inches
Inches × 2.54	=	centimetres	Centimetres × 0.3937	=	inches
Feet × 0.3048	=	metres	Metres × 3.281	=	feet

Area

Sq. inches × 6.452	=	sq. cm.	Sq. cms × 0.155	=	sq. in.
Sq. feet × 0.0929	=	sq. metres	Sq. metres × 10.76	=	sq. feet

Volume

Cubic ft. × 0.02832	=	cubic metres
Cubic metres × 35.311	=	cubic ft.

Mass

Pounds × 0.4536	=	kilograms	Kilograms × 2.205	=	pounds
Tons × 1016	=	kilograms	Kilograms × 0.0009844	=	tons
Tons × 0.9844	=	tonnes	Tonnes × 1.016	=	tons

Appendix VI:
CIE luminaire symbols

Floodlight
A luminaire with a beam angle of 100° or more

Special floodlight
A luminaire with a beam angle of less than 100°

Reflector spotlight
A luminaire with a variable beam produced by movement of the lamp in relation to its reflector, e.g. Beamlight

Sealed beam light
A unit where the filament, reflector and lens are all fixed in relation to each other, e.g. Par 64, etc.

Lens spotlight
A luminaire with a variable beam using a lens with combined lamp and reflector movement, e.g. PC unit

Fresnel spotlight
The same principle as the lens spotlight but uses a 'stepped' Fresnel lens to give a softer beam edge

Profile (ellipsoidal)
A luminaire which has a hard edged beam. The shape of the beam is variable by the use of diaphragms, shutters or silhouette cutouts

Effects spotlight
Projects stationary or moving objects, produces an even field by using an objective lens

Soft light
A luminaire with a large lit surface area to produce a diffused light with indefinite shadow boundaries.

Further reading

BS 5550: Location Lighting, British Standards Institution, 1996.

BS 7671: 1992 plus amendments (IEE Wiring Regulations, 16th Edition), British Standards Institution, 1994.

Control Systems for Live Entertainment, John Huntingdon, Focal Press (America), 1994.

Focal Guide to Safety In Live Performance, George Thompson, Focal Press, 1995.

Guide to Acoustic Practice, BBC Engineering 1990.

Handbook of Electrical Installation and Practice, Parts 1 and 2, Various, Granada, 1983.

Light and Colour, R Daniel Overheim, David L Wagner, John Wiley & Sons, 1982.

Light, Michael I Sobell, University of Chicago Press, 1987.

Lighting the Stage, Frances Reid, Focal Press, 1995.

Low Voltage Directive (73/23/EEC), European Community Publication, C199, July 1994.

Set Lighting Technicians Handbook, Harry C. Box, Focal Press (America), 1993.

The EMC Directive (89/336/EEC), European Community Publication, L139, May 1989.

The Reproduction of Colour in Photography, Printing and Television, RWG Hunt, Fountain Press, 1995.

The Stage Lighting Handbook (Third Edition), Francis Reid, A&C Black, 1987.

The Supply of Machinery (Safety) (Amendment) Regulations No. 2063, HMSO, 1994.

The Supply of Machinery (Safety) Regulations No. 3073, HMSO, 1992.

The Technique of Lighting for Film and Television, Gerald Millerson, Focal Press, 1991.

Theatre Lighting in the Age of Gas, Terence Rees, The Society for Theatre Research, 1978.

Theatres, Roderick Ham, The Architectural Press (1987).

Thorn Technical Handbook (Various), Thorn Lighting.

Index